English MPs

English MPs

Legislators and Servants of their Constituents, 1750–1800

Michael McCahill

BLOOMSBURY ACADEMIC
LONDON • NEW YORK • OXFORD • NEW DELHI • SYDNEY

BLOOMSBURY ACADEMIC
Bloomsbury Publishing Plc
50 Bedford Square, London, WC1B 3DP, UK
1385 Broadway, New York, NY 10018, USA
29 Earlsfort Terrace, Dublin 2, Ireland

BLOOMSBURY, BLOOMSBURY ACADEMIC and the Diana logo are trademarks of
Bloomsbury Publishing Plc

First published in Great Britain 2023
This paperback edition published in 2024

Copyright © Michael McCahill, 2023

Michael McCahill has asserted his right under the Copyright,
Designs and Patents Act, 1988, to be identified as Author of this work.

For legal purposes the Acknowledgements on p. viii constitute an
extension of this copyright page.

Cover image © English House of Commons in 1793. Hand-coloured woodcut.
North Wind Picture Archives / Alamy Stock Photo

All rights reserved. No part of this publication may be reproduced or transmitted
in any form or by any means, electronic or mechanical, including photocopying,
recording, or any information storage or retrieval system, without prior permission
in writing from the publishers.

Bloomsbury Publishing Plc does not have any control over, or responsibility for, any
third-party websites referred to or in this book. All internet addresses given in
this book were correct at the time of going to press. The author and publisher regret any
inconvenience caused if addresses have changed or sites have ceased to exist,
but can accept no responsibility for any such changes.

A catalogue record for this book is available from the British Library.

A catalog record for this book is available from the Library of Congress.

ISBN: PB: 978-1-3503-3228-7
ePDF: 978-1-3503-3229-4
eBook: 978-1-3503-3230-0

Typeset by RefineCatch Limited, Bungay, Suffolk

To find out more about our authors and books visit www.bloomsbury.com
and sign up for our newsletters.

Contents

List of Figures		vi
List of Tables		vii
Acknowledgements		viii
1	MPs and Legislation in Late Eighteenth-Century Parliaments	1
2	Knights of the Shire	29
3	Contentious Constituencies: Plymouth, Kingston-upon-Hull, Bristol and their MPs	55
4	Successful and Less Significant Legislators: Blackstone, Newdigate and Windham	79
5	Thomas Gilbert: Legislator *Par Excellence*	97
6	Essex Imbroglios	117
7	Interest Groups: The West India Interest	129
8	Lobbies: Birmingham, The Chamber of Manufacturers and the Fisheries	159
9	Parliamentary Reform: Instructions and Representation	183
10	The Commons and the Lords: A Legislative Partnership?	211
11	Conclusion	233
Bibliography		245
Index		259

Figures

2.1 Sir George Savile, English Whig politician, 1770. Etching by B. Wilson and J. Basire, after a painting by B. Wilson. Photo by SSPL/Getty Images.   37

3.1 Portrait of British statesman and orator Edmund Burke (1729–1797), a member of British Parliament who advocated a liberal treatment in the government of the American colonies and supported the abolition of the Atlantic slave trade, 1780s. Photo by Stock Montage/Getty Images.   66

9.1 William Beckford, James Townshend and John Sawbridge seated at a table and conversing, engraving, 1830. From the New York Public Library. Photo by Smith Collection/Gado/Getty Images.   196

Tables

1.1	Numbers of MPs who conducted legislation through the House of Commons in nine sessions. 1765–7, 1772–4, 1786–8.	9
1.2	Numbers and percentage of MPs overseeing the passage of legislation over three sessions. 1765–7, 1772–4, 1786–8.	10
1.3	Number of bills carried by active MPs through one or more steps, 1765–7 1772–4, 1786–8.	10
2.1	Levels of legislative activity of English county MPs in comparison to the total English contingent of 491 MPs, 1765–7, 1772–4, 1786–8.	31
2.2	Numbers of county members who promoted legislation in one or more of the sessions, 1765–7, 1772–4, 1786–8.	31
2.3	Numbers of bills promoted by county members, 1765–7, 1772–4, 1786–8.000	32
7.1	MPs with West Indian connections sitting for English constituencies, 1754–1790.	134

Acknowledgements

While preparing this book I have received assistance and advice from many people. Marshall Moriarty and Professor Fred Leventhal were the first to read portions of my manuscript when they kindly agreed to make sense of the Introduction which badly needed their thorough, insightful editing. Once they had completed their handiwork, I sent the chapter to Clyve Jones, who over the years had published my articles in *Parliamentary History* and my books in the journal's Texts and Studies series. In this case, he had urged me to send him the early version of the Introduction which he in turn forwarded to a reviewer who provided well-chosen critiques and recommendations that I later incorporated. I am forever grateful to Clyve for his support and encouragement over the years and miss him, both as a fellow historian of the eighteenth century and a friend. Since 1968 when I embarked on my PhD dissertation on the House of Lords, John Sainty has provided answers and guidance whenever I approached him with questions. This project coming over 50 years after our first meeting was no exception, and I am fortunate to be able to draw upon his limitless knowledge of the functioning of eighteenth-century parliaments, thereby saving myself from making any number of errors. He has been always willing to help, as has Professor Grayson Ditchfield who not only read and commented upon Chapter 5 but answered my questions as I slowly worked my way towards completing the book, with recommendations as to where I should send the manuscript for publication with happy results. He is invariably patient and helpful in responding to my queries. I am fortunate to have such good and informed colleagues and friends. Drs Stephen Farrell and E.A. Wasson answered my questions, recommended what I should read and suggested what issues I should address. In so doing they broadened my approach. I am grateful to Francesca Giacchino, Harvard's Reference Librarian, who took enormous amounts of time to find material that I needed to secure the permissions required to quote from various sources in Harvard's Widener Library. As I worked my way through the manuscript, Professor Eric Beerbohm of Harvard's Government Department read each chapter and discussed it with me. I appreciated his enthusiasm for the task, the points he raised in our discussions and the encouragement he invariably provided. Though not an eighteenth-century specialist, he is knowledgeable about Burke and the subject of representation. I benefited enormously from our sessions which kept me going before and during the pandemic. I am also grateful to Professor Richard D. Brown of the University of Connecticut for reading Chapter 7 to make sure that I did not make errors in my brief discussions of colonial American issues, and to Professor Andrew Kaufman of the Harvard Law School who secured books and other materials from the Law School's Library, sometimes via inter-library loan, sometimes by having short sources copied for me. My computer skills are limited, and I had the good fortune to be able to call upon several friends who helped to overcome my deficiencies: Lance

Latham located the images that appear in this book, and David Cooper assisted in locating the information regarding those images for Bloomsbury Academic while Howard Winkler worked hard to unravel several other intractable issues others were unable to resolve. Finally, I am grateful to Emily Drewe, Abigail Lane and Meghan Harris at Bloomsbury Academic for helping me prepare my case for the referees who would evaluate my book proposal and later guiding me through the early stages of preparing the manuscript for publication. They were invariably helpful, wise and patient. Finally, I am grateful to Tom Bedford, an extraordinarily patient and careful editor who more than compensated for my deficiencies in that area. I am especially fortunate to have been able to work with him.

American students of eighteenth-century Britain are also fortunate to be able to conduct their research in the country's many archives. I am grateful to the staff of the Birmingham Archives for their assistance during my visits and Geoff Burns for granting me permission to quote from the Matthew Boulton general correspondence. Similarly, during several days working at the Bristol Archives the staff was invariably helpful in dealing with my requests, and I appreciate the archivist, Malcolm Boyns, granting me permission to quote from the manuscripts of the Society of Merchant Venturers. Over the years I have spent months in the Manuscripts Room of the British Library reading the letters of eighteenth-century politicians. I am grateful to have access to its incomparable collections and to the staff who provide such excellent service to the readers. I also thank Zoe Stansell for extending me permission to quote from the additional manuscripts collections cited in my bibliography. Katherine Fox granted me permission to use passages from the Stephen Fuller Letterbooks in the Joseph J. Williams, SJ ethnological collection, MS.2009.030, at the John J. Burns Library, Boston College, and Katrina Dean provided permission on behalf of the Syndics of the Cambridge University Library to quote from the Vanneck of Heveningham Papers (Vanneck-Arcedeckne Mss). I was fortunate to be able to spend many days working at the David M. Rubenstein Rare Book and Manuscript Library at Duke University on this and a previous project, reading Stephen Fuller's letterbooks. It is a wonderful place to work, and I thank Amy McDonald, the University's Assistant Archivist, for permission to quote from their Fuller Papers. I am grateful as well to the Duty Officer of the Essex Record Office for allowing me to quote from Hilda Grieve's *The Sleepers and the Shadows: Chelmsford, Its People and Its Past*, Vol. 2 (Essex Record Office) and to the Record Office and Lord Rayleigh, depositor of the collection, for allowing me to quote from the Strutt MSS. Paul Seward gave me permission to use extracts from the eighteenth-century volumes of the *History of Parliament*, while Victoria Oakman, Collections Officer at the Northamptonshire Archives and Heritage Centre, permitted me to quote from the Fitzwilliam Papers, and Mrs Jaime McMurtie, Archivist at Inspire Nottingham Archives, also gave me leave to include several passages from the Savile-Foljambe Mss. Professor Richard Gaunt, editor of *Parliamentary History*, allowed me to include passages of various lengths from its publications, while Tim Knebel, archivist at the Sheffield City Library, allowed me to quote from certain series of records in the Wentworth Woodhouse Muniments Collection, including the 2nd Marquis of Rockingham papers (where the letter in question comes from); an additional specific acknowledgement is required to the Sheffield City Council as follows: This was an original stipulation which formed part of the agreement with the Estates Office when the records first came to us many decades ago. The collection in question is Wentworth Woodhouse Mss R1/1232. Cambridge University Press has permitted me to use a passage from a chapter by Mark Knights: 'Participation and representation before democracy: Petitions and addresses in premodern Britain', in *Political Representation*, ed. Ian Shapiro, Susan S. Stokes, Elizabeth Jean Wood and Alexander S. Kirshner (2009); in addition, Oxford University Press extended me permission to use several passages from *The Writings and Speeches of Edmund Burke: Party, Parliament and the American War, 1774–1780*, iii, ed. W.M. Elofson, W.M. and John A. Woods (1996), other passages from Paul Langford's *Public Life and Propertied Englishman, 1689–1798* (1991), and one letter from *The Correspondence of Edmund Burke, 1778–1782*, iv, ed. John A. Woods (1974), pp. 273–4. Likewise, the Enquiry Officer at the University of Nottingham's Manuscripts and Special Collections Library allowed me to quote from PwF 6884 and PwF 9003 (Portland Mss), while Naomi Sackett, Archivist of the Wiltshire and Swindon History Centre, permitted me to quote from The Letters of Thomas Prowse to Peter Lovell, 1749–1767. Samantha Ryan on behalf of the Warwickshire County Record Office gave me permission to quote from the Newdigate Mss on deposit there; Kim Leichner, the Rights Administrator at the University of Pennsylvania Press gave me permission to include several passages from Andrew Jackson O'Shaughnessy's *An Empire Divided: The American Revolution and the British Caribbean*, and, finally, Jane de Gruchey, Archivist, Somerset and Devon Archives and Local Studies extended permission to quote from the Dickinson Mss in Taunton.

I must give very special thanks to three people. Denie Weil made her Covent Garden flat available to my wife and me whenever we needed it. It was the perfect *pied-à-terre*, comfortable and well-stocked, with all sorts of tips regarding shopping, restaurants and medical care, within walking distance of the Institute of Historical Research and Waterloo Station and just a short bus ride to the British Library. The two of us could not have had a more comfortable and perfectly located base from which to do my research in the London area and through England. We owe Mrs Weil a great deal for the many happy and comfortable times we spent in London – my research went all the better because of her kindness. Ever since I started on my studies on the House of Lords and the peerage my wife, Barbara Ann, has travelled with me to and around Britain while I visited its many records repositories. Fortunately, she is a Tudor historian and an avid traveller, so for the most part, has never been at a loss for things to do while I worked. She has also been a booster, offering encouragement, reading drafts and making suggestions when I have been stuck and always travelling around Britain when she might have occupied herself elsewhere. More recently, as I completed this project and prepared the manuscript for publication, she coped with the move and settling into a new community with only limited assistance from me. Finally, and above all, I am indebted to my daughter, Elizabeth McCahill, a distinguished historian of the Roman Renaissance, who again and again took time out from her family and her own work to read, edit and comment upon my chapters. An elegant writer herself, she advised me on my prose and made me focus my arguments more carefully and not bury them in detail. Above all she encouraged me to make my case more forcefully, and at the outset, and not leave it to the reader to discover my point. Again and again, she saved me from my technological inadequacies, enabling me to prepare a manuscript that began to meet the criteria set by my editors, something I could not have done on my own. For her ongoing encouragement, help, advice and historical insight I dedicate this work to her with love and appreciation.

1

MPs and Legislation in Late Eighteenth-Century Parliaments

William Wilberforce[1] did not stand for re-election for Yorkshire in 1812 because of ill health. After serving his Yorkshire constituents for 28 years, they made no mention of his efforts to abolish the slave trade, but thanked him for overseeing 'the private business of the county',[2] by which they meant the specific and local bills a knight of the shire was expected to carry through the House. Nor was this sort of reaction unusual. In the *Staffordshire Advertiser*'s notice following Thomas Gilbert's[3] death the authors ignored his service as the leading poor law reformer of the age and his undisputed expertise on canal legislation, and instead celebrated Gilbert's zealous application

> to the amendment of the roads, and although he did not succeed in his original plan of procuring a general Act for their improvement yet he carried through the House many provincial bills which tended to make travelling in the counties of Northampton, Warwick, Stafford and Derby, the places to which he particularly directed his attention, infinitely more commodious and agreeable: indeed it is well known, that before his time, the highways were the worst in the Kingdom.[4]

These testimonials testify to the degree to which relatively minor bills consumed the attention of eighteenth-century MPs and loomed large in the minds of their constituents. Individual turnpike bills were of little significance, but taken together Gilbert's turnpike legislation transformed the midlands' highways into a system of transport that was useful in meeting the needs of the region's burgeoning agricultural and industrial economy. Similarly improvement acts passed during these years were an integral part of eighteenth- and nineteenth-century urbanisation as improvement commissioners stepped in to lay out streets which were paved and lit. The commissioners provided for central markets, new sewage systems and bridges; by these and other

---

[1] William Wilberforce (1759–1833), MP, Kinston-upon Hull, 1780–4. Yorkshire, 1784–1812, and Bramber, 1812–25.
[2] Quoted in Paul Langford, *Public Life and Propertied Englishman, 1689–1989* (Oxford, 1991), p. 164.
[3] Thomas Gilbert (?1719–98), MP, Newcastle-under-Lyme, 1763–8, and Lichfield, 1768–94; paymaster of charity for the relief of widows of naval officers, 1753–98; comptroller of the great wardrobe, 1763–82; chairman of ways and means, 1784–94.
[4] *Staffordshire Advertiser*, 12 Jan. 1799.

means they transformed the remnants of medieval towns into what began to resemble modern cities.

Rosemary Sweet argues that a by-product of the many local acts was that MPs and their urban constituencies '…were locked into a much more complex set of relationships and reciprocal obligations'.[5] Members responded to the torrent of specific and local legislation in the decades after 1750 and fulfilled expectations of neighbours and constituents who looked to them either to promote or oppose a variety of measures and not just local improvement acts. These interactions, as Sweet points out, created reciprocal relationships and norms of conduct that became more complex and pervasive. Once it became usual for MPs to respond to the instructions of neighbours and constituents regarding specific legislation, it gradually became more common for them to treat constituent instructions regarding new taxes or commercial policies with similar attention and respect, as we shall see in Chapters 9 and 10.

Constituent instructions were not new to the period.[6] During those years, however, a shift occurred in the number of MPs who responded to them, and in how the House reacted to members who indicated that their stance on issues was shaped, at least in part, by constituents' instructions. Had they made such statements a decade or two earlier, members would have faced criticism and ridicule.[7] By the mid-1780s, after a decade of Wilkite agitation, Association petitioning and a disastrous war, members justified their positions on important national questions by citing instructions, usually without provoking heated responses regarding the legitimacy of their conduct. Colleagues might challenge their approach, but MPs cited constituent views as a legitimate determinant of their own positions on new taxes, commercial agreements and other questions of national importance.[8]

In doing so they challenged the position of Edmund Burke, who famously told his Bristol constituents in 1774 that MPs were virtual representatives of the entire nation. For this reason, their narrow preoccupations had to give way to a broader vision that an MP attained from attending to the range of opinions expressed in the Commons and, on the basis of these, coming to his own informed views. What Burke offered was an ideal vision of the proper conduct of members of Parliament. This inquiry, however, has found ample examples to show that practical considerations and, to a much lesser

---

[5] Rosemary Sweet, *The English Towns, 1680–1840: Government, Society and Culture* (Harlow and New York, 1998), p. 59.
[6] For discussion of instructions to eighteenth-century MPs, see Paul Kelly, 'Constituents' instructions to members of Parliament in the eighteenth century', in *Party Management in Parliament, 1660–1784*, ed. Clyve Jones (New York, 1984), pp. 169–89; and Nicholas Rogers, *Whigs and Cities: Popular Politics in the Age of Walpole and Pitt* (Oxford, 1989), pp. 68, 98–9, 103–4, 120–1, 240–4.
[7] See, for example, *Parliamentary History [PH]*, xxiii, cc. 998–1016.
[8] For Burke's views on the MP and his relations to his constituents, see Edmund Burke, 'To the electors of Bristol on being declared by Sheriffs, duly elected one of the representatives of Parliament for that city' [1774], in *The Writings and Speeches of Edmund Burke*, general ed. Paul Langford, Vol. II, ed. W.M. Elofson with John A. Woods (Oxford, 1996), pp. 68–70; Lucy Sutherland, 'Edmund Burke and relations between members of Parliament and their constituents', in *Politics and Finance in the Eighteenth Century*, ed. Aubrey Newman (1984), pp. 281–97; P.T. Underdown, 'Bristol and Burke', in *Bristol in the Eighteenth Century*, ed. Patrick McGrath (Newton Abbot, 1972), pp. 41–62. Burke, however, acknowledged the right of constituents to instruct MPs on matters relating to specific legislation and local business.

degree, reforming enthusiasm shaped the legislative behaviour of English MPs during the last quarter of the eighteenth century. The following chapters, and in particular Chapters 9 and 11, show that for many MPs Burke's vision gave way to the needs and opinions of constituents, pressure from family and the pleas of neighbours, friends and patrons. Thus, the same Parliament which refused to heed appeals from metropolitan radicals and Yorkshire reformers to enlarge the political nation and make MPs more directly responsible to 'the people' addressed the needs of significant segments of the nation.

I: Methodology

Given the important impact of the seemingly modest individual bills which collectively represented about three-quarters of Parliament's annual output during the eighteenth century, it is not surprising that Paul Langford remarked 30 years ago that 'research into Parliament as a legislative institution is in its infancy'.[9] Since that time Julian Hoppit and Joanna Innes have enriched our understanding of the nature, volume and variety of the legislation it enacted.[10] They also surveyed the ways in which the House coped with the wave of legislation once annual meetings of Parliament became the norm after 1689.[11] Langford has also shown that MPs took up legislative projects promoted by those who lived in the neighbourhood of their estates but outside of the boundaries of Parliamentary boroughs, thereby providing underrepresented regions access to Westminster.[12] Together these and other scholars have enlarged our understanding of the legislative business of the House and some of the ways its members coped with the vast increase in its business. Their work, however, has concentrated primarily on defining the volume of legislation, its nature and the processes the Commons created to handle the increase in legislation once petitioners discovered that the Parliamentary statute became the most reliable and inexpensive means of 'remodelling and revising property rights'.

Thus, we still know little about how and to what degree the great body of MPs participated in the legislative business of the House. The biographies of MPs in the volumes of the *History of Parliament*[13] for this period make only intermittent reference to the members' activities as legislators. It is as if the editors of those volume considered the Commons' legislative role as of minimal importance.[14] Fortunately, Langford, Hoppit and others have inspired a number of articles which investigate either the

---

[9] Paul Langford, *Public Life and Propertied Englishmen, 1689-1798* (Oxford, 1991), p. viii.
[10] Julian Hoppit, Joanna Innes and John Styles, 'Towards a history of Parliamentary legislation, 1660-1800', *Parl. Hist.*, xiii (1994), 213–221; and Hoppit and Innes, 'Introduction', in *Failed Legislation, 1660-1800*, ed. Hoppit (London and Rio Grande, Ohio, 1997), p. 3.
[11] Hoppit and Innes, 'Introduction', *Failed Legislation*, pp. 5–6.
[12] Langford, *Public Life*, pp. 192-201; and 'Property and "virtual representation" in eighteenth-century England', *HJ*, xxxi (1988), 83–106.
[13] *History of Parliament: The House of Commons 1754-1790 [HPC]*, ed. Sir Lewis Namier and John Brooke (3 vols, 1964).
[14] For more on this point, see David Cannadine, 'The history of Parliament: Past and present – and future', *Parl. Hist.*, xxvi (2007), 366–86.

legislative work of individual MPs or the legislative activity relating to particular issues, including Parliament and the regions, enclosure and canals, poor relief, penal and penitentiary reform, interest groups, and the promotion of trade. Indeed, in the last several years, my unscientific sense is that the output of such articles has accelerated. With the exception of Professors Langford, Hoppit and Innes no authorities have attempted a synthesis of this work that focuses on the full range of legislation.[15] My goals are to pull this material together along with the results of my own research to explain how English MPs who sat between 1754 and 1790 viewed their legislative responsibilities and to what the extent they fulfilled them by taking an active part in carrying bills through their various stages in the Commons.[16]

In answering these questions, my focus differs from that of T.K. Moore and Henry Horwitz, authors of an important study of the Commons' 'working' members, in large part because I focus exclusively upon English MPs' participation in the legislative business of the Commons. By contrast their conclusions derived from data they collected for the 1691-2 and 1692-3 sessions in order to identify 'working' members:[17] their criteria included telling divisions, participation in debates and nominations to second reading committees as well as to committees of investigation. Claiming that their focus was on 'public affairs', they explicitly ignored proceedings relating to specific legislation.[18] My book, by contrast, studies how and why members undertook the management of specific bills, which by the late eighteenth century accounted for almost three-quarters of the legislation that annually reached the statute book.[19]

---

[15] Hoppit, 'Reforming Britain's weights and measures, 1660-1824', *English Historical Review [EHR]*, cvii (1993), pp. 82, 94-5; Innes, 'Parliament and the shaping of eighteenth-sentury social policy', *Transactions of the Royal Historical Society [TRHS]*, 5th ser., cl (1990), pp. 63-92. Both articles stress that governments were wary of initiating general legislation on these questions, which was instead initiated by backbench MPs.

[16] England returned 489 MPs from 40 counties, 203 boroughs and the two universities. *History of Parliament: The House of Commons, 1754-1790*, ed. L.B. Namier and J. Brooke (3 vols, 1964), i, 2. To this group I added Edward Kynaston and Ralph Congreve, both of whom sat for Welsh constituencies in the 1761 Parliament. Congreve, whose principal estate was in Berkshire, was described by constituents as 'a person who was not so much as known' in Cardiganshire. *HPC, 1754-1790*, iii, 15, ii, 242. Because of the scope of the project, I focused this study on MPs sitting for English constituencies between 1754 and 1790.

[17] T.K. Moore and Henry Horwitz, 'Who runs the House? Aspects of Parliamentary organization in the later seventeenth century', *JMH*, xliii (1971), 205-27. Between 1714 and 1760 Parliament passed 2635 specific acts and 914 general acts; during the years 1760-1800 the numbers of each increased substantially to 6206 specific acts and 2145 general ones. About 74.3 per cent of the measures enacted in the period on which this book focuses were specific. Hoppit, 'Patterns of Parliamentary legislation, 1660-1801', *Historical Journal*, xxxix (1996), p. 117.

[18] Instead they collected data on who told divisions, participated in debates or were nominated to its second reading committees and committees of investigation. Moore and Horwitz, 'Who runs the House?', pp. 206-8, 210

[19] Hoppit, 'Patterns of Parliamentary legislation, 1660-1801', Table 1, p. 117. Like Hoppit, I use the terms specific, general or national as opposed to public and private to describe different categories of bills. For his rationale for this usage, see, 'Patterns', p. 116. For the problems with 'public and private', see also, Langford, *Public Life*, pp. 164-5, Sheila Lambert, *Bills and Acts: Legislative Procedure in Eighteenth-Century England* (Cambridge, 1971), pp. 29-30, 84-5; and Peter Thomas, *The House of Commons in the Eighteenth Century* (Brookfield, VT, 1992), pp. 45-7.

To identify members who conducted the legislative business of the House I collected data from the *Journals of the House of Commons* for three sets of three consecutive sessions[20] – 1765–67, 1772–74 and 1786–88[21] – and identified each MP who carried measures through one or more stages over their journey through the chamber. Unlike Moore and Horwitz I did not collect data relating to those who tallied those voting for and against a motion at divisions, nor did I compile lists of who spoke in debates because the local and specific legislation provoked few recorded debates and fewer divisions, whose outcomes were rarely recorded.[22]

By and large my study emphasises the contributions of backbench MPs and less frequently those of the leading politicians and others who held offices under the Crown. Authors of monographs or the biographies in the volumes of the *History of Parliament* have made some effort to chronicle the latter's legislative exploits. In this book I focus on the work of the many backbench MPs in promoting the specific and local legislation of constituents, neighbours and other clients and family members. From time to time individuals within the group were called upon by ministers to assist in moving their controversial measures through the House. In addition, I followed the efforts of politicians and other officials who promoted specific and local legislation at the behest of constituents and other clients and assisted backbench MPs in steering their own general measures through Parliament.

Despite our differing focus and our using varying criteria to identify 'working members', I identified one of my groups that was similar to one of their two 'working' groups. The first of their groups consisted of MPs who spoke frequently in debates, had considerable Parliamentary experience and took a Whiggish or Country line in the proceedings; for the most part they held or aspired to office and usually sat for constituencies with smaller numbers of electors; the second group consisted of those who chaired second reading committees. As a group, they were less experienced than the debaters, and more likely to sit for large constituencies than the debaters.[23] These MPs were not unlike the small active group who carried 11 or more bills over two sessions in one of my three-session groupings. Like Moore and Horwitz's second reading groups, my most active group of MPs for the 1760s and 1770s with a few exceptions

---

[20] I opted to collect data for three sets of three consecutive sessions in order to identify patterns that characterised the eighteenth-century legislative process as well as the numbers of and manner in which MPs participated in it.

[21] I selected the years 1765–7 and 1772–4, because they represented the high tide in upsurge in the number of legislative initiatives that commenced in the 1750s and continued through the early 1770s (in the case of turnpikes) to later in the 1770s or early 1780s for canals, enclosures or estate bills. Those who have studied the creation of turnpike and canal networks as well as the incidence of enclosure and estate legislation agree that rising interest rates, credit shortages and disruptions in trade led to a drop in the numbers of these bills that came before Parliament in the mid to late 1770s or early 1780s; they also agree that recovery to levels of the peak periods did not occur until the late 1780s or the early 1790s: William Albert, *The Turnpike Road System in England, 1763–1840* (Cambridge, 1974), pp. 51–4; McCahill, Michael, 'Estate acts of Parliament, 1740–1800', in *Institutional Practice and Memory*, ed. Clyve Jones (Chichester, 2013), p. 149; Michael Turner, *English Parliamentary Enclosure* (Folkestone, Kent and Hamden, CT, 1980), pp. 66–9; J.R. Ward, *The Finance of Canal Building in Eighteenth-Century England* (1974), p. 4.

[22] Moore and Horwitz, 'Who runs the House?', p. 208.

[23] Moore and Horwitz, 'Who runs the House?', pp. 216–7, 224–5.

were returned from constituencies with 1000 constituents and like Moore and Horwitz's second reading contingent showed no inclination to attain political office. While most were independent country gentlemen, a few had strong political connections, and unlike Moore and Horwitz' relatively inexperienced members, mine already had served an average of 11 years in the House by 1766 and 13 years by 1773. What the two shared in common is that they were both useful to the nation at large!

II: The Legislative Process

The legislative process for specific and local bills got underway when an MP moved for the House to receive the petition for such a measure.[24] Petitions were usually prepared by the attorney employed by the group organising the project.[25] Once the petition was finalised, the MP who would subsequently take charge of the bill presented it to the House. It was referred to a select committee, whose membership was chosen by nomination, based on pertinent local, personal and professional knowledge, and chaired by the measure's sponsor. The committee, having set dates for subsequent sessions, examined the points of the petition and counter-petitions, if they were forthcoming. The chair delivered his report from the bar of the House; after he had done so, a clerk presented a summary of the evidence, and the chair moved for leave to bring in the bill, which was then read for the first time. The first reading was usually a formality. Standing orders of 1699 required that there be at least three days between each reading of specific and local bills to prevent surprises, so the crucial phases of the measures' journeys through the House were predictable. The bill's sponsor moved for the second reading, providing the House its first opportunity to consider the measure's principle. Usually it was at this point that the House heard petitions against the principle. After the House determined that the reasons given by promoters to justify the need for legislation were valid, the sponsor moved seven days later to have the bill committed. In a select committee, its members examined the bill's contents in detail, filled in the blanks and made additional amendments, sometimes in response to counter-petitions. At the completion of the proceedings, the chairman moved that the report be received on a specified day. He presented the report at the bar of the House. Once the House accepted the report and adopted any amendments, the sponsor moved that the bill should be engrossed, which meant putting it in its final form, after which the bill would receive a third reading and when further amendments might be added, or sometimes on the same day he moved 'that this bill shall pass'. Once that was adopted, the bill was carried to the House of Lords.

---

[24] Petitions for so-called private bills were required by Standing Order 25 (1685).
[25] Bramwell, *The Manner of Proceeding on Bills in the House of Lords* (1831), p. 36. Members of the committee to build a canal from the River Calder to Barnsley in Yorkshire appointed a solicitor to prepare the draft of their bill which they reviewed over three days, making alterations and adding several clauses before approving a final draft. They then sent their solicitor to make the application to Parliament along with several of their own numbers to attend its passage. TNA, RAIL 806/3, ff. 18–19, Barnsley Canal Minute Book, 3–5 Jan. 1783. See also, Lambert, *Bills and Acts*, pp. 62–3.

Unlike the case with 'private' bills, new pubic bills did not require a petition. All that was necessary was for the member to apply for leave to bring in his bill, at which point it would receive its first reading. With public bills there was no specified three-day hiatus between each reading, and they went into a Committee of the whole House instead of a select committee following their second reading. Otherwise, the two sorts of measures went through similar stages.

In chronicling the work of individual MPs, I recorded the names of those who chaired the petition committees, presented their reports, moved to bring in the bill and moved for its first reading. I did not record the names of those assigned by the House to prepare bills, because for the most part that task had already been accomplished by the measure's promoters and their attorney. The exceptions were those MPs who introduced their own legislation; in those cases, as we shall see, the members, depending upon the circumstances, worked with a variety of local or ecclesiastical officials, but usually had drafts of their measures vetted by the Crown's legal officers before presenting them to the House. I also noted all those who chaired the second reading committees of bills and delivered their reports, but did not attempt to keep track of those who attended those committees, mainly because the House ceased to keep a record of attendance at select committees after 1768, and in any case few of those originally assigned attended their sessions.[26] I did, however, make a note of those who moved for the third reading of bills and later moved that 'the bill shall pass' and carried it to the Lords when it did. What all these steps had in common was that they required some degree of activity on the part of the member. They not only had to be present and familiar with the contents of their measure, but also knowledgeable regarding the orders of the House and capable of handling the complaints of counter-petitioners and the pressures of the Commons' schedule.[27]

III: Backbench MPs and General Measures

Sponsors of general measures, initiated by ministers or backbenchers, sometimes relied upon backbenchers with special experience and skills to oversee their progress, particularly in the second reading committees of the whole House. Among the more important of these individuals in the 1760s was Edward Kynaston.[28] During the 1765 session Kynaston oversaw the passage of eight pieces of specific legislation and chaired

---

[26] Lambert, *Bills and Acts*, pp. 96–7, 99–101; Thomas, *House of Commons*, pp. 50–2.
[27] The *Journals* are not always precise in making clear which member was involved at a particular point. Usually they identify MPs by their surnames, though in cases in which members shared them, efforts were made to add a first name as well. There were seven Mr. Townshends in the Commons at some point between 1761 and 1790; two were the Hon. Mr. Townshend; there were also three Mr. Lascelles (Daniel, Edwin and Edward) between 1761 and 1780. On a few occasions, guesswork was needed to determine who was who, and it is unlikely that all my guesses were accurate; inevitably in the tedious process of recording and transcribing I made further errors. Still, my data, collected over nine sessions, provides a broad and largely accurate survey of the portion of hundreds of members of the House of Commons.
[28] Edward Kynaston (1709–72), MP, Bishop's Castle, 1734–41 and Montgomeryshire, 1747–72.

committees of the whole House on 12 general bills, including Thomas Gilbert's bill 'for the better relief of the poor',[29] one of his bills for the preservation of the nation's roads and highways, a third to encourage the growth of madder[30] and a militia bill, whose primary object was to compel delinquent counties to fulfil obligations laid out in the militia acts of 1757 and 1762.[31] Presented by Sir George Savile,[32] one of the chamber's principal proponents of the militia, the measure owed its existence to similarly minded MPs, who were sufficiently numerous to carry it against colleagues from inland counties that wished to avoid the expense of supporting a force they believed was needed only to defend their coastal neighbours.[33]

The general acts Kynaston guided through the committee in 1765 were the work of backbench MPs. Overseeing these measures compelled him to attend the House almost daily between 12 February and April 22, 1765. Namier in his short biography of Kynaston noted that upon his resignation George Grenville[34] told Kynaston 'I shall always be ready to bear witness to your constant attendance at the House'. Yet, Sir Lewis seems not to have consulted the *Journals* and discovered what it was that necessitated Kynaston's attendance.[35]

While his legislative work in these instances was apolitical, Rose Fuller's[36] was not. Though he held no office in the Rockingham administration, he was selected in 1766 to chair another committee of the whole House on which the government relied to make its case for the Stamp Act's repeal. Fuller performed the task with admirable skill, selecting and scheduling witnesses who from the outset of the committee's sessions made the case for the Stamp Act's repeal. At his instigation witnesses with West Indian connections detailed the damage the Stamp Act had done to the Caribbean economy.[37]

IV: MPs' Level of Legislative Activity

Data derived from my survey of MPs' participation in the legislative business of the House reveals notable consistency in the numbers and percentage of those who took

---

[29] See, Innes, 'Parliament and social policy', pp. 88–9. Though the bill was passed by the Commons, it was rejected in the Lords by those who wished to embarrass the Duke of Bedford and George Grenville. *HPC, 1754–1790,* i, 181.

[30] The root of a madder plant was used to produce a reddish-purple dye.

[31] J.R. Western, *The English Militia in the Eighteenth Century: The Story of a Political Issue, 1660–1800* (Oxford, 1958), pp. 196–7.

[32] Sir George Savile, 8th Bt. (1726–84), MP Yorkshire 1759–83.

[33] *Journals of the House of Commons [CJ]*, xxx, 422. The act failed to compel all counties to fulfil their obligations. Derbyshire and Worcestershire only raised a militia in 1770 and 1773. Western, *English Militia*, p. 199.

[34] George Grenville (1712–70), MP, Buckingham, 1741–70; Ld. of Admiralty, 1744–7 and of Treasury, 1747–54; Treasurer of Navy, 1754–5, 1756–7 and 1757–62; Sec. of State, 1762; First Ld. of Admiralty, 1762–3; First Lord of the Treasury, 1763–5.

[35] *HPC, 1754–1790,* iii, p. 15.

[36] Rose Fuller (?1708–77), member of the Jamaican assembly, 1735 and of the council, 1737; MP, New Romney, 1756–61; Maidstone, 1761–8 and Rye, 1768–77.

[37] Peter D.G. Thomas, *British Politics and the Stamp Act Crisis: The First Phase of the American Revolution, 1763–1767* (Oxford, 1975), p. 226; *HPC, 1754–1790,* ii, 479. For a more extended discussion of Fuller's role as chairman, see Chapter 7.

Table 1.1 Numbers of MPs who conducted legislation through the House of Commons in nine sessions, 1765–7, 1772–4, 1786–8

1765 – 133	1772 – 128	1786 – 122
1766 – 105	1773 – 122	1787 – 94
1767 – 111	1774 – 108	1788 – 105

part in the legislative process. Table 1.1 shows that the number who did so never exceeded 133, and that it only once fell below 100. Likewise, the percentage of English MPs who participated in legislative business ranged from 19.1 in 1787 to 27.1 in 1765. On average, slightly over 23 per cent of these members actively engaged in the legislative business of nine sessions. Levels of individual participation varied widely. William Baker[38] was largely inactive in 1774. In late March, however, he presented a bill to allow the export of wheat meal, oats, barley, pease, beans and malt to Hudson's Bay and three days later carried the bill to the House of Lords after its passage in the Commons (14 George III, c. 2). The more taxing job of shepherding the measure through its second reading committee fell to his friend, Frederick Montagu,[39] a seasoned Parliamentarian.

At the other extreme was Lord Brownlow Bertie,[40] who possessed a talent for moving Lincolnshire enclosure, drainage and navigation bills through the House. In 1774, a relatively light year for him, he guided seven enclosure bills and a measure to make the River Witham navigable to passage between 4 April and 17 May. In the same session Sir Thomas Clavering[41] undertook a more challenging load that included oversight of a disputed estate bill and three other proposals, one of which was the controversial Town Moor enclosure bill.[42] In addition Clavering chaired two committees of the whole House relating to the health and discharge of prisoners from gaol.[43]

---

[38] William Baker (1743–1824), MP, Plympton Erle, 1768–74, Aldborough, 1777–80, Hertford, 1780–4, and Hertfordshire, 1790–1802, 1805–7. Sheriff, London and Mdsx, 1770–1. Baker was a member of the committee of the Hudson's Bay Company which promoted the legislation in order to remove the prohibition of the export of the staples to the colonies that was included in the Corn Act of 1773 (13 George III, c. 43). Donald Grove Barnes, *A History of the English Corn Laws from 1660–1846* (1930), p. 49.

[39] Frederick Montagu (1733–1800), MP, Northampton, 1759–68 and Higham Ferrers, 1768–90; Ld. of Treasury, 1782, 1782–3.

[40] Lord Brownlow Bertie (1729–1809), MP, Lincolnshire, 1781–79; succ. as 5th Duke of Ancaster, 1779; Ld. Lt., Lincolnshire, 1779–1809.

[41] Sir Thomas Clavering, 7th Bt. (1719–94), MP, St. Mawes, 1753–4, Shaftesbury, 1754–60 and Durham Co., 1768–90.

[42] The measure arose out of a controversy following the decision of the Corporation of Newcastle-upon-Tyne in 1772 to enclose a portion of the Town Moor for cultivation, an act that threatened the customary rights of the town's freemen. Some of the latter were arrested after breaking fences and gates on the enclosed areas. Brought to trial in 1773, their counsel, Serj. John Gylnn (MP, Middlesex), defended the freemen's customary rights, which the Northumberland assizes upheld and ordered that an agreement reached between the lessee and the freemen be incorporated into a bill to be obtained at the Corporation's expense. Though opposed by the town's MPs, the bill passed. H.T. Dickinson, *Radical Politics in the North-East of England in the Later Eighteenth Century* (Durham County Local History Society, 1979), 7–8; see also, Kathleen Wilson, *The Sense of the People: Politics, Culture and Imperialism in England, 1715–1785* (Cambridge, 1995), pp. 343–5.

[43] 14 George III, c. 20 and 59.

Ultimately the House approved these controversial bills. His most arduous assignment, however, was to chair a committee appointed to investigate the state of the linen trade in Great Britain and Ireland. Though the committee got underway on 1 March, Clavering was unable to produce an interim report until April 25 because the issue provoked innumerable petitions from proponents of the industry and from representatives of trades that feared concessions to the linen industry would harm their own prospects.[44]

These individual examples do not, however, convey the range of legislative activity throughout the nine sessions. Tables 1.2 and 1.3 address that question from two different perspectives: levels of participation during each of the three-session segments and the number of bills promoted by individual MPs over the three-year groupings. The percentage of English members promoting legislation ranged from 41.1 in the 1780s to 45 in the 1770s, and 42.4 between 1765 and 1767. Table 1.3 also shows that there was remarkable consistency in the number of bills carried by English MPs in the three-session blocks of the 1760s and the 1770s.

Moreover, the decline in the number of enclosure, estate, turnpike and canal bills promoted by the active legislators in the 1780s resulted from rising interest rates that

Table 1.2 Numbers and percentage of MPs overseeing the passage of legislation over three sessions, 1765–7, 1772–4, 1786–8

	1 Session	2 Sessions	3 Sessions	Total Active MPs
1765–7	102 (49.0%)	60 (28.8%)	46 (22.1%)	208 (42.4%)
1772–4	108 (48.9%)	59 (26.7%)	54 (24.4%)	221 (45.0%)
1786–8	128 (63.3%)	45 (22.3%)	29 (14.4%)	202 (41.1%)

Table 1.3 Number of bills carried by active MPs through one or more steps, 1765–7, 1772–4, 1786–8

	1 Bill	2–5 Bills	6–10 Bills	Over 11 Bills
1765–7	62 (29.8%)	94 (45.2%)	29 (13.9%)	23 (11.3%)
1772–4	67 (30.5%)	98 (44.5%)	32 (14.5%)	23 (10.5%)
1786–8	93 (46.0%)	65 (32.2%)	27 (13.4%)	17 (8.4%)

[44] The inquiry over which Clavering presided responded to the declining fortunes of the linen industry in Ireland and Scotland, due, its supporters maintained, to competition from foreign markets and the failure of credit following on the financial crisis of 1772–3. Scottish members pressed for bounties to encourage exports. Cotton manufactures contended bounties would give a preference to linen over their products; representatives of woollen manufacturers protested linen needed no protection because no other manufacture was in such good shape. Debrett, *Parl. Reg.*, vii, pp. 274–6, 279–80, 282–3. Parliament proposed some action on the issue after the presentation of an inconclusive interim report. *CJ*, xxxiv, 677. Lord Frederick Campbell presented a fuller report on behalf of the linen industry on 25 May 1773. 'Report from the Committees appointed to present state of the linen trade in Great Britain and Ireland', *House of Commons Sessional Papers*, ed. Sheila Lambert, pp. 387–438. For the petitions presented against concessions to the linen industry, see *CJ*, xxxiv, 522, 525–6, 540, 548, 551, 556, 565, 574, 578, 582; and Univ. of Bristol, Special Collections, Arts and Sciences Library, 'Matthew Brickdale Parliamentary diary', Vol. 9, ff. 46–7, Vol. 10, ff. 3–6, 14.

accompanied the war with the North American colonies. The number of these bills did not begin to return to their earlier levels until the mid to late 1780s and early 1790s.

What most of the active members had in common was that they represented populous constituencies – counties or boroughs with electorates of 1,000 or more voters: three-quarters met that criterion in the 1760s, as did two-thirds in the 1770s. The data presented in Tables 1.2 and 1.3 also highlight the fact that there were at least three levels of legislative 'workers'. To identify the most active group, I selected members who managed legislation in at least two sessions and over the same period guided 11 or more bills through their stages for passage. Between 1765 and 1767 there were 23 of these members,[45] and in the next decade there were 22.[46] Only Peter Burrell,[47] Nathaniel Cholmley[48] and Henry Shiffner[49] among the active MPs in the 1760s represented constituencies with under 350 electors, and in the 1770s, Cholmley and Beaumont Hotham[50] at Wigan represented 100 or fewer constituents, Sir Cecil Wray at East Retford[51] about 150, and Whitworth at Minehead had about 300. Mackworth[52] and Brudenell[53] represented larger constituencies with about 500 and 800 constituents respectively. As a group the most active legislators were experienced – their median level of service being 11 years in 1766 and 13 in 1773.

Within each group there were significant variations in levels of activity. While most oversaw legislation in each of the three sessions and a minimum of 11 bills over those periods, there were differences. Between 1765 and 1767 Lord Brownlow Bertie and John Hewett[54] guided 30 bills through one or more of steps in their passage through

[45] Edward Bacon (Norwich), Sir William Beauchamp Proctor (Middlesex), Lord Brownlow Bertie (Lincolnshire), Peter Burrell (Launceston), Lord George Augustus Cavendish (Derbyshire), Nathaniel Cholmley (Aldborough), Sir John Hynde Cotton (Cambridgeshire), William Fitzherbert (Derby), Rose Fuller (Maidstone), Thomas Gilbert (Newcastle-under-Lyme), Lord Grey (Staffordshire), John Hewett (Nottinghamshire), Edward Kynaston (Montgomeryshire), Sir Robert Ladbroke (London), Edwin Lascelles (Yorkshire), Richard Lowndes (Buckinghamshire), Sir Joseph Mawbey (Southwark), Frederick Montagu (Northampton), Sir Charles Mordaunt (Warwickshire), Hon. Edwin Sandys (Westminster), Sir George Savile (Yorkshire), Sir Francis Vincent (Surrey), Thomas Whichcot (Lincolnshire).

[46] Sir Edward Astley (Norfolk), Edward Bacon (Norwich), Lord Brownlow Bertie (Lincolnshire), George Bridges Brudenell (Rutland), Lord George Augustus Cavendish (Derbyshire), Nathaniel Cholmley (Boroughbridge), Sir Thomas Clavering (Durham Co.), Sir John Hynde Cotton (Cambridgeshire), Thomas DeGrey (Norfolk), Sir William Dolben (Northamptonshire), William Dowdeswell (Worcestershire), Thomas Gilbert (Lichfield), Charles Gray (Colchester), Thomas Harley (London), Beaumont Hotham (Wigan), Sir Herbert Mackworth (Cardiff Boroughs), Sir George Savile (Yorkshire), Sir Thomas Skipwith (Warwickshire), Sir Francis Vincent (Surrey), Sir Charles Whitworth (Minehead), Hon. Thomas Willoughby (Nottinghamshire), Sir Cecil Wray (East Retford).

[47] Peter Burrell (1723–75) MP, Launceston, 1759–68 and Totnes, 1768–74; surveyor-general of Crown lands, 1769–75.

[48] Nathaniel Cholmley (1721–91), MP, Aldborough, 1756–1768 and Boroughbridge, 1768–1774.

[49] Henry Shiffner (1721–1795), MP, Minehead, 1761–1768.

[50] Beaumont Hotham (1737–1814), MP, Wigan, 1768–1774, succ. bro as 2nd Baron Hotham [I] and 12th Bt., 1813; Baron of the Exchequer, 1775–1805; Commr. of the Great Seal, Apr–Dec. 1783.

[51] Sir Cecil Wray, 13th Bt. (1734–1805), MP, East Retford, 1768–1780 and Westminster, 1782–1784; cornet, 1 Drag. 1755; ret. 1757.

[52] Sir Herbert Mackworth (1737–1790), MP, Cardiff Boroughs, 1766–1790; cr. Bt., 1776.

[53] George Bridges Brudenell (?1725–1801), MP Rutland, 1754–1761 and 1768–1790 and Stamford, 1761–1768; Equerry to King, 1746–61; Clerk Comptroller of the Household, 1765–8; Clerk of the Board of the Green Cloth, 1768–82.

[54] John Hewett (1721–87), MP, Nottinghamshire, 1747–74.

their house, whereas Peter Burrell, Sir John Hynde Cotton,[55] Joseph Mawbey[56] and Thomas Whichcot[57] oversaw the progress of only 11. In the 1770s, Charles Whitworth[58] oversaw 71 measures, not surprising given his role as chairman of ways and means; far behind him were Bertie and Sir George Savile, both of whom promoted about 34, and George Bridges Brudenell who helped to forward over 30, whereas Thomas DeGrey,[59] Thomas Gilbert and Sir Cecil Wray promoted 11.

Though the active group for 1786–8 was smaller than its counterparts for the 1760s and 1770s, it had similar characteristics. Most of the 16 active legislators sat for large constituencies (14[60] for counties and two[61] for boroughs) whose electorates numbered 1000 or more. Only Gilbert sat for a smaller borough. In comparison to members of the active groups for the 1766 and 1773 sessions, the active legislators in 1787 were more experienced (median years of service: 19) and older (median age: 53). They were also less active legislators than Bertie and Hewett; only Henry Duncombe[62] and William Mainwaring[63] took charge of 20 or more bills over the three sessions.

My data finally highlight the fact that active legislators in one decade were likely, so long as they remained healthy, to legislate actively in subsequent sessions. Twelve[64] of the MPs who actively legislated in the three sessions in the 1760s did the same in the 1770s, and three[65] who promoted substantial amounts of legislation in the sessions of the 1770s did the same between 1786 and 1788.

At the other extreme were members who advanced only one bill in one of the three sessions of the three-session groupings. This relatively inactive cohort included 65 MPs in the 1760s, 72 between 1772 and 1774, and 98 in the 1780s. Representatives of small constituencies (with about 200 or fewer voters) predominated among this group in all three decades. Yet a significant portion of MPs, ranging from 34.7 per cent in the 1780s, to 30.6 per cent in the 1770s and 31.7 per cent in the 1760s, were returned from counties

---

[55] Sir John Hynde Cotton, 4th Bt. (?1717–95), MP, St. Germans, 1741–7, Marlborough, 1752–61 and Cambridgeshire, 1764–80.
[56] Sir Joseph Mawbey, Bt. (1730–98), MP, Southwark, 1761–74 and Surrey, 1775–90; cr. Bt. 1765.
[57] Thomas Whichcot (c. 1700–76), MP, Lincolnshire, 1740–74.
[58] Sir Charles Whitworth (c.1721–78), MP, Minehead, 1747–61 and 1768–74, Bletchingley, 1761–8, East Looe, 1774 and Saltash, 1775–8; Lt.-Gov. of Gravesend and Tilbury; Chair, ways and means, 1768–78.
[59] Thomas DeGrey, (1717–81), MP, Norfolk, 1764–74.
[60] John Blackburne (Lancashire), Lord G.A. Cavendish (Derbyshire), John Crewe (Cheshire), Henry Duncombe (Yorkshire), John Peach Hungerford (Leicestershire), Jervoise Clarke Jervoise (Hampshire), William Mainwaring (Middlesex), Hon. Charles Marsham (Kent), Thomas Master (Glouncestershire), Sir Joseph Mawbey (Surrey), Edward Phelips (Somerset), John Rolle (Devon), Sir John Thorold (Lincolnshire) and William Wilberforce (Yorkshire).
[61] Sir Matthew White Ridley (Newcastle-upon-Tyne) and Brooke Watson (London).
[62] Henry Duncombe (1728–1818), MP, Yorkshire, 1780–96.
[63] For a fuller discussion of Duncombe and Mainwaring, see Chapter 2.
[64] Edward Bacon, Lord Brownlow Bertie, Nathaniel Cholmley, Sir John Hynde Cotton, Rose Fuller, Hon. Thomas Harley, Richard Lowndes, Sir George Savile, Lord Charles Spencer, Hon. Frederick Vane, Sir Charles Whitworth and Sir George Yonge. Six of the 12 were knights of the shire for their full Parliamentary tenure; Sir Thomas Harley sat for London from 1761 to 1774 and Herefordshire from 1776–1802.
[65] Members of the 1770s/1780s group were Lord G.A. Cavendish, Sir William Dolben and Sir Matthew White Ridley.

and boroughs with electorates of 1,000 or more. MPs who promoted only one bill in the three-session sequences were not equally inactive. Of the 72 members who attended one session and were involved in the passage of one bill, 38 limited themselves either to presenting a bill or carrying it to the House of Lords.

The question has arisen regarding why I chose to focus on certain MPs and certain constituencies. Insofar as I was able, the legislative portraits of MPs provided throughout the book provided justifications for their inclusions. Not all of the latter were effective legislators. Indeed, that is why I included Sir William Blackstone and William Windham, men who achieved considerable prominence during the 1780s, and in Windham's case went on to attain cabinet office. Yet neither during the 1780s was notable for his legislative achievements, and Chapter 4 offers explanations for why this was the case. On the whole, however, I have taken a fairly benign view of the legislative accomplishments of the eighteenth-century legislator, which is why I added Chapter 6, focusing on MPs who represented several Essex constituencies as well as the county. Self-interest as well as personal and political rivalries undermined the implementation of a potentially useful navigation bill in the late 1760s while the same considerations resulted in a needlessly expensive county gaol that in the end had to be torn down and replaced. Otherwise, I chose Bristol because its constituents made such demands upon their MPs, including Edmund Burke; Plymouth because Lord Barrington was not only an effective administrator in the War Office but for 24 years was an attentive constituency MP who in the 1770s became embroiled in a local controversy regarding a divisive improvement bill; and finally Kingston-upon Hull, whose local leaders struggled unsuccessfully to provide the town with adequate dock facilities, a problem that was eventually resolved by the town's MPs with the assistance of William Pitt (Chapter 3). Otherwise constituencies became a matter of focus because of the particular issues that arose: for example, I examined the role of Lincolnshire MPs when they introduced legislation to allow the export of fleeces; or Lancashire and Liverpool while considering the legislative achievements of Thomas Stanley.[66]

V: Case Studies

The most interesting among the active legislators were those who promoted general legislation in two of the three sessions during the 1770s. In addition to overseeing the progress of the staples of the legislative agenda – enclosures, roads and turnpikes, navigations and improvement bills – they initiated a variety of general measures on their own or with other MPs. Sixty members promoted legislation in at least two sessions during the 1770s. They were returned from a variety of constituencies: 21 represented English counties; ten others represented large boroughs, while 15 sat for constituencies with 100 or fewer electors. Some promoted as many as 13 or 14 bills while less active colleagues managed only two or three.

---

[66] Thomas Stanley (1749–1816), MP, Lancashire, 1780–1812.

Sir Thomas Charles Bunbury[67] was busy during the 1772 session when he oversaw the passage of a bill to repair a turnpike from Bury St. Edmunds to Newmarket, promoted an enclosure bill and carried the Dee Navigation Bill to the House of Lords. He was notable in the House of Commons, however, primarily as a penal and penitentiary reformer.[68] In November 1770 Sir William Meredith[69] moved for an inquiry 'into the state of the kingdom's criminal laws'.[70] The Commons subsequently appointed a committee on the subject on 27 November. As its chair Bunbury subsequently recommended the repeal of four statutes that mandated the death penalty. Because Parliament was prorogued the same day, the committee resumed its work on 31 January 1772, again with Bunbury as the chair. He presented the group's recommendation for the repeal of four additional capital statutes.[71] The House accepted the report and assigned him and seven other MPS with the task of preparing a bill.[72] Bunbury subsequently presented what became known as the Penal Laws Bill, chaired proceedings in the committee of the whole House, reported its amendments to the House on May 20 and, the next day, carried it to the House of Lords where it lapsed.[73]

Undeterred, Bunbury pressed ahead with proposals for reform. Due in large part to the outbreak of the war with the American colonies, transportation as a punishment for serious crimes was becoming unfeasible. Instead in 1776, William Eden[74] introduced legislation to sentence convicted criminals to hard labour and imprisonment on two hulks anchored on the Thames. He told Burke, that 'it has become expedient in point both of Humanity and common Sense to find some means of employing of the unhappy People who are the Objects of this Bill... for short terms in the Service of the Trinity House, and by giving them a sum of money on their Discharge after teaching them a Habit of Industry'.[75] Bunbury was assigned to bring in the bill.[76]

---

[67] Thomas Charles Bunbury, 6th Bt. (1740-1821), MP, Suffolk, 1761-84 and 1790-1812. A leading patron of the turf.

[68] According to Simon Devereaux, Bunbury was in the forefront of penal reform in Parliament. 'The making of the Penitentiary Act, 1775-1779', *HJ*, xlii (1999), 418. It is notable that the short entry on Bunbury in the *Oxford Dictionary of National Biography [ODNB]* makes no mention of his career as a penal reformer. *ODNB*, viii, 672.

[69] Sir William Meredith, 3rd Bt. (?1725-1790), MP, Wigan, 1754-61 and Liverpool, 1761-80; Ld. of Admiralty, 1765-6 and Comptroller of Household, 1774-7.

[70] *PH*, xvi, 1124-7.

[71] Sir Leon Radzinowicz, *A History of English Criminal Law and its Administration from 1750. Vol 1: The Movement for Reform* (1948), pp. 427-9. According to Radzinowicz, the acts had little in common except that they were no longer used. The list presented by the committee for repeal was the first instance in the history of criminal law reform of such a recommendation. *English Criminal Law*, i, 429-30.

[72] *CJ*, xxxiii, 365, 612, 695.

[73] *CJ*, xxxiii, 772, 774-5, 777. The Lords could not proceed on the bill in 1772, as Parliament was prorogued the day it was brought up.

[74] William Eden (1744-1814), MP, New Woodstock, 1774-1784 and Heytesbury, 1784-93; Under-Sec. of State, 1772-8; Ld. of Trade, 1776-82; Commissioner for Negotiations with America, 1778-9; Sec. to Ld. Lt. of Ireland, 1780-2; Vice-Treasurer of Ireland, 1783; envoy to France to negotiate commercial treaty, 1785-8; Ambassador to Spain, 1788-9 and to United Provinces, 1789-93; Jt. Postmaster General, 1798-1804; Pres., Bd. of Trade, 1806-7; cr. Baron Auckland [I], 1789 and [GB], 1793. Author of *Principles of Penal Punishment* (1771).

[75] *The Correspondence of Edmund Burke, 1774-1778*, ed. G.H. Guttridge (Cambridge, 1961), iii, 251.

[76] *CJ*, xxxv, 694. According to Devereux, the Hulks Act (16 George III, c. 43) was 'a striking innovation in itself' and also an attempt to forestall more radical innovations that Eden realised could never succeed. 'Penitentiary Act', p. 520. For the text of the 'Hulks Act', see *Commons Sessional Papers*, xxvii, 295-310.

The passage of the Hulks Act rekindled Bunbury's determination to reform of the criminal code. Recent fires at Portsmouth and Bristol harbours and pressure from Bristol merchants induced Richard Combe[77] to propose making arson in the dockyards a capital crime. The measure provoked a strong opposition in the House. Meredith, in an important speech,[78] argued that cruel laws did not prevent crimes, that new capital laws engendered others, that the aim of all punishment was example, and that he preferred hard labour to capital punishment. Bunbury's attempt to make Combe's proposed offense clergiable[79] failed. Nevertheless, the bill lapsed after receiving two readings. In 1778, Bunbury chaired a committee established to assess the operations of the Hulk Act.[80] While noting initial high levels of mortality, the committee's report recommended a one-year extension of the Act, which the Commons adopted.[81]

At this point, Bunbury and his allies appear to have reversed themselves. In 1779, he chaired another committee that recommended the reintroduction of transportation. He and his allies amended the Penitentiary Bill – the work of Eden and Sir William Blackstone[82] – in order to remove a number of its compromises and add clauses to assure that standards of health and cleanliness required by acts of 1774[83] were enforced. Whereas Eden and Blackstone had taken care not to provoke local interests by placing additional financial burdens upon them, Bunbury and his allies, according to Devereaux, did the opposite.[84] Thus, when the Penitentiary Bill reached the House of Lords, peers refused to proceed until the Commons removed those provisions.[85] The Act[86] that emerged from this process was never fully implemented. Nevertheless, Beattie claims that it provided a model for local authorities who in the 1780s embarked on the reconstruction and reform of prisons.[87]

Another of the reforming MPs, Jacob Pleydell-Bouverie, Viscount Folkestone,[88] was, according to Langford, a model of late eighteenth-century aristocratic piety.[89] Folkestone was notable in the House for his political independence. His diary clarifies

---

[77] Richard Combe (1728–80), MP, Milborne Port, 1772 and Aldeburgh, 1774–80; member of the Society of Merchant Venturers, Bristol and Treasurer of the Ordnance, 1780.
[78] A published version of Meredith's speech went through six editions and sold 60,000 copies. *History of Criminal Law*, i, 474, 476.
[79] A 'clergiable' offense was one that provided 'benefit of clergy', in other words exemption from the ordinary courts of law because of membership of the clergy, or later, according to the *OED*, 'exemption from sentences for certain offences because of literacy or scholarship'.
[80] *PH*, xix, 234–5, 241, 971. For the work of the 1778 committee and another chaired by Bunbury in 1779, see J.M. Beattie, *Crime and the Courts, 1660–1800* (Princeton, NJ, 1986), pp. 573–4. For the report of the 1779 committee, see *Commons' Sessional Papers*, xxxi, 363–92.
[81] *CJ*, xxxvii, 306–15; Devereaux, 'Penitentiary Act', 405–33.
[82] Sir William Blackstone (1723–80), MP, Hindon, 1761–8 and Westbury, 1768–70; Vinerian Professor of English law, 1758–66; Principal of New Inn Hall, Oxf., 1761–6; Solicitor-General to Queen Charlotte, 1763–70; Justice, King's Bench, 16 Feb. 1770 and common pleas, 22 June 1770.
[83] 14 George III, c. 20 and 59.
[84] For the report of Bunbury's committee, see *House of Commons Sessional Papers*, xxxi, 363–97.
[85] Devereaux, 'Penitentiary Act', 431–2
[86] 19 George III, c. 74.
[87] Beattie, *Crime and the Courts*, p. 576.
[88] Jacob Pleydell Bouverie, Viscount Folkestone (1750–1828), MP, Salisbury, 1771–1776; succ. fa. as 2nd Earl of Radnor, 1776; Ld. Lt. Berkshire, 1791–1819; chairman of the bench in Berkshire and Wiltshire.
[89] Langford, *Public Life*, pp. 573–5.

the reasons: in a debate on 15 February 1774, he charged that a British expedition which resulted in the death and displacement of many Caribs on the island of St. Vincent was undertaken without sufficient provocation.[90] A month later he refused to support a motion to sanctioning the £234,000 that Lord Clive received from an Indian nawab in 1757, because, he argued, it came through 'the influence of the powers he was entrusted with'.[91]

During his brief term as an MP Folkestone was also an advocate for the poor and the imprisoned. During the 1774 session, he was a prime mover of a bill to prevent the unjust removal of labourers whom poor law authorities feared would become charges on the parish. Following its second reading, he chaired the committee of the whole House on the measure; despite his efforts, the House refused to consider the committee's report with the result that the bill, which aimed to mitigate the harshness of the law of settlement, failed.[92] He was more successful in helping to carry Alexander Popham's[93] two acts, inspired by the investigations of the influential prison reformer, John Howard.[94] The first regulated prisons and eliminated fees owed by released prisoners;[95] the second set standards for gaol's cleanliness and prisoners' nutrition in order to reduce gaol fever. According to his diary, Folkestone seconded Popham's motion to bring in his original bill and spoke against a motion to delay its consideration.[96] He also supported efforts to reform the criminal law. On 8 April, 1772 he backed Bunbury's motion for the repeal of 21 Jac. I, c. 17, a statute which declared that concealment of the birth of a bastard child constituted proof that the mother had murdered the child, making her liable for execution. This and subsequent attempts to repeal the act failed, first in the Commons and in two subsequent instances in the Lords.[97] Folkestone also tried to protect the poor from the effects of high food prices. In 1772 he opposed a measure that would have increased the base price of wheat and during the same session was added to the committee appointed to bring in a bill 'to remedy evils caused by forestallers'.[98]

---

[90] *PH*, xvii, 731. For tensions between Caribs and white settlers on St. Vincent, see Andrew J. O'Shaughnessy, *An Empire Divided: The American Revolution and the British Caribbean* (Philadelphia, PA, 2000), pp. 41–44; and P.J. Marshall, 'A polite and commercial people in the Caribbean: The British in St Vincent', in *Revisiting the Polite and Commercial People*, ed. Elaine Chalus and Gauci (Oxford, 2019), pp. 184–6.

[91] Wiltshire and Swindon History Centre [WSHC], Folkestone diary, 4 May 1772, 15 Feb, 21 Mar. 1773.

[92] The act, inspired by reports of authorities removing young working men once they intended to marry, was the work of William Graves (?1724–1801), MP, West Looe, 1768–74 and East Looe, 1775–83, 1784–6, 1796–8; *CJ*, xxxvi, 546, 549; *PH*, xvii, 843–5; WSHC, Folkestone Diary, 2, 8, 9 Mar, 1774. For the text of Graves' bill see *Commons' Sessional Papers*, xxiv, 124–8 and as amended, 129–32.

[93] Alexander Popham (?1729–1810), MP Taunton, 1768–80, 1784–96; chair of the Somerset quarter sessions. For the text of the first of these acts (14 Geo. III, c. 20) see *Commons' Sessional Papers*, xxiv, 133–6.

[94] John Howard (1726–90), leading prison reformer. Author of *State of the Prisons* (1777). For an assessment of his influence, see Beattie, *Crime and the Courts*, pp. 569–73.

[95] Popham's initial attempt to carry the bills failed in 1773. According to the Webbs, only after Popham enlisted Howard to give evidence on their behalf in the next session did the Commons approve them. Sidney and Beatrice Webb, *English Prisons under Local Government* (London and New York, 1922), pp. 35–6.

[96] WSHC, Folkestone diary, 17 Feb., 15 Mar. 1774.

[97] Radzinowicz, *Criminal Law*, pp. 483–4; *LJ*, xxiii, p. 445, 692.

[98] WSHC, Folkestone diary, 8 May 1772; *CJ*, iii, 591.

Amidst all this activity, Folkestone was an active constituency MP, supporting locally initiated road, enclosure and estate bills, even as their proceedings dragged on through the House.⁹⁹ To assist Salisbury weavers who had petitioned against extending favours to the linen industry, he saw to it that their petition was referred to the select committee on trade,¹⁰⁰ supported their request to have its second reading committee on April 26 and was present at its third. Richard Glover¹⁰¹ represented them before the committee and opposed a proposal to give a bounty on printed and stained linen exported from Britain or Ireland.¹⁰² He also carried a bill to permit the exchange of advowsons between his father and Queen's College, Oxford, moved the bill's first reading, chaired its second reading committee, delivered the report and finally carried the measure to the Lords.¹⁰³ Situations in which MPs promoted measures and presided over committees on bills introduced for family members, close friends or patrons, were, as we shall see, common between 1750 and 1790.

Unlike Folkestone, Frederick Montagu was a friend of leading politicians and adhered to the Rockingham party. Because he was a knowledgeable legislator, his colleagues turned to him for help in carrying their own measures. As already noted, in 1774 he chaired the committee of the whole House on William Baker's bill to export corn for the benefit of the Hudson's Bay Company and delivered its report.¹⁰⁴

On 25 February 1774, Admiral Lord Howe¹⁰⁵ presented the petition of Richard Arkwright,¹⁰⁶ Nottingham spinners of cotton and manufacturers of British white stuffs. The petitioners sought to bring in a bill that would legalise white cotton stuffs, set the excise duty at three pence, and grant cotton stuffs the drawback¹⁰⁷ allowed on British and Irish linen.¹⁰⁸ Because of lobbying by woollen and linen interests, the petition lay on the table for six weeks before being referred to a committee which included Howe and John Plumptre.¹⁰⁹ Montagu, a Nottinghamshire landowner, and Howe were charged with preparing and presenting the bill, and it was Montagu who chaired the committee of the whole House and eventually reported from the committee a bill to remove duties on printed cottons made in Britain or Ireland.¹¹⁰ The act of 1774 (14 Geo.

---

⁹⁹ For example, he presented the petition for the Titcombe enclosure on 16 February 1774, was present at the bill's first reading on 21 March, at its second reading on 29 March, and reported the measure from its second reading committee the next day. WSHC, Folkestone diary.

¹⁰⁰ *CJ*, xxxiv, 546.

¹⁰¹ Richard Glover (1712-85), MP, Weymouth and Melcombe Regis, 1751-8. Appeared before select committees of the House of Commons on the linen business in 1774 (*CJ*, xxxiv, 661; and *PH*, xvii, 1111-3).

¹⁰² WSHC, Folkestone diary, 10, 16 Mar. 1774.

¹⁰³ *CJ*, xxxiv, 673; WSHC, Folkestone diary, 25 Apr. 1774.

¹⁰⁴ *CJ*, xxxiii, 687, 768.

¹⁰⁵ Admiral Lord Richard Howe, 4th Visct. [I] (1726-99), MP, Dartmouth, 1757-82; Ld. of Admiralty, 1763-5; Treasurer of Navy, 1765-6, 1766-70; C.-in-C. America, 1776-8; First Ld. of Admiralty, 1783-8; cr. Visct. Howe [G.B.], 1782 and Earl, 1788; K.G., 1797.

¹⁰⁶ Sir Richard Arkwright (1732-92), inventor of the water frame; with Jedediah Strutt, proprietor of mills at Cromford; Chorley in Lancashire, Wirksworth in Derbyshire and New Lanark in Scotland.

¹⁰⁷ A drawback is the amount of duty remitted on imported goods that were re-exported instead of being sold domestically.

¹⁰⁸ *CJ*, xxxiv, 496.

¹⁰⁹ John Plumptre (1711-91), MP, Penryn, 1758-61 and Nottingham, 1761-74.

¹¹⁰ *CJ*, xxxiv, 730, 774, 787, 9, 19, 27 May 1774.

III, c.72) overturned longstanding restrictions imposed by a series of earlier acts and established the industry on a firm legal footing by permitting cotton cloth to be dyed, printed and sold in Britain. Montagu's contribution to its enactment had momentous consequences.[111] The successful legislation is but one example of local MPs taking up the cause of neighbouring manufacturers and merchants to enable them to secure legislation they required to expand and improve their businesses. Further examples of such partnerships are discussed in Chapters 3, 4 and 8.

Given his knowledge of the Commons' legislative procedures, Montagu was chosen to chair the select committee appointed to consider rules 'to be observed by persons applying for private bills'. To protect property rights his committee proposed alterations to the orders aimed at assuring there would be public notices of proposed projects prior to the introduction of enclosure, turnpike or navigation bills. On 30 March 1774, he reported one of the committee's recommendations – that promoters of enclosure bills post notices of their intentions on church doors for three weeks in the summer prior to the opening of the next session and that commissioners, appointed to implement terms of the bill, be required to account for funds used in the fulfilment of their duties.[112] Given his mastery and the range of his connections, Lord North approached him in 1780 about taking the speakership despite Montagu's being a political opponent. Though the Marquess of Rockingham pressed him to take the post, Montagu declined the honour, citing health concerns and his belief that the post 'has much Labour & no entertainment in it...'.[113]

Samuel Whitbread,[114] the moving force behind the largest and most up to date brewery in England, lived in two different worlds. Having accumulated a fortune, he built a Bedfordshire estate, centred on Cardington, his birthplace where he ultimately invested over £250,000 in surrounding properties and established a sufficient presence to secure election from Bedford in 1768. At Westminster he attended to the legislative needs of Cardington and promoted a series of naturalisation bills, most likely for London business associates.[115] Seven other London brewers[116] sat in Parliament between 1754 and 1790. According to Peter Mathias, these powerful porter brewers became the interest's spokesmen on import duties and bounties. In addition to negotiating with ministers over issues such as excise duties on malt and beer, brewer

---

[111] R.S. Fitton and A.P. Wadsworth, *The Strutts and the Arkwrights 1758-1830: A Study of the Early Factory System* (Manchester, 1958), pp. 69–70, 485; Patrick O'Brien, Trevor Griffith and Philip Hunt, 'Political components of the Industrial Revolution: Parliament and the English cotton textile industry, 1660–1774', *EcHR*, n.s., xliv (1991), 395–423.

[112] The committee made similar recommendations regarding turnpikes – requiring prior notice of their routes. In the case of canals, requirements included that applications be made to the owners and occupiers of lands through which the canal would pass and the presentation of lists of those who assented to and opposed the plans. *CJ*, xxxiv, 608–9, 649; Sheila Lambert, *Bills and Acts*, pp. 134–5, 141. Almon, *Political Register*, iii, 78; *Commons' Sessional Papers*, xxx, 3–8.

[113] *HPC, 1754–1790*, iii, 154–5; British Library [BL], Camelford Papers, Add. MS, 69293, f. 69, Montagu to Thomas Pitt, 24 Sept. [1780].

[114] Samuel Whitbread (1720–96), MP, Bedford, 1768–74, 1775–90 and Steyning, 1792–6.

[115] *CJ*, xxxiii, 729, 744, 681–2.

[116] John Calvert, Sr, John Calvert, Jr, Nicolson Calvert, William Calvert, Sir John Hynde Cotton, William Hammond and Henry Thrale.

MPs invariably sat on Parliamentary committees investigating their industry to make sure that opposing interests did not control the selection of witnesses and the subsequent report.[117] They also endeavoured to see that there were sufficient supplies of malt and hops for the industry at a reasonable price. Thus, on 24 February 1774 Whitbread presented a petition from hops merchants and brewers of London and Westminster complaining that planters of hops packed their produce in coarse bagging, weighing 20 to 40 pounds, so that purchasers paid as much for the bags as for the hops in them. Despite their complaint, the petition foundered in committee. Charles Marsham,[118] who stood as MP for Kent, the leading producer of hops, at the 1774 election, presented another bill on behalf of hops farmers.[119] The result was a classic case of competing interests. Like his business counterparts in the House, Whitbread promoted legislation advantageous to his particular industry.

Active MPs were, in their own way, experts, called upon by neighbours, family members, constituents and a variety of interests to manage the progress of a range of bills because of their demonstrated willingness and proven ability to complete the task successfully. Of course, not all who agreed to undertake the business did so effectively. George Selwyn,[120] for example, unwillingly took the chair on the Sedgemoor enclosure bill at its second reading committee in December 1775. When he reported the bill, its opponents' motion to have the measure withdrawn carried by a vote of 59 to 34. The reason for this setback was that the proposal circulated among owners for their assent was different in at least 20 respects from the bill reviewed by the committee.[121] Selwyn blamed the bills' agents, the measure's complexity and the failure of the clerks to point out the discrepancies, but never noticed the problems himself, despite taking responsibility for carrying the bill.[122]

VI: Impact of Specific and Local Legislation

The majority of measures that MPs carried through the House were narrowly limited in their scope. They, like many navigation, enclosure, estate and improvement bills,

---

[117] Peter Mathias, *The Brewing Industry in England, 1700–1830* (Cambridge, 1959), pp. 332–8.
[118] Hon. Charles Marsham (1744–1811) MP, Maidstone, 1768–1744 and Kent, 1774–1790; Ld. Lt. Kent, 1797–1808; succ. fa. as 3rd Baron Romney, 1793; cr. Earl of Romney, 1801.
[119] *CJ*, xxxiv, 531, 582, 594, 654, 748, 754, 775. For the circumstances leading to the setting aside of one bill and the introduction of another, see, Langford, *Public Life*, p. 174.
[120] George Augustus Selwyn (1719–91), MP, Ludgershall, 1747–54, 1780–91, and Gloucester, 1754–80; registrar of court of chancery in Barbados, 1753–91; paymaster, Bd. of Works, 1753–82; Surveyor Gen. of Crown Lands, 1784–91.
[121] There was an intense local opposition to the bill. Though 213 persons signed the petition in support of it, 749 signed a counter-petition. To address the latter's grievances, the Commons added many amendments. G.E. Mingay, *Parliamentary Enclosure in England: An Introduction to its Causes, Incidence, and Impact, 1750–1850* (Harlow, 1997), p. 52.
[122] The measure was backed by Lord Stavordale, the Earl of Ilchester and Viscount Bolingbroke, who expected that profits from the enclosure would cover portions of their gambling debts. *HMC, Carlisle MSS*, pp. 304, 307, 309–10. Over the nine sessions for which I collected data, Selwyn took charge of one other measure, an uncontroversial name bill that the House of Lords had already passed.

reflected eighteenth-century Parliament's preference for specific measures that were limited in their application. With the exception of canal bills, measures of this sort rarely provoked serious discord at Westminster after 1760. Indeed, James Harris[123] reported to his son in 1779 that 'there reigns at this instant a most wonderful tranquility in Parliament. Houses are made up with difficulty, and nothing done but turnpikes and enclosures'.[124]

Yet, this was just the sort of work that kept Harris and other MPs busy for much of a session. His wife, in another letter to the son, noted 'Your father constantly attends the House of Commons: nothing has been done there this week except committees on private bills'.[125]

The implication of the Harris' messages was that this type of business, while requiring the attention of MPs, was of secondary importance, an outlook also reflected in the published reports of Parliamentary proceedings compiled by John Almon and John Debrett. Almon ignored those proceedings, and Debrett's early volumes periodically note that business on a particular day was limited to private and local business without providing details. As Ian Harris remarks in his recent article on Parliamentary reporting in the London press, 'private business did not usually feature prominently, and Parliamentary committees, except committees of the whole House, might go unreported'.[126]

However insignificant the individual measures promoted by Harris or other MPs may have been, the collective impact of the many specific bills that made their way through eighteenth-century Parliaments was substantial.[127] Improvements in communications were vital to the growth of towns and industries, particularly coal.[128] Beginning in the 1750s a turnpike network in South Yorkshire and North Derbyshire linked Sheffield and other towns to river ports, lead mining regions of the Peak to the coalfield, to agrarian districts and ultimately to London. Iron foundries depended upon improved transport to secure their raw materials and distribute their output; the production of coal and lime was stimulated by the construction of roads and canals, as were markets and fairs for livestock and cereals.[129]

The Aire and Calder Navigation, with Leeds at its western edge, made the town 'an inland port serving the industrially expanding West Riding hinterland', while the expansion of its turnpike network in the 1740s and 1750s linked it to the other West Riding wool towns. According to Christopher Chalklin, these transportation improvements enabled Leeds to maintain its leadership among regional cloth towns

---

[123] James Harris (1709–1780), MP, Christchurch, 1761–80; Ld. of Admiralty, 1762–3 and of Treasury, 1763–5; Sec. and Comptroller to Queen, 1774–80.
[124] *A Series of Letters of the First Earl of Malmesbury, his Family and Friends from 1745 to 1820*, ed. Earl of Malmesbury (2 vols, 1870), i, 401.
[125] *A Series of Letters*, i, 341.
[126] Ian Harris, 'What was Parliamentary reporting? A study of aims and results in London daily newspapers, 1780–1796', *Parl. Hist.*, xl (2020), 272.
[127] Cf. Langford, *A Polite and Commercial People*, Chapter 9.
[128] For the impact of canals on coal producers and consumers, see Michael W. Flinn, *The History of the British Coal Industry* (Oxford, 1984), ii, 181–8.
[129] G.H. Hopkinson, 'Road development in South Yorkshire and North Derbyshire, 1700–1850', *Transactions of the Hunter Archaeological Society*, x (1971), 19–30.

throughout the eighteenth century.[130] Likewise, the prosperity of ports such as Liverpool and Hull depended upon their improved connections to the hinterlands which provided them with raw materials and products for export and absorbed their imports. Canals and waterways linked Liverpool to Cheshire salt, Lancashire coal fields, Staffordshire potteries and ironmasters, and to textile manufacturers across the north of England. By providing cheap transportation for coal, corn and building materials they also accelerated Liverpool's urban growth.[131] Nor were improvements in communications vital just to northern ports and industrial or mining centres. By the 1770s Maidstone had the best wholesale shops in Kent: access to the town's hinterland, which was provided by turnpikes and new waterways linking it to the Weald and eastern Sussex, earned Maidstone's shopkeepers £100,000 annually.[132]

Improvements in communications also spurred the growth of spas and other resorts. To expand, both Bath and Cheltenham needed good connecting roads to make visitors' journeys easier. Nor were the required turnpike acts their sole legislative priorities. Both initiated improvement bills to provide clean, well-lit streets and promenades. Bath's came first, in 1757 (30 Geo. II, c. 65) and 1766 (6 Geo. III, c. 70), followed by Cheltenham's in 1785 (26 Geo. III, c. 116) and 1792 (32 Geo. III, c. 83). Improvement acts were pivotal to the transformation of the two towns into fashionable spas. Bath's 1766 act empowered its corporation to make compulsory purchases, widen and light streets, and link the lower to the upper town.[133] In addition amenities such as the Pump and Assembly Rooms and new baths were provided as a result of the 1789 Bath Improvement Act (29 Geo. III, c. 11). The 1766 and 1789 acts also laid the groundwork for private developers to build additional housing.[134]

In addition, Bath's principal developer, Sir William Pulteney,[135] transformed his wife's Bathwick property into a fashionable residential area. To accomplish his goal of creating a planned development, Pulteney secured three estate acts[136] (1769, 1772,

---

[130] Christopher Chalklin, *The Provincial Towns of Georgian England: A Study of the Building Process, 1740–1820* (Montreal, 1974), pp. 38–9; cf. Penelope Corfield, *The Impact of English Towns, 1700–1800* (New York, 1982), p. 11. Authorities note that the growth of Exeter and Hereford was impeded by their lack of good internal communications: Robert Newton, *Eighteenth-Century Exeter* (Exeter, 1984), pp. 66–7; *The Cambridge Urban History of Britain. Vol II: 1540–1840*, ed. Peter Clark (3 vols, Cambridge, 2000), 106–7; Peter Clark and Lyn Murfin, *The History of Maidstone: The Making of a Modern County Town* (Stroud, 1995), pp. 75–79.

[131] Alan Dyer, 'Midlands', in *The Cambridge Urban History*, II, 94–5; Baron F. Duckham, 'Canals and river navigation', in *Transportation in the Industrial Revolution*, p. 132; Gordon Jackson, *Hull in the Eighteenth Century*, pp. 9–11; F.E. Hyde, *Liverpool and the Mersey: An Economic History of a Port* (Newton Abbot, 1971), pp. 13, 73–5.

[132] C.W. Chalklin, 'South East', in *Cambridge Urban History*, II, pp. 62–3.

[133] Bryan Little, 'Gloucestershire spas: An eighteenth-century parallel', in *Essays in Bristol and Gloucestershire History*, ed. Patrick McGrath and John Cannon (Bristol, 1976), 189–98; Phyllis Hembry, *The English Spa, 1560–1815: A Social History* (London and Cranbury, NJ 1990), pp. 114, 126, 128.

[134] P.J. Corfield, *The Impact of English Towns, 1700–1800* (New York, 1982), pp. 52–8.

[135] Sir William Pulteney (1729–1805), MP, Cromartyshire, 1768–74 and Shrewsbury, 1775–1805; m. Frances, d. and h. of Daniel Pulteney, cousin of William Pulteney, Earl of Bath 1760; took name Pulteney, 1767 on wife's succeeding to estates of Lord Bath; succ. as 5th Bt., 1774.

[136] For the details of these acts, see R.S. Neale, *Bath, 1680–1850: A Social History* (London and Boston, MA, 1981), pp. 229–30, 232.

1774). These empowered the trustees of his wife's estate to raise mortgages to cover the cost of a bridge over the Avon to Bath, as well as connecting roads on each shore with shops and stables on and adjoining the bridge.[137] Empowered to raise funds and grant leases and backed by a Corporation authorised to make compulsory purchases, Pulteney was able to launch what one Bath historian describes as 'the development of an urban estate equal in range if not in the scale of his activities, to the Duke of Bedford in London'.[138]

Julian Hoppit's data indicate that a quarter of all acts that reached the statute book between 1660 and 1800 concerned the economy. Of these 70 per cent were enclosure acts.[139] It is generally recognised that enclosure, drainage and land reclamation, along with mixed farming, more advanced crop rotation and improved animal husbandry, combined to produce increases in agricultural output in the century after 1740. But the impact of enclosure was not confined to agriculture. Just as enclosure at Cheltenham was a necessary prelude to constructing housing there, it was also the prelude, according to John Beckett, to new housing in Radford on Nottingham's western edge and Sneinton to its east.

Estate acts that empowered land owners to make long-term building leases were another necessary prelude to those developments. The Duke of Bedford's act of 1776 opened the way for the construction of Bedford Square, just as the Colmore estate act (20 Geo. II, c.16) enabled the family to grant the long-term leases on 100 acres on the northwest edge of Birmingham. Similarly, an act of 1766 (6 Geo III, c. 61) enabled Sir Thomas Gooch to grant 120-year leases on about 150 acres to the west and south of Birmingham's centre in advance of the city's building boom in the 1770s.[140] Finally, enclosure acts were often the necessary preliminary to the development of mineral resources. Those secured by the Dudleys between 1776 and 1796 were, according to T.J. Raybould, 'the cornerstone of the industrial empire'. They gave the family access to coal, iron and limestone. Legislation was vital to the growth of one of the great aristocratic mineral and industrial estates.[141]

On a broader level Patrick O'Brien and his colleagues maintain that eighteenth-century market forces operated within 'a framework of legislation promulgated and enforced by the central government in London'. The nature of legislation that emerged from this process was the result of bargaining among the pertinent interest groups, 'constrained by Parliament's perception of strategic and political necessities and conditioned by the ideological preconceptions of a mercantilist age'.[142] The Act of 1774, which permitted the sale of dyed and printed cotton cloth throughout Britain, was the

---

[137] Hembry, *English Spa*, pp. 126–8.
[138] Neale, *Bath, 1680–1850*, pp. 218–9, 229–32, 237–41.
[139] Hoppit, 'Patterns of Parliamentary legislation', 120.
[140] John Beckett, 'An industrial town in the making, 1750–1830', in *A Centenary History of Nottingham*, ed. Beckett (Manchester and New York, 1997), pp. 212–214; John Beckett, *The Aristocracy in England 1660–1914* (Oxford and New York, 1986), pp. 270, 280.
[141] T.J. Raybould, *The Economic Emergence of the Black Country: A Study of the Dudley Estate* (Newton Abbot, 1973), pp. 35–451, 52–7.
[142] Patrick O'Brien, Trevor Griffiths, Philip Hunt, 'Political components of the Industrial Revolution: Parliament and the English cotton textile industry, 1660–1774', *EcHR*, n.s., xliv, 395–423.

culmination of a series of legislative contests that extended over three-quarters of a century. The act of 1774 was a contingent product, not the outcome of a grand, encompassing vision. It came about as a result of adept lobbying on the part of Richard Arkwright and other cotton masters, who were fortunate enough to have advocates such as Plumptre, Howe and Montagu.

VII: Motivations

It remains necessary to explain what moved MPs to become actively involved in the legislative process. While the profiles of MPs discussed earlier hint at some of the motivations, I surveyed the lists of non-governmental bills promoted by backbench MPs to identify factors that might explain their interventions. It was often impossible to identify a sole motive instigating members' promotion of various bills, for in many cases there were several factors that seemed to influence them. Moreover, motivations relating to the numerous naturalisation, name or estate bills were unclear because the connection between the petitioners and the members who managed them remained murky. Thus, some speculation was involved on my part, but the *Journals*, biographies in *House of Commons, 1754–1790* and the more complete ones in the subsequent Thorne volumes along with relevant manuscript and printed correspondence provided useful clues. For example, if petitioners for a bill included 'leading' gentlemen of a constituency or its mayor and other town officials, the member was most likely responding to constituents. The need to serve constituents and neighbours accounted for almost half of the instances in which MPs promoted legislation in the House. The next chapter demonstrates that knights of the shire saw it as a principal part of their duty to forward measures promoted from their respective counties. In addition, some MPs were chosen by their fellow members or constituents to take up legislation because of their demonstrated mastery of the procedures of the House and their record of steering legislation to passage. These included especially active knights of the shire, such as Lord Brownlow Bertie, and successive chairs of ways and means, including Sir Charles Whitworth and Thomas Gilbert, along with particularly knowledgeable MPs including Frederick Montagu, Sir Thomas Clavering, Edward Kynaston and Sir Brownlow Bertie.

Four other factors influenced significant portions of MPs in each decade. Members returned by noble patrons often took charge of their patron's legislation as it made its way through the Commons. In addition, the frequent tendency of MPs to promote legislation in which they or their families had a direct stake was usually easy to identify, though still probably underestimated in this study, because of the difficulty in making a connection between MPs and the petitioners for enclosure bills. In some instances in each decade, members were to carry legislation by political considerations. Moreover, in the 1770s, and to a much greater extent in the 1780s, notable numbers of MPs were activated by their desire to promote reforms, many of which were apolitical.

There were exceptions, however, and those exceptions increased in number after the mid-1780s resulted in increased tensions between the two Houses, especially as the Lords persisted in obstructing measures such as the abolition of the slave trade, which enjoyed broad public support. This problem intensified in the early nineteenth century as the Commons, responding to public pressure, enacted legislation to eliminate parts of what became labelled 'Old Corruption', which the elite had eagerly promoted and ministers of the Crown had relied upon to bind supporters to administrations of the day. Again and again, the more adamant Lords threw out those bills, provoking outcries in the lower House and raising questions about the legitimacy of the Lord's veto of legislation that enjoyed broad support among the public and large majorities in the Commons.

Thirty years ago Paul Langford noted that both peers and MPs promoted measures initiated from the regions of their estates and country residences, and that by so doing, gave under-represented areas of the country access to Parliament.[143] The difficulty of identifying the dispersed properties of so many MPs and connecting their locations to specific pieces of legislation means that the degree to which MPs' propertied interests affected their legislative conduct is underestimated in my data. Yet, among the various considerations in shaping their legislative activity, this factor probably ranked just behind constituent pressure during each of the three decades.

VIII: Conclusions

The largest number of MPs responded to initiatives from their constituencies – a point reiterated throughout this book and especially in its final chapters. This finding reinforces points made by Frank O'Gorman, who maintained that MPs' hold on their seats depended in part upon their serving the legislative needs of constituents. Langford agreed that MPs were expected to promote the specific measures brought forward by their constituents, neighbours, patrons and family members.[144]

Demands upon MPs to carry legislation through the House were the inevitable consequence of the establishment of Parliamentary sovereignty. The appeal of legislation for those who petitioned for enclosures, turnpikes, canals or improvement bills was, according to Paul Langford, that Parliamentary enactment gave them 'cast-iron legal security at a relatively modest cost'.[145] As demonstrated in Table 1.2, English MPs for the most part took at least a fairly active part in furthering the legislation that was pressed upon them by those who elected them, by neighbours or other clients.

Parliament's generally sympathetic treatment of specific bills and of general measures relating to trade and the encouragement of particular industries also encouraged a number of applications. Manchester petitioners, for example, noted that 'the very great Attention shewn by the House to the Commercial Interests of this Kingdom'. Their awareness in turn caused its merchants and manufacturers to send delegations to London whenever legislation pertaining to trade came before the

---

[143] Langford, 'Property and "virtual representation"', *HJ*, 83–106.
[144] Frank O'Gorman, *Voters, Patrons and Parties: The Unreformed Electorates of Hanoverian England, 1734–1832* (Oxford, 1989), pp. 66, 240; Langford, *Public Life*, pp. 190–2.
[145] Langford, *Private Life*, p. 168.

Commons.[146] Manchester was not unique in this respect. According to Richard Wilson, members of the Leeds merchant community were able to present their views to committees on all legislation relating to the Yorkshire woollen industry. They generously funded lobbying activities and were always ready to head to London to present their case to Yorkshire MPs as well as ministers. The demands upon members from constituencies with a variety of interests and large electorates were especially heavy – as shown in the discussion of members for Bristol in Chapter 3 and in the chapters on the various interest groups.[147] Failure to attend to constituents' business could jeopardise members' hold on their seats.

While highlighting members' willingness to promote the projects of their constituents and neighbours and their sponsorship of a range of reforms, it is necessary to acknowledge in completing their portrait as legislators that MPs including Sir William Pulteney spent substantial amounts of time devising and securing support for and then carrying his legislation for the Bathwick development projects, despite the fact that the project had nothing to do with the needs of his Shrewsbury constituents. While few of his compatriots undertook such elaborate projects on their own behalf, many, like Pulteney, successfully promoted measures that would benefit them or their families. Such self-interested conduct was generally regarded an unexceptionable. The only cases I found of the practice being curtailed occurred in the House of Lords, where one argument for strengthening the position of the Lord Chairman of the Committees was that in so doing he would be able to limit the capacity of individual peers to influence the shape of legislation to their own advantage.[148]

The ability of cotton masters, brewers and other interest groups to gain access to Parliament and secure the legislation they required from a landlord-dominated Parliament to promote their businesses confirms the conclusions of Langford, Hoppit and H.T. Dickinson and others who have shown that members of the landed elite were ready to take up the needs of merchant and manufacturing communities.

In concluding this chapter, it is essential to emphasise that no group of English MPs restricted their attention to one branch of legislation. North was attentive to the legislative needs of Banbury, his constituency, as well of those of Oxford University, of which he was Chancellor. He was active and effective in securing the Oxford Canal Bill which was promoted by the University's heads of houses, and ultimately ran though Banbury; Charles Fox likewise promoted several pieces of specific legislation on behalf of his Westminster constituents, and Pitt, at the behest of his friend Wilberforce and other allies, was instrumental in finally securing the legislation that provided Hull with a dock that met its needs. If backbench MPs devoted much of their legislative energies to securing the specific and local legislation promoted by constituents, neighbours and local interest groups, a number also introduced general legislation, some of which had national ramifications. The authors of these measures usually submitted those bills to a

---

[146] Quoted in Langford, *Private Life*, pp. 173–4.
[147] See, for example, *Politics of the Port of Bristol in the Eighteenth Century. The Petitions of the Society of Merchant Venturers, 1698–1805*, ed. W.E. Minchinton (Vol. xxiii, Bristol Record Society, 1963).
[148] See McCahill, *The House of Lords in the Age of George III*, pp. 326–32.

judge or one of the Crown's law officers for review and amendment before presenting them to the house. If the measure was designed to be a part of county administration, they would also send it to the appropriate county bench or militia officers if they wished to secure its passage. In some instances, their bills even became government measures after undergoing suitable amendment: because Pitt shared Wilberforce's concern about the rising tide of murders in the metropolis in the early 1780s, he bestowed the government's blessings upon the latter's Felon's Anatomy Bill after the measure underwent revision at the hands of the Crown's law officers.[149] Occasionally, ministers also drafted backbench MPs to chair special committees on controversial national questions and many participated in proceedings on important national questions, ranging from the Wilkes cases in the 1760s and the early 1770s, to questions relating to the reform of Parliament in the 1770s and the 1780s, or the relaxation of restraints on Protestant Dissenters and Roman Catholics. A number took an active part in questions relating to the North American and West Indian colonies, on the Cider Tax and the Stamp Act in the 1760s or later the Coalition's Receipts Tax and Pitt's Shop Tax in the early 1780s, both of which were unpopular in urban areas. Many of these MPs were responding to the petitions, instructions or other appeals of their constituents, neighbours and various interest groups. These same groups later encouraged many of them to intervene on a range of contentious commercial issues including the export of woollen fleeces, a contest that divided counties such as Lincolnshire, with large numbers of graziers from the older woollen industries of the southwest and East Anglia. On the other hand, efforts by Lord North and later William Pitt to form a closer economic bond between England and Ireland provoked widespread opposition throughout England and Scotland, initially thwarting North and ultimately dooming Pitt's proposals. However, strong support for the commercial treaty with France in 1786 from among the more technologically and/or structurally advanced manufacturing communities, including Birmingham, the potteries and the textile manufacturers of Lancashire and the West Riding, helped Pitt to overcome opposition from the more traditional craft industries of the south and southeast. Again, MPs were made aware of the views of local interests and constituents through petitions, instructions, personal letters, conversations and a variety of other means. MPs intervened in the legislative process when they felt impelled to do so either out of personal interest, political conviction or because pressure, usually applied by constituents, one or more interest groups, political allies or, as Paul Langford described in his frequently cited article, by neighbours or other connections who lived within the vicinity of their country houses and estates. There can be no doubt their legislative accomplishments contributed not only to the progress and stability of late eighteenth century England, but also enhanced the legitimacy of the Commons in a difficult and tumultuous period.

In this respect my conclusions regarding the impact of English legislators are substantially reinforced by those of Moore and Horwitz regarding the impact of their

---

[149] For a fuller discussion of proceedings on this measure, see Chapter 10; Simon Devereux, 'Inexperienced humanitarians? William Wilberforce, William Pitt and the execution crisis of the 1780s', *Law and History Review*, xxxviii (2015); and Peter King, *Punishing the Criminal Corpse, 1700-1840: Aggravated Forms of Death Penalty in England* (London, 1988), pp. 138–42.

'working' members who chaired second reading committees. They write in the final pages of the article that:

> the presence of members whose service as second reading men must often have rebounded to the benefit of their constituencies and a variety of sectional interests, and hence enhanced the usefulness of the Commons to the country at large. Thus, though the House usually appears to us as the forum for high politics, to limit our view of its activities and those who transacted them to this sphere may lead us to overlook some of its less visible sources of its strength as an institution in the later seventeenth century and for many years thereafter.[150]

---

[150] Moore and Horwitz, 'Who runs the House?', pp. 226–7.

2

Knights of the Shire

MPs representing England's 40 counties enjoyed special prestige during the eighteenth century. For this reason, country gentlemen vied for the chance to hold one of those seats. Bamber Gascoyne,[1] for example, told an associate in 1768 that 'to have represented the county would have been the highest honour and I should have made it the greatest task of my life'.[2] Established families spent large sums to return a scion, and aspirants including Sir George Savile declined invitations to stand for boroughs in order to wait for an open seat in Yorkshire.[3] Unlike most of their Parliamentary colleagues, members for the counties represented large electorates – 20,000 or more in Yorkshire, 8,000 in Kent, Lancashire or Somerset,[4] and the task of the county MPs, as described by Namier, was to support the king's government as long as they honestly could, after impartially assessing the business that came before them without reference to party or faction.[5]

Given his preoccupation with high politics, Namier ignored the fact that novice county MPs confronted burdensome legislative obligations upon their arrival at Westminster. Whatever their backgrounds, knights of the shire acknowledged it was their duty to oversee the passage of measures promoted by neighbours and constituents. According to J.V. Beckett, Sir James Lowther[6] returned to the Commons in 1708 because his earlier experience confirmed that his presence there was crucial to the advancement of the needs of Cumberland. Forty-five years later he oversaw the passage of six Cumbrian turnpike acts in one session, not because it was to his special interest to improve roads, but because he believed it was his responsibility as member for the county to do so.[7] Sir George Savile was renowned for his even-handed efforts to promote bills initiated by his Yorkshire constituents. Even when he supported the

---

[1] Bamber Gascoyne (1725-91), MP. Maldon, 1761-3, Midhurst, 1765-8, Weobley, 1770-4, Truro, 1774-84 and Bossiney, 1784-6; Ld. of Trade, 1763-5, 1772-9; Ld. of Admiralty, 1779-82; Receiver Gen. of Customs, 1786-9.
[2] *HPC, 1754-1790*, ii, 489.
[3] *HPC, 1754-1790*, iii, 406.
[4] *HPC, 1754-1790*, i, 514
[5] L.B. Namier, 'Country gentlemen in Parliament, 1750-1787', in *Crossroads in Power. Essays on eighteenth-century England* (1962), pp. 31-2.
[6] Sir James Lowther, 4th Bt. (1673-1755), MP, Carlisle, 1694-1702, Cumberland, 1708-22, 1727-55, and Appleby, 1723-7.
[7] J.V. Beckett, 'A back-bench MP in the eighteenth century: Sir James Lowther of Whitehaven', *Parl. Hist.* (1982), i, 81-2; and *Coal and Tobacco: The Lowthers and the Economic Development of West Cumberland, 1660-1760* (Cambridge, 1981), pp. 175-7.

proprietors of the Aire and Calder navigation against the Leeds-Selby canal bill and secured that measure's defeat, its proponents acknowledged his fairness and concern for the county's well-being.[8] A group of them told Savile that they regarded him as their representative in general but regarded him as the county's particular patron; as such they had every confidence that Savile would 'work for the general Interest of the Commercial Concerns' of those who would now depend upon the navigation.[9]

Neither Savile nor Lowther were typical knights of the shire: Lowther noted in 1753 that very few other members attended as much as he did because of his work on the six road bills.[10] Similarly in his panegyric, Edmund Burke said of Savile that his

> private benevolence, expanding itself into patriotism, renders his whole being the estate of the public, in which he had not reserved a *peculium* for himself of profit, diversion, or relaxation. During the Session, the first in, and the last out of the House of Commons, he passes from the senate to the camp [as a militia commander], and seldom seeing the seat of his ancestors, he is always in the senate to serve his country, or in the field to defend it.[11]

Even if county members did not define their roles as expansively as those two, they had many constituents with innumerable projects to serve. These could energise otherwise unremarkable legislators. Edward Eliot,[12] for example, attended intermittently prior to his election as member for Cornwall, but following his election in 1775 Thomas Pitt[13] remarked that 'by the independent line he has taken in Parliament, and by the zeal with which he has assisted every object of the County, [Eliot] has in my opinion entitled himself to our support'.[14]

Paul Langford agreed that the rising volume of specific legislation imposed heavy burdens on knights of the shire.[15] Data presented in Table 2.1 establish that knights of the shire were regularly the most active group of legislators in the House. Whereas an average of 23.1 per cent of all English MPs took an active part in carrying bills through the House during at least one of the nine sessions I surveyed, between 1765 and 1767, an average of between 38 and 55 per cent of the knights of the shire were equally active. Moreover, the rate of the county MPs' participation in legislative business was consistent

---

[8] For the legislative battles between the proprietors of the Aire and Calder and their many critics, see R.G. Wilson, 'The Aire and Calder Navigation. Part III. The Navigation in the second half of the eighteenth century', *The Bradford Antiquary*, xliv (1969), 215–43; and Nottinghamshire Archives, Savile-Foljambe MS, DD/FJ/11/1/7/194/2, George Oates to Savile, 7 Mar. 1774.

[9] Notts. Archives, Savile-Foljambe MS, DD/FJ 11/1/7/193/3, Rev. Robert Charlesworth to Savile, 6 Mar. 1774.

[10] Beckett, *Coal and Iron*, pp. 176–7.

[11] Notts. Archives, Savile-Foljambe MS, DD/FJ 11/1/1/pt.2, ff. 1–2, 'The character of Sir George Savile by the Right Honble. Edmund Burke'.

[12] Edward Eliot (1727–1804), MP, St. Germans, 1748–68, 1774–5, Liskeard, 1768–74, and Cornwall, 1775–84; Receiver Gen. of Duchy of Cornwall, 1749–1804; Ld. of Trade, 1759–76; cr. Baron Eliot, 1784.

[13] Thomas Pitt (1737–93), MP, Old Sarum, 1761–8, 1774–84 and Okehampton, 1768–74; Ld. of Admiralty, 1763–5; cr. Baron Camelford, 1784.

[14] *HPC, 1754–1790*, ii, 388.

[15] Langford, *Private Life*, p. 200.

Table 2.1 Levels of legislative activity of English county MPs in comparison to the total English contingent of 491 MPs, 1765–7, 1772–4, 1786–8[16]

	1	2	3	4
	Total No. of Active Eng. Legislators	No. and % of Active Co. MPs	Col. 2 as % of Col. 1	Col. 2 as % of 491 Eng. MPs
1765	133	44 (55.0)	33.1	8.96
1765–6	105	36 (45.0)	34.3	7.33
1766–7	111	30 (37.5)	27.0	6.11
1772	128	43 (53.8)	33.6	8.76
1773	122	38 (47.5)	31.1	7.74
1774	108	37 (46.3)	34.3	7.54
1786	122	43 (53.8)	35.2	8.76
1787	94	38 (47.5)	40.4	7.74
1788	105	37 (46.3)	35.2	7.54

over three decades, reflecting the fact that their core group had a clear vision of its legislative obligations which nearly half and often more performed each year, except during the 1766–7 session.

As a group 80 county legislators constituted 16.3 per cent of the total English contingent (491) in the House. The 44 county MPs were active during the 1765 session and made up a third of the English members who promoted legislation. Nor was the 1765 session an aberration. During the next session 36 county MPs (42 per cent of the group's total contingent) formed 35.2 per cent of the total number of active English legislators, and even in 1766–7 the 30 active county legislators comprised over a quarter of the 111 English MPs who promoted legislation though they constituted just over 6 per cent of the total English contingent.

Data presented in Tables 2.2 and 2.3 indicate, however, that levels of legislative activity among knights of the shire varied widely, often depending on the numbers of

Table 2.2 Numbers of county members who promoted legislation in one or more of the sessions, 1765–7, 1772–4, 1786–8

	1 Session	2 Sessions	3 Sessions	None in Any Session
1765–7	13	20	24	42 (31)[17]
1772–4	13	21	19	46 (31)[18]
1786–8	26	18	21	25 (18)[19]

[16] 'Active' legislators were those who took one or more bills through at least one stage on which my counts focused during their journey through the House.
[17] Eleven of the county members returned in 1761 could not promote bills between 1765 and 1767 because they died or received a peerage before 1765.
[18] Fifteen of the members returned in 1768 died, were unseated or were advanced to the House of Lords by January 1772.
[19] Seven of the 89 county MPs returned in 1784 were not in the House between 1786 and July 1788 either because they died or were elevated to the peerage.

Table 2.3 Numbers of bills promoted by county members, 1765–7, 1772–4, 1786–8

	No Bills	1–4	5–9	10–14	15–20	Over 20
1765–7	31	27	17	6	4	4
1772–4	45	22	21	2	4	5
1786–8	25	35	13	7	6	5

turnpike, enclosure and navigation bills presented from each county during the particular session. Table 2.3 shows that there was a significant increase in the level of relatively inactive county MPs after 1774, due to the financial crisis which resulted in higher interest rates and a consequent reduction in the numbers of interest-sensitive infrastructure projects, as discussed in subsequent paragraphs.

I: Active County Legislators

The active county members, who legislated each of the sessions in my three-session sequences or promoted ten or more bills over one of the three-year periods, were either adept at the business of legislation or represented counties with an extensive agenda. According to Michael Turner, Yorkshire, Lincolnshire and Norfolk each produced over 300 enclosure bills between 1760 and 1820. By contrast an average of only about four per cent of the land of nine counties[20] was affected by Parliamentary enclosure according to Gordon Mingay, and knights of the shire returned from three of those counties (Cornwall, Devon and Shropshire) were among the least active legislators of the group in the 1760s and 1770s). Similarly, almost 60 per cent (30 of 52 acts) of the navigation bills that reached the statute book between 1759 and 1774 were constructed in the Midlands or the North.[21] When Josiah Wedgwood and other promoters considered appeals to Parliament for those acts, they approached the members for the counties which their canals would be most likely to affect.[22]

Not surprisingly the geographic distribution of the most active legislators among the ranks of knights of the shire between 1765 and 1767 and 1772 and 1774 broadly coincided with the geographic distribution of enclosure and navigation acts. W.E. Tate claims that county members, rather than borough MPs, dealt with enclosure bills.[23] So it is logical that seven of the 11 most active county legislators in the 1770s were returned from counties that produced large numbers of enclosure and navigation bills: two of

---

[20] Michael Turner, *English Parliamentary Enclosure: Its Historical Geography and Economic History* (Folkestone, Kent and Hamden, CT, 1980), pp. 176–7. Cheshire, Cornwall, Devon, Hereford, Kent, Lancashire, Monmouthshire, Shropshire and Sussex. G.E. Mingay, *Parliamentary Enclosure*, p. 17.
[21] Duckham, 'Canals and river navigations', p. 105.
[22] See, *Letters of Josiah Wedgwood*, ed. Katherine Eufemia Farrer (Disbury, Manchester, 1903), i, 85–6; and T. Willan, *The Navigation of the River Weaver in the Eighteenth Century* (Manchester, 1951), pp. 63–67.
[23] W.E. Tate, 'Members of Parliament and their personal relations to enclosures: A study with special reference to Oxfordshire enclosures', *Agricultural History*, xxiii (1949), 220.
[24] Sir William Beauchamp Proctor, Middlesex and Sir Francis Vincent, Surrey.

the others represented populous metropolitan counties,[24] and the other two represented Staffordshire and Derbyshire, counties that submitted numerous turnpike and navigation bills.[25] Between 1765 and 1767 ten of the 11 county members who shepherded ten or more bills through the House sat for counties whose proprietors submitted 300 or more enclosure bills between 1760 and 1820, and one was returned for Surrey, a metropolitan county with an extensive legislative agenda.[26]

Among the group of active legislators, Lord Brownlow Bertie stands out for the level of his activity. Between 1765 and 1767 he promoted 36 bills (23 enclosure, eight road and five drainage bills), and between 1772 and 1774 he promoted another 34 (29 enclosures, four drainage and an estate bill). Bertie's legislative agenda reflects Lincolnshire's agricultural and commercial priorities after 1750. Enclosure was at the core of the county's agricultural revolution. According to David Grigg, Parliament in the two decades after 1762 approved 45 enclosure acts affecting 100,000 acres in the southern portion of the county.[27] Fenland drainage was a necessary preliminary to enclosure and other improvements. In addition to enlarging fenland acreage, drainage provided relief from the flooding that was endemic to the region.[28]

Improved access to other regions was another essential part of Lincolnshire's improvement. The crucial period in the upgrading of the county's 'terrible' roads by means of turnpike trusts occurred between 1755 and 1765. Grigg maintains, however, that improvements in river navigations, which often accompanied drainage projects, had the greatest impact on the county's farming economy because navigations offered farmers inexpensive access to the West Riding, West Midland markets and, above all, to London.[29]

Bertie did not carry 71 bills through the House of Commons unassisted. Coningsby Sibthorp[30] restricted his legislative exertions to enclosures, reporting from a petition committee on one and presenting two bills which Bertie subsequently carried through the House. Between 1772 and 1774 Charles Amcotts[31] and Sir Brownlow Cust[32] relieved Bertie of a bit of his burden. The former reported from the second reading committee on an enclosure bill in 1774 and carried two others to the House of Lords in 1774, while Cust presented a drainage bill which Bertie guided through the House. Over six sessions Bertie must have carried 65 bills singlehandedly. His focus was the promotion of legislation serving the interests of Lincolnshire landed proprietors, including his

---

[25] Lord George Augustus Cavendish, Derbyshire and William Bagot, Staffordshire.
[26] Sir Edward Astley, Norfolk, Lord Brownlow Bertie, Lincolnshire, Sir John Hynde Cotton, Cambridgeshire, Sir William Dolben, Northamptonshire, Edwin Lascelles, Yorkshire, Richard Lowndes, Buckinghamshire, Sir Charles Mordaunt, Warwickshire, Sir George Savile, Yorkshire, Thomas Skipwith, Warwickshire, Sir Francis Vincent, Surrey, Thomas Whichcot, Lincolnshire.
[27] David Grigg, *The Agricultural Revolution in South Lincolnshire* (Cambridge, 1966), p. 33.
[28] Because water was not efficiently removed from major drains due to the poor conditions at the outfalls, flooding remained a problem for generations. Grigg, *Agricultural Revolution*, pp. 33-5. For one early proposal to address the outfall problem, see Ancaster MSS: 2ANC 10/4/1: Meeting at Sleaford, 2 Nov. 1763 regarding heads of a bill to restore outfall of River Witham.
[29] Grigg, *The Agricultural Revolution*, pp. 3-45; and T.W. Beastall, *The Agricultural Revolution in Lincolnshire: History of Lincolnshire*, viii (Lincoln, 1978), pp. 6-7, 14-15, 20-23.
[30] Coningsby Sibthorpe (1706-79), MP Lincoln, 1734-41, 1747-54, 1761-8.
[31] Charles Amcotts (1729-77), MP, Boston, 1754-61, 1766-77.
[32] Sir Brownlow Cust (1744-1807), MP, Ilchester, 1768-74 and Grantham, 1774-6; cr. Baron Brownlow, 1776.

family. At least five measures he forwarded authorised the enclosure of manors belonging to the dukes of Ancaster – manors he inherited when he succeeded to the dukedom in 1779.

Bertie's attention to legislation that served the interests of his family and other Lincolnshire landlords was not unusual for knights of the shire during this period. According to J.M. Martin, Sir Charles Mordaunt[33] reported from the second reading committees on 22 of 38 Warwickshire enclosure bills that passed the Commons during his 40-year tenure.[34] In this respect, he was typical of his colleagues. Between 1730 and 1779, Warwickshire proprietors initiated 70 enclosure bills: according to Martin, in over half the cases the principal petitioners were connected to at least one of the MPs who participated in the proceedings on their measures. For example, the Earl of Denbigh[35] complained to Mordaunt that the Willey enclosure 'would be so great a nuisance to my house, Grounds & Plantations'. As a result, he urged Mordaunt in December 1767 'to pour cold water on the petition' and postpone deliberations on the bill. A messenger later assured Denbigh that Sir Charles would give him notice so that the Earl would have time to mount an opposition to any further proceedings.[36]

By contrast, Sir John Hynde Cotton was, according to Namier, 'the prototype of the country gentleman'.[37] He was an active legislator during the 1760s and 1770s: between 1765 and 1767 he promoted 14 bills (seven road bills, three enclosure bills, three drainage bills and another to incorporate Cambridge's Addenbrooke Hospital), and his activity increased between 1772 and 1774 when he oversaw the progress of 21 bills, including two road, two enclosures, a naturalisation and ten drainage, and the others on miscellaneous subjects. Cotton was also a regular attendant at Quarter Sessions, where he served as an intermediary between the county's magistrates and his patron, the 2nd Earl of Hardwicke.[38] He used these occasions to fashion agreements that provided the basis for future legislation – some of which he later guided through the House. During the summer of 1766, he led meetings which produced an agreement on the governance for the future Addenbrooke Hospital. On 17 February 1767, he chaired the committee on the petition of the future hospital's trustees, presented the bill and subsequently carried it to the House of Lords.[39]

By 1774 Cotton's health was deteriorating. After taking his seat in the new Parliament, he informed Hardwicke that he was ready for the Earl's nephew and heir,

---

[33] Sir Charles Mordaunt, 6th Bt. (?1697–1778), MP, Warwickshire, 1734–74.

[34] J.M. Martin, 'Members of Parliament and enclosure: A reconsideration', *Agricultural History Review*, xxvii, 103–4, 106

[35] Basil Feilding (1719–1800), succ. as 6th Earl of Denbigh, 1755; Master of the Harriers, 1761–82; Ld. of the Bedchamber, 1763–1800.

[36] Warwickshire County Record Office, Denbigh Letterbook, C 2017/243, Denbigh to Mordaunt, 9 Dec. 1767; Denbigh to John Townley, 9 Dec. 1767, f. 97; John Mordaunt to Denbigh, 12 Dec. 1767, f. 96.

[37] Namier, *England in the Age of the American Revolution* (1961), pp. 9–10.

[38] Philip Yorke, Visct. Royston (1720–90), MP, Reigate, 1741–7 and Cambridgeshire, 1747–64; succ. as 2nd Earl of Hardwicke, 1764; Ld. Lt., Cambridgeshire, 1757–90; Teller of Exchequer, 1738–90; High Steward of Cambridge University, 1764–90.

[39] *CJ*, xxxi, 160, 206.

Philip Yorke,[40] to take his seat. By 1779 the time had come.[41] Cotton had been a useful agent of the Yorke family, and when county opinion demanded it, he was capable of pushing the Earl to take steps he wished to avoid.[42]

Philip Yorke did not enjoy the freedom to cross his uncles.[43] For decades the Yorkes had put a premium on the fact that its members spoke with one voice politically – a quality that impressed George III.[44] Thus, Yorke struggled to balance the interests of family against those of constituents. His uncles expected him to join them in opposing political and 'economical' reform. Many constituents, however, looked to the county's MPs to support both questions and later the repeal of the Test and Corporation Acts as they applied to dissenters. Conflict arose in February 1781 over Burke's 'economical' reform bill which Uncles John and Sir Joseph opposed. Yorke believed Burke's act would 'quiet the minds of the People'.[45] Hardwicke relented, telling him there was little harm in an independent member 'shewing that he does not strictly set his watch by the Court Dial'.[46]

Still, the pressure remained. The issue came to a head in January 1783 when Yorke was pressed to present a county petition in support of the Parliamentary reform. Sir Joseph insisted his nephew consult the Speaker if it was improper for an MP 'to present a petition without supporting it'. The Speaker replied that this sort of thing occurred frequently. Yorke went ahead and presented the petition without obtaining Hardwicke's permission because he feared if he refused, the reform party would 'disturb the tranquility of the County'; he declined, however, to speak on its behalf.[47]

In December 1783 the family split over the controversial India Bill,[48] – which Yorke eventually opposed – and the turmoil which followed its defeat. It pained Hardwicke in January 1784 that his brother John and his nephew took opposite positions during the early phases of William Pitt's new administration because 'that will not tend to procure the Family Consideration' either from the Pitt camp or Fox's.

Disagreements arose in 1785 over Pitt's proposals for Parliamentary reform and, two years later, on the question of removing the restrictions on Dissenters in the Test and Corporation Acts. On this question, Yorke was unable to resist the popular cry and

---

[40] Philip Yorke, (1757–1834), MP, Cambridgeshire, 1780–90; succ. as 3rd Earl of Hardwicke, 1790; Ld. Lt., Cambridgeshire, 1790–1834, Ld. Lt., Ireland, 1801–6; High Steward, Cambridge University, 1806–1834.
[41] BL, Hardwicke Papers, Add. MS 35680, f. 343, Cotton to Hardwicke, 28 July 1774.
[42] BL, Hardwicke Papers, Add. MS 35681, ff. 160–1, Cotton to Hardwicke, 4 Nov. 1779.
[43] In addition to Hardwicke, the uncles included the Hon. John Yorke (1728–1801), MP Higham Ferrers, 1753–68 and Reigate, 1768–74 and the Hon. Sir Joseph Yorke (1724–92), MP East Grinstead, 1751–61, Dover, 1761–74 and Grampound, 1774–80; Gen. 1777, Col. 1st Life Guards, 1789–92; K.B., 1761; cr. Baron Dover, 1788; Minister at the Hague, 1751–61; Ambassador, 1761–80.
[44] The King told the Earl in 1765 'that We were right to act in concert, – that We kept our Weight by it, & that He approved of Union in all Families. More especially in ours'. BL, Hardwicke Papers, Add. MS 35360, ff. 230–1, Hardwicke to Charles Yorke, 22 Nov. 1765.
[45] BL, Hardwicke Papers, 35379, ff. 274–5, 312–3, Yorke to Hardwicke, 2 Jan [1781], 21 Feb [1781].
[46] BL, Hardwicke Papers, Add. MS 35379, ff. 310–13, Hardwicke to Yorke, 10 Feb. 1781.
[47] BL, Hardwicke Papers, Add. MS 35381, ff. 22, 24, 32–2, Yorke to Hardwicke, Jan. 1783, Monday night, Tuesday night [1783].
[48] HPC, 1754–1790, iii, 683; BL, Hardwicke Papers, Add, MS 35382, 156–7, 161–5; Hardwicke to Yorke, Yorke to Hardwicke, 14, 21 Nov. 1783.

he supported Henry Beaufoy's motion to repeal the Test and Corporation Acts.[49] A month earlier, Cambridgeshire dissenters had petitioned for relief. Yorke had informed Hardwicke that 'their case is ably stated' and he thought their demands

> reasonable, and that no harm can arise but from intemperate opposition, that might raise the flame, increase their numbers and render them more disaffected to the establishments of Church and State.

He added that 'we have a great many Dissenters in Cambridgeshire who would be much pleased if my opinion should coincide with their wishes'.[50]

Even as he struggled to assert his independence, Yorke received many requests from constituents to intervene on a variety of specific and local measures. While he was of little use in tending to requests to permit the export of woollen fleeces and other matters, he was dutiful and successful in attending to other matters. For example he was able to delay the progress of a bill that would have enabled landowners to impose 'exorbitant' tolls on paths along the River Ouse until he arranged for the opposing parties to meet and reach a mutually satisfactory resolution to their disputes.[51] He also oversaw the passage of the Cambridge Improvement Bill, which was first introduced in 1769 as a result of pressure exerted by principal inhabitants on the Corporation. Nothing happened at that point, though the measure's sponsors had planned to reintroduce a bill in 1785. Finally, in 1788 an Improvement Bill came before the House which Yorke reported with amendments from its second reading committee. He later chaired sessions of a committee of the whole House which added additional amendments. Following its passage in the Commons, he carried the measure to the House of Lords.[52] The act provided for the paving, cleansing and lighting of Cambridge's streets, which, prior to the act, were described as 'primitive'[53] (28 Geo. III, c. 42).

II: Sir George Savile

The career of Sir George Savile stands in contrast to the tentativeness of Philip Yorke or a preoccupation with the projects of landowners that characterised Brownlow Bertie and Sir Charles Mordaunt. He was among the Commons' notable figures, respected for his independence and integrity, for his commitment to core beliefs and his attention to the needs of constituents, who saw him as their invariable advocate.

He was also among the active the knights of the shire in the 1760s and 1770s. From 1765 through 1767 the *Journals* show that he promoted over 20 bills – most of which represented the county member's standard legislative fare (12 enclosure, two road, two

---

[49] *PH*, xxvi, cc. 781–817.
[50] *HPC, 1754–90*, iii, 684–5.
[51] BL, Hardwicke Papers, Add. 35685, ff. 113, 150, 160, W. Fisher to Yorke, 1 Feb., Group letter to Yorke, 27 Mar. and 14 Apr. 1790.
[52] For proceedings on the bill and Yorke's work on its behalf, see *CJ*, xliii, 158, 258, 420, 458.
[53] Arthur Gray, *Town of Cambridge* (1925), pp. 153, 155.

Figure 2.1 Sir George Savile, English Whig politician, 1770. Etching by B. Wilson and J. Basire, after a painting by B. Wilson. Photo by SSPL/Getty Images.

navigation, and two drainage bills). With members for Newcastle, Northumberland and Yorkshire colleagues he promoted a bill to regulate the loading of ships with coals at Newcastle and Sunderland, and in 1766 he took charge of the Bath Improvement Bill. His legislative burden increased between 1772 and 1774 when he took 26 bills through one or more of their stages, including 15 enclosure, four road, three drainage bills, the Calder-Kingsmill Navigation Bill and three measures ranging from the establishment of legal quays at Hull to a bridge over the River Aire at Carlton. Finally, in 1775 Parliament passed Savile's Act (15 Geo. III, c. 18),[54] a measure designed to address Yorkshire's chronic shortage of cash by prohibiting the issue of notes below £1.[55]

This unexciting list of measures does not reflect Savile's legislative achievements. Those grew out of his core beliefs and commitments including his determination to promote the needs of his constituents and protect the property rights of individuals and of enterprises, his commitment to religious freedom and, most important, his belief in the rights of electors. Savile introduced legislation to secure these rights and institutions and supported the efforts of MPs who shared his commitments.

As noted in Chapter 1, Savile, a passionate defender of the militia, was instrumental in establishing that institution on a firm legal foundation. Following the passage of George Townshend's Militia Act in 1757, the militia was unpopular and its future existence was uncertain. In this environment Savile's priority was to assure its survival. In 1761, when Townshend's Act was approaching its expiration, a contest arose as to whether and for how long its life would be extended. Some wished to extend it in perpetuity; more moderate supporters favoured an extension for five to seven years. The court, however, opposed its existence. Savile set the context for the debate with his pamphlet, *An Argument Concerning the Militia*.[56] He attacked the ballot as an unfair tax which failed to assure that the ablest men were enrolled. He argued that men of property had an obligation to serve so proposed that each parish be empowered to levy a rate and enlist the required number of men. A bill incorporating his points soon emerged, including the requirement that drills occur either in two two-week sequences or for an extended period of 28 days, rather than on odd days as in the original system. Under the act martial law was to become the means of maintaining discipline. The eventual passage of the act (2 Geo. III, c. 20)[57] with the extension of the force for seven years, indicated, according to J.R. Western, that the militia was ceasing to be a divisive political issue. Threats of a French invasion and interventions by Sir George and Lord Strange,[58] both of whom understood what was needed to make the militia an effective force, were crucial in ensuring its on-going existence.[59] Savile's efforts in 1761–2 were not the end of his attempts to make the militia effective. As noted in Chapter 1, he

---

[54] The text is in *Commons Sessional Papers*, xxiii, 63–70.
[55] R. Wilson, *Gentlemen Merchants*, p. 155.
[56] Sir George Savile, *An Argument Concerning the Militia* (1762).
[57] For the Commons' proceedings on the 1762 Act, see Walpole, *Memoirs of the Reign of George III*, i, 67.
[58] James Smith Stanley, Lord Strange (1717–71), MP, Lancashire, 1741–71; Ld. Lt., Lancashire, 1757–71; Chancellor, Duchy of Lancaster, 1760–71. For his efforts to strengthen the militia, see Western, *English Militia*, pp. 190, 194, 198.
[59] Western, *English Militia*, pp. 185–93.

presented a bill in 1765 to compel recalcitrant counties to meet obligations imposed on them by acts of 1757 and 1762. He also promoted the Act of 1769 (9 George III, c. 49) which finally established the militia on a permanent basis and also dealt with defaulting counties.[60]

Savile was also a forceful advocate of the sanctity of established property rights. To this end, he did battle in the House in 1773 and 1774 to uphold rights granted to the undertakers of the Aire and Calder Navigation by earlier acts of Parliament. This involved his opposing the Leeds-Selby Canal Bill because it would infringe upon the rights granted in earlier acts to the Aire and Calder. He did so even though the Leeds-Selby Bill enjoyed broad support among West Riding merchants and manufacturers due to the Aire and Calder's reputation for high rates and record of poor maintenance.[61] To address the navigation's critics, Savile assured the bill's supporters that in the event the bill was defeated the Aire and Calder's undertakers would 'render the navigation of the said River as complete as possible'. Because of his reputation in the county, many of the bill's supporters accepted the assurances.[62]

The same concern for property rights that led Savile to defend the Aire and Calder induced him to bring in the Nullum Tempus Bill in 1768. Its purpose was to secure the rights of the Crown's lessees. The measure underwent a detailed scrutiny in the House. According to James Harris, the debate in committee 'was informing, and full of legal history, but to many of the hearers, I should imagine, dry and fatiguing'.[63] The bill was eventually defeated by Sir James Lowther[64] and his allies, but Savile reintroduced it in 1769 when he secured its passage (9 Geo III, c. 16).[65]

Throughout the 1770s Savile, a Unitarian, maintained that the essence of Protestantism was its aversion to persecution. In 1772 he supported the petition of the Feather's Tavern group of Church of England clergy and laity who appealed to Parliament to release them from their obligation to subscribe to the 39 Articles. He maintained that several of the articles had no Scriptural foundation and that others were inconsistent with reason.[66] In a thundering speech he opposed proposals to impose a test in return for lifting the requirement to subscribe:

> What! man, a poor contemptible reptile, talk of raising barriers about the church of God! He might as well talk of guarding omnipotence... The church of God, Sir, can protect itself. Truth must, if a fair trial be but allowed it, prove victorious... If the things which are necessary to salvation are not plainly revealed, then there is

---

[60] Western, *English Militia*, pp. 197–99.
[61] In part because of Savile's opposition, the Leeds-Selby Bill remained in its second reading committee for 46 days, producing 800 pages of evidence. Langford, *Private Life*, p 201.
[62] R. Wilson, 'The Aire and Calder Navigation', *Bradford Antiquary*, 221–2, 229–31; Inspire Nottingham Archives, Savile-Foljambe MS, DD/FJ/11/1/7/193/3, Savile to Rev. Robert Charlesworth, 9 Mar. 1774 and DD/FJ/11/17/194/1, Savile to George Oates, 10 Mar. 1774.
[63] Quoted in Thomas, *House of Commons*, p. 227. For the proceedings on the measure, see also Walpole, *Memoirs*, iii, pp. 204–5.
[64] Sir James Lowther, 5th Bt. (1736–1802).
[65] For the background to the measure, see David Wilkinson, *The Duke of Portland: Politics and Party in the Age of George III* (Basingstoke, 2003), pp. 23–4.
[66] *PH*, xvii, 289–93.

no way of salvation revealed to the bulk of mankind at all. Whatever is obscurely revealed, will always be obscure, notwithstanding our decisions... We should not therefore set bars in the way of those who are willing to enter and labour in the church of God... Did [Christ] ask... whether they were Athanasians, or Arians, or Arminians? No – he delivered that admirable and comprehensive maxim: He that is not against me is for me: go ye and say likewise.[67]

His final contribution to the cause of religious liberty came in 1778 when he introduced legislation to free Roman Catholics from some of the penal code's restrictions on their ownership of property and right to receive Catholic educations. Introducing the measure on 14 May 1778, he told the House that a principal goal was to show that persecution 'was, or ought to be, wholly adverse to the Protestant religion'. Colin Haydon has noted that the act was a 'limited measure' that left Catholics subject to penalties from the Elizabethan era.[68] Still, his work on issues relating to religious liberty earned Savile accolades, including from the Unitarian Theophilus Lindsey.[69] The day after the House rejected the Feather's Tavern petition, Lindsey, having travelled from Yorkshire, reported that 'Sr. G. Saville, Mr Dunning[70] and Mr Wedderburne[71] delivered such speeches as were worth going 240 miles to hear'. Likewise, reporting on the introduction of Savile's bill for the relief of Roman Catholics, Lindsey wrote that 'You would have been delighted with ye feeling and humanity and justice that Sir George spoke with'.[72]

Among his various causes, Savile's commitment to upholding the rights of electors took priority. Proceedings against John Wilkes[73] in 1764 were, he believed, a direct attack on those who had returned him, as he explained to his constituents:

> it is the duty of Parliament to see that no part of the Parliament be treated illegally; for every part of the Parliament is part of the Kingdom represented... The member of Parliament being illegally us'd; his Constituents are so. If Privilege have Sense in it, it is this, that the Rights of the Constituents are virtually united in the person of

---

[67] Quoted in W.R. Ward, *Georgian Oxford: University Politics in the Eighteenth Century* (Oxford, 1958), pp. 248–9.

[68] Colin Haydon, 'Parliament and popery in England, 1700–1780', in *Parliament and the Church, 1529–1960*, ed. J.P. Parry and Stephen Taylor (Edinburgh, 2000), p. 57.

[69] Theophilus Lindsey (1723–1808), Ordained a deacon in the Church of England, Lindsey assisted in raising the Feather's Tavern petition in 1771–2. Following its rejection, he left the Church and presided over the Essex Chapel in London.

[70] John Dunning (1731–1783), MP, Calne, 1768–82; Solicitor-Gen. 1768–70; Chancellor, Duchy of Lancaster, 1782–3; cr. Baron Ashburton, 1782.

[71] Alexander Wedderburn (1733–1805), MP, Ayr Burghs, 1761–8, Richmond, 1768–9, Bishop's Castle, 1770–4 and 1778–80, and Okehampton, 1774–8; Solicitor Gen., 1771–8; Chancellor to the Queen, 1771–80; Attorney Gen., 1778–80, C.J. Common Pleas, 1780–93; First Commissioner of the Great Seal, Apr.–Dec. 1783; Lord Chancellor, 1793–1801; cr. Baron Loughborough, 1780 and Earl of Rosslyn, 1801.

[72] *The Letters of Theophilus Lindsey (1723–1808). Vol. 1: 1747–1788*, ed. G.M. Ditchfield (2 vols, Church of England Record Society, Woodbridge, Suffolk, 2007), no. 79, p. 124, no. 182, p. 258.

[73] John Wilkes (1725–97), MP, Aylesbury, 1757–64 and Middlesex, 4 Feb. 1768, 16–17 Feb. 1769, 1774–90; alderman of London, 1769; sheriff, 1771–2; Ld. Mayor, 1774–5; City Chamberlain, 1779–90.

the Member. The Parliament will vindicate those rights violated in his person, and assert the privilege necessary to enable him to defend those Rights.[74]

Given these views, it was inevitable that Savile would condemn Wilkes' arrest and his subsequent expulsion from the House in 1764 after he was convicted of blasphemy and libel. In 1768 and 1769 Middlesex electors returned him three times, but the House instead seated Henry Lawes Luttrell[75] because Wilkes had been declared an outlaw in 1764. Savile declared in 1770 that the House was 'sitting illegally after its illegal act' in overturning Wilkes' election and that 'they have betrayed their trust'.[76] From 1771 until Wilkes finally took his seat in 1774, Savile annually introduced legislation to secure the rights of electors.

Savile had a unique view of his relationship with his constituents. He maintained that he held 'a leasehold under my constituents'.[77] Acting upon this belief, he refused to advise those attending Yorkshire's county meeting in 1769 on how to deal with the Commons' response to Middlesex electors. Instead, he told Lord Rockingham:[78]

> when attending... my part will be not to lead or advise: or I think even support any proposition, but I am duty bound, as their delegate returned from his Errand, to take any part of the transaction that might be desir'd.[79]

Not surprisingly his approach frustrated his more partisan allies. Frederick Montagu reported after attending Nottinghamshire's county meeting where Thomas Willoughby[80] took a line similar to Savile's. The result, Montagu feared, would be inaction; he added, 'If Sir G.S. would be active & take the lead it would facilitate every thing extremely'.[81] That was not Savile's approach. His duty was to carry out the wishes of his constituents, not tell them how to act.

In one of his last acts as Yorkshire's member, Savile on 8 February 1780 presented the county's petition in support of the Association and 'economical' reform. After noting the numbers who had signed the petition and their great property, he condemned

---

[74] Notts. Archives, Savile-Foljambe MSS, Savile's letter to his constituents on general warrants, DD/FJ 11/1/7/358.
[75] Henry Lawes Luttrell (?1737–1821), MP, Bossiney, 1768-9 and 1774–84, Middlesex, 1769–74, Plympton Erle, 1790–94 and Ludgershall, 1817–21; army, 1757; Col., 1777; Major Gen. 1782, Lieut. Gen. of Ordnance, Ireland, 1787–97; Col. 6 Drag. Gds, 1788–1821; Lt. Gen.1793; C.-in-C. [I] 1796–97; Master Gen. of Ordnance [I] 1797–1800; Gen. 1798; succ. father as 2nd Earl of Carhampton [I], 1787.
[76] HPC, 1754–1790, iii, 407.
[77] PH, xvii, cc. 318–9; HPC, 1754–1790, iii, 407.
[78] Charles Watson-Wentworth (1730–82), succ. as 2nd Marquess of Rockingham, 1750; Ld. of the Bedchamber, 1757–62; Ld. Lt. West Riding, 1765–82; First Lord of the Treasury, 1765–6, 1782.
[79] Sheffield Archives, WWM/ R1-1232, Savile to Rockingham, 24 Sept. 1769. Reproduced with permission from the Milton (Peterborough) Estates Company and the Director of Culture, Sheffield City Council (the Wentworth Woodhouse Papers have been accepted in lieu of inheritance taxes by HM Government and allocated to the Sheffield City Council).
[80] Hon. Thomas Willoughby (1728–81), MP, Nottinghamshire, 1762–74; succ. as 4th Baron Willoughby, 1774.
[81] University of Nottingham, Manuscripts and Special Collections, Pw F. 6884, Montagu to Portland, 3 Oct. 1769.

colleagues who were more attentive to enclosure bills and business of that sort than attending to the great concerns of the nation. The 8000 who signed the Yorkshire petition clearly showed, 'that... the people have heard that a regard to private interests, in this House, is a great enemy to the discharge of our public duty'.[82] The account of Savile's speech recorded in *Parliamentary History* noted he spoke softly because he had a cold and a sore throat and continued with the following:

> The House was remarkably still and attentive. The character of the speaker, the importance of the subject, the novelty of the occasion, fully counter-balanced the distemper that would have proved fatal to the eloquence of a member less popular speaking on a lighter subject: such was the deep silence that prevailed on both sides of the House, that the venerable patriot was heard without much difficulty.[83]

As Burke wrote, Sir George Savile was unique in his lifetime. He stood out on account of his integrity, his adherence to core values and the esteem in which he was held by his colleagues in the House and by his Yorkshire constituents.

III: Active County MPs, 1780s

As noted in Chapter 1, the numbers of enclosure[84] and navigation bills declined significantly from the mid-1770s and did not regain the levels they had achieved until the early 1790s. This shift accounts, in part, for the lower number of members representing midland and northern counties among the active group of legislators in the 1780s. Both of the knights of the shire from Yorkshire and Derbyshire[85] remained in that cohort, as did Sir John Thorold.[86] But the group included representatives of counties that had not previously produced active legislators. Among these were Henry James Pye,[87] John Crewe,[88] John Rolle[89] and Charles Marsham.

Several of these men followed traditional patterns and devoted their legislative energies to promoting enclosure and turnpike bills. Lord George Augustus Cavendish[90] was the sole MP in the group to promote 11 or more bills over the three-year periods for each decade. He focused on projects initiated by his family and by propertied

---

[82] *PH*, xx, c. 1374.
[83] *PH*, xx, c. 1374.
[84] According to G.E. Mingay, Parliament passed averages of 22 enclosure bills a session between 1755 and 1764, and 64 a year in the 1770s. Those averages fell to 24 in the 1780s. *Parliamentary Enclosure*, p. 22.
[85] Henry Duncombe and William Wilberforce represented Yorkshire in the Parliament of 1784. Edward Miller Mundy (1750-1822), MP, Derbyshire, 1784-1822; Col. 2nd Regt., Derbys. Militia, 1803 along with George August Cavendish, already cited.
[86] Sir John Thorold, 9th Bt. (1734-1815), MP, Lincolnshire, 1779-1816.
[87] Henry James Pye (1745-1813), MP, Berkshire, 1783-1813.
[88] John Crewe, MP, Stafford, 1765-8 and Cheshire, 1768-1802; cr. Baron Crewe, 1806.
[89] John Rolle (1756-1842), MP, Devon, 1780-96; cr. Baron Rolle, 1796.
[90] Lord George Augustus Cavendish (1727-94), MP, Weymouth and Melcombe Regis, 1751-4 and Derbyshire, 1754-80 and 1781-94; Comptroller of Household, 1761-2; Ld. Lt. Derbyshire, 1766-82.

constituents. Between 1786 and 1788 he promoted eight turnpike bills and 11 enclosures, mostly originating in Derbyshire.

During these years Sir John Thorold promoted ten turnpike bills, six enclosures, a bridge over the Trent at Gainsborough and a drainage bill – a typical record for a Lincolnshire MP and not dissimilar to his predecessor Lord Brownlow Bertie during the 1760s and 1770s. With Bertie he also led constituents' opposition to a series of controversial general measures that had important implications for Lincolnshire graziers and the woollen industry.[91]

The issue arose in the 1780s because of the fluctuating price of raw wool and the declining fortunes of woollen manufacturers of the southwest. Weak demand for the fleeces led to the establishment of committees in Lincolnshire and Norfolk in October 1781. Out of those sessions came applications to Parliament for leave to export the surplus raw wool. The complaint was not a new one. Even as manufacturers urged the Walpole administration during the 1720s and into the 1740s to make the export ban more effective, publications against it appeared in the 1740s, most notably John Smith's *Memoirs of Wool* (1747); Smith pressed in his correspondence with John Cust for the export of wool and highlighted problems in the trade in fleeces, including complaints about their disfiguring and jobbers' frauds in their packing and weighing of the product.[92] Thus, the Lincolnshire petition to Parliament in 1782, appealing for a relaxation of the prohibition and permission for limited exports of raw wool to Europe, did not break new ground.

West Riding manufacturers, however, responded to the committee's proposals with formidable political muscle and an array of counter arguments. The contests between the two sides culminated in February 1782 when about 200 people, including 50 MPs, converged on the Thatched House Tavern in London. Lincolnshire observers warned that their group lacked effective, well-prepared political spokesmen. According to one observer 'our county members will not be able to undertake it and more that they would not conduct it ably.... [T]he lead must devolve to some member, perhaps the member for Lincoln, who though a man of business, is not well attended to in the House'.[93] 'The Manufacturers on the other hand attended in a well arrang'd body of members of the house of Commons headed by several good Business men who well [k]new how to arrange the Ideas of the whole proceeding'.[94] Needless to say, the business did not go as the graziers had hoped.

---

[91] Bertie, by now the 5th Duke of Ancaster, rallied Lincolnshire wool growers. On 17 Oct. 1781 he chaired a landowners meeting that resulted in the establishment of a committee 'to consult what immediate relief can be given to the present distress and what remedy it may be proper to seek, to amend the general state of our wool trade for the future'. James Bischoff, *A Comprehensive History of the Woollen and Worsted Manufactures* (2 vols, 1842), i, 207–8.

[92] Lincolnshire Archives, Frownlow MSS, Personal Correspondence, BNLW/BQ/106, John Smith to John Cust, 7, 18 Oct., 1747; Julian Hoppit, *Britain's Political Economies: Parliament and Economic Life, 1660–1800* (Cambridge, 2017), pp. 227–33. For Smith's work, see p. 233.

[93] Quoted in Sir Francis Hill, *Georgian Lincoln* (Cambridge, 1966), p. 94.

[94] Quoted in Hoppit, *Britain's Political Economies*, pp. 236–7. For the opposition of West Riding and Norwich merchants and manufacturers, see Bischoff, *Comprehensive History*, i, 209–213.

During the middle years of the decade the west and southwest agitated for restrictions. A meeting at Bath in 1784 linked rising prices for fleeces to the export of sheep and wool. Two years later high prices for wool led Norwich manufacturers and those from the southwest to petition for a bill to eradicate the smuggling of fleeces. Sir Harbord Harbord[95] introduced the measure in June 1786, but because Yorkshire manufacturers suspected its intent was to curtail their supply of wool, the measure failed.[96]

A similar bill appeared in 1788 at the instigation of Exeter. John Rolle reported the petition from its committee. Once leave was given by the House to bring in a bill 'to make more effective an Act of 23 Henry VIII and reduce to one act several laws to prevent export of sheep and wool', five members for counties with a woollen industry were instructed to bring in the measure. According to Richard Wilson, Lincolnshire's MPs once more made ineffectual efforts to defeat the bill. The exception was Thorold, who conducted what he described as a 'spirited' opposition.[97] Drawing upon pamphlets by Sir Joseph Banks and others, Thorold accused manufacturers of exaggerating the amount of wool exported illicitly; he also objected to the harshness of a measure that imposed fines and imprisonment on graziers who lived near the sea on the mistaken assumption that they were smugglers. The bill, he charged, was 'incorrigibly bad, originating in a mean and rapacious spirit of avarice and monopoly, and consequently producing acts of injustice and oppression'. Despite his impassioned remarks, the House approved the bill at its third reading.[98]

The main portion of the active group of county members during the 1780s had two notable attributes. Among its members were MPs who represented counties in the southeast, southwest (Kent, Somerset and Devon) or the northwest (Cheshire, Lancashire), counties which had not, for the most part, during the 1760s or 1770s returned notably active legislators. Moreover, the careers of the 1780 MPs seem to have been informed to a greater degree than their predecessors by their experiences in local government as magistrates or by their willingness to serve as spokesmen for the needs of large towns, including Manchester, Liverpool and Birmingham.

The career of Thomas Stanley[99] highlights the limitations of relying on a record of legislative activity over a three-year span in assessing the impact of an MP. Between 1786 and 1788 he promoted only three Lancashire road bills and two enclosures, yet he was celebrated during his tenure as an effective spokesman for Lancashire's manufacturers and merchants, after supporting a bounty on cotton exports and the

---

[95] Harbord Harbord (1734–1810), MP, Norwich, 1756–86; cr. Baron Suffield, 1786.
[96] Hoppit, *Failed Legislation*, p. 490. For Yorkshire's suspicions, see Northamptonshire Archives, Fitzwilliam Papers, Box 38, Pemberton Milnes to Earl Fitzwilliam, 1 Aug. 1786 and Richard Wilson, 'Newspapers and industry: The export of wool controversies of the 1780s', in *The Press in English Society from the Seventeenth to the Nineteenth Centuries*, ed. Michael Harris and Alan Lee (Cranbury, NJ and London, 1986), pp. 100–1.
[97] Wilson, 'Newspapers and industry', pp. 102–3. *The Sheep and Wool Correspondence of Sir Joseph Banks, 1781–1820*, ed. Harold C. Carter (1979), pp. 49, 59.
[98] *PH*, xxvii, cc. 382–3, 389. In addition to the works of Banks, Thorold drew upon pamphlets by Thomas Pownall, Arthur Young and Lord Sheffield for his points. Hoppit, *Britain's Political Economies*, p. 239.
[99] Thomas Stanley (1749–1816), MP, Lancashire, 1780–1812.

removal of taxes on cotton goods.[100] His major contributions came in 1785. On 11 March he presented the petition of Manchester manufacturers and workers demanding the repeal of Pitt's fustian tax which came after the presentation of a petition for that step.[101] His efforts on behalf of repeal later earned him and two of the town's delegates to the committee of the House on the offensive tax a celebratory dinner at the Manchester Hotel.[102] Constituent pressure and the partisan campaign of his Foxite compatriots led Stanley to oppose Pitt's plan to allow Ireland greater access to the British market in 1785. In 1787 he supported the commercial treaty with France in 1787, giving up, he confessed, his own opinions to the wishes and instructions of my constituents'.[103] From 1788 he upheld the interests of Liverpool slave traders by opposing efforts to regulate or abolish the slave trade. Stephen Fuller,[104] who complained of the reluctance of MPs tied to the West Indies to attend sessions of the Commons' select committee on the trade, cited Stanley as one of the few who actively participated in its prolonged sessions.[105]

IV: County MPs and General Legislation

Joanna Innes, David Eastwood and Richard Connors have shown how MPs drew on their experiences as magistrates or memberships in voluntary societies to present legislation that was national in its scope.[106] These connections along with more traditional motivations brought knights of the shire for Devon, Somerset, Kent, Middlesex and Yorkshire into the forefront of legislative activity in the 1780s. According to Innes, about 1,000 bills relating to social policy were submitted to the Commons in the 100 years after 1690, half of which reached the statute book. A significant portion

---

[100] *HPC, 1754-1790*, iii, 472-3. In 1780 Stanley reported from a select committee established to consider the petition of Manchester cotton workers complaining of low wages. Their spokesmen before the committee attributed the wage problem and unemployment throughout Lancashire to extensive use of new machinery. The report concluded on every point in support of the manufacturers' position. It asserted there was no want of employment for the industrious poor and that an upsurge in demand for British cotton products would not have occurred without the use of new 'patent machines'. The report concluded: 'if Manufacturers were deprived the use of Patent Machines, it would be the means of transferring these evident advantages into the Hands of foreign Nations'. *Commons Sessional Papers*, xxxi, 393-8.
[101] The petition was signed by 80,000 Lancashire manufacturers and workers. Stanley claimed that the tax of eight per cent on exported goods deprived Manchester of its overseas markets and forced workmen to emigrate. *PH*, xxv, cc. 350, 362.
[102] W.E. Axon, *The Annals of Manchester: A Chronological Record from the Earliest Times to the End of 1885* (Manchester, 1886), p. 112.
[103] *HPC, 1754-1790*, iii, 475.
[104] Stephen Fuller (1716-1806), agent for Jamaica, 1764-95. *The Correspondence of Stephen Fuller, 1788-1795: Jamaica, the West India Interest at Westminster and the Campaign to Preserve the Slave Trade*, ed. M.W. McCahill (Chichester and Malden, MA, 2014), pp. 26-39.
[105] *Correspondence of Stephen Fuller*, pp. 137, 142.
[106] Innes, 'Parliament and English social policy', *TRHS*, 5th ser., xl (1990), 80-1; David Eastwood, 'Men, morals and the machinery of social legislation, 1790-1840', *Parl. Hist.*, xiii (1994), 190-205; Richard Connors, 'Parliament and poverty in mid-eighteenth-century England', *Parl. Hist.*, xxi, 207-32.

of these measures were introduced by backbench MPs., many of them county MPs.[107] County MPs often worked together to promote bills for the relief of the poor and imprisoned debtors, the better operation of the militia, and, in the case of Wilberforce and several compatriots, for the abolition of the slave trade. In doing so, they often cited the wishes of constituents, local authorities or voluntary societies with which they were associated in explaining why they were introducing the measures.

John Pollexfen Bastard[108] and John Rolle Devon's knights of the shire formed a productive legislative partnership during the late eighteenth century. Bastard presented a bill to prevent frivolous and vexatious suits in ecclesiastical courts on 23 February 1786.[109] His initial goal was to set a time limit within which charges of immorality could be brought before the ecclesiastical courts. Opposition from Lloyd Kenyon[110] and Burke forced him to withdraw it in May, but he reintroduced an expanded version that included restrictions on the initiation of suits for the recovery of small tithes if the sum involved was below a specified low level.[111] This bill made its way through the Commons with Rolle chairing its second reading committee. In the upper House Archbishop Cornwallis[112] and Bishop Warren[113] attacked the bill for putting the court under such restraints 'that it could scarcely exercise its jurisdiction', and it was defeated. Undeterred, Bastard reintroduced his bill the next session. He condemned 'the arbitrary and remorseless Ecclesiastical Courts, for what they chose to represent as a contempt of their authority', citing many instances of what he called their oppression, and Rolle came to his defence after Bastard was attacked by Kenyon and John Scott. The bill became law only after Bastard removed the tithe clauses (Ecclesiastical Suits Act:, 27 Geo. III, c 44).[114]

Bastard oversaw five other measures between 1786 and 1788: the Keyberry Road Bill, again with Rolle. He the chaired a committee on the petition of Denys Rolle[115] for a bill to build a new Devon gaol (Devon Gaol Act, 27 Geo. III, c. 59)[116] and carried an enclosure and a naturalisation bill. He also chaired the committee of the whole House on William Mainwaring's bill to extend provisions of an earlier measure to reduce the terms of imprisonment of debtors in London and Westminster and abolish fees they

---

[107] Innes, 'Parliament and the shaping of social policy', 69; According to Peter Jupp, between 28 and 42 per cent of the general legislation introduced between 1760 and 1839 was presented by backbench MPs. Between 18 and 25 per cent of those measures became law. Jupp, *The Governing of Britain, 1688–1848: The Executive Parliament and the People* (Abingdon, 2006), p. 221.

[108] John Pollexfen Bastard (1756–1816), MP, Truro, 1783–4 and Devon, 1784–1816.

[109] *CJ*, xli, 249.

[110] Lloyd Kenyon (1732–1802), MP, Hindon, 1780–4 and Tregony, 1784–8; C.J, Chester, 1780–4; Attorney Gen., 1782–3, Dec. and Jan. 1783–4; cr. Bt.,1784; Master of the Rolls, 1784–8; C.J., King's Bench, 1788–1802; cr. Baron Kenyon, 1788.

[111] For the text of the bill, see *Commons Sessional Papers*, xlvii, 219–26.

[112] Frederick Cornwallis (1713–83) Archbishop of Canterbury, 1768–83.

[113] John Warren (1730–1800), Bishop of Ely, 1772–9, St. David's, 1779–83 and Bangor, 1783–1800; sometime chairman of the of the Lords' committees, 1793–4.

[114] *PH*, xxvi, cc. 623–5, 1005–7; Ditchfield, 'The Quakers and the tithe question', *Parl. Hist.*, iv, 90–1.

[115] Denys Rolle (?1725–97), MP, Barnstaple, 1761–74.

[116] The Webbs noted that by 1804 Devon was one of the ten counties which devoted the most attention to prison administration. S. and B. Webb, *English Prisons under Local Government* (New York, 1922), p. 56, n.2.

paid to their gaolers. Once it received the Commons' approval, he carried the bill to the Lords.[117]

Bastard's partner, Rolle, was a colourful figure and the inspiration for the *Rolliad*.[118] A blunt, inarticulate speaker whose 'hand and foot were said to have been the largest in the kingdom',[119] Rolle was an obvious target for a satirical lampoon. He was also the largest landholder in Devon, attentive to the needs of his constituents, especially those of the poor. In addition to the measures he forwarded with Bastard, Rolle promoted during the late 1780s a road, an estate and a naturalisation bill along with a measure to rebuild All Saints Church in Newcastle-upon-Tyne along with the already noted bills to bar the export of sheep and raw wool. In addition, his biography in the *History of Parliament* volumes notes that on 30 April 1787, at 'the express desire of his constituents' he proposed a bill for 'a more comfortable subsistence for the poor', and a reduction of 'the very heavy and increasing poor rates'. These objectives were to be achieved through friendly societies 'successfully established, and advantageously adopted to the comfort of the poor'.[120] Rolle said he wished to establish

> one general club or fund throughout the kingdom, with permanency to the body, and security to the capital… to be raised by obliging the rich in a certain limited proportion to become contributors to the benefit of the poor, and to oblige the poor, whilst young and in health, to contribute towards their own support when disabled by sickness, accident, or age.[121]

Though given leave to bring in his bill, the House postponed hearing the report of the second reading committee.[122] Undeterred, Rolle offered another poor bill in 1788, which also failed,[123] but he successfully promoted a bill at the behest of the overseers of the poor in Exeter 'to render more effectual an act of 25 George III for erecting hospitals and workhouses' (Exeter Poor Relief Act, 28 Geo III, c. 76). Bastard, along with the members for the town helped him to prepare and present the bill, but Rolle carried it through the rest of its stages. With the exception of one minor compounding bill he promoted for a constituent, it was the last measure he carried though the House between 1786 and 1788.

Between 1786 and 1788 Henry Duncombe and William Wilberforce, Yorkshire's MPs, together promoted 29 bills. Over the three years, Duncombe promoted 22 bills, two of them with Wilberforce – the unsuccessful Bridlington Harbour Bill and another unsuccessful bill to better ascertain persons eligible to vote in elections for members of the counties. Duncombe was again unsuccessful in 1788 in his effort to secure legislation to regulate the loading of coals at Newcastle and Sunderland, an exercise

---

[117] Mainwaring introduced the bill on February 27. For Bastard's work on it, see *CJ*, xli, 567, 656.
[118] The *Rolliad* initially appeared in segments in the *Morning Herald* in 1784 and 1785.
[119] *HPC, 1790–1820*, v, 35.
[120] *HPC, 1754–1790*, iii, 373–4.
[121] Quoted in *HPC, 1754–1790*, iii, p. 374.
[122] Hoppit, *Failed legislation*, p. 492.
[123] Hoppit, *Failed legislation*, p. 496. For its text, see *Commons Sessional Papers*, xlviii, 421–44.

that provoked a number of counter-petitions.[124] He was not alone in failing on this question. Lord Mulgrave in 1787 and Sir Matthew White Ridley[125] in the following session introduced similar measures only to see them defeated.[126] Beyond these measures, Duncombe carried a promissory notes bill in 1786, nine enclosure bills, two estate and three road bills; he was one of a group of MPs to steer the controversial wool bill through the House in 1788 when he also promoted the Shropshire Canal Bill.

Even a member of Wilberforce's national standing attended to the routine business of constituents when he was able. After surrendering his county seat in 1812, his Yorkshire constituents thanked him for supervising 'the private business of the county'.[127] Between 1786 and 1788 he promoted three roads, one drainage, two enclosures, a Leeds paving and the two failed measures he pursued with Duncombe. In 1786 he presented on his own initiative and carried through the House a bill to regulate the disposal of the bodies of executed criminals, which failed in the Lords. After 1787, Wilberforce, however, became heavily involved with two new projects – the Proclamation Society[128] and the abolition of the slave trade. As a result, he had less time for the routine legislative business of the county MP.[129]

If the work of the Proclamation Society partially diverted Wilberforce's attention from Yorkshire's local business, the cause of abolition was all-consuming. There were consultations with Pitt and other opponents of the trade, and attendance at meetings of the Abolition Society. When Sir William Dolben encountered opposition to his controversial Slave Trade Regulation Bill, Wilberforce came to his assistance. During his long campaign he had to deal with defenders of the trade – collecting evidence 'upon which to ground the first attack on the trade' before the committee of the Privy Council.[130] Subsequently, he had prolonged consultations with Pitt and William Grenville as he prepared for his first major address on the slave trade on 12 May 1789, when he presented 12 resolutions justifying its abolition. Following the address, the House established a select committee to investigate the trade, proceedings which consumed several years of his attention.[131] In April 1790, for example, Stephen Fuller reported to Jamaica that 'the Members who attended [the committee] on the part of the Abolishers were Mr Wilberforce, Sir William Dolbin, Mr [Frederick] Montagu, &

---

[124] Hoppit, *Failed Legislation*, pp. 494–5.
[125] Sir Matthew White Ridley, 2nd Bt. (1745–1813), MP, Morpeth, 1768–74 and Newcastle-upon-Tyne, 1774–1812, Mayor of Newcastle, 1774, 1782, 1791.
[126] Hoppit, *Failed Legislation*, pp. 494–5.
[127] Cited in Langford, *Public Life*, p. 164.
[128] For the Proclamation Society, its objectives and Wilberforce's work on its behalf, see Joanna Innes, 'Politics and morals: The reformation of manners movement in later eighteenth-century England', in *The Transformation of Political Culture: England and Germany in the late Eighteenth Century*, ed. Eckhart Hellmuth (New York, 1990), pp. 57–118.
[129] Nevertheless, Wilberforce and Duncombe were successful in behind the scenes efforts to secure an acceptable plan for a new dock for Hull in the 1790s.
[130] The Privy Council committee was Pitt's idea. He hoped that the committee's report would make the case for abolition. John Ehrman, *The Younger Pitt*, p. 496.
[131] Despite the Privy Council's report, independent MPs and conservative Whigs demanded in May 1789 that the Commons undertake its own inquiry, because it would be 'unparliamentary' to rely upon information obtained by the Privy Council. *PH*, xxviii, cc. 81–92. For the demands made by this select committee on Wilberforce's time in 1790, see *Wilberforce*, i, pp. 266–7, 270, ii, pp. 167–8.

Mr Smith M.[ember] for Sudbury.[132] They met every day, without missing one day, precisely at eleven, and sat till three, sometimes longer'.[133]

While Wilberforce concentrated on abolishing the slave trade, William Mainwaring,[134] a member of the Society's committee, found time to forward portions of the Society's agenda even as he promoted some of the business of Middlesex. Though a contemporary described him as among 'the more useful and respectable members of the Commons',[135] most of the 15 bills Mainwaring promoted between 1786 and 1788 would have been standard fare for a member for Middlesex. They included a paving bill, a new church for Paddington, another to license Sadler's Wells, and others to regulate the slaughtering of horses in London and renew the Westminster Paving Act. As already noted, he tried to alleviate the situation of imprisoned debtors, by introducing legislation on 14 March 1786 to reduce their terms of incarceration and abolish fees they owed their gaolers.[136] The previous session he had joined other Middlesex and Westminster magistrates in opposing Pitt's bill for the reform of metropolitan policing. While acknowledging that crime was widespread, Mainwaring questioned the practicality of the legislation, complaining there were already too many penal laws. What was needed, he claimed, was better enforcement of existing laws. Given the local resistance to the proposal, it failed.[137]

Mainwaring's commitment to the goals of the Proclamation Society, which, according to Simon Devereux included the reduction of the reliance upon hanging as a punishment for capital crimes,[138] is reflected in his 'Interludes Bill', introduced in 1786. The measure's purpose was to amend 10 George II and reduce to one act laws relating to rogues and vagabonds. It also proposed to amend 25 George II by regulating places of entertainment in London and Westminster. The measure failed to pass in 1786, but Mainwaring reintroduced it in 1787 when it made its way through

---

[132] Fuller was likely referring to William Smith, who partnered Wilberforce in this phase of the abolition campaign and subsequently sat for Sudbury.
[133] *The Correspondence of Stephen Fuller*, p. 137.
[134] William Mainwaring (1735–1821). MP, Middlesex, 1784–1802; Lincoln's Inn, 1754, bencher, 1795; first protonotary, court of common pleas, 1768–94; chair, Middlesex and Westminster quarter sessions, 1781–1816.
[135] Quoted in Ian R. Christie, *British 'Non-Elite' MPs 1715–1820* (Oxford, 1995), p. 175.
[136] For its text, see *Commons Sessional Papers*, xlviii, pp. 111–14 (26 George III, c. 44).
[137] Hoppit, *Failed Legislation*, pp. 490–1, 496–7. Radzinowicz criticised Mainwaring for his role in wrecking the bill. According to Innes, however, he wanted to arm magistrates with powers 'to suppress vice', a priority of the Proclamation Society. He had described the bill at its introduction as a 'cold, feeble measure, that might do some good, but a great deal of mischief'. He complained that it imposed no regulations on alehouses. Innes, 'Politics and morals', 96; *PH*, xxix, 1179–80.
[138] The King's proclamation of 1787 'required all subjects and magistrates to enforce laws against the profanation of the Sabbath, excessive drinking, blasphemies and cursing, licentious gatherings and lewd publications'. By these Wilberforce hoped to reduce the scale of capital punishment. 'The barbarous custom of hanging has been tried too long… The most effectual way to prevent greater crimes' he told Christopher Wyvill, 'is by punishing the smaller, and by endeavouring to repress the general spirit of licentiousness which is the parent of every evil'. Quoted in Simon Devereux, www.cambridge.org/core/journals/law-and-history-review/article/inexperienced-humanitarians?-william-wilberforce-william-pitt-and-the-execution-crisis-of-the-1780s/DA5821170E59D63DF61 D543291A285DA

both chambers before the lower House failed to approve amendments added by the Lords.[139]

Mainwaring became embroiled in further legislative controversy tied to the Proclamation Society in March 1794 when he introduced a bill to amend an act of Charles II regarding the observance of the Sabbath. The original measure imposed a fine of five shillings for breaking the law and granted a third of that sum to the informer or prosecutor who identified the violation. In presenting his bill, Mainwaring asked the House to consider 'how very inadequate an inducement the third part of five shillings was for the prosecutor to take upon himself the trouble of seeing the law carried into effect'. He proposed instead that justices be authorised to pay a prosecutor's expenses and prohibit bakers from working on Sundays except from 10 am to 1 pm. The bill that came before the House was quite different from Mainwaring's proposals. It was drafted by Sir William Dolben, another member of the Society, and made a breach of Sunday a misdemeanour, punishable by a fine and imprisonment. Pitt and Pepper Arden[140] attacked the bill which was defeated in the Commons.[141]

Michael Ignatieff praised Mainwaring for superintending the construction of a house of correction at Clerkenwell on the John Howard model after securing the necessary legislation.[142] The Coldbath Prison, however, became a subject of controversy in 1798 when Sir Francis Burdett[143] charged that Aris, its governor, treated political prisoners in an inhumane fashion. Mainwaring replied by rejecting the charges and demanding an inquiry. A prison in which inmates suffered cold, hunger and abuse had failed to fulfil its promise, though members of the inquiry refused to admonish its authorities. The effect of the management scandals was that 'Penitentiary and Bastille' became linked in the popular imagination, and Mainwaring lost his seat at the 1802 election.[144]

V: Complexity of Legislating

A problem with much of the previous discussion is that for the most part it makes MPs' task of legislating seem all too simple. Even the mundane turnpike bill could cause complications, requiring the members responsible for guiding those bills through the chamber to negotiate 'deals' with local potentates in order to ensure their passage. In

---

[139] Hoppit, *Failed Legislation*, pp. 490–1.
[140] Richard Pepper Arden (1744–1804), MP, Newton, I.o.W., 1783–4, Aldborough, 1784–90; Hastings, 1790–4 and Bath, 1794–1801; Welsh judge, 1776–82; Solicitor Gen. 1782–3, Dec. 1783–Apr. 1784; Attorney Gen. and C.J. Chester, 1784–88; Master of Rolls, 1788–1801; C.J. Common Pleas, 1801–4; cr. Baron Alvanley, 1801.
[141] Radzinowicz, *A History of English Criminal Law and its Administration from 1750. Vol. 4: Grappling for Control* (1968), pp. 186–7.
[142] Michael Ignatieff, *A Just Measure of Pain*, p. 78; Innes, 'Politics and morals', pp. 117–18.
[143] Sir Francis Burdett (1770–1844), MP, Boroughbridge, 1796–1802; Middlesex, 1802–4 and 1805–6; Westminster, 1807–37 and Wiltshire North, 1837–44; succ. gdfa. as 5th Bt., 1797.
[144] *HPC, 1790–1820*, iv, 525; Innes, 'Politics and morals', pp. 117–18; Ignatieff, *A Just Measure of Pain*, p. 142.

1792 William Dickinson[145] was informed that the residents of Butleigh opposed including the town in the Somerton Act. James Grenville[146] protested that they had not received the necessary notices and asked to 'review' the matter with Dickinson. The session must have gone well, for within a month, Grenville informed Dickinson that he had received a copy of the amended bill which contained a new clause with no toll gate in the vicinity of Butleigh. 'This clause', Grenville wrote, 'perfectly satisfies us, and I can see no cause for objecting to any part of the Bill in its present form'. On the basis of their agreement, Grenville trusted Dickinson to add gentlemen to his list of Commissioners 'to protect our interests' when the measure went into its second reading committee.[147]

Issues that provoked James Grenville in 1792 upset the 10th Earl of Westmorland[148] in 1800. Despite his modest abilities, Westmorland ornamented a succession of cabinets for 28 years, so his concerns necessitated Dickinson's attention. The measure in question was the Crewkerne Turnpike Bill, and once again Dickinson was to chair its second reading committee. Westmoreland had petitioned to postpone the committee's sitting which Dickinson opposed, partly because a postponement would entail additional expenses for the turnpike's trustees. Instead, he recommended that the Earl's agent, who had previously declined to negotiate, 'talk substance' in order to reach an agreement.[149]

What took place between Dickinson and James Grenville, and what Dickinson proposed that Westmorland's agent undertake, was the sort of horse trading that enabled eighteenth-century Parliaments to function. Disputes of the sort Dickinson encountered arose frequently throughout the eighteenth century, and his ability to negotiate settlements involving opposing parties was crucial to the operation of the Commons as a legislative institution.

Legislators not only had to settle disagreements that stood in the way of the passage of legislation, but had to confront the impatient, uninformed complaints of constituents. In 1749 Thomas Prowse[150] became embroiled with his Somerset constituents over the Bristol Turnpike Bill. Discontent became so intense that his friends feared the business would prejudice his electoral interest. Rioters, outraged by new tolls, were tearing down toll gates and, according to Prowse, threatening 'the little we have left of Liberty or Property'.

Constituents insinuated that was he responsible for the bill when it was in fact initiated by Bristol's corporation. Prowse assured them he took no part in the proceedings until they instructed him to add certain commissioners to the bill along

---

[145] William Dickinson (1745–1806), MP, Great Marlow, 1768–74, Rye, 1777–90 and Somerset, 1790–1806.
[146] James Grenville (1742–1825), MP, Thirsk, 1765–8, Buckingham, 1770–90 and Buckinghamshire, 1790–7; Ld. of Treas., 1782–3 and of Trade, 1784–1825; cr. Baron Glastonbury, 1797.
[147] Somerset and Devon Archives and Local Studies, Dickinson Papers, DD/DN 4/2/7, ff. 21, 31, Grenville to Dickinson, 9 Feb. 11 Mar. 1792
[148] John Fane, 10th Earl of Westmorland (1759–1841), Postmaster-Gen, 1789; Ld. Lt., [I], 1789–95; Master of Horse, 1795–8; Lord Privy Seal, 1798–1806 and 1807–27.
[149] Somerset Archives and Devon Local Studies, William Dickinson Papers, DD/DN/4/2/7, f. 97, Dickinson to Westmorland, 8 Mar. 1800.
[150] Thomas Prowse (1707–67), MP, Somerset, 1740–67.

with some additional clauses. Yet, they then instructed him to try to throw out the measure without realising, he complained, that 'turnpikes are at present the favourites of Parliament, and... a suggestion only that the County of Somerset did not approve would be no argument even in a Courtier's mouth against passing this Law'. His final complaint was that he received contradictory signals from Somerset. While 200 gentlemen and freeholders had sent him and his fellow MP a petition demanding they add the commissioners, the document made no mention of issues that subsequently upset them. To pacify his constituents, Prowse highlighted alterations he had made that gave the county the upper hand over Bristol which they had earlier failed to comprehend or appreciate.[151]

Prowse endured other challenges, some as stressful as the harassment he endured over the Bristol Turnpike Bill. In December 1749, after presenting the case of Somerset graziers to the Duke of Dorset,[152] he managed after intense lobbying to secure the repeal an order of the Privy Council that would have imposed an embargo on the admission of cattle from the south, southwest and west of England into the London market.[153] So his constituents, despite their occasional intemperance, appreciated his efforts on their behalf and returned him to Parliament without opposition in 1754 and 1761.

VI: Conclusion

Most county members diligently fulfilled their legislative obligations to their constituents. Roles that required mastery of the standing orders of the House or chairing contentious second reading committees were usually left to the most active and experienced knights of the shire including Lord Brownlow Bertie, Lord George Augustus Cavendish, Frederick Montagu or Prowse. These MPs were also likely to be designated by promoters to settle details of bills prior to their presentation or to negotiate agreements with parties whose objections threatened their passage.

With the exception of Sir George Savile, Sir Thomas Bunbury, and a few other active county members, most knights of the shire during the 1760s and early 1770s focused their energies on shepherding the priorities of fellow landlords through the House. Those priorities, as we have seen, included enclosure, drainage, turnpike, estate, navigation and some local improvement bills. Yet this sort of legislation never represented the totality of the county MPs legislative agenda, especially in the 1770s and 1780s. The Webbs noted the importance of a series of acts[154] obtained between 1785 and 1788 for rebuilding county gaols, all of which were modelled on principles

---

[151] WSHC, Letters from Thomas Prowse to Peter Lovell 179-1767, Prowse to Peter Lovell, 14 Sept. 1749.
[152] Lionel Cranfield Sackville (1688-1765), succ. fa. as 7th Earl of Dorset and 2nd Earl of Middlesex, 1706; Groom of Stole, 1711-17, Constable of Dover Castle, 1714-30; Lord Warden of Cinque Ports, 1714-17; cr. Duke of Dorset, 1720; Lord Steward, 1725-30 and 1737-45; Ld. Lt. [I], 1731-7 and 1751-5; Ld. President of Council, 1745-50; Ld. Lt. Kent, 1746-65.
[153] WSHC, Prowse MSS, Prowse to Lovell, 23 Dec. 1748, 4, 18 Jan. 1749.
[154] Webbs, *English Prisons under Local Government* (1922), pp. 39-40.

derived from the Penitentiary Act of 1779.[155] Most of the acts were introduced and carried through the House by county members. As already noted, Sir George Savile and Lord Strange were instrumental in ensuring the permanence of the militia and managed to drag recalcitrant counties into fulfilling their obligations to the militia system. Savile's Catholic Relief Act was a first step in restoring to English Roman Catholics rights to ownership of property and a Catholic education.

Though it was usually borough MPs who assisted county colleagues with their heavy legislative burdens, knights of the shire Sir Robert Lawley[156] and Sir George Augustus Shuckburgh[157] attended to Birmingham's many legislative needs after 1780. As noted in this chapter, Thomas Stanley was a useful advocate for the interests of Manchester cotton barons, and Frederick Montague took a leading part in steering Arkwright's legislation to legalise the production of white stuffs through the House in 1774, thereby putting cotton cloth on the same legal basis as its woollen and linen competitors. In the end Wilberforce's campaign bill to abolish the British slave trade limited his capacity to serve the more mundane legislative projects of his Yorkshire constituents. Nevertheless, they appreciated his efforts on behalf of their 'private' bills.

Their legislative diligence is also a testament to the county members' commitment to their constituents. As noted at the chapter's outset, those who secured county seats for the most part acknowledged their obligation to forward their constituents' business through the House. A principal goal of this chapter is to show that many of them fulfilled this obligation diligently and effectively, though the bulk of the burden fell upon a small portion of the group. They had little hesitation in undertaking these tasks because most acknowledged that constituents could call upon their members to forward their specific and local business. As was clear in the discussion of Philip Yorke, there were questions as to what degree constituents could press MPs to follow their directions on national questions, against the wishes of patrons, family members or the member's informed judgment. This is an issue discussed at greater length in subsequent chapters, but for a variety of reasons Yorke, by the mid-1780s, began to break free of his uncles and respond to the voices of constituents on such questions as the Coalition's India Bill and the appeals of Cambridgeshire dissenters to support the repeal of the Test and Corporation Acts in 1787.

---

[155] Devon Gaol Act (25 Geo. III, c. 10: (Bastard carried the bill)), Gloucestershire Gaol Act (26 Geo III, c. 24), Middlesex Gaol Act (27 Geo III, c. 58, (Mainwaring carried), Shropshire Gaol Act, (26 Geo. III, c. 55, (R. Hill carried), Staffordshire 27 Geo III, c. 8, (Gilbert carried) and Sussex (27 Geo. III, c. 60, (Mainwaring carried); Webbs, *English Prisons*, p. 39.
[156] Sir Robert Lawley, 5th Bt. (1736–1793), MP, Warwickshire, 1780–1793.
[157] Sir George Augustus Shuckburgh, 6th Bt. (1751–1804), MP, Warwickshire, 1780–1804. For Lawley's and Shuckburgh's work on behalf of Birmingham at Westminster, see Chapter 8.

3

Contentious Constituencies: Plymouth, Kingston-upon-Hull, Bristol and their MPs

This chapter focuses on members for three constituencies – Bristol, Kingston-upon-Hull and Plymouth. With 5,000 voters Bristol was England's third largest urban constituency. Hull's 1,200 voters were described as 'a large and unruly electorate'.[1] By contrast, the right to vote at Plymouth was vested in approximately 200 freemen whose appetite for government patronage exhausted Lord Sandwich.

Each of these constituencies expected its MPs to forward its needs in Parliament and with the relevant government departments. Problems arose regarding various proposals to extend Hull's dock or Plymouth's controversial improvement bills. The battles raged on each issue for years, placing Lord Barrington[2] and later the members for Hull between each town's opposing camps. MPs' correspondence reveals, however, that they, for the most part, worked successfully to achieve the goals of substantial bodies of their constituents; Edmund Burke, while dutifully attending to constituency business, claimed in 1730 to find the task tiresome and degrading – an outlook that weakened his hold on his Bristol seat.

I: Plymouth

Lord Barrington represented Plymouth for 24 years, forwarding residents' applications for appointments to a variety of local posts and tending the constituency's business at Westminster. On 31 January 1770 the town's Mayor, aldermen, common council and principal inhabitants petitioned for a bill to light and pave the town's streets; it was presented to the Commons and referred to a petition committee that included Barrington. Within eight days, however, another group of town officials and principal inhabitants presented a counter-petition; later the mayor and a group of town officials complained that the improvement bill 'will be attended with Numberless Oppressions

---

[1] *HPC, 1754–1790*, i, 258.
[2] William Wildman, 2nd Viscount Barrington [I] (1717–93), MP, Berwick-on-Tweed, 1740–54 and Plymouth, 1754–78, Ld. of Admiralty, 1746–54; Master of Great Wardrobe, 1754–5; Sec. at War, 1755–61, 1765–78; Chancellor of Exchequer, 1761–2, Treasurer of Navy, 1762–5; Postmaster Gen. 1782.

and pernicious Consequences to the Corporation and Inhabitants in General, and will (very probably) tend to the Utter Ruin of the Said Town'.[3] Within weeks of the measure's passage, both sides assured Barrington that the Improvement Act (10 Geo. III, c. 14) would require amendment.[4] What followed were contests that extended over four years and resulted in a second Improvement Act two years later (12 Geo. III, c. 14) and a Streets Act (14 Geo III, c. 8) and endless squabbling, leaving Barrington, who had supported the initial measure, struggling to find resolution to the on-going dissension.[5]

Initially, he had tried to maintain his neutrality: he presented each side's petitions to the House, held conferences with its agents and local leaders, giving the group his advice on how to proceed. Even as the two sides made tactical errors, Barrington maintained his impartiality, but eventually he supported the bill because more aldermen and common councilmen supported than opposed it.

His declaration of support did not defuse the opposition to the measure. In January, 1772 the opponents petitioned the Commons, accusing the new improvement commissioners of unjust taxation. They also asserted that the Act was 'a manifest violation of the Town's Charter', adding that the mayor and Corporation 'have full Authority to put into execution every necessary and needful Purpose for the good Government and real Benefit of the Town'.[6] The result was the second improvement bill, which amended the original measure by making provision for 30 additional commissioners chosen by ratepayers to be added to the existing group. Disputes of this sort disrupted many communities as Parliament empowered local paving commissioners to levy rates, remove obstructions by compulsory purchase and pave, light and cleanse, often at considerable expense.

The backlash against the improvement bill became political. A fellow naval officer warned Barrington's brother that

> sometime in March last year when Lord Barrington had just got the Amendments of the Paving Bill postpon'd, & was thought by me & others not to have held the balance exactly even between the Corporation and the Commissioners, a Gentleman with whom I happen'd to fall in company, observing me to be a little chagrin'd, proposed an opposition to his lordship at any future election, & ask'd me for my vote.[7]

Throughout the struggle, Barrington, though aware that prominent members of the community opposed his stance, assured his correspondents that he acted 'invariably by

---

[3] BL, Barrington MSS 73676, f. 66, Samuel Peter and six others to Barrington, 10 Jan. 1770.
[4] *CJ*, xxxiii, 128; BL, Barrington MSS, Add. MS 73676, ff. 103, 107, 109; 15, 27, 29 Jan. 1771. The House, however, agreed not to proceed with the revisions, probably because the two sides were so far apart. Barrington to Tolcher, 19 Mar. 1771, f. 188.
[5] BL, Barrington MSS, Add. MS 73676, ff. 84–5, Barrington to Samuel Peters, 5 Apr. 1770.
[6] *CJ*, xxxiii, 522. For reliance upon chartered rights as a justification for opposition to improvement acts, see Rosemary Sweet, 'Local identities and a national Parliament, c. 1688–1835', in *Parliaments, Nations and Identities in Britain and Ireland, 1660–1850*, ed. Julian Hoppit (Manchester, 2003), pp. 48–63. For the backlash against what some called 'the Epidemical Madness of New Paving' see Langford, *Public Life*, pp. 223–27.
[7] BL, Barrington MSS, Add. MS 73680, f. 24, J. Musgrave to Capt. Samuel Barrington, 9 Aug. 1771.

the directions of the upper Bench, and by what I understood by them, to be the general inclination of my Constituents'. Assured of this support, He approached Lord North and the Admiralty to secure the government's financial assistance in rebuilding the walls at Mountbatten.[8] He called upon the minister at the request of local shopkeepers to take steps to protect them from the allegedly fraudulent practices of hawkers and pedlars and was able to get the necessary act passed in the 1772 session.[9] The Corporation relied upon him in 1775 to defeat Sir John St. Aubyn's plan to secure an act to divert water from the town's reserve to supply his tenants at Plymouth Dock.[10] Residents deluged him with applications for appointments, reminding him, 'there are many poor Freemen of this Town, to whom those little appointments made for 'very comfortable retirements'.[11] Given the esteem with which he was held by North, Sandwich and George III, the patronage continued to flow, and Barrington's position remained secure until he retired in 1778. He was a fine constituency MP even as he tended for years to the needs of the army.

II: Hull

The consuming legislative issue in Hull in the second half of the eighteenth century related to docking and the harbour's congestion. In March 1772 merchants of six counties demanded that a port be established at Gainsborough because of the inadequacy of the dock facilities at Hull, and the same year the Customs threatened to bring in the necessary legislation if the town failed to present a bill of its own. The reason for these demands was that Hull's port lacked the facilities to handle its fourfold increase in tonnage over the previous 30 years and a legal quay to handle its foreign trade.[12] Because the Corporation lacked the funds to build the required facilities, the privately funded Hull Dock Company secured the needed legislation in 1772 to create an independent entity to build a new dock. In 1774 pressure from the commissioners of the Customs led to the introduction of legislation for a dock which also empowered the king to assign space on the west side of the harbour for the only lawful quay for goods in overseas trade. Since the new facility would form part of the military dock, the Customs advanced £15,000 towards its construction. Though previously criticised by his constituents for a 'want of activity', William Weddell[13] steered the legislation (14 Geo III, c. 56) through its stages, a process which extended from 21 March to 9 May, when he was able to carry the bill to the House of Lords.[14]

---

[8] BL, Barrington MS, Add. MS 73681, ff. 36-7, 40-1, 9 principal inhabitants to Barrington, 31 Jan. 1772 and reply, 6 Feb. 1772. *HPC, 1754-1790*, i, 258.
[9] BL, Barrington MSS, Add. MS 73680, f. 62, Petition of the shopkeepers of Plymouth to the Mayor of Plymouth, asking corporation to instruct the town's representatives to support such legislation, 13 May 1772.
[10] BL, Barrington MSS, Add. MS 73679, f. 12, J. Nicholls and seven aldermen to Barrington, Dec. 1775.
[11] BL, Barrington MSS, Add, MS 73678, f. 148, Ralph Mitchell to Barrington, 2 Feb. 1776.
[12] Gordon Jackson, *Hull in the Eighteenth Century*, pp. 241-2.
[13] William Weddell (1736-92), MP, Kingston-upon-Hull, 1766-74 and Malton, 1775-84, 1784-92; *HPC, 1754-1790*, iii, 617.
[14] *CJ*, 576, 579, 584, 672, 680, 683-4, 684, 713.

Though the new dock was the largest in England to date, it soon became inadequate. Proprietors of the Dock Company were unwilling undertake the expenditure necessary for its expansion without the promise of the large return they were unlikely to obtain. Because they enjoyed a monopoly, no other consortium could undertake the task. The result was a prolonged stalemate. On 28 March 1787 Samuel Thornton[15] presented the petition of the Mayor, officials and merchants of Hull to enlarge the dock and gradually transfer ownership of the Dock Company to a public company by purchasing the company's stock at half its market value. Thornton subsequently presented petitions from numerous manufacturing and commercial centres, all supporting the bill.[16] Nevertheless, the measure provoked an outcry from the Dock Company, whose chairman appealed to Earl Fitzwilliam[17] for his assistance and that of his friends in protesting against an attempt to deprive it of rights conferred on it by Parliament; he later attributed the postponement of the bill's second reading for several months to Fitzwilliam's friends and the 'never to be forgotten assiduity of Sir Thomas Dundas'.[18] The company's victory 'represented a clear victory of private over public interest'.[19]

Over the next decade Hull's MPs struggled to find a compromise that would permit an expansion of port facilities and satisfy ship owners, the town and the Dock Company's shareholders. To this end they negotiated with William Pitt for grants of land and financial support for new construction.[20] Promoters of a new dock, the Mayor and the chairman of the Dock Company responded in detail to the different dock proposals of the MPs, adding their own recommendations.[21] The process resulted in a bill which enjoyed almost unanimous support, at least until the 3rd Duke of Richmond,[22] the Master General of the Ordnance, unexpectedly announced that the government would grant a portion of the garrison site for the expansion of the dock. While the offer was acceptable to the Dock Company, it was not to other parties and hopes for expansion collapsed.[23]

In the meantime, owners of ships unable to find space at quays refused to pay dock duties and presented their proposal for a dock at a new site 'between the west end of the Present Dock and the Humber with an entrance into it from the Humber'. Three

---

[15] Samuel Thornton (1754–1838), MP, Kingston-upon-Hull, 1784–1806 and Surrey, 1807–12, 1813–18; Dir., Bank of England, Gov. 1799–1801; Gov., Russia Co, 1810–38.

[16] *CJ*, xlii, 609–12, 664, 686, 689; Jackson, *Hull in the Eighteenth Century*, pp. 252–3.

[17] William Wentworth Fitzwilliam (1748–1833), succ. as 4th Earl Fitzwilliam, 1756; succ. to estates of his uncle, 2nd Marquess of Rockingham, 1782; Ld. President, 1794, 1806; Ld. Lt. [I],1794–5; minister without portfolio, 1806–7; Ld. Lt., West Riding, 1798–1819.

[18] Sir Thomas Dundas, 2nd Bt. (1741–1820), MP, Richmond, 1763–68 and Stirling, 1768–94; cr. Baron Dundas, 1794; Ld. Lt. and V. Adm., Orkney and Shetland, 1794–1820. Northamptonshire Archives and Heritage Services, Fitzwilliam Papers, Box 34, Hammond to Fitzwilliam, 5 May 1787.

[19] Rosemary Sweet, 'Local identities and a national Parliament', p. 54.

[20] TNA, Pitt Papers, PRO 30/8/180, f. 121, Walter Spencer Stanhope to Pitt, 12 Dec. 1787.

[21] Barnsley Archive, Spencer Stanhope Papers, 60575/1, 2, 4, 5, Six promoters of a new dock to Spencer Stanhope, 11 June, 1788; Thomas Westerdell (Mayor) to S. Thornton, 21 June, 1788; William Hammond to Thornton, 11 July, 1788.

[22] Charles Lennox (1735–1806), succ. as 3rd Duke of Richmond, 1750; General, 1760; Ambassador to Paris, 1765–6; Sec. of State (south), 1766; Master Gen. of Ordnance, 1782–3, 1783–95.

[23] Jackson, *Hull in the Eighteenth Century*, pp. 252–5.

surveyors appointed by the Treasury likewise reported that the new dock should have a communication with the Humber.

The Mayor and Burgesses pressed ahead presenting yet another petition for a bill on 10 February 1794. On 7 March, Thornton delivered the committee's report in favour of bringing in a bill, which was presented five days later. Innumerable towns and groups of manufacturers and merchants petitioned in support of the bill, but the Company demanded the right to be heard by counsel against the measure, once again citing its property rights. On 9 April the House adopted a motion to put off the second reading of the measure for two months, effectively killing it.[24]

At this point Yorkshire's knights of the shire and Thornton, acting in concert with the Pitt and the Smith family, prominent bankers both in Hull and nationally,[25] at last stepped in to break the stalemate. They offered a proposal similar to that of the aggrieved ship owners – for a dock 'between the west end of the Present Dock and the Humber with an entrance into it from the Humber.[26] The prestige and wealth of this group and their connections to Pitt enabled them to impose a settlement on a fractious community that was unable to negotiate one itself.

Nevertheless, the war meant that the necessary legislation did not make its way through Parliament for years, in part because of the project's complexity and huge expense. It required the expertise of John Rennie[27] to overcome problems of silting, and the town and the Company to come up with over £233,000 to cover the eventual costs. The necessary legislation was not secured until 1802 (42 Geo. III, c. 9), and the need for additional funds from the Dock Company required another act in 1805 (45 Geo. III, c. 42). The plan devised by the MPs in 1794–5 was finally implemented, but at enormous cost.[28]

III: Bristol

In the eighteenth century, Bristol was, according to Kenneth Morgan, the leading metropolis of the west and 'the magnet for the economic life of her region'. The key to her prosperity was the city's dominant role in the transatlantic trade. North American and the West Indies shipping each accounted for between a quarter and a third of tonnage arriving at Bristol's port in the decades prior to 1775. Though its transatlantic trade declined relative to that of rival west-coast ports, it remained more valuable than Liverpool's for most of the century. Nor was Bristol's wealth exclusively commercial. According to Morgan the city was a centre of growth industries, including sugar

---

[24] *CJ*, xlix, 149, 307, 320, 448.
[25] Those who presented the ultimatum were Wilberforce and Henry Duncombe, Yorkshire's MPs, Samuel Thornton, E.J. Eliot, MP, Liskeard; Robert Smith, MP, Nottingham, partner in the family bank, close friend of Pitt; Samuel Smith, brother of Robert, partner in the family bank, MP, Leicester; John Smith, owner of 23 shares in the Dock Company. Jackson, *Hull in the Eighteenth Century*, p. 257.
[26] Jackson, *Hull in the Eighteenth Century*, pp. 254–6.
[27] John Rennie (1761–1821), civil engineer who designed many docks, bridges and canals; pioneer in use of structural cast iron.
[28] Jackson, *Hull in the Eighteenth Century*, pp. 258–61.

refining, soap making, glass and pottery refining and metal industries.[29] Despite its broad ranging commerce and energetic industrial sector, Bristol remained notable for its parochialism, complacency and its conservatism. Liverpool and Birmingham after 1760 were at pains to expand links to their hinterlands.[30] By contrast, Bristol's merchants were slow to adapt to changing circumstances. According to Morgan too much of the city's capital remained invested in the Caribbean.[31]

IV: Bristol and its MPs

From the 1750s through the early 1770s the city's most effective MP was Robert Nugent.[32] A minor political potentate,[33] he maintained close connections to the Grenville family and at various points held posts at the Treasury and the Board of Trade, posts that left him well positioned to serve Bristol's merchant community which dominated the political life of the city.

Nugent was never subservient to the city's dominant merchant interest. To the contrary he was emphatic in instructing his constituents on how to proceed with their Parliamentary business. On 21 November 1764, for example, Bristol's Society of Merchant Venturers (SMV) petitioned the Treasury for relief from import duties on sugar imported from the ceded islands.[34] The issue was of concern to Bristol and Liverpool merchants who had lent money to promote cultivation on the islands. Almost a month after the delivery of their petition, Nugent forwarded a report from the commissioners of customs to the SMV indicating that until their application was made to Parliament relative to duties on the ceded islands' sugars, they would be warehoused. When Nugent wrote in January 1765 to notify his constituents that the petition for importing sugars from the islands was before the House, he emphasised that London merchants and West Indians had proposed a cut-off date of May for duty-free importation, as opposed to October which Nugent had proposed on behalf of Bristol and other holders of the ceded island debt. He admonished his constituents to exert themselves on their own behalf by providing him with the information he needed to make their case in the House.

---

[29] Kenneth Morgan, *Bristol and the Atlantic Trade in the Eighteenth Century* (Cambridge and New York, 1993), pp. 9–13, 220–2.

[30] Walter Minchinton, 'The port of Bristol in the eighteenth century', in *Bristol in the Eighteenth Century*, ed. Patrick, McGrath (Newton Abbot, 1972), pp. 156–7.

[31] Morgan, *Bristol and the Atlantic Trade*, p. 422.

[32] Robert Nugent (1709–88), MP, St. Mawes, 1741–54 and 1774–84; Bristol, 1754–74; Comptroller of Household of Prince of Wales, 1747–51; Ld. of Treasury, 1754–59; Jt. Vice-Treasurer [I], 1760–5; First Ld. of Trade, 1766–8; Jt. Vice-Treasurer [I], 1768–82; cr. Visct Clare [I], 1767 and Earl Nugent [I]. 1776.

[33] In addition to controlling two seats at St. Mawes in Cornwall, there were four MPs, including his son Edward Nugent, Edward Eliot, T.E. Drax and J.E. Colleton, in the Parliament of 1761 who were connected to Nugent by blood or marriage, for whom he served as the liaison to administration. HPC 1754–1790, iii, 219.

[34] Minchinton, *Petitions of the SMV*, pp. 88–9. The ceded islands were obtained from France in 1763 and included Dominica, Grenada, St. Vincent and Tobago.

I think there is no Probability of our succeeding, but if your Demand... be of Sufficient importance... you must dispatch to town, without Loss of Time, some Person with Proofs of the Debts remaining due to you. It was asserted in the House that Notice was sent to Bristol,... of the intended Application above a Month ago, and no Answer received... I hope to have a more explicit and particular answer to my former letters than your previous express brought. I doubt I must present your Petition, as it will be thought odd you should not interest yourselves in the passage of the Bill if you be not concerned in the Event.[35]

More important than his assertive tone was Nugent's skill as a legislative tactician which enabled him to secure his constituents' points even in the face of strong opposition. On 4 April 1766, the SMV petitioned the House of Commons for a bill to make Dominica a free port; Liverpool and Lancaster had already done so, hoping by this means to gain access to the produce of the islands of foreign powers.[36] Because sugars produced on the French islands sold for lower prices than those of the British West Indies, their planters opposed the proposal as did many British members. Fearing that the Rockingham ministry, which supported free ports, would soon collapse, Nugent insisted on pressing ahead with the proposal. A deputation from Bristol hastened to London to assist in drafting a bill to present in late May by which time Nugent had been named to the committee to prepare and bring in the measure. In fact, the bill was hurried through both Houses and received the royal assent on 6 June (6 Geo. III, c. 58).[37]

This sort of legislative legerdemain was one of Nugent's notable traits. The leaders of Bristol were invariably concerned with assuring sufficient food supplies to prevent high prices that could cause urban disorder. Consequently, they pressed MPs almost annually to secure legislation to permit the importation of Irish salt beef, pork and butter. Responsibility for carrying those measures usually fell to Nugent because the legislation encountered opposition from the landed interest whose spokesmen argued the imports harmed 'the whole body of English farmers'.[38] William Beckford,[39] Sir William Meredith and Nugent, spokesmen for large cities, maintained that high prices necessitated such measures.[40]

In 1766 food shortages resulted in strong measures, including a royal proclamation banning the export of domestic wheat. In addition, the SMV urged the city's members to support legislation permitting the importation of wheat and flour duty free from Europe and the American colonies. Nugent had cope with landed representatives who refused to extend the duty-free entry beyond 1 June while the large towns demanded

---

[35] Bristol Record Office [BRO], SMV, 2/4/2/9/11, Nugent to the Master, 17 Jan. 1765.
[36] *CJ*, xxx, 704.
[37] Minchinton, *Petitions of the SMV*, pp. 105–6; cf. P.D.G. Thomas, *British Politics and the Stamp Act Crisis*, pp. 267–9.
[38] *CJ*, xxix, 57, 59.
[39] William Beckford (1709–70), MP, Shaftesbury, 1747–54 and London, 1754–70; alderman of London, 1752; sheriff, 1755–6; Ld Mayor, 1762–3, 1769–70; substantial Jamaican proprietor.
[40] Hampshire Archives and Local Studies, Malmesbury MS, Parliamentary diary of James Harris, 9M73/G/708, 1, 2 Dec. 1761 and G713, 8 Feb. 1764; *CJ*, xxix, 82, 88.

the period of exemption continue into the autumn. On 18 November 1768 he informed the master of the SMV that though he had been confined by gout, he had managed to attend the House in time to defeat a clause to permit the export of corn within six months.[41]

For the most part Nugent acted on his own in these battles, without seeking assistance from other Bristol MPs. Among these was Jarrit Smith, an attentive but rather insignificant member. Smith informed the Society when business of potential interest was likely to come before the House and notified its members of the progress of such legislation. He dispatched copies of bills and other relevant items to the Hall. Periodically, he informed the master when it would be appropriate to petition in support of a bill in which the SMV might have a stake. In 1759, however, 19 gentlemen thanked him for the effective assistance he provided them in securing the passage of a bill for the free importation of Irish tallow.[42] In 1765, he helped to carry one naturalisation bill through the House of Commons, and in 1766 he oversaw the passage of the Bristol Streets Bill through most of its stages in the Commons – altogether an unexceptionable record.[43]

Matthew Brickdale[44] was a more formidable figure, though he never had the skill or authority that Nugent demonstrated. A Bristol clothier and undertaker, Brickdale attended to Bristol's commercial interests, and the SMV relied on him during the life of the 1768 Parliament when he worked closely with Nugent. In 1773, he received a letter on behalf of the Dominica Society reminding him of its intention to bring in a bill to encourage foreigners to lend money on security of estates in the British West Indies. The Society believed that such an act would foster loans, thereby enabling Dominican proprietors to develop their properties. They requested that Brickdale inform Bristol merchants of the measure and send them copies of their petition.[45] The SMV in turn petitioned the Commons in support of the bill, which was presented on 20 January, and the act was passed on 16 March (13 George III, c. 38).[46] Brickdale was also instrumental in securing the passage of additional legislation for the renewal of the Jamaica free port act. The previous year, he had already encouraged the Society to send a memorial to the Treasury in favour of renewal. When the matter came up in the House, the act relating to Dominica was renewed to 1780; Jamaica's, however, was renewed only for a year (13 George III, c. 33). Clare presented Bristol's case for a more extended renewal in 1774, while Brickdale was one of those who drafted the bill which passed through the Commons without opposition (14 George III, c. 41).[47]

---

[41] BRO, SMV 2/4/2/13/2, Clare to the Master, 18 Nov. 1768. Nugent was created Viscount Clare [I] in 1767.
[42] BRO, Jarrit Smith Papers, AC/JS/95/1, Gentlemen of Soapmakers Hall of Bristol to Smith, 12 Apr. 1759.
[43] BRO, SMV, 2/4/2/7/1, 3, 13, 14; SMV, 2/4/2/8/4, 5, 6, 12, 23; SMV, 2/4/2/9/10.
[44] Matthew Brickdale (1735–1831), MP, Bristol, 1768–74, 1780–90; common councillor, Bristol, 1767–84.
[45] BRO, SMV, 2/4/2/17/1, Arthur Jones to Brickdale, 31 Dec. 1772.
[46] Minchinton, *Petitions of the SMV*, p. 122; *CJ*, xxxiv, 53, 198; BRO, SMV, 2/4/2/18/3, Brickdale to Master, 21 Feb. 1774.
[47] Minchinton, *Petitions of the SMV*, pp. 124–5; BRO, SMV, 2/4/2/18/3, Brickdale to Isaac Elton, 26 Feb. 1774.

Brickdale did not always partner with Clare. In 1769 the SMV, at his recommendation, petitioned the House requesting that privileges sought by London regarding bounties on raw silk imported from America be extended to Bristol. Together with James Laroche[48] and Liverpool's MPs, Brickdale approached the Treasury on the issue and learned that the Treasury would make concessions. To secure these, however, he and his allies first had to secure the repeal of 23 Geo II, c. 20 (Growth of Silk Act) in the next session. In the meantime, London secured the passage of its act (Silks Act, 1769, 9 Geo III, c. 38). Not to be outdone, Brickdale and Sir William Meredith gave notice that they would apply for legislation in the next session to secure similar bounties for their cities.[49]

Amidst all this activity, Nugent remained a legislative force. In the wake of the banking crisis of 1772 a small group of London bankers introduced a bill that would have imposed severe limits on merchant bankers and did nothing to limit speculators in the funds. The bill made no progress in the 1773 session, but was reintroduced with minor revisions on 31 March 1774.[50] The SMV's petition against the bill which was presented on 6 May attacked it's main points:

> the said Bill is partial to a very great Degree, being calculated to favour and serve a particular Set of Men, who call themselves Bankers only, and that in Prejudice of the Merchant Bankers..., and that the Partiality of the said Bill in Favour of the Persons who stile themselves Bankers only is further evident in that it lays no Restraint on the worst Species of Trade in this Kingdom, which has injured Thousands, and ruined many, and which is chiefly exercised by a Set of Men dealing speculatively in the Public Funds.

Bristol was joined in its opposition by other London bankers who petitioned against the bill, which failed to progress beyond its first reading.[51]

Ultimately it was Clare who secured the proposal's defeat, according to his admirer, Dean Tucker.[52] In his encomium to Clare following his decision to give up his seat at Bristol, Tucker wrote that his patron was:

> the sole Instrument of rejecting... a Bill framed by the Bankers of London, and supported by all their Interest, for the laudable Purpose of bringing all the deposited Money of Great Britain to their Shops, to the total destruction of the Banking Business in Bristol, and all other Towns except the Metropolis, and the Stagnation of

---

[48] James Laroche (1734-1804), MP, Bodmin, 1768-80; sheriff, Bristol, 1764-5 and Master, SMV, 1782-3. According to Madge Dresser, Laroche was England's most important slaving agent. Dresser, *Slavery Obscured: The Social History of the Slave Trade in an English Provincial Port* (London and New York, 2001), p. 106.

[49] Minchinton, *Petitions of the SMV*, pp. 112-13; BRO, SMV, 13/23, 24, Brickdale to Master, 23, 24 Apr. 1769.

[50] *CJ*, xxxiv, 297, 501. L.S. Pressnell, *Country Banking in the Industrial Revolution* (Oxford, 1956), pp. 501-2.

[51] *CJ*, xxxiv, 711, 701.

[52] Rev. Josiah Tucker (1713-99), Rector of All Saints, Bristol, 1739 and St. Stephen's, Bristol, 1749-90; Dean of Gloucester, 1759; author of pamphlets on matters relating to commerce and politics.

Manufacture and Commerce, unenlivened and unfed by Money or Credit, all to be swallowed up in that devouring Vortex.[53]

With Brickdale's assistance Clare continued to carry the usual bill to import salted beef, pork and butter from Ireland;[54] in 1773, it was Brickdale, however, who reported from the committee on the petition to deepen Bristol's harbour and later presented Bristol's Playhouse Bill.[55]

Despite their service in Parliament on behalf of the city's and the SMV's legislative needs, neither Clare nor Brickdale were returned at the 1774 election, largely due to their support for the government's policies against the American colonies. In addition, a radical party had emerged in Bristol. A public meeting there in March 1769 instructed citizens to follow the radical agenda supporting shorter Parliaments, limiting the number of placemen and excluding pensioners and contractors from the House. Neither Clare nor Brickdale supported the demands. Instead in early 1774 Bristol radicals selected Henry Cruger as their candidate. Clare withdrew following the first day of polling in 1774 when some of his supporters apparently deserted him. Suffering from gout, he made the decision to withdraw to St. Mawes, where 'he was perfectly safe': 'Five-sixths of the borough is his own property, his constituents were his tenants, and he was sure of his election'.[56]

The Rev. Josiah Tucker, by no means an unbiased source, praised Clare's tenure as member for Bristol in a pamphlet published in 1775, maintaining that Clare was:

> the unwearied Advocate for the Freedom of Trade, the faithful Representative of the City of Bristol, and the zealous Promoter of its internal Prosperity, and a generous and impartial Benefactor of its distressed and decayed Citizens.

To the latter end, Clare,

> whenever the price of Corn began to rise above a moderate Pitch, he used to propose first to stop the Stills at Home, and then the Exportation Abroad, and last of all to admit of an Importation Duty free. And as the private Interest of landed Gentlemen, often led them to oppose these salutary Measures,... he has been

---

[53] Josiah Tucker, *Review of Lord Vis. Clare's Conduct as Representative of Bristol* (Gloucester and Bristol, 1775), p. 11.

[54] *CJ*, xxxiii, 527; *ibid.*, xxxiv, 499, 524, 527–8, 532. Clare reported to Isaac Elton on 25 Feb. that 'Mr. Brickdale moved yesterday for a Bill to continue the Irish Provision Act. It was to be included in a Bill for continuing Expiring Laws, but was omitted thro' some unaccountable neglect. Let the Importers be cautious until the Bill passes as it certainly will'. BRO, SMV, 2/4/2/18/5.

[55] Though ill, Clare sent a letter opposing the bill. Brickdale reported from the committee on the petition and counter-petition (*CJ*, xxxiv, 147, 178), but in the face of opposition from the city's Quaker community, he adopted a neutral position, writing: 'I will do no more than be a common friend to both, and be only the medium of conveyance of each of their wishes to the House for them to be determined on, for as the common representative of All, it would be unbecoming me to do otherwise in a disputed matter'. P.T. Underdown, 'Religious opposition to licensing the Bristol and Birmingham theatres in the eighteenth century', *University of Birmingham Historical Journal*, vi (1957–8), 151–2.

[56] *HPC, 1754–1790*, iii, 220–1, i, 239.

known to have solicited, and to have obtained, through Dint of Importunity and Perseverance, two bills in the same Session for stopping the Distillation of Corn, and two More for preventing the Exportation of it.

Clare, according to Tucker, secured for the outports bounties on imported indigo, thereby preventing London from establishing another monopoly. He was also one of the architects of the free port system in the British West Indies.[57]

Brickdale had no safe borough to which he could retreat. Instead he contested the election. In the aftermath of Clare's withdrawal, however, Richard Champion, a merchant, leading Quaker and moderate Whig, nominated Edmund Burke, who received the support of other Whigs who disliked Cruger.

V: Burke and Bristol

Burke was the leading theorist and spokesman for the Whig party. His 'Thoughts on the cause of the present discontents', that attributed the subversion of the integrity of several ministries during the 1760s to the growing influence of the Crown, became the core belief of the Whig party for generations. As secretary to the Marquess of Rockingham and his heir, Earl Fitzwilliam, Burke tied his fortunes to the family for more than two decades. At Bristol, however, Burke owed his victory to Cruger's voters, many of whom gave him their second votes. Brickdale, who ended only 51 votes behind Burke, petitioned to overturn the result on the grounds the election was irregular, but without success. Thus, Burke moved to Bristol from Wendover, a borough dominated by Lord Verney,[58] where electors lived rent-free so long as they gave their votes to Verney's nominees.[59] By contrast Bristol had one of the most numerous electorates in the kingdom. Burke was proud to represent so populous a borough and eager to create a constituency for the Rockingham Party. At the outset, however, he informed constituents, who in the past had never hesitated to inform their representatives of their legislative needs, that:

> it ought to be the happiness and glory of a Representative, to live in the strictest union, the closest correspondence,... with his constituents. But, his unbiased opinion, his mature judgement, his enlightened conscience, he ought not to sacrifice to you; to any man, or to any set of men living. These he does not derive from your pleasure; no, nor from the law and the Constitution. They are a trust from Providence, for the abuse of which he is deeply answerable. Your Representative owes you, not his industry only, but his judgement; and he betrays, instead of serving you, if he sacrifices it to your opinion.[60]

---

[57] Josiah Tucker, *A Review of Lord Vis Clare's Conduct as Representative of Bristol*, pp. 6–11.
[58] Ralph Verney (1714–91), succ. as 2nd Earl Verney [I], 1752, MP Wendover, 1753–61, Carmarthen, 1761–8 and Buckinghamshire, 1768–84, 1790–1.
[59] *HPC, 1754–1790*, i, 217
[60] *The Writings and Speeches of Edmund Burke: Party, Parliament and the American War, 1774–1780*, ed. W.M. Elofson and John A. Woods (Oxford, 1996), III, 68–9.

Figure 3.1 Portrait of British statesman and orator Edmund Burke (1729–1797), a member of British Parliament who advocated a liberal treatment in the government of the American colonies and supported the abolition of the Atlantic slave trade, 1780s. Photo by Stock Montage/Getty Images.

According to P.T. Underwood, Burke was attentive to the needs of his constituents and successful in securing their objectives, despite the fact that he was an opposition MP. Indeed, Underdown compares his record favourably to that of Clare and notes that Burke was successful in preventing London merchants from gaining preferential treatment at the expense of the outports and in ensuring that Bristol was treated on equal terms with other cities and ports in Britain.[61]

Still Burke faced difficulties as a member for Bristol. Not the least of these was the fact that his most important constituents were merchants who had a myriad of legislative needs and emphatic views as to how they should best be fulfilled. They also remembered how Clare and Brickdale had performed services for them not just in response to their petitions for local needs but on issues of national concern. While they might object to the administration's policies towards the American colonists for fear these would disrupt their profitable trade, they could not afford to offend ministers on whose protection and patronage they relied. The result was that Burke found that few were prepared to support him in the sort of opposition that became a hallmark of the Rockingham Party.

From the time that he entered the House, Burke stood out as an orator. By the end of the 1760s, his only rivals in debate were George Grenville and Lord North, a former and future prime minister; according to Paul Langford, neither could rival Burke's learning or his rhetorical panache.[62] As the American war approached he had established himself as the leader of the Whig party in the Commons. The only contender, Lord John Cavendish, preferred fox hunting to the rigours of Parliamentary debate.

In any case, it was Burke, according to Langford, who defined and articulated the party's views on America in two speeches which he delivered over 11 months in 1774 and 1775 and subsequently published anonymously. He argued for the advantages of a policy of co-operation as opposed to confrontation, the core which would involve repealing Britain's offensive taxes and promising not to impose any others in the future. Instead, he recommended a return to the Whig policy of living and working in partnership, for the Americans were descendants of English settlers with an inheritance of English rights and customs.[63]

The task of upholding these positions in the Commons at the same time that his new constituents expected him to secure a range of seemingly insignificant legislation or favours from ministers who were the authors of the policies he abhorred placed enormous burdens on Burke. Tending to what he later called 'little things' was time consuming, often unappreciated and had the effect of diverting Burke from business he considered to be of real importance. Tending to constituents' needs sometimes required him having to secure favours from Lord North or lesser government officials whom he scorned. It was a process he found distasteful and degrading. At the same time, his opposition put him at odds with a minister on whose good will some of his constituents depended.

---

[61] P.T. Underdown, 'Edmund Burke, the commissary of his Bristol constituents, 1774–1780', *EHR*, lxxiii (1958), 269.
[62] *ODNB*, viii, 824.
[63] The first speech was in April 1774 and the second in March 1775. *ODNB*, viii, 826.

Yet Burke was, as far as possible, diligent in attending to constituents though the results were not always happy. He was criticised in 1775 for failing to secure the passage of an Irish salted provisions bill which Clare had usually introduced and carried. Burke assumed that Clare would again perform the task and did not move for the measure's renewal. To justify his inaction, he asserted that it was 'uncivil' to take up bills that other MPs had routinely taken responsibility of carrying through the House.[64] This was a disingenuous attempt at self-justification since Jarrit Smith and Brickdale had earlier carried the measures on behalf of the SMV. Worse still, once the bill finally secured Parliament's approval, the Collector of Customs at Bristol, a Clare nominee, refused to allow the Irish ship to unload its supplies until the bill received the royal assent. Burke blamed Clare and the Collector; he was unwilling to admit that he had mishandled a routine chore. He came in for a good deal of criticism for failing to make sure the measure received Parliament's sanction before it lapsed because the city's poor depended upon the Irish provisions.

To compound the effect of his fumbling on the salted provisions, Burke casually ignored the pleas of Bristol soapmakers, his political allies. The Master of the Bristol Chandlers and Soapmakers Hall approached the city's MPs on 12 January regarding a petition of London soapmakers who sought to change the manner in which soap duties were collected. The Bristol petitioners feared the change would be detrimental to their businesses. Burke's friends sent reminders of the urgency of the business early in February. Cruger replied in March, but Burke sent no answer until early April by which time his inattention had provoked adverse comment.[65] In a sense his shortcomings did not matter because the Board of Excise ruled against the London petitioners, but his casual approach on a point of importance to his supporters was an additional cause for complaint during his first full troubled session.

For Burke these issues were understandably subsidiary to the main question of the day – America. At the beginning of 1775 he organised merchants to support a petition against the administration's policy towards the colonies, but the triumph, such as it was, proved to be short lived. In a letter to Champion on 10 January, 1775, he remarked, after attending a meeting of London merchants, that he was unable to identify any feelings of resentment which they ought to feel against ministers who had initiated so many calamities. If Bristol manifested a similar lack of ardour, he advised Campion and his other allies in the city against trying to enlist support for the petition that Burke had drafted, for there was little likelihood that they would support it.[66]

Rather than endorse Burke's plan, the SMV resorted to delay. Champion and his allies, however, summoned a second Hall to approve Burke's petition. When it reached London, it, with others opposing North's policies, was left to lie unconsidered on the Commons' table.[67]

---

[64] *Burke Correspondence*, iii, 144, n. 58.
[65] Underdown, 'Burke, commissary of his Bristol constituents', 261–2.
[66] *Burke Correspondence*, iii, 95–6.
[67] P.T. Underdown, 'Bristol and Burke', in *Bristol in the Eighteenth Century*, ed. Patrick McGrath (Newton Abbot, 1972), pp. 53–5; Almon, *Parliamentary Register*, i, 106.

American business consumed Burke's attention for the remainder of 1775. After learning that North would introduce legislation prohibiting trade with colonies in revolt, Paul Farr, one of his political allies and chair of the SMV, pressed Burke to secure amendments to the bill to prevent unnecessary hardship for Bristol merchants. To do so he instructed Burke to work with Cruger, Sir James Laroche and Richard Combe, the last of whom were government supporters. Burke was able to serve Farr on his own by applying to Sir Grey Cooper[68] who advised him to go directly to North since the bill was already in the final stages of passage. The minister accepted two of four proposed alterations, indicating that the others were unnecessary. Both amendments were adopted in the House of Lords on 19 December and accepted in the Commons when the measure was returned. Burke told Champion it was unpleasant negotiating with ministers on a measure he abhorred, but consoled himself with the thought that several honest men might save themselves from ruin as a result of his efforts.[69]

Throughout the 1776 session he worked harmoniously with his Bristol supporters, though not with Cruger. At the opening of the session, he had to help carry a Bristol Port Bill again promoted by Farr. Cruger presented the petition just prior to the last date the House had set for receiving them. Thereafter, Burke carried the petition through its committee, delivering the report on 7 March. Cruger presented the bill on the 11th, which was read a second time on the 18th and referred to a committee including Burke, Cruger and Richard Combe.[70] Cruger reported it from the second reading committee on 29 March, after which the bill passed through the Commons, and on 1 April Burke carried it to the Lords where it passed without amendment. Burke's task was complicated when on 14 March the Bristol firms of Cruger and Mallard and Peach[71] and Henderson petitioned against the measure, claiming they had lacked the time to amend the original plan. In a letter to Champion on 3 April Burke wondered what might have induced Cruger to oppose a measure that he himself had brought into the House. Such an act only confirmed for him that there was no limit to his fellow member's impertinence and indecency.[72]

Though Cruger had slipped in amendments during the second reading committee, which he chaired, an unamended bill received royal assent on 13 May (16 George III, c. 43).

The harmonious relationship Burke enjoyed with his constituents in 1776 was strained in 1777 again over the American war. In early January, city leaders hesitated as to whether they should petition condemning the war or send addresses in support of the administration's policies. On 18 January the Corporation voted an address in support of the administration. Burke found Bristol's official position on the war

---

[68] Sir Grey Cooper (c. 1726–1801), MP, Rochester, 1765–8, Grampound, 1768–74, Saltash, 1774–84 and Richmond 1786–90; Sec. to Treasury, 1765–82; K.C., Duchy of Lancaster, 1765–1801; Ld. of Treasury, 1783.
[69] *Burke Correspondence*, iii, pp. 238–9.
[70] *CJ*, xxxv, 540, 635–6, 660.
[71] Samuel Peach was Cruger's father-in-law.
[72] The partners claimed that several clauses in the bill relating to restricting the landing of certain commodities at specified places were injurious to their businesses. Minchinton, *Petitions of the SMV*, pp. 137–9; *Burke Correspondence*, iii, pp. 248–9, 259.

illogical. He indicated to Champion that he had hoped that burdensome taxes, losses in trade and military setbacks would make them angry with the authors of the current war policies. Instead, he found that Bristol's citizens regarded the series of military and naval setbacks as they would unavoidable natural misfortunes.[73]

Earlier that spring Burke's friends in Bristol had expressed their dissatisfaction with the Commons' failure to oppose the administration's bill for the partial suspension of habeas corpus. The reason for the failure was due in part to the fact that the Rockinghams had seceded from the House because they recognised further opposition in the face of the government's overwhelming majorities was counter-productive. In reply to a critical entry in *Felix Farley's Bristol Journal* for 22 February, Burke told Champion that government was ruining England, and that debate would only make things that were destructive momentarily plausible.[74]

Equally annoying in the eyes of his Bristol followers was his failure yet again to support Bristol's soapmakers. On 19 February 1777 Fry, Fripp & Co., the city's leading firm, wrote that the town's MPs should watch out for a bill relating to duties on soap, which was introduced on 15 May and passed on 2 June. When admonished by Champion for his failure to act, Burke offered excuses. He attended to minor matters, 'small tithes', he called them, with greater attention than most members who conducted the nation's principal business. He went on to explain to Campion that it astounded him how much importance his constituents attached to 'little' things and how little to the great questions that came before the House. Indeed, they judged him exclusively in terms of how he met their special needs.[75]

Burke's letter highlights his dilemma at Bristol. For the most part he was diligent in dealing with his constituent's 'little things', but sometimes he performed the tasks grudgingly because he was distracted by American questions. He attended promptly to the business interests of Richard Champion but was seemingly less concerned about the challenges posed by London competitors of the precarious businesses of his Bristol soapmaker allies. In fact, rumours reached Bristol that he had supported the offensive measures of their rivals. When challenged by Champion, his only excuse for his failure in 1777 was that because he worked a great deal on the business of the House, he was liable to forget things – this despite the fact he and the Rockinghams had seceded for much of the 1777 session. Nor is it likely that the partners of Fry, Fripp & Co. could take much consolation in his promise to Champion that he would henceforth attend to the most trifling business of the most insignificant person in Bristol.[76]

By contrast, Burke performed a substantial favour for Champion during the same session. On 10 February 1777 Richard Yates, manager of a Birmingham theatre, applied to Parliament for a license. Burke supported the first reading of the Birmingham Bill, partly because its chief opponent was his nemesis, Sir William Bagot. Richard Champion and the Bristol Quakers had earlier united to defeat a similar proposal for Bristol and feared that if the Birmingham Bill succeeded, supporters of a Bristol

---

[73] *Burke Correspondence*, iii, 367.
[74] *Burke Correspondence*, iii, 330.
[75] *Burke Correspondence*, iii, 356.
[76] *Burke Correspondence*, iii, 361–2; Lock, *Burke*, i, 412.

playhouse would use its passage as a precedent for their own measure.[77] On 29 April, Burke explained to his friend, the actor David Garrick, who had urged him to support Yates, that the pressing applications of his most loyal constituents compelled him to act in a manner contrary to that which Garrick had recommended.[78] Moved by their instructions, Burke voted against the measure at its second reading while defending Yates. He spoke, however, in favour of theatres and ridiculed Bagot for his attack on them.[79]

The issue which created the sharpest breach between Burke and his Bristol allies was a motion introduced by Earl Nugent[80] for a relaxation of the restrictions on Ireland's trade. On 8 and 9 April 1778 a committee of the Commons approved proposals allowing for the direct import of Irish goods except for woollens into the colonies, colonies' products except for tobacco and indigo into Ireland, and the export of Irish products with a few restrictions into Britain. Burke optimistically wrote to Samuel Span, Master of the SMV, and up to this point one of his principal supporters, that he was confident that Bristol merchants would certainly recognise that a 'great Empire' could not survive on narrow or restricted commerce and, therefore, would open themselves to the plan.[81]

In this he was wrong. Span and his colleagues feared that Ireland's low taxes would give its merchants and manufacturers advantages over British competitors. They were so opposed to the bill they would prefer union with Ireland to seeing it reach the statute book. Thus, Span informed Burke and Cruger that, given the interests of their constituents and, more generally, of English manufacturers, both should oppose the plan.[82]

Throughout 1778 Bristol's opposition to the proposal remained unabating. There were open meetings devoted to the question, three petitions to Parliament, deputations to the House of Commons from the SMV, the Common Council, approaches to other members of Parliament, letters of opposition to every city and borough in the kingdom and correspondence in the press.[83] A century and a quarter later John Lambert wrote that 'every leading merchant who had supported Burke, with the exception of Richard Champion, seems to have been offended by his conduct'.[84]

Burke was surprised by the outcry against him. Baffled, he wondered how he had offended Span and his other friends at Bristol who, he thought, had come to share his views and would cooperate with him on a matter in which he was as good a judge as they, though he acknowledged that they knew their own affairs better than he. While proclaiming that he would never wish to harm Bristol, on matters relating to Ireland

---

[77] P.T. Underdown, 'Religious opposition to licensing of the Bristol and Birmingham theatres in the eighteenth century', *University of Birmingham Historical Journal*, vi (1957–8), 149–55.
[78] *Burke Correspondence*, iii, 335–6.
[79] *Writings and Speeches*, iii, 337–8.
[80] Clare was made Earl Nugent [I] in 1776.
[81] *Burke Correspondence*, iii, 426.
[82] *Burke Correspondence*, iii, 429.
[83] Underdown, 'Bristol and Burke', pp. 56–7.
[84] Lambert, *Annals of Bristol*, p. 433. Joseph Harford, whom Burke tried to convince to stand in 1780 for the seat he had held at Bristol, wrote on 12 May, 1778: 'We are sorry to say, we do not yet find one amongst us, who can declare in favor of thy Sentiments under the present situation of things'.

he must act in relation to the whole, confident that in the end, his constituents would see their error.[85]

Confronted by Bristol's united opposition, Burke asserted his independence. On 23 April, he assured Span and the SMV that he had never forgotten his responsibility to uphold the interests of his constituents. He regretted that his conduct on the Irish issue had been a cause of uneasiness among them. At the same time, he reiterated that he was unable to oppose a plan so perfectly in accord with his declared opinions. He went on to declare that what made his abilities of use was that he was not prepared to forsake his opinions for momentary political convenience, but rather that he served in Parliament to promote the well-being of the nation, whatever the cost to himself. Only by taking such a path could he preserve his integrity.[86]

Burke's reactions to the episode display on the one hand the degree to which he had lost touch even with his closest Bristol supporters, most of whom he had not visited since 1776. He corresponded with a small coterie of friends and then about issues of immediate concern to them. His response displays his commitment to the ideals he outlined in his address following his election in 1774: he was prepared to serve his constituents but not at the expense of his principles. Confronted by these, the merchants of Bristol and their commercial anxieties would have to give way.

Though the Commons' committee considering Nugent's resolutions managed to find a compromise that enabled them to recommend the proposal to the full House on 19 May, opposition to his proposals throughout the country resulted in their being dropped in Parliament. Nevertheless, Lord North early in 1779 offered more concessions to the Irish. Bristol opposed them, and the SMV dispatched a representative to London to reiterate its opposition. Burke, suspicious of anything presented by the administration, stood aside.[87] The situation resolved itself ironically.

North, who waffled when Nugent made his proposals the previous year, was faced when Parliament reassembled in November with an Ireland defended by a Volunteer force of 40,000 armed men, formed ostensibly to protect the country from a French invasion, but composed of patriots seething over the refusal of Westminster to accede to Nugent's proposals. What North offered the Irish on 9 December 1779 in the face of this situation was a fundamental change in Anglo–Irish commercial relations. Included were the removal of restrictions on the export of Irish woollens and glass to Britain and the opening of Irish trade to British colonies with the same duties as those enjoyed by British merchants. Ironically, Bristol merchants who had protested in 1778 found North's more radical recommendations unexceptionable.[88]

Despite the Irish fracas, Burke returned to promoting the projects of those he had alienated during the previous year. In April 1779 he intervened with Philip Stephens[89] to secure protection against impressment for a ship belonging to a former ally, John

---

[85] *Burke Correspondence*, iii, 430.
[86] *Burke Correspondence*, iii, 436.
[87] Minchinton, *Petitions of the SMV*, p. 147; Lock, *Burke*, i, p. 429.
[88] R.B. McDowell, *Ireland in the Age of Imperialism and Revolution 1760–1801* (Oxford, 1979), pp. 255–71; Minchinton, *Petitions of the SMV*, p. 149.
[89] Philip Stephens (1723–1809), MP, Liskeard, 1759–68; Sandwich, 1768–1806; Asst. Sec. in Victualling Office; 2nd Sec. to Admiralty 1759–63; Sec. to Admiralty 1763–95; Ld. of Admiralty, 1795–1806; cr. Bt., 1795.

Noble, which was to sail to Quebec. Stephens at Burke's behest also guaranteed that there would be a ship stationed to protect vessels, such as Noble's, involved in the Labrador trade.[90] In addition Burke successfully intervened against legislation introduced by Shropshire gentlemen to regulate the Severn salmon fishery. According to its Bristol opponents, the bill would severely limit the city's supplies of fish. The Corporation's petition against the bill pressed for an amendment to the measure, and on 17 March Burke informed Sir John Durbin, Bristol's mayor, that he had constantly attended the bill to make sure a clause would satisfy the mayor. Despite many petitions against the revised measure, the bill passed with his amendment (18 George III, c. 33).

The same pattern continued into the 1779–80 session. Burke and Cruger, in a rare instance of mutual co-operation, applied to the Admiralty for a force to be dispatched to Newfoundland to protect Bristol ships involved in the fishery. More importantly, he played a part in amending a clause which the SMV found objectionable in the administration's Smuggling Bill. The Hall maintained that under the clause as written ship owners became subject to the loss of their ship, even though their captains at sea could not be made aware of the new law's terms prior to its implementation. Burke called upon one of the secretaries of the Treasury to present the SMV's objections and was able to postpone proceedings on the measure until the arrival of the SMV's agent, John Powell, in London.[91] The latter was dispatched to oversee the negotiations for alterations and met with Combe and Laroche, who informed him it was essential to meet at once with North and Sir Grey Cooper as the SMV's proposed amendment was inadmissible. Nevertheless, a meeting was set for the next morning, and at the last moment Powell reported that Burke appeared and promised to attend the session. Powell anticipated that it would be difficult framing a clause the ministers could accept.[92] On 28 May, however, Burke informed the master that Powell believed the changes he secured to the disputed provisions would satisfy the SMV. In short, he played a crucial role in gaining the SMV's points, demonstrating in the process that he was an adept negotiator and Parliamentary maneuverer (19 Geo. III, c. 69).

Nevertheless, he invited controversy by refusing to oppose Lord Beauchamp's bill to alter the law relating to the imprisonment of insolvent debtors. The measure, which never reached the statute book, would have required creditors to pay an allowance to the debtors they jailed and have empowered courts to discharge debtors lacking the resources to pay their debts. The measure provoked protests and a public meeting at Bristol which petitioned against it. Burke presented the Bristol petition and postponed consideration of it to give time for Bristol's opponents to make their case against the bill. In the second reading committee, he presented Bristol's objections and emphasised to the chair of the Bristol committee the measure's experimental nature, adding that he was committed to support what he claimed posed little hazard to creditors.[93]

[90] *Burke Correspondence*, iii, 424.
[91] BRO, SMV, 2/4/2/20/22/31, Burke to Miller, 25 May, 1779.
[92] BRO, SMV 2/4/2/20/22/33, John Powell to Miller, 27 May, 1779.
[93] *Burke Correspondence*, iv, 232. When in September, 1780, Burke responded to criticisms of his constituents on the eve of the election, he remarked that the charge that he supported Beauchamp's bill was the 'most prevalent'. *Writings and Speeches*, iii, 643. For the text of Beauchamp's bill before and after amendments were added, see *House of Commons Sessional Papers*, xxix, 325-32 and, as amended, 335-59.

As the 1780 election approached, Burke's prospects in Bristol were problematic. Local Tories united behind the candidacies of Brickdale and Richard Combe. Cruger had informed Burke that he would stand on his personal interest. With ample funding from his father-in-law and likely to receive the support of Bristol's shopkeepers and artisans, his prospects were good. Burke, who enjoyed the support of most members of the Corporation, was reluctant to cede the seat to Cruger. He also suspected that Combe might die before the poll, in which case his supporters would possibly give their votes to him rather than see the radical Cruger returned to Westminster.[94]

In the end, however, Burke chose to withdraw from the contest. He lacked the resources to undertake a costly contest and was in any case in a weak position to do so. He had offended many of his supporters, not only on the Irish issue, but by taking up the cause of Roman Catholics and later Beauchamp's bill; he was an opponent of the slave trade in one of its capitals and had become increasingly out of touch with a number of his supporters as he devoted more and more time to his campaigns in the Commons.[95] Indeed he may have had doubts about his suitability for a constituency such as Bristol. In a letter to the Duke of Portland, he confessed that:

> I have a notion that men who take an enlarged line on publick Business, and upon Grounds of some depth, and that require at every instant, the appearance of doing something, in *appearance* wrong, in order to do what is really and *substantially* right, ought not to sit for these great busy places. Besides their local agency is vexatious, and sometimes humiliating. I have lookd back at my Conduct and its relation to the publick for some years past; and if I had followd the humours of this town, which are called opinions, I should have been more frequently wrong, than even if I had been guided by the Court; for I should have fallen into not a few of their Mistakes, and have had an whole Class of Errors of another kind to answer for into the Bargain. Indeed as I grow older, my temper grows in some Sort the more different from that of old men. I hope I never shall reject the principles of general publick prudence;... But as to leaving to the Crowd, to choose for me, what principles I ought to hold, or what Course I ought to pursue for their benefit – I had much rather, innocently and obscurely, mix with them, with the utter ruin of all my hopes (which hopes are my all) than to betray them by learning lessons from them. They are naturally proud, tyrannical, and ignorant; bad scholars and worse Masters.[96]

Even as he disavowed the public voice, Burke identified himself as a reformer, endeavouring to steer his economic reform bill through Parliament. For such a member to forsake Bristol for Malton would, he acknowledged, appear to be 'a piece of Buffoonery'. He was devastated by having to withdraw, yet he had no choice.

[94] *HPC, 1754–1790*, i, 286.
[95] *ODNB*, viii, 829.
[96] *Burke Correspondence*, iv, ed. John A. Woods (Cambridge, 1974), pp. 273–4.

VI: Bristol: 1780–90

During the two Parliaments of the 1780s, Matthew Brickdale shouldered most of the burden of carrying Bristol's legislation through the House.[97] He focused with varying energy and effectiveness on the issues that most concerned his Bristol constituents in the four areas – the West Indies, opposition to Pitt's Irish commercial propositions, efforts to abolish the slave trade and attending to Bristol's infrastructure improvements.

A primary focus for Bristol was the state of the Caribbean islands which suffered during the American war and in the years that followed. To aid in their recovery Bristol's MPs managed to revive the free port system with help from Liverpool and several manufacturing centres. The Dominica free port act had lapsed in 1780, but in 1785 Bristol merchants dispatched a memorial to the Treasury, pressing for its renewal. A new free ports act that also applied to Jamaica and Grenada passed both Houses and received royal approval in 1787 (27 George III, c. 27).[98]

Between 1786 and 1788 Brickdale and to a lesser extent Cruger carried bills relating to Bristol streets, bridges and churches. In 1786 the SMV sent a petition to the House in favour of a bill to render more effective an earlier measure to rebuild the bridge over the Avon. Brickdale and Cruger assisted in drafting the bill: opposition in the city, however, forced its withdrawal, and a new measure was introduced on 28 April, which Brickdale eventually carried to the Lords (Bristol Bridge Act, 26 George III c. 66).[99] The following year he chaired the committee on a petition for a bill to divide the parish of St. James and raise money for a new church, and on 13 March he delivered the committee's report (St. James' Parish Bristol Act, 27 Geo. III, c. 49).[100] Finally, in 1788 Brickdale chaired the second reading committees of the Bristol Improvement Bill, the Guildhall Bill and a measure to regulate buildings in the city, and subsequently carried the latter measure to the Lords[101] (Bristol Improvement Act, 28 Geo. III, c. 65, Bristol Building Act, 28 Geo. III, c. 66 and Bristol Guildhall Act, 28 Geo. III, c. 67).

When abolitionists pressed for the regulation and then the abolition of the slave trade, Bristol's members gave voice to the town's resistance in the Commons. Petitions began to pour into the House of Commons in support of abolition in 1788, and the House took up Sir William Dolben's Slave Trade Regulation Bill – the first attempt to impose regulations on the trade in 300 years. Not surprisingly, the SMV dispatched a memorial to the Board of Trade emphasising the importance of the slave trade; it also

---

[97] Bristol's other members between 1780 and 1790 were Sir Henry Lippincott, 1st Bt. (1737–80) MP, Sept. 1780–Dec. 1780; George Daubeny (1742–1806), Feb. 1781–84 and Henry Cruger, 1784–90.
[98] The Free Port Act of 1766 initially opened ports in Dominica and Jamaica to foreign shipping. By the 1780s British manufacturers' demand for raw materials and new markets led to the expansion of the system in 1787. J.R. Ward, 'The British in the West Indies', in *The Oxford History of the British Empire: Volume II: The Eighteenth Century*, ed. P.J. Marshall (Oxford, 1998), p. 423. For more on this system, see below, Chapter 7.
[99] *CJ*, xli, 214, 281, 637, 839; Minchinton, *Petitions of the SMV*, p. 157.
[100] *CJ*, xlii, 412, 542, 558–9
[101] *CJ*, xliii, 456, 463, 502 526.

petitioned the House on 12 May 1789 expressing its alarm at the possibility of abolition.[102]

Cruger took the more decisive part in representing Bristol's case in support of the trade.[103] He stated that evidence introduced by both sides regarding the trade was 'overcharged'; instead of abolishing the trade, he felt that it was necessary gradually to eliminate its abuses, for he considered the idea of abolition to be 'ruinous in the extreme'. Over the remaining months of his term, he worked with the West India interest to defeat Dolben's bill and kept in touch with the Hall on steps that were taken to achieve that end.[104]

The recurring task of securing cheap provisions for the poor demanded Brickdale's attention throughout the 1784 Parliament. The first occasion came in 1785 when the SMV claimed that clauses in a pending corn bill would hurt Bristol because areas around the city could not produce sufficient wheat to meet its needs. The Corporation petitioned, and because of widespread opposition the export bill was defeated at its second reading.[105] Four years later another corn bill, this one regulating the import and export of corn and the duty on foreign corn, led to petitions from the SMV, the Corporation and many other towns. All were referred to the bill's petition committee whose members struggled to prepare a bill that addressed the various objections. Brickdale reported to the master that he had received the Society's objections to an objectionable clause and had joined with MPs from London and other towns to combat it 'but without effect, [as] Mr. Pitt & the Attorney & Solicitor general defending it, & carrying it by a division'. On 1 June, however, opponents managed to put off the motion to receive the committee's report on the amended bill for three months, thus assuring its defeat.[106]

VII: Conclusion

What the three constituencies discussed in this chapter shared were attentive and demanding constituents who expected their MPs to attend to their legislative needs. A fundamental difference, however, was that the issues that concerned Plymouth and Kingston-upon-Hull were primarily local whereas Bristol, whose residents promoted many measures of local concern, also instructed their members on contentious

---

[102] The petition accompanied Wilberforce's presentation of his 12 resolutions relating to the abolition of the slave trade on 12 May, 1789 – the formal opening of his campaign to end the trade. P.J. Marshall discusses the background to the petition and its contents in 'The anti-slave trade movement in Bristol', in *Bristol in the Eighteenth Century*, ed. P. McGrath (Newton Abbot, 1972), pp. 199–200. For Wilberforce's resolutions and his motion for the abolition of the slave trade, see *Parl. Reg.*, 2nd ser., xxvi, 130–54; or *PH*, xxviii, cc. 41–67.

[103] Marshall, 'Anti-slavery in Bristol', p. 200.

[104] *PH*, xxvii, 578–9; *Parl. Reg.*, 2nd ser., xxvi, 198–9; for Cruger's efforts to defeat Dolben's bill, see Marshall, 'Anti-slavery in Bristol', 202–34.

[105] *CJ*, xl, 931, 1000; Minchinton, *Petitions of the SMV*, pp. 155–6; Hoppit, *Failed Legislation*, pp. 482–3.

[106] BRO, SMV/2/4/2/29a/29, Brickdale to master, 26 May, 1790; *CJ*, xlv, 543; D.G. Barnes, *History of the English Corn Laws*, pp. 53–4.

national questions. Whereas Burke and most of his colleagues acknowledged their obligation to follow the instructions on specific and local business, they generally reserved to themselves the right to form their positions on issues of national concern. Thus, Burke differed with the SMV's support of the North administration's American policy in 1777 and resisted Bristol's persistent opposition to Nugent's Irish proposals in 1778. All of the MPs discussed in this chapter recognised that it was one of their prime responsibilities to forward the projects that loomed so large in the eyes of their supporters, though Burke found this obligation burdensome and one that sometimes diverted him from more important business.

Burke was in a more fragile position in Bristol than the members for other constituencies. Key to the success of Lord Barrington in Plymouth was the support he enjoyed from a succession of ministers and George III. With that sort of influence Barrington remained secure in Plymouth where he continued to secure favours for his constituents. Thus, he could back controversial local legislation without jeopardising his seat. He was also fortunate to have in Francis Holbourne and Sir Charles Hardy[107] competent and diligent colleagues. Samuel Thornton and Walter Spencer-Stanhope similarly benefited as members for Kingston-upon-Hull from the support of William Pitt and the longstanding friendship of William Wilberforce. Moreover, Thornton had established family and banking connections in Hull. Similarly, William Weddell, an uninspired legislator, could still rely on the backing of his friend, Earl Fitzwilliam – heir to the Rockingham interest in Yorkshire. These political, family and banking ties were instrumental in securing legislative solutions to Hull's dock problems as the previous discussion suggests.

The situation of Robert Nugent at Bristol was not dissimilar to that of Barrington at Plymouth, though Nugent never enjoyed the same degree of favour with the King nor the same degree of support in Bristol as Barrington did in Plymouth. More servant of the Crown than a politician, Barrington did not stake out controversial political positions, as Nugent did on the American and Irish questions. Matthew Brickdale followed an independent political line and lacked Nugent's force but was a reliable friend to the SMV and its programme. Though he proved to be a less than ardent defender of the slave trade, he ably forwarded legislation of use to the SMV and to the City. Jarrit, Laroche and Combe were inconsequential legislators who, unlike Burke, had strong connections in the Bristol merchant community.

Throughout his time at Bristol, Burke had few steadfast political allies aside from Campion. Unlike Barrington, Nugent or Brickdale, he worked at a disadvantage in trying to secure many of his constituents' objectives because both he and his principal patrons (Rockinham, Fitzwilliam and the Duke of Portland) were in opposition during the years he represented Bristol. These difficulties were compounded because he lacked an effective legislative ally to assist him in attending to Bristol's legislative needs: He and Cruger often worked at cross purposes, and he had little use for Combe or Laroche. Yet despite these disadvantages, Burke gained much of what his constituents requested

---

[107] Sir Charles Hardy (c. 1714–80), MP, Rochester, 1764–8 and Plymouth, 1771–80; navy, Capt. 1741, R.-Adm. 1756, V.-Adm 1759, Adm. 1770; Gov. New York, 1755–7 and Greenwich Hospital, 1771–80; C.-in-C. Channel Fleet 1779–90.

from North and his officials, a testament to his commitment to Bristol, his hard work, political skills and guile. Nevertheless, he seems never to have entered into the task of tending to the 'little things' with any enthusiasm. It was integral to his role as a member for Bristol. Burke, as already noted, found it 'vexatious and sometimes humiliating'. For this reason, he was, as he came to recognise, probably unsuited for the constituency.

4

Successful and Less Significant Legislators: Blackstone, Newdigate and Windham

This chapter focuses on three members who achieved prominence in their own right between 1754 and 1790 though only in one instance as a legislator. William Blackstone is remembered as the author of *Commentaries on the Laws of England*, the systematic study of the common laws. In an age that revered the independent member, Sir Roger Newdigate was, along with Sir George Savile, one of the notable independents of his era; unlike Sir George, he was also one of the most controversial. Finally, William Windham briefly achieved political prominence and cabinet office, yet he was, in the words of Henry Brougham, 'too often the dupe of his own ingenuity'. The careers of two of the three demonstrate that great abilities or profound knowledge of the law did not necessarily result in the MP becoming a notable or successful legislator.

I: William Blackstone[1]

His relative poverty forced William Blackstone to become the legal advisor for the Bertie family, Earls of Abingdon. Through their influence he became recorder of Wallingford and assumed the roles of steward and business manager to the family whose fortunes were undermined by debts left by the 3rd Earl in 1760 and the extravagance of his successor.[2] In these positions Blackstone negotiated the sale of properties and arranged new loans. He oversaw the construction of roads linking Wallingford to Oxford and Reading, thereby providing for the growth of the town's trade. He also served as the 4th Earl's manager for the Parliamentary borough of Westbury. In this position he devised a scheme to purchase burgage tenements and leases that gave Abingdon electoral control and Blackstone a seat that freed him from the dominion of Lord Bute, through whose influence he had previously sat for Hindon.[3]

---

[1] William Blackstone (1723–1780), MP, Hindon, 1761–8 and Westbury, 1768–70; Recorder, Wallingford 1749; Vinerian Professor of Law, Oxford Univ., 1758–66; Principal of New Hall, Oxford, 1761–6; Solicitor-Gen. to Queen, 1753–70; Judge, Common Pleas, 9 Feb. 1770 and King's Bench, 16 Feb. 1770; Judge, Common Pleas, 1770–80.

[2] Willoughby Bertie, 3rd Earl of Abingdon (1692–1760); Willoughby Bertie, 4th Earl of Abingdon (1740–99).

[3] Anthony Taussig, *Blackstone and his Contemporaries* (Austin, TX, 2009), pp. 77, 80, 83.

As Vinerian Professor of Law Blackstone began to convert his lectures into the *Commentaries*, the first volume of which appeared in November 1765.

During the 1760s Blackstone's role as an active legislator was shaped either by his connection to the Berties or by his legal interests. He was an indifferent orator. According to Wilfred Prest, he was insufficiently articulate to be a first-rate debater, and Namier dismissed him as 'an indifferent speaker', whose speeches were 'mostly on subjects of secondary importance'. They showed, he concluded, 'a lack of common sense'.[4] The result was that he was ill-equipped to shape the proceedings of the House on major public measures. He excelled, however, in detailed committee work and plunged into their proceedings with relish. Between 10 January 1765 and the end of March he was named to nearly 50 different Commons' committees. Most of them dealt with minor issues – approving petitions for enclosures, the naturalisation of foreigners or the establishment of turnpike trusts. He also dealt with business on a mixed array of projects, including the turnpiking of the road between Wallingford and Farringdon. Most notably, he drafted Thomas Gilbert's 1765 poor law which served as a model for the latter's ultimately successful 1782 Act.[5]

Blackstone made his most extensive legislative efforts on behalf of the Earls of Abingdon and other members of the family. He drafted and oversaw the passage of bills to provide jointures for wives and portions for younger children.[6] More importantly, he set out to enhance the profitability of the family's estates by replacing a ferry with a toll bridge over the Thames between Swimford in Berkshire and Eynsham in Oxfordshire, a project that ultimately required several separate pieces of legislation before it was completed.

In February 1765 he and Richard Jackson[7] endeavoured to secure a bill 'to enable ecclesiastical persons, or bodies politic, corporate and collegiate, to exchange their lands under certain restrictions'. Blackstone forwarded an amended copy to Thomas Townshend,[8] MP, for Cambridge University, in hopes of securing his support. On 18 March, the bill passed through its final stage in the House of Commons after a motion opposing its third reading was defeated by a vote of 113 to 95.[9] The measure failed in the House of Lords because it was opposed by Archbishop Secker[10] of Canterbury and other prelates.[11]

---

[4] Wilfred Prest, *William Blackstone: Law and Letters in the Eighteenth Century* (Oxford, 2008), pp. 204, 227; *HPC, 1754–1790*, ii, 96.

[5] Prest, *William Blackstone*, pp. 204, 227.

[6] Prest, *William Blackstone*, p. 189.

[7] Richard Jackson (?1722–87), MP, Weymouth and Melcombe Regis, 1762-8 and New Romney, 1768-84; Agent for Connecticut, 1760–70, for Pennsylvania, 1763–70, and Massachusetts, 1765–70; Sec. to Chancellor of Exchequer, 1763–5; Counsel to Board of Trade, 1770–82; Counsel to Cambridge Univ. 1771–87; Ld. of Treasury, 1782–3.

[8] Hon. Thomas Townshend (1701–80), MP, Winchelsea, 1722–7 and Cambridge University, 1727–74; Undersec. of State, 1724–30; Teller of Exchequer, 1727–74; Sec. to Duke of Devonshire as Ld. Lt. of Ireland, 1759.

[9] *CJ*, xxx, 259.

[10] Thomas Secker (1693–1768), Bishop of Bristol, 1734, tr. to Oxford, 1737, Dean of St. Paul's, 1750; Archbishop of Canterbury, 1758.

[11] Hoppit, *Failed Legislation*, pp. 398–9; Prest, *William Blackstone*, pp. 228–9.

Blackstone had a productive 1766–7 session when he reported from the Commons' committee appointed to consider Lord Abingdon's petition for the bill to build a toll bridge and road across the Thames at Swimford, west of Oxford. The bridge became a part of an elaborate scheme which eventually included a repaired Botley Causeway linking the bridge to the west end of Thames Street in Oxford, thereby providing the city a route to the west, and, finally, the landmark Oxford improvement commission. The whole project was unusually complex for the period and required for its completion the united effort of Blackstone, Wetherell, the University's Vice-Chancellor and the City of Oxford. Not surprisingly the bridge committee delivered a favourable report on a measure drafted by its chair, and on 9 December, 1767 Blackstone presented the bill.[12] The second phase of the project involved repairing the public carriageway which extended from Thames Street in Oxford over Botley's Causeway to the turnpike road near Firfield in Berkshire. Once again Blackstone drafted the legislation, presented the bill and managed its passage (7 George III, c. 6). In addition, he used his influence to secure some of the funding for the Causeway project from Oxford and the universities' colleges.[13]

Once passed, it turned out that the Botley Act required amending, a not uncommon phenomenon, so Blackstone introduced another bill in December 1767 with the necessary alterations. Despite being house-bound with gout and contending with witnesses who were unable to appear to give evidence on account of fevers, Blackstone managed from his bed, with the help of Newdigate Poyntz,[14] to see that the measure made its way through both Houses (8 Geo. III, c. 34).[15]

Though the University did not become directly involved in the Botley project, the Chancellor provided support and various members offered financial backing. According to *Jackson's Oxford Journal* Blackstone's bill also led to discussions about adding a toll bridge at Magdalen College to the draft proposal.[16] Convocation rejected an idea which three years later formed the centrepiece of the Oxford Improvement Bill for which the University and the City of Oxford jointly petitioned in January 1771.

Blackstone's various projects contributed little to restoring the fortunes of the Bertie family, but, according to Prest, they, in conjunction with the Oxford Improvement Act of 1771, made their mark locally because their physical results mark the first stages in Oxford's transition from the town's medieval past.[17]

Blackstone was less successful in securing the passage of two other bills he presented in 1767. The first followed on from an unsuccessful effort by George Prescott[18] and

---

[12] *CJ*, xxxi, 24, 40, 43. The Bridge Act passed the Commons on 11 December (7 George III, c. 63).

[13] Prest, *William Blackstone*, p. 223; the bridge and causeway had opened by 4 Aug. 1769.

[14] Newdigate Poyntz (1715–72), Commons' committee clerk and Parliamentary agent.

[15] *Blackstone Letters*, xiv, 119–22.

[16] *Jackson's Oxford Journal*, 27 Nov. 1767; L.S. Sutherland, 'The administration of the university', in *History of the University of Oxford. Vol. 5: The Eighteenth Century*, ed. Lucy Sutherland and L.G. Mitchell (Oxford, 1986), pp. 223–4.

[17] The previous discussion is based on I.G. Doolittle, *William Blackstone: A Biography* (Haslemere, 2001), pp. 68–78; Julian Munby and Hugh Walton, 'The building of New Road', *Oxoniensia*, iv (1990), 123–30; L.S. Sutherland, 'The administration of the university', pp. 222–5; *Blackstone Letters*, pp. 117–123; and Prest, *William Blackstone*, p. 223.

[18] George Prescott (c. 1711–90), MP, Stockbridge, 1761–1768, and Milborne Port, 1772–4.

would have eased the payment of creditors by drawing on the estates of deceased debtors, including the real property of merchants and other traders. Blackstone introduced the measure on 10 April, 1767 after submitting it to Charles Yorke,[19] 'for any observations he may have Leisure to make'. The practice of legal reformers seeking the opinion of the Crown's law officers was a routine one, and the bill passed the House after receiving detailed scrutiny in its second reading committee. It later foundered in the Lords after its second reading in May.[20] Blackstone subsequently introduced a similar bill, but the measure did not progress beyond its second reading because Parliament was prorogued.[21] His subsequent legislative efforts involved plans for the Oxford canal, and, as noted in Chapter 1, significant prison reforms, but the latter occurred when he became a judge.

Though hardworking and adept at manoeuvring his measures through the House, Blackstone was neither a significant Member of Parliament nor a notable legislator. Prest shows that he busied himself in the work of the Commons' committees, but insofar as he worked to forward legislation, he did so mainly on behalf of members of the Bertie family. His act to rebuild the Botley Causeway and his secondary role in carrying the Oxford Improvement Act initiated the transformation of Oxford's layout of streets from their medieval pattern, but this achievement was purely local. Sir William Holdsworth hailed his creditors' relief bills of 1767 as 'radical relief in the law relating to the administration of assets';[22] their radicalism, however, likely meant that the judges in the upper House would throw them out.

Blackstone's most significant legislative contribution came after he left the House and was serving as a judge. Beginning in 1775 he joined with William Eden in drafting what became the Penitentiary Act of 1779, as noted in Chapter 1. Over four years he prepared drafts of the measure, taking a lead in the business in 1778, while Eden was in America. Jeremy Bentham, the most scathing critic of the *Commentaries*, nevertheless praised the drafts of their Hard Labour Bill, which came before Parliament in 1778, as 'a capital improvement in penal legislation'.[23]

Blackstone's legislative achievements as an MP, though useful in a few cases, were limited in their scope and failed to earn him the recognition he gained as author of the *Commentaries*. Ill-suited to the give and take of the Commons' debate, he was, according to Namier, ponderous and tending to lecture. Because he lacked a lucrative legal practice, he could not afford to remain an MP, and even while he was one, he had to devote a disproportionate amount of his time to the legal affairs of the Bertie family. His legislative career was something of a disappointment.

---

[19] Hon. Charles Yorke (1747–70), MP, Reigate, 1747–1768 and Cambridge University, 1768–70; Clerk of the Crown in Chancery, 1747–70; Solicitor-Gen. to Prince of Wales, 1754–6; Solicitor Gen. 1754–61; Attorney-Gen. Nov. 1761–3; Aug. 1765–Aug. 1766; Ld. Chancellor, 1770.
[20] Hoppit, *Failed Legislation*, pp. 398–9.
[21] Prest, *William Blackstone*, pp. 230–1.
[22] Cited in Prest, *William Blackstone*, p. 230.
[23] Cited in Prest, *William Blackstone*, p. 298.

II: Sir Roger Newdigate, 5th Bt.[24]

Sir Roger is best known as a member for his fierce and, from his point of view, largely successful opposition to attempts during the 1770s to relax restrictions that would, according to him, undermine the Church of England. These involved efforts to exempt laity and clergy of the Church from having to subscribe to its 39 articles, providing similar exemptions to Oxford and Cambridge undergraduates at their matriculation, or exempting Dissenting ministers and teachers who were required to subscribe to the articles until legislation was passed freeing them from the obligation in 1779. Newdigate also thwarted attempts to end the annual commemoration of the so-called 'martyrdom' of Charles I. Though his role in these campaigns has been recorded in detail by many scholars,[25] it is worth reiterating as an example of his commitment to the Church, and his refusal to allow backsliding on the part of the universities, Lord North and the episcopal bench. His victories also highlight his prowess as a legislative warrior and his attentive representation of what he saw as the interests of his Oxford University constituents.

On 6 February 1772 Sir William Meredith moved that the petition of the Feather's Tavern group of 250 laymen and clergy, praying for an end to the requirement that they subscribe to the 39 articles, might lie on the table of the House. The motion was rejected by a vote of 217–71. In responding to Meredith, Newdigate resorted to the emphatic rhetoric that became characteristic of the tone he adopted on such occasions. He proclaimed that what was in the petition would open the door to 'the Arian, the Socinian, the Papist, the 5th Monarchy Man' venting 'their pernicious doctrines to the confusion of Church and State'. His success in this case was gratifying for, as he told his wife in a letter:

> everything relating to the debate has turned out beyond my wish or expectation. I had the good fortune of dragging the M[i]n[instr]y to do what everyone agrees they ought but did not intend to do. I learn besides today that there was a meeting of Lord North, the Archbishop & others to which I was to have been sent for, who agreed to let the Petition be brought up. If I had been there I should have found it difficult to resist such authority. I was absent, & luckily by my standing saved them and myself from reproach of lack of warmness, at least in such a cause.[26]

Another challenge soon followed when a county meeting at Morpeth applied to Parliament to end the *Nullum Tempus* privileges of the Church of England. These gave the Church the right to reclaim property currently in private hands that had once belonged to it. Henry Seymour[27] introduced legislation to abolish this ecclesiastical

---

[24] Sir Roger Newdigate, 5th Bt. (1719–1806), MP, Middlesex, 1742–7 and Oxford University, 1751–80.
[25] G.M. Ditchfield, 'The Subscription issue in British Parliamentary politics', *Parl. Hist*, vii (1988), 45–80; L.G. Mitchell, 'Politics and revolution, 1772–1800', in *History of the University of Oxford. Vol. 5*, pp. 165–184; W.R. Ward, *Georgian Oxford: University Politics in the Eighteenth Century* (Oxford, 1958), 162–88.
[26] *The Correspondence of Sir Roger Newdigate of Arbury, Warwickshire*, ed. A.W.A. White (Vol. XXXVII, Stratford-upon-Avon, 1995), pp. 178–9.
[27] Henry Seymour (1729–1807), MP, Totnes, 1763–8, Huntington, 1768–74 and Evesham, 1774–80; Groom of the Bedchamber, 1763–5.

privilege, just as a similar right belonging to the Crown had been abolished by an act introduced by Sir George Savile in 1768. Nathan Wetherell,[28] speaking for the Heads of Houses, appealed to Newdigate to exert all his powers for the Church and the universities against Seymour's proposed bill. The measure's adversaries at Oxford distributed 500 copies of a pamphlet by Dean Tucker and sent circular letters to all Oxford MPs. In the end the measure was defeated on 17 February by a vote of 117 to 141.[29] Wetherell immediately sent his thanks and those of the heads of colleges to Newdigate and Francis Page[30] for their triumph, adding that he hoped the House would leave the 'Church to itself'.[31]

Those hopes were overly sanguine, for within two days of the letter, Thomas Nowell, Oxford's Regius Professor of Modern History, became the object of an attack, launched by Thomas Townshend.[32] He moved on 21 February that Nowell be censured for a sermon delivered on 30 January commemorating the execution of Charles II. The sermon, according to Townshend, smacked of divine right theory.

Newdigate, in a letter to his wife describing proceedings in the House on 25 February, inveighed against appointing a man to preach, moving thanks in the House and ordering that the sermon be printed and then reversing itself with an order that it be removed from the *Journals*. When Frederick Montagu went further, announcing that he would give notice to abolish the observation of the day, Newdigate told his wife '... I moved the Order of the day & was beat 152 to 101'. On 2 March, the House reconsidered Montagu's motion, which Newdigate opposed with his usual heat, arguing that there should be no revision of the Book of Common Prayer. With the support of North, Montagu's motion was defeated by a vote of 97 to 125.[33]

Despite Newdigate's triumphs London's Dissenting ministers were heartened that during the Commons' previous discussions of subscription distinctions were made between Anglican clergy who should be required to subscribe and Dissenters who might legitimately be exempted from that obligation. Some assumed Lord North had implied this in a speech he had delivered. Thus, London Dissenters moved for a bill to relieve their compatriots from the obligation. Leave to bring in a bill was granted on 3 April 1772 with only Newdigate and Sir William Dolben[34] opposing; during the debate Newdigate inveighed against subversive Presbyterianism. Because leave was

---

[28] Nathan Wetherell (1726–1808), Master of University College; Vice-Chancellor of Oxford University, 1768–71; Dean of Hereford, 1772–1808.

[29] WCRO, Newdigate MSS, CR136/B 2558a, Wetherell to Newdigate, 18 Feb., 1772; Mitchell, 'Politics and revolution', p. 250; *CJ*, xxxiii, 482.

[30] Francis Page (?1726–1803), MP, Oxford University, 1768–1801.

[31] WCRO, Newdigate MSS, CR136/B2359, Wetherell to Newdigate, 19 Feb., 1772.

[32] Thomas Townshend (1733–1800), MP, Whitchurch, 1754–83; Clerk of the Household of Prince of Wales, 1756–60; Clerk of Green Cloth, 1760–2; Ld. of Treasury, 1765–7; Jt. Paymaster Gen. 1767–8; Sec. at War, 1782; Home Sec. 1782–3, 1783–9; Chief Justice in Eyre, south of Trent, 1789–1800; cr. Baron Sydney 1783 and Viscount, 1789; Leader of the House of Lords, 1783–9.

[33] *Newdigate Correspondence*, p.182; J.C.D. Clark, *English Society 1688–1832: Ideology, Social Structure and Political Practice during the Ancient Regime* (Cambridge and New York, 1985), pp. 212–14; Hoppit, *Failed Legislation*, 418–19.

[34] Sir William Dolben, 3rd Bt. (1727–1814), MP, Oxford University, Feb.–Mar.1768 and 1780–1806), Northamptonshire, 1768–74.

inevitable, Lord North absented himself from the proceedings. The King initially urged him to oppose the measure in the House without pressing his supporters who had large blocks of Dissenters among their constituents to join him. Both knew the Lords would throw out such a bill, which it did in 1772 and 1773. North, however, declined to oppose the measure, so proceedings in the Commons were sedate; in fact only nine members opposed at its second and third readings.[35]

The Feather's Tavern Petition, in addition to raising the issue of clerical subscription, provoked debates at the universities on whether it was appropriate to compel undergraduates who did not anticipate entering the Church's ministry to subscribe. At Cambridge, Richard Watson,[36] the Regius Professor of Divinity, attacked the university's requirement.[37] Even Oxford found itself divided on the issue throughout 1772, with one camp favouring an end to subscription, another proposing that entrants acknowledge they were members of the Church and a third opposing any revision.[38]

This confusion threatened to play into the hands of Sir William Meredith, who in February 1772 gave notice of his intention to bring in a bill to end university subscription while the apparent willingness of the universities to modify their statutes caused Newdigate to intervene at Oxford. In November he informed the new Vice-Chancellor, Thomas Fothergill, in a letter that was read at Convocation that 'if we flatter ourselves that any concession whatsoever can abate their ill will, we shall find ourselves much mistaken'.[39]

Invigorated by Newdigate's letter, defenders of the status quo defeated proposals for change at the University's convocation on 4 February 1773. The Prime Minister initially seemed disinclined to oppose an alteration, and even Francis Page believed that some modification was necessary while the University debated. Once its position was clarified, the positions of these two stiffened. Meredith could no longer expect reform from within the universities and had to proceed on his own. By the end of 1772, Newdigate was negotiating with him as to when he would renew his motion. In introducing his bill, Meredith cited the general approval in the House during the previous session for ending academic subscriptions; Newdigate, however, charged that the goal of his motion had been 'to set open the doors of the church, and to admit within her pale, dissenters of every denomination ... to wound our ecclesiastical establishment, to overturn her fences, and lay her bulwarks in ruins'.[40] On 23 February 1773 the motion to go into committee on the bill was defeated by a majority of 159 to 67.[41]

---

[35] CJ, xxxiii, 668; Ward, Georgian Oxford, pp. 254–5; for background to the bill, see Ditchfield, 'Subscription issue', pp. 52–3. Ditchfield has lists of the Lords voting for and against the bill at its second reading on 19 May, pp. 66–70 and of MPs against the bill at its second reading on p. 70.
[36] Richard Watson (1737–1816), Professor of Chemistry, Cambridge, 1764; Regius Professor of Divinity, 1771; Bishop of Llandaff, 1782.
[37] A Second Letter to the Members of the Honourable House of Commons Relating to the Subscription Required of Graduates in the Universities (1772).
[38] Mitchell, 'Politics and revolution', p. 175
[39] WCRO, Newdigate MSS, CR 136/B2381, Newdigate to Thomas Fothergill, 18 Nov. 1772.
[40] Quoted in Ward, Georgian Oxford, p. 267.
[41] PH, xvii, c. 758; CJ, xxxiv, 148.

Nevertheless, the London Dissenters renewed their campaign to free themselves from subscription. On 2 March 1773 Sir Henry Hoghton[42] presented his bill to relieve Dissenting clergy and teachers from that requirement.[43] The measure differed from its 1772 predecessor in the hope that it would gain wider support.[44] Its introduction, however, provoked counter-petitions from Calvinist Dissenters who claimed that the bill was unnecessary and posed a threat to articles 'on which the Reformation was founded'. Supporters of the bill cited the petitioners' low social standing in an attempt to discredit them, though Newdigate estimated their numbers ranged from 'many hundreds' to 'over 2,000'.[45] On 10 March at the bill's second reading the minority opposed to it rose to 34, up from 9 in 1772. Still the measure was never in danger in the lower House and passed the House by a vote of 65 to 14, only to fail in the Lords.[46] Given the large majorities against the bills in the House of Lords in 1772 and 1773, no similar attempt was made in 1774.

As the situation in America deteriorated and discontent with the North administration, its mismanagement of the war and the burden of taxation to meet its cost mounted at home, impatience with government increased. The outbreak of the war with France and unrest in Ireland made it clearer that North and his colleagues were not in a position to offend England's large Dissenting communities, especially after Roman Catholics received relief from some of the strictures of the penal code in 1778. Several bishops of the established Church had considered introducing legislation that modified the existing practices relating to Dissenters.[47] Their supporters in the House of Commons brought in a bill which continued the requirement to subscribe to the doctrinal articles, but bestowed on those who refused to do so all the freedoms provided under the Toleration Act. There was no widespread Dissenting campaign on behalf of the measure as there had been in 1772 and 1773, only approaches to sympathetic MPs. The fact that the administration took a neutral position, and that some bishops were unlikely to oppose or might even support the measure, meant that Newdigate and other adversaries could not count on the Lords to block the measure.[48]

Instead, High Churchmen resolved to include a test in return for the concession. The Rev. George Horne[49] wrote to Newdigate that 'we cannot but be of opinion *here*, that ... an unbounded license for preaching and teaching, without so much as a general declaration of belief in the Scriptures as a Revelation of God's will, is more than a

---

[42] Sir Henry Hoghton, 6th Bt. (1728–95), MP, Preston, 1768–95.
[43] *CJ*, xxxiv, 164.
[44] For the differences, see Ditchfield, 'Subscription issue', p. 57.
[45] Ditchfield, 'Subscription issue', p. 58.
[46] For the list of the minority in the Commons on 25 March, see Ditchfield, 'Subscription issue', pp. 71–2. For the list of those for and against the bill in the Lords on 2 April 1773, see *ibid.*, pp. 68–70.
[47] According to Bishop Porteus, some bishops were prepared in 1778 to introduce their own bill to release dissenting ministers and school masters from their obligation to subscribe, providing they could supply testimonials of good character. When a draft measure was circulated among the episcopal bench, differences arose, so it was not presented. Lambeth Palace Library, Porteus Notebooks, MSS 2098, ff. 69–72.
[48] Ditchfield, 'Subscription issue', pp. 61–2.
[49] George Horne (1730–93), President of Magdalen College, Oxford, 1769; Vice-Chancellor, 1776–9; Chaplain to George III, 1771; Dean of Canterbury, 1781; Bishop of Norwich, 1791.

Christian Government ought to grant'.[50] Responding to this concern Newdigate sent a public letter to the University and then took a lead in orchestrating its response to the bill. On 30 March Convocation adopted a petition that questioned 'the licensing of men to preach and teach, without any declaration whatever of their belief in the doctrines of Christianity, or of the divine authority of the Scriptures'. Oxford's amendment to the bill was moved by its Chancellor, Lord North, and carried by a vote of 88 to 55.[51]

As a result of his many interventions in the House on their behalf, Sir Roger is best known for his unrelenting defence of the Church and the University and his strident opposition to proposals that hinted at undermining the supremacy. At the same time, he was assiduous in attending to the University's more mundane legislative business which ranged from the repair and extension of Oxford streets and bridges to protecting its interests in a variety of enclosure bills and the other mundane business of the University.

As an active, improving landlord, Newdigate steered bills through the House that contributed to the improvement of his region and his estates. According to J.M. Martin, he took a lead in the drafting of a number of enclosure bills, including one in 1769 for the enclosure of Bedworth,[52] where his father had developed coal mines.[53] He drafted the measure and subsequently guided it through the House. This sort of situation was, as already noted, not unusual. Sir Roger had chaired select committees on a number of enclosure bills that he drafted. Thus, he was well versed in the intricacies of enclosure legislation as well as in the tricks of lay proprietors. All of this was useful experience for one of the University's members, since enclosure bills presented special difficulties for Oxford colleges given the tendency of lay proprietors to infringe on the rights of tithe holders.[54] Newdigate was called upon to make sure that New College did not find itself burdened with undue fees in the implementation of its enclosure and was later urged to arbitrate between Lincoln College, impropriator of the Parish of Twyford in Buckinghamshire and Lord Wenman,[55] the parish's principal proprietor and petitioner for an enclosure act whose terms were unsatisfactory to the college. In both instances Sir Roger settled the issues in ways that satisfied the distressed masters.[56]

Members of the University also called upon Newdigate for details of pending legislation. Wetherell, who was unaware of the details of the Botley Turnpike Bill, enquired if anything in the bill indicated the turnpike would extend through Oxford and necessitate the installation of a gate at Magdalen Bridge. With exemplary dispatch,

---

[50] WCRO, Newdigate MSS, B136/B1759, Horne to Newdigate, 27 Feb. 1779.
[51] *CJ*, xxxvii; Mitchell, 'Politics and revolution', pp. 179–80. Theophilus Lindsay believed it was Newdigate who stirred up the Oxford dons and that without him, they would not have 'meddled in the business'. Ditchfield, 'Subscription issue', pp. 62–3.
[52] For the Bedworth enclosure petition, see *CJ*, xxxii, 303.
[53] J.M. Martin, 'Members of Parliament and enclosure', *Agriculture History*, p. 104.
[54] Langford has an excellent short discussion on the various problems and the difficulties they posed in relation to enclosure bills in *Public Life*, pp. 328–9.
[55] Philip Wenman, 4th Viscount Wenman [I], (1742–1800), MP, Oxfordshire, 1768–96.
[56] WCRO, Newdigate MSS, CR136 B1734, Thomas Hayward to Newdigate, 19 Apr. 1766 and CR 136/B1702, B. Hallifax to Newdigate, 12 Mar. 1774.

Newdigate replied the next day that he knew of no intention to extend the Botley Turnpike Bill beyond the limits of the Petition, which was, in fact, signed by Wetherell himself.[57]

Among his most challenging duties as the University's member was steering the controversial Oxford Improvement Bill (also known as the Mileways Act) through the chamber during the 1771 session. The act is notable for a number of reasons: among its legacies are such Oxford landmarks as the reconstructed Magdalen Bridge, the construction, widening and repaving of a number of the city's streets, as well as lighting, drainage, traffic regulation and refuse disposal.[58] The act is notable also because it outlawed the slaughtering of animals on the public streets. Henceforth butchers were congregated in a Covered Market that ended street trading and opened in November 1774. Finally, it brought an end to a longstanding rivalry between the university and the city by providing that a committee including six representatives of each would share responsibility for the act's implementation and management.

Nathan Wetherell informed Newdigate in November 1770 that Convocation had unanimously agreed to petition Parliament for leave to bring in the improvement bill and requested Newidgate's patronage of the measure, 'which will be of great service to the University'.[59] The bill engendered strong opposition from farmers in the eastern regions of Oxfordshire. Confronted with this resistance, Newdigate, who had opposed any compromise with Dissenters, suggested it would be wiser to come to some arrangement rather than driving the critics into opposition by pushing ahead with the bill.[60] His caution bore fruit in a victory in the committee on the petition on 4 February 1771, which earned plaudits from Wetherell, who thanked Newdigate and Page 'for service already done' on behalf of the University, adding he was sure that friends of the University would support its passage throughout its progress through the House'.[61] Wetherell, however, was disturbed by the strong attack mounted against the measure at its second reading – according to Sutherland 'by forces outside the city'. In the face of this resistance, convocation granted Newdigate and Page 'the direction and promotion of the Bill', with the proviso that:

> the Application of the Tolls shou'd extend to the making of a commodious way into the Town thro: St Clements, to the repairing or rebuilding Madg: Bridge, the removing of the several nuisances specified in the Bill, &c, the new Paving of the streets leading to the great Roads, mentioned in the Schedules. These are looked upon as *Essentials*; & unless we are able to carry these Points, it will not be worth our while to tax ourselves, for after all the great Burden will lie upon the Inhabitants of the Place.[62]

---

[57] WCRO, Newdigate MSS, CR136/B2332, Wetherell to Newdigate, 10 Dec. 1767 and CR136/B2333, Newdigate to Wetherell, 11 Dec. 1767.
[58] T.W.M. Jaine, 'The building of Magdalen Bridge, 1779–1790', *Oxoniensia*, xxxvi (1971), 59.
[59] WCRO, Newdigate MSS, CR136 B2340, Wetherell to Newdigate, 21 Nov. 1770.
[60] *Newdigate Correspondence*, p. 167.
[61] WCRO, Newdigate MSS, B136/B2343, Wetherell to Newdigate, 4 Feb. 1771.
[62] Sutherland, 'The administration of the University', p. 224; WCRO, Newdigate MSS, CR136/B2345, Wetherell to Newdigate, 14 Feb. 1771.

The Vice-Chancellor need not have worried, for a reduction of tolls on carriages loaded with grain on market days orchestrated by the University MPs and a few other minor amendments pacified the eastern portion of the county and enabled the measure to pass on 28 March.[63]

Throughout these proceedings, Newdigate showed a willingness to compromise in a manner that softened the opposition of the measure's opponents and allowed the measure to proceed towards passage. He displayed all the suppleness and moderation in these proceedings that was absent in his conduct during the proceedings on the subscription question, and on several occasions prevented the University from pressing its opponents unnecessarily. Not without reason Wetherell wrote to congratulate him and Page for relieving the University of the burden of managing the bill's passage – for their 'zeal, activity & good management of the Bill in every stage of it'.[64]

Also of significance was Newdigate's campaign on behalf of the Oxford Canal, which members of the University promoted as a means of securing cheaper coal and freeing themselves from the bondage of what Wetherell called 'our monopolizing bargemen'. As well as meeting the needs of the University, completion of the canal enabled Sir Roger to ship coal from his mines at Griffe in Warwickshire to Oxford and from there throughout the country. His diary shows that throughout 1768 he met with Warwickshire and Oxfordshire officials and landowners to enlist support for the project and counteract the Chamber of London which established its own committee. The London Chamber regarded Newcastle coal as superior to that of the Midlands and proposed to include a clause in the Oxford bill prohibiting coal from proceeding from the proposed canal into the Thames below Oxford. The Chamber acknowledged, however, that the canal would bring benefits to London by reducing the cost of moving Birmingham iron products to London almost by a half.

The fear that a canal link to the Midlands coal fields would cause a reduction of shipments from Newcastle also raised the alarm that such a reduction would cut into the coastal trade, thereby undercutting a prime source of the navy's manpower. These and other charges by the Chamber and its allies received an answer in a letter that appeared in *Jackson's Oxford's Journal* on 24 June 1769. Its forceful prose is reminiscent of speeches Sir Roger delivered in the Commons as he confronted those he regarded as the enemies of the Church. It is a skilful piece – purportedly by 'an Oxford Freeholder', but one in which Sir Roger likely had a hand.

The bill's petition was presented on 29 November 1768. Newdigate and Lord North were among those named to its committee.[65] Reporting from the petition committee, Newdigate noted that Joseph Parker, an engineer, testified that the route proposed for the canal was 'practicable'. Both Newdigate and North were later part of the group assigned by the House to prepare and bring in the bill. Newdigate took the chair of the

---

[63] For other amendments proposed by Newdigate, see WCRO, Newdigate MSS, CR136/B2436b Newdigate to Wetherell, 14 Feb. 1771 (draft).

[64] WCRO, Newdigate MSS, B136/B2348a, Wetherell to Newdigate, 20 Feb. 1771.

[65] *CJ*, xxxii, 78, 87–8. North sat for Banbury through which the canal would pass. Hugh J. Compton, *The Oxford Canal* (Newton Abbot and North Pomfret, VT, 1976), pp. 10–11. Newdigate presented the bill on 8 December, *CJ*, xxxii, p. 94.

second reading committee, and when it came time for the report on 15 March, he noted that the committee had met on 14 occasions.[66] The next day a motion to put off the report for three months was rejected by a vote of 89 to 37. The pressure of other business meant the additional investigation was postponed until 4 April. Nevertheless, the House passed the bill the next day, and Newdigate carried it to the Lords where it passed on 19 April and went on to receive the royal assent on 21 April (9 Geo III, C. 70).

Prior to the bill's passage, Sir Roger had made innumerable visits to London to enlist support for the measure in both houses. Among these meetings was one at Marlborough House where he met with the Dukes of Marlborough and Bridgewater and Earl Gower, both of the latter being influential promoters of canals. More than any other MP, Sir Roger exerted his local influence and applied his talents in Westminster to assemble the funds and the political support to assure the passage of the Bill.

In addition to his work on behalf of the University, Sir Roger promoted bills that would further the development of his Warwickshire estates. He reported from the committee on the petition for the enclosure of the parish of Chilvers Coton, a necessary preliminary to opening coal mines on the family's property.[67] Like other MPs he exploited his position as a Member of Parliament either to secure the passage of measures in which he had a direct interest or to thwart those that he saw as harmful to local or personal interests. That he was able to do so is another sign of his legislative attentiveness and the degree to which he and other MPs exploited their positions as legislators of personal or familial purposes.

III: William Windham[68]

Though he eventually rose to national prominence and a seat in the cabinet, William Windham did not enter the House of Commons with a clear sense of direction or with priorities for himself as a member for Norwich. The result was that during his first six years in the Commons, he pursued an unsteady path as a legislator, because of ill health, lack of confidence and indecision as to whether he would pursue the life of a politician, that of a scholar or disciple of Burke. His diaries show that insofar as he had a goal it was to make a mark as an orator, yet while taking unusual care to prepare his remarks, an immobilising terror sometimes overtook him as the opportunity to speak approached. For example, he recorded in his diary for 18 April 1785 that he was prepared 'with so much thought' to deliver remarks on Pitt's proposals for the reform of Parliament, but once he arrived in the House, its heat 'disordered' his powers to the extent that he was unable to rise to his feet.[69]

---

[66] *CJ*, xxxii, 220–1; Compton, *Oxford Canal*, p. 13.
[67] See *Newdigate Correspondence*, pp. 123–35 for negotiations relating to the preparation and presentation of the bill.
[68] William Windham (1750–1810), MP, Norwich, 1784–1802, St. Mawes, 1802–6, New Romney, 1806–7 and Higham Ferrers, 1807–10; Chief Sec. to Ld. Lt [I], 1783; Sec at War, 1794–1801; Sec. for War and Colonies, 1806–7.
[69] BL, Add. MS 51710, Holland House papers, ff. 32–3, 18 Apr. 1785. *The Diary of the Right Hon. William Windham, 1784 to 1810*, ed. Mrs. Henry Baring (1866), p. 51.

Windham's diaries show that his focus as an MP, especially during the early years of the Parliament, remained on his speaking and the agenda of his Whig allies, particularly that of Edmund Burke. Fanny Burney noted that Windham's 'real driving force was his 'excess of friendship and admiration for' Edmund Burke, 'his mentor in politics'.[70] Because of these preoccupations he sometimes ignored business of importance to Norwich and was regarded by his allies as occasionally careless in attending to routine constituency matters. His Norwich agent, for example, noted that if Windham 'had been at all remiss it has been by inattention to your interest in not coming down oftener at Mich[elma]s Sessions for instance'.[71]

Still, after Robert Partridge, Norwich's mayor and chair of the city's association of merchants, manufacturers and dealers in wool, called upon the city's MPs to forward to William Pitt their petition regarding the illicit smuggling of raw wool and live sheep in 1784, the minister asked for information regarding processes in the local manufacturing, which Partridge promised to forward to Pitt through Windham and Harbord.[72]

Thereafter Windham's diary, correspondence and Parliamentary speeches indicate that he devoted little attention to Norwich business. In a short speech on 27 January 1784 he dismissed as lavish a ministerial proposal to spend £700,000 on fortifying the dockyards,[73] and on 21 March 1785 he went to the House to attend the presentation of a Norwich petition that advocated for Parliamentary reform, including the restoration of triennial Parliaments. On subsequent occasions, however, he joined Burke in opposing Parliamentary reform.[74] Windham intended to speak during the debate on Pitt's proposals for reform on 18 April, but, as noted above, became suddenly overwhelmed and could not rise to the occasion. He joined his Whig colleagues in opposing Pitt's Irish propositions, remaining in the House on the night of 20–21 May until 7 am, when he managed to speak.[75] Ten days later, he acknowledged his obligation to his constituents in a debate on the controversial Shop Tax, which MPs for towns had attacked for several sessions. During a debate on the measure's third reading Windham declared 'that he was instructed by his constituents to oppose it [the bill's passage], and their instructions were perfectly consistent with his own private sentiments'.[76] Given this happy coincidence, he was able to vote against the bill and follow their guidance. He wasn't always so obliging. On 16 May 1786 during the debate on a bill to explain the Hawkers and Pedlars Bill, he told the House that despite his constituents' instructions,

---

[70] HPC, 1790–1820, vi, 608.
[71] BL, Windham MS, Add. MS 37873, Elias Norgate to Windham, 9 Dec. 1784, f. 100.
[72] BL, Windham MS, Add. MS, 37873, ff. 102–3, 105 106, Partridge to Harbord and Windham, 29 Dec. 1784, 5 Jan. 1785. The two MPs received the thanks of Norwich's merchants and manufacturers for their interventions with Pitt regarding his forthcoming Irish propositions. BL, Add. MS. 37873, ff. 111–14, Partridge to Windham and Harbord, 16 Jan. 1785.
[73] PH, xxv, 1155.
[74] Windham Diary, p. 45. The petition 'wishing to have the original Excellence of the Constitution of this Country restored, maintained and perpetuated by a Recurrence of the genuine Principles on which it was founded'. The petitioners asked for a restoration of triennial Parliaments. CJ, xl, 747, 21 Mar. 1785.
[75] Windham Diaries, pp. 52–3.
[76] PH, xxv, 792.

he would oppose Pitt's Bill, remaining confident that he would retain their good will.[77] Like Burke, he rejected the notion that he was bound by instructions. He had informed Norwich electors in a pre-election speech in 1784 that 'his own *dispassionate judgement*' would be 'the sole and fixed rule' of his Parliamentary conduct, causing his opponent, Henry Hobart,[78] to declare that he would be invariably attentive to his constituents' wishes.[79] Norwich independents sent Windham intermittent assessments of his political conduct during his early years in the House. There is no indication that he felt any obligation to follow their instructions.

Windham's occasional casualness got him into a difficult wrangle in 1787, when the following appeared in the *Norfolk Chronicle* on 26 February:

> ... with Regard to his Constituents in General he [Windham] had only to observe that if some few Persons had given the Approbation of the Treaty, he knew of several of them, distinguished as much as any men could possibly be, for their Abilities, Information and Judgement, who gave their decided Opinions against the Measure.[80]

These remarks were reportedly made during a Commons' debate on the French commercial treaty, which he opposed along with his Whig colleagues.[81] The city's manufacturers and merchants, however, claimed that during the debate he had misrepresented their opinions of the treaty and its probable effects on their businesses.[82] In the weeks subsequent to their protest, Robert Partridge's letters to Windham revealed that their MP knew little about the organisation and workings of Norwich's primary industry and failed to recognise the depth of their resentment at his misrepresentation of their opinions. While Partridge was reluctant to press him too hard,[83] the manufacturers expected a retraction from Windham and clarification of their views to the House of Commons.

The result of the confrontation was a six-week standoff between Windham and his constituents in which Windham claimed that he was unaware of the circumstances in which the group had adopted its resolution and that his words had been misrepresented in the press. For their part the merchants and manufacturers framed their case in a series of letters, culminating in one dispatched by Partridge on 20 March. Of concern to the group 'was the Slight supposed to be cast on the General Meeting [of the Merchants and Manufacturers]'.[84] The source of the problem, in the view of Partridge

---

[77] *PH*, xxvi, 13–14.
[78] Hon. Henry Hobart (1738–1799), MP, Norwich, 1786–7, 1787–1799.
[79] Quoted in Wilson, *Sense of the People*, pp. 428, 429.
[80] BL, Windham MSS, Add MS 37873, f. 133, inserted in letter of Robert Partridge to Windham, 9 Mar. 1787.
[81] I was unable to find such a statement in the relevant volumes of the *Parliamentary Register* or Cobbett's *Parliamentary History*. Windham, himself, claimed the statement that appeared in the *Chronicle* was an inaccurate report of his remarks.
[82] BL, Windham MSS, Add. MS, 37873, f. 133, Partridge to Windham, 9 Mar. 1787.
[83] BL, Add. MS, 37873, f. 138 Windham Papers, Partridge to Windham, 11 Mar. 1787.
[84] BL, Add. MS, 37873, f. 137. Windham Papers, Partridge to Windham, 14 Mar. 1787.

and his colleagues, arose during the debate in question, after Pitt asked Windham about the views of Norwich regarding the treaty. Windham's critics charged he had not made himself

> sufficiently acquainted with the prevalence of their Opinions, but gave too much Consequence and Weight to casual Communications with Individuals and by dwelling with particular Energy on them Sunk the Importance of the Resolutions.
>
> ...You have admitted, that we sought not to involve You in Difficulties, we meddled not with Political investigations: we did not Require your Vote, nor ask You to give any strength to our Resolutions, but what your Situation as our local Member demanded; but that our Sentiments should have been stood simply, with all their inherent Evidence we think we had a Title to expect.[85]

Windham had sought out the views of his constituents, views which coincided with those of his Whig colleagues who also opposed the Treaty. If they represented only those of a small portion of the community, Windham was careful to note that his sources were 'distinguished as much as any men could be for their Abilities, Information, and Judgement'.

Norwich merchants and manufacturers complained of Windham's presumption in taking their good will for granted in the face of their complaints while devoting his time to Burke's crusade against Warren Hastings and other matters. In February and March 1786 he was preoccupied with preparing speeches on India and Ordnance issues.[86] Though legitimate matters they had little to do with Norwich. His diary indicated that on 2 July he was 'obliged to go to meeting about wool at Crown & Anchor', because the wool manufacturers of Norwich and the southwest were in the process of preparing a bill to prevent the smuggling of fleeces, which his compatriot Harbord introduced on 19 June.[87]

Still, Windham had 'focused all his attention' on questions relating to the Hastings case, reading the charges against him with an eye to selecting the one that he could move when it came time to bring forward the impeachment. It was not until 4 April that he formally moved his charge after devoting ten days to its preparation.[88] Nor did the 1787 contretemps with his constituents significantly alter his focus during the last years of the 1784 Parliament. Having impeached Hastings, he joined Burke and the others in conducting the trial. When he spoke in the House, it was on a range of minor measures, including a measure to prevent robbery of gardens[89] or moving to revive an inquiry regarding the export of corn.[90] In 1790 he managed to follow the progress of a succession of wool bills.[91]

---

[85] BL, Add, MS 37873, ff. 140-2, Windham Papers, Partridge to Windham, 20 Mar. 1787.
[86] *Windham Diary*, pp. 73-7.
[87] *Windham Diary*, p. 78; BL, Add. MS 51710, ff. 38-9.
[88] *Windham Diary*, pp. 101-2, 104-5.
[89] *PH*, xxvii, c. 143.
[90] Windham noted in his diary he had 'received hand bills relating to what I had said about the exportation of Corn'. BL, Add. MS 51710, Holland House Papers, f. 73.
[91] *Windham Diary*, pp. 102, 104-5, 108-9, 111, 136, 163, 174, 193-4.

Moreover, his views on issues of importance to his numerous Nonconformist constituents were what John Phillips described as 'variable and sometimes paradoxical'.[92] An example of this occurred during the debate on Henry Beaufoy's motion to repeal the Test and Corporation Acts in May 1787. Charles Fox had said 'that it would not be proper to exclude men from a participation of power on account of his religion'. Windham responded that 'he thought that this exclusion was not to be considered as a punishment, but as the noble lord [Lord North] had termed it, as an act of self-defence'. He voted against the motion. Yet, in 1789 he reversed himself and voted for a motion to repeal the Test Act.[93] While sitting for a borough whose electors had in 1785 expressed a preference for a return to triennial Parliaments,[94] Windham on 4 March 1789 opposed Henry Flood's motion for Parliamentary reform.[95]

These votes, among others, highlight the fact that by the end of the 1780s Windham was at odds with his constituents on several important political issues.[96] Though he was returned in 1790 at Norwich's quietest election in years, his re-election was due, according to Phillips, in part to the understandable confusion among the electors regarding Windham's views.

That confusion did not last long. As the French Revolution became more violent and radical, Windham's opposition to reform became emphatic, as he explained in a long letter to John Gurney, a Norwich constituent. The occasion for the letter was to explain his conduct during the debate on Charles Grey's motion for reform on 26 April, 1792. Windham rejected the insinuation that he would oppose any motion for Parliamentary reform. The reason for his intense opposition in this instance was that he anticipated the commencement of civil unrest:

> My own serious opinion is that unless men of all descriptions unite to say they will not ..., consent to change the state of things which has produced, and is still producing, a degree of happiness, security and liberty unknown hitherto in the world, we shall, before we are aware of it, be involved in all the horrors of civil confusion. If we are, it will be an example of human folly and madness, such as the world has never yet exhibited.[97]

IV: Conclusion

The three men discussed here were in different ways significant figures in late eighteenth-century England, but among the three only Sir Roger Newdigate made an

---

[92] John Phillips, *Electoral Behavior in Unreformed England: Plumpers, Splitters, and Straights* (Princeton, NJ, 1982), p. 297.
[93] PH, xxviii, c. 40; HPC, 1754–1790, iii, 650.
[94] CJ, xl, 747.
[95] PH, xxviii, 465–6.
[96] For the political attitudes of the late eighteenth-century Norwich electorate, see Kathleen Wilson, *The Sense of the People*, pp. 424, 432; and Phillips, *Electoral Behavior*, pp. 291–305.
[97] *Correspondence of Edmund Burke and William Windham with Illustrative Letters in the Windham Papers in the British Museum*, ed. J.B. Gilson (Roxburghe Club, Cambridge, 1910), pp. 29.

impact as a legislator. A lack of substantial income forced William Blackstone to enter the service of the Earls of Abingdon as their steward and political manager. Once in Parliament, he threw himself into the committee work of the House, where he established his mastery of the detailed business of legislation. Yet aside from his legislative efforts on behalf of the Berties, including the Swinford Bridge and the Botley causeway, measures undertaken to improve the fragile the financial position of the Bertie family, he achieved little as an MP. His legal reforms while potentially useful were thwarted by the Lords and his major prison reform came after he became a judge. It was the acclaim that accompanied the *Commentaries* and his loyalty to the governments of the day that secured him a seat on the court of common pleas.

Ideological considerations had a vital part in shaping the legislative involvement of Sir Roger Newdigate and William Windham. Newdigate was uncompromising on questions relating to the supremacy of the Church of England and to Oxford University. William Windham, though waffling curiously on issues such as the repeal of the Test and Corporations Acts, delivered speeches against political reform in 1785 and 1792 that were consonant with his growing attachment to Burke and his principles. In neither instance, however, do these ideological positions represent the sum total of the legislative participation of these two members.

Instead Windham and Sir Roger represent an interesting contrast as members for their constituencies. Sir Roger was an ideal member for Oxford University. He had, according to L.G. Mitchell, a 'monumental integrity' which appealed to the University and not just because he espoused its views on subscription and the other controversial questions that came before the House during the 1770s.[98] In several instances where the University seemed unsure or even wavered in the face of attacks on points that were dear to the Church and the University, Sir Roger took the strong line and gave direction to his hesitant constituents. As demonstrated, he was a tireless promoter of the University's improvement, as seen in his work on enclosure and canal bills that had an impact on it and played a pivotal part in guiding the Oxford Improvement Bill to enactment. In these last endeavours he revealed himself to be an adept negotiator, who pacified opponents so as to assure the passage of contested legislation sought by the town and the university. He had a keen sense of when not to press opponents and when to make the deal that accommodated the needs of the other side. He was also attentive to his own affairs, but never, apparently, at the expense of the University's needs. In all his work for Oxford, Newdigate displayed a mastery of the legislative process and procedure which stood him in good stead both in the serving the University and in pursuing his personal and political goals.

By contrast, Windham was a raw, sometimes lazy legislator with few settled principles at least until the end of the 1784 Parliament. He had a rather shaky relationship with his constituents who were moving ideologically, according to Phillips, in a direction that was increasingly incompatible with his Burkean ideas. Windham attended to some of the concerns of his constituents, especially their desire to prevent the export or smuggling of wool, but in this respect, he played a secondary role in

---

[98] L.G. Mitchell, 'Politics and revolution, 1772–1800', pp. 163–4.

comparison to his colleague, Harbord, who did most of the work on the issue. His diaries and speeches in the House testify to his preoccupation with the impeachment and later the trial of Warren Hastings and his somewhat flippant and intermittent attention to Norwich's business. He was not the author nor was he a prime mover of legislation of interest to Norwich. He might comment upon it, and if it was of interest to Norwich make an appearance, sometimes in support of the business but usually as a spectator. As is clear from his diaries, Windham's priority was to make a name for himself in the Commons' debates as a spokesman on behalf of Whig causes, especially those espoused by Burke rather than as an advocate for the needs and interests of his Norwich constituents.

5

Thomas Gilbert:[1] Legislator *Par Excellence*

Thomas Gilbert deserves a chapter to himself because of the range and importance of his extra-Parliamentary career and the mark he made as a legislator. He was acknowledged by his fellow MPs and later historians to be the leading authority on the poor law, for which he initiated a series of measures, including his Relief of the Poor Act of 1782 (22 Geo. III, c. 83). The list of acts I identified that he introduced during his 31-year tenure, though incomplete, testifies to the range of his legislative interests and to the extent and breadth of the reforms he initiated.[2]

Though Gilbert was a prolific author of pamphlets and spoke in the House on issues in which he was interested, he was a private man who revealed little of himself. His correspondence with his principal associates, including Earl Gower,[3] the 3rd Duke of Bridgewater,[4] Matthew Boulton, and his brother, John, insofar as it exists, focuses on the business at hand. Unlike most assessments of Gilbert, this chapter provides an overview of his work in order to show how his record as the agent for two aristocratic estates, a creator of his own businesses and a pioneer of canal transportation shaped his legislative career.

It is possible to lay out a fairly full picture of what Gilbert accomplished during his 31 years in the House. His legislative work was shaped by his legal background, the experience he derived from his work as agent for Gower and Bridgewater and from the business enterprises he launched with his brother. The political experience he gained in the house was also crucial, as were his wide-ranging connections among magistrates and poor law reformers throughout the country. These motivated him to undertake the range of reforms he initiated during his Parliamentary career and also shaped the manner in which he undertook those efforts. In addition to his poor law reforms, they included attempts to standardise and sort out the body of turnpike and

---

[1] Thomas Gilbert (1719?-98), MP, Newcastle-under-Lyme, 1763-8 and Lichfield, 1768-94; Inner Temple, 1740; called to the bar, 1744; paymaster of the charity for the relief of widows of naval officers, 1753-98; Comptroller of the Great Wardrobe, 1763-1782; Chairman of Ways and Means, 1784-94.
[2] The list is appended to this chapter.
[3] Granville Leveson-Gower (1721-1803), Visct. Trentham, MP, Bishop's Castle, 1744-7, Westminster, 1747-54 and Lichfield, 1754; succ. as 2nd Earl Gower, 1754; Master of Horse, 1757-60; Master of Great Wardrobe, 1760-3; Lord Chamberlain, 1763-5; Lord President of the Council, 1767-79, 1783-4; Lord Privy Seal, 1784-94; cr. Marquess of Stafford, 1786.
[4] Francis Egerton, (1736-1803); succ. as 3rd Duke of Bridgewater, 1748.

highway legislation, legislation to provide low-interest loans for the construction of housing for poor curates, a proposal to impose a tax on the income of officials and placemen as a means of restoring financial order to the nation, and plans for the reform of the court of George III that were never implemented. I rely upon Gilbert's own words in an attempt at the end of the chapter to identify the motivations that linked his wide-ranging endeavours and sustained his reforming energies over 31 years in the Commons.

Gilbert was a man of his age – an empiricist who believed that good legislation should be founded on data relevant to the question. In 1775 a committee he chaired recommended that to determine which buildings of existing poor law authorities would be best suited for his proposed houses of industry and workhouses, the Commons should call for returns throughout the country of the nature of poor law buildings, the use of their apartments and other details, 'with many other particulars respecting the maintenance, and employment of the poor'. From these returns, Gilbert declared 'it is expected great improvements may be made, and a more perfect system formed, from the experience of those houses'.[5]

He was impatient with arguments based on tradition, especially when the traditions cited were invalidated by experience and evidence. Though he joined Earl Gower in supporting most of the governments of the day, Gilbert was a reformer who on occasion could be independent in his critiques, even of administrations in which Gower held office. He believed in progress and that good legislation could improve the lot of the country's poor, the operation of George III's household, the nation's system of road and canal transport and, as the result of the licensing of dogs and the restriction of alehouses, England's public health.

According to the *Staffordshire Advertiser* Gilbert 'never made any very conspicuous figure, either in the courts at Westminster, or on circuit'.[6] Instead, he made use of his father's connections to the Leveson-Gower family and became the election advisor to the 2nd Earl Gower. To reduce their burden of election expenses, Gower, on Gilbert's advice, invested a huge sum to purchase burgage properties at Lichfield during the 1750s. These investments established the Leveson-Gower hold on one seat there until 1821.[7] Because of this work he was elevated in 1758 to the position of steward of the family's estates with a salary of £300 a year, a position he retained until 1788. At about the same time he became the general agent to Gower's brother-in-law, the Duke of Bridgewater, the famous canal Duke, for whom Gilbert's brother John[8] already served as estate agent. Eric Richards describes Gower 'as an aristocrat/industrialist *par excellence*', but adds that the Gilbert brothers were the ones who organised the large

---

[5] *Observations upon the Orders and Resolutions of the House of Commons with Respect to the Poor, Vagrants, and Houses of Correction* (1775), pp. 30–1. The House declined to undertake these surveys.
[6] *Staffordshire Advertiser*, 12 Jan. 1799.
[7] J.R. Wordie, *Estate Management in Eighteenth-Century England* (1982), pp. 239–46; Peter Lead, *Agents of Revolution: John and Thomas Gilbert – Entrepreneurs* (Stoke-on-Trent, 1989), pp. 31–3.
[8] John Gilbert (1724–95) apprenticed to Matthew Boulton, father of the engineer; recommended building a canal to drain Bridgewater's mines and transport their coal; later appointed Bridgewater's agent and engineer; worked with James Brindley to design and build the Bridgewater canal; manager of the Duke's Lancashire mines and industrial enterprises.

capitalist enterprises on his estates.⁹ Gower provided the capital for the development of his properties, while Thomas and John oversaw the exploitation of the mineral resources. In 1764, for example, the Earl leased the operations of his Lilleshall estate to the brothers, reserving one half of the profits to himself and retaining a 50 per cent stake in what became Earl Gower and Company,¹⁰ with the remaining shares divided between Thomas and John Gilbert. The brothers' most important achievement, according to Peter Lead, was to convert Gower and Bridgewater to the idea that canals were a practical mode of transportation.¹¹ Their pivotal decision at Lilleshall was to build the Donnington Wood Canal connecting the Earl's coal mines and lime quarries to the Wolverhampton-Newport turnpike. One immediate consequence of the canal's construction was that Richard Reynolds,¹² the Coalbrookdale ironmaster, erected an iron furnace near the canal on the Earl's estate, resulting in greater demand for the estate's raw materials.¹³ Under the brothers' management rents on the Lilleshall estates increased by 31 per cent between 1758 and 1788.¹⁴

Even as they managed Earl Gower and Company, the brothers developed their late father's interests in North Staffordshire collieries, lime quarries and copper mines, and on Bridgewater's mines at Ecton and the Woodhead seam near Cheadle. In 1760 they leased a smelting mill from the Earl of Shrewsbury before forming a partnership in 1762 that included the Duke of Devonshire¹⁵ and others in the area. This partnership was the work of Thomas who was, according to B.L. Anderson, 'a money scrivening attorney, characterised as much by his familiarity with business practice and local affairs as by his knowledge of the law'.¹⁶

Thomas entered the service of the 3rd Duke of Bridgewater in 1753 and became his factor in 1758. According to the Duke's biographer, Gilbert, with the exception of Gower, 'had more influence over Bridgewater than any other man'.¹⁷ He encouraged the development of the Duke's canal, mining and industrial enterprises, served as his principal financial legal advisor and as well as his auditor. He drafted the Duke's canal bills and had oversight of John Gilbert's work on the canal system in addition to serving in effect as Parliamentary solicitor for the Duke's first two canal bills. According to

---

9   Eric Richards, 'The industrial face of a great estate: Trentham and Lilleshall, 1780-1840', *EcHR*, xxvii (1974), 415.
10 Wordie, *Estate Management*, 113. Renamed Marquess of Stafford and Company in 1786 when Gower received an advance in the peerage.
11 Lead, *Agents of Revolution*, pp. 53-7, 65-8.
12 Richard Reynolds (1735-1816), iron master, promoter of the Shropshire canal and Quaker philanthropist.
13 Lead, *Agents of Revolution*, pp. 47-8, 115-17.
14 These comparatively modest gains (on Gower's Trentham estate they rose by 95 per cent during the same period) were due to the fact that so much of the Lilleshall estate was leased rather than rack rented. Wordie, 'Estate management' pp. 50-1.
15 William Cavendish, 4th Duke of Devonshire (c. 1720-64), MP, Derbyshire, 1741-5.; Master of the Horse, 1751-5; Ld. Treasurer (I), 1754-5, 1761-3; Ld. Lt. (I) 1755-6; Ld. Lt., Derbyshire, 1756-64; First Lord of the Treasury, Nov. 1756-July 1757; Ld. Chamberlain, 1757-62.
16 B.L. Anderson, 'The attorney and the early capital market in Lancashire', in *Capital Formation in the Industrial Revolution*, ed. Francois Crouzet (1972), p. 228.
17 Hugh Malet, *Bridgewater, the Canal Duke, 1736-1803* (Manchester, 1977), p. 35.

Lead he also took the lead in obtaining the Duke's early canal acts before he entered Parliament.[18] Together with his brother, he was responsible for recruiting James Brindley[19] to work for Bridgewater.

As he entered the House, Gilbert had mastered the intricacies and procedures of canal legislation and was a leading proponent of their benefits as a means of promoting commerce and economic development throughout Britain. He took a lead in carrying the major canal projects of the 1760s, including the Trent and Mersey Canal Bill, which ultimately linked London to Hull via Birmingham and the potteries, Liverpool and Leeds.

The impetus behind that project came from Josiah Wedgewood and his fellow potters who saw it as a means of distributing their fragile products at reduced costs. According to Malet the Egerton-Gower connection was planning a similar project before Wedgwood took up with his plan, and it was Thomas Gilbert who convinced Bridgewater of the advantages of joining his canal to the Trent and Mersey at Runcorn in Cheshire.

While Wedgwood recognised that he and his allies needed the political weight of the Gower and Bridgewater interests to carry the necessary legislation through Parliament, he was wary of allowing them control of the project and was initially suspicious of Gilbert.[20] Eventually Gower stepped in, acknowledged Wedgwood's concerns and promoted a partnership.[21] Thereafter Wedgwood and Gilbert worked together to assure that the necessary legislation secured Parliament's sanction. Key to their partnership was their mutual recognition of the need to build public support for the project. This recognition led to the preparation of a case statement to distribute to the public and members of each House. Wedgwood enlisted his associate James Bentley to draw up the case for the proposed canal in a pamphlet, the first edition of which appeared in 1765.[22] Wedgwood soon saw the need for a second edition with wider distribution than the first. Gilbert, in turn, pressed Wedgwood to have the pamphlet sent to his house as soon as possible as he had a gentleman 'who is exceedingly clever in these matters'.

Late in 1765 when Wedgwood moved for a mobilisation of the forces supporting the canal to counteract a mounting opposition, Gower hesitated to appear at an upcoming Staffordshire meeting. Gilbert convinced the Earl to attend and the meeting was successful in rallying Staffordshire's gentlemen behind the proposal. Gilbert chaired the bill's second reading committee, delivered its report and carried the

---

[18] Lead, *Agents of Revolution*, p. 85.
[19] James Brindley (1716–62), pioneering engineer of English canal construction; the Duke of Bridgewater appointed him as consulting engineer for a canal linking the coal mines at Worsley to Manchester, 1759; the canal was notable for its tunnelling and an aqueduct over the River Irwell; he also oversaw the construction of England's Grand Trunk System in the 1760s and 1770s, including the Trent and Mersey, the Staffordshire and Worcestershire, the Coventry and Oxford canals, which ultimately linked London to Liverpool and Hull and ultimately to Birmingham and Bristol.
[20] Malet, *Bridgewater*, p.107; *Letters of Josiah Wedgwood*, ed. Katherine Eufemia, Lady Farrer, (3 vols, Manchester, 1903–6), i, pp. 19–23, 40–3; Lead, *Agents of Revolution*, pp. 72–8.
[21] *Wedgwood Letters*, i, 19–23.
[22] Thomas Bentley, *A View of the Advantages of Inland Navigations: With a Plan of a Navigable Canal for a Communication between the Ports of Liverpool and Hull* (1765).

amended measure to the House of Lords where Bridgewater undertook its management. Despite strong opposition, the bill eventually received Parliament's sanction on 14 May 1766 (6 George III, c. 96).[23] In the wake of the measure's passage, Gilbert, who owned ten shares in the new company, became its chairman, a post he retained until disputes with the Wedgwood faction led to his resignation in 1785.[24]

Following the passage of the Trent and Mersey Bill Gilbert assumed a commanding position on canal business in the House. He provided important assistance to a number of canal promoters, including those behind the proposed Birmingham Canal. The canal committee's notes indicate that Matthew Boulton along with the company's counsel met Gilbert at Lichfield late in 1768. During the meeting Gilbert 'offered his services to the committee to consider and settle a petition to be sent to him by the Committee'.[25] That support resulted in the committee thanking Gilbert 'for the extraordinary Service he has rendered us in the Bill in general, but particularly in obtaining a reduction of the Warfage'. Minutes of a meeting of 3 February 1769 further noted that Gilbert had 'offered his services to the proprietors to consider and settle a Petition to be sent up to him by the Committee [of proprietors]'. The committee, having considered two rough drafts of the petition, then:

> Resolved that both such Drafts be sent up to Mr White, Clerk in parliament with whom Mr Gilbert undertook to settle and adjust the same, outlining the particular reasons contain'd in the matters of such petition, and requesting the favour that Mr Gilbert will assist Mr White in settling the same and return it to the Committee as early as possible.[26]

When they had obtained their Act, the proprietors resolved that 'Letters of thanks be transmitted from the Committee to Lord Beauchamp, Mr. Gilbert, and Lord Dartmouth[27] for their assistance in conducting our amended bill through both Houses of Parliament'.

I: Early General Reforms

In his roles as steward to Gower and Bridgewater, Gilbert had also been involved in the promotion of turnpikes. Indeed, the author of his obituary in the *Staffordshire Advertiser* noted that Gilbert:

---

[23] *CJ*, xxx, 521, 645.
[24] Lead, *Agents of Revolution*, pp. 7-81. Lead claims it was because of 'the growing significance of canal projects during the 1760s that Thomas Gilbert was brought into Parliament by the Leveson-Gower interest' (p. 85). Gilbert subsequently served as the chair of the Caldon Canal Company, built by the Trent and Mersey Co. in 1778, and also chaired the Shropshire Canal Company once its act was passed in 1788.
[25] TNA, Birmingham Canal Minute Book, RAIL 810/1, f. 66, special meeting of the committee, 16 Jan. 1769.
[26] TNA, Birmingham Canal Minute Book, RAIL 810/1, ff. 16, 66.
[27] William Legge (1731-1801), succ. grandfather as 2nd Earl of Dartmouth, 1750; First Ld. of Trade, 1765-6, 1772-5; Sec. of State, Colonies, 1772-5; Lord Privy Seal, 1775-82; Lord Steward, 1783.

zealously applied himself to the amendment of the roads, and although he did not succeed in his original plan of procuring a general Act for their improvement yet he carried through the House many provincial bills which tended to make travelling in the counties of Northampton, Warwick, Stafford and Derby, the places to which he particularly directed his attention, infinitely more commodious and agreeable: indeed it is well known, that before his time, the highways were the worst in the Kingdom.[28]

Gilbert's early experience in coping with road and turnpike bills and his impatience with the confusion that resulted from what the Webbs described as an intolerable 'chaos of statutes'[29] relating to this branch of legislation led him and a group of like-minded MPs to try to sort out the mess. The result was an act that came less than three years after Gilbert entered Parliament. The Highways Turnpike Roads Act of 1766 (6 Geo. III, c.43), dismissed by the Webbs as 'an unsatisfactory essay', was followed shortly by the General Turnpike Act (13 Geo. III, c. 84) and the accompanying Highways Act (13 Geo. III, c. 78) of 1773. The Turnpike Act consolidated earlier measures, placing trusts under sessional control. It tried to make the statute force more equitable, ventured into the contentious issue of regulating the weight of vehicles and width of wheels as a means of preserving the roads, and provided standard clauses for future highway and turnpike bills, ensuring some degree of standardisation. The law, however, was widely condemned because of its complexity and ambiguity.[30]

If the 1773 Turnpike Bill failed to eliminate the chaos that had enveloped eighteenth-century turnpike administration, it testified to Gilbert's willingness, even as a raw member, to streamline this branch of the legislation as a means of making future measures easier to obtain and administer. He told the House on introducing his motion to bring in his turnpike bill that though immense sums were collected annually to keep the roads in repair, 'many were notoriously, & shamefully neglected'.[31] Complaints of this sort came up again and again as Gilbert moved for reform not just of the poor laws but other areas as well.

Gilbert introduced a number of bills that had no apparent connection to his work as an estate agent. The legislation is interesting for its range and for the variety of partnerships he formed in pursuing this legislation. Most of the business was of limited significance, and relatively little in the end reached the statute book or achieved the ends he desired if it did. Still, the work attests to his willingness to serve a variety of causes, even those opposed by his patrons and employers.

---

[28] *Staffordshire Advertiser*, 12 Jan. 1799.
[29] Sidney and Beatrice Webb, *English Local Government. Vol. 5: The Story of The King's Highway* (Hamden, CT, 1963), p. 121.
[30] Sidney and Beatrice Webb, *The King's Highway*, pp. 121–2; William T. Jackman, *The Development of Transportation in Modern England* (1962), pp. 220–3; Eric Pawson, *Transport and Economy: The Turnpike Roads of Eighteenth-Century Britain* (London, New York and San Francisco, 1977), pp. 74–5; Langford, *Public Life*, p. 163.
[31] As an example, he cited the case of an act that authorised tolls amounting to £2500 a year; 'yet the roads which brought this annual receipt were scarcely passable'. *Bath Chronicle and Weekly Gazette*, 4 Mar. 1773.

In 1772 Gilbert undertook the management of the Quaker Tithes Bill, according to Professor G.M. Ditchfield at the request of the Quaker Meeting of Sufferings. The measure would have restrained tithe owners from proceeding at law for remedies against Quakers for recovery of tithes below £10.[32] It received its first and second readings, but in its second reading committee, which Gilbert chaired, amendments were added that were unacceptable to the sponsors. As a result, they advised Gilbert to withdraw the bill, which he did on 24 May.[33] The principal reason for its failure was that leaders of the established church recognised that measures of the sort Gilbert was promoting posed a threat to ecclesiastical property and the status of church courts, which were already under attack.[34]

Gilbert subsequently revealed that he believed in the importance of religion as a foundation for social stability and good conduct. Among bills that spoke to that conviction were the Residence House Acts (17 George III, c. 52 and 21 George III c. 66) which promoted the residence of poor curates by enabling incumbents of small livings to secure loans from Queen Anne's Bounty at low rates of interest for the construction of glebe houses. Under the act, the Bounty could loan up to £100 to livings under £50 a year interest free. In fact, the Bounty's board made no loans until after 1810 when it undertook an extensive programme based on Gilbert's Act. By 1826 it had loaned over £224,525.[35] The 1781 act was merely an amending act. Neither its timing nor that of the first bill was coincidental, for in 1781 Gilbert introduced the first version of his most famous poor law reform which reached the statute book the following year.

The likely connection between the poor law reforms and Residence House Acts was that Gilbert was eager to install educated clergy in the parishes where they might fill positions of leadership in his new scheme in place of existing overseers of the poor for whom he and others had a low opinion. He must have hoped that a resident clergy, in proximity to struggling parishioners, would fill the voids in poor law leadership.

II: Political and Court Reforms

After his patron Earl Gower took office in 1767, Thomas Gilbert supported the governments of which the Earl was a part, but there is little evidence that he participated in political debates. Nevertheless, on 23 Feb. 1778, he informed the House:

> that the affairs of the public were greatly neglected, and that, a committee should be appointed to enquire into the expenditure of public money particularly into the exorbitant contracts and abuses of office, and the exorbitancy of office fees; he

---

[32] The text of the bill is printed in *Commons Sessional Papers*, xxii, 365–9.
[33] *CJ*, xxxiii, 727.
[34] This paragraph is based on conversations with Professor Ditchfield and his 'Parliament, the Quakers and the tithe question, 1750–1835', *Parl. Hist.*, iv (1985), 90.
[35] This discussion is based on G.F.A Best, *Temporal Pillars: Queen Anne's Bounty, The Ecclesiastical Commissioners and the Church of England* (Cambridge, 1964), pp. 204, 217.

declared his resolution, to propose a tax on one-fourth upon the incomes of all placemen.³⁶

On 9 March Gilbert moved his tax, excepting only the Speaker, some judges, along with foreign ministers, officers in the army and navy, and those whose salary was not more than £200 a year. His proposal was carried in the committee of supply by a vote of 100–82, but the North administration rallied its forces and narrowly overturned Gilbert's proposal by a vote of 147–141 when the committee made its report.³⁷ According to Horace Walpole, Gower and Bridgewater went to great lengths to persuade Gilbert not to introduce his motion, but he told them he would be uneasy if he did not propose it.³⁸

Protests of this sort were a recurrent part of Gilbert's conduct. He moved the reform of the highway and turnpike legislation because so much of the country's wealth was being squandered on wasteful, ill-managed projects. Similar motives led him to undertake revisions of the nation's poor laws and his attempts to reform George III's Household. Gilbert repeatedly proclaimed his abhorrence of waste and the burden it placed both upon England's taxpayers and its poor.

For several months in 1782–3 Thomas Gilbert joined with Lord Shelburne³⁹ in an effort to reform the royal household. Gilbert had opposed Edmund Burke's initial efforts to enact Parliamentary regulations affecting the household because he and other MPs were reluctant to impose such measures upon their sovereign. According to one of Shelburne's biographers, Gilbert was chosen for the task, partly because he had led the opposition to Burke's plan and partly because he had drawn up his own outline of household reforms while holding the post of Comptroller of Accounts to the Treasurer of the Chamber. Shelburne was also eager to enlist the support of Earl Gower for his new administration.⁴⁰

Gilbert's task was to prepare plans for the different branches of the Household, and draw up lists of people who would lose their offices and their compensation. He went about his work with gusto, searching for offices that might be eliminated,⁴¹ and drafting 'his Majesty's instructions for the Great Offices of his Household which are essentially necessary'.⁴² Gilbert's background in managing the businesses of Gower and

---

[36] PH, xix, 803.
[37] PH, xix, 873.
[38] Horace Walpole, *Memoirs of the Reign of George III*, ed. Derek Jarrett (4 vols, New Haven, CT, and London, 2000), i, 129–30.
[39] William Petty-Fitzmaurice (1737–1805), Visct. Fitzmaurice, army, Maj.-Gen. 1765, Lt.-Gen. 1772, Gen. 1783; MP, Chipping Wycombe, 1760–1; succ. fa. as 2nd Earl of Shelburne [I] and Baron Wycombe [GB], 1761; First Ld. of Trade, 1763; Sec. of State, South, 1766–1768; Home Sec. Mar.–July, 1782; First Ld. of Treasury, July 1782–Apr. 1783; cr. Marquess of Landowne, 1784.
[40] John Norris, *Shelburne and Reform* (London and New York, 1963), p. 179.
[41] Gilbert, for example, discovered that Henry Fane held the office of Surveyor of the King's Roads, one 'of very little Duty' for which he received £918 a year. He recommended the immediate abolition of the post. BL, Bowood MS, Add. 88906, f. 107, Gilbert to Shelburne, 6 Sept, 1782. Fane was a son of the 8th Earl of Westmorland and MP for Lyme Regis from 1772–1802; Earl A. Reitan, *Politics, Finance and the People: Economical Reform in England in the Age of the American Revolution, 1770–92* (Basingstoke, 2007), p. 117.
[42] BL, Bowood MS, Add. MS, 88906, f. 111, Gilbert to Shelburne, 15 Dec. 1782.

Bridgewater may have led him to conclude that if economies were to be achieved, accounts would have to be submitted to a new officer – the Superintendent of the Household and Paymaster of the Civil List – who would oversee contracts and supervise clerks in each department. This proposal provoked outraged responses from the Lord Carlisle, the Lord Steward and the Duke of Manchester,[43] the Lord Chamberlain. Gilbert informed Shelburne after his meeting with Manchester that the Duke:

> did not at all relish the Idea of having any person to superintend, or inspect the business of his Office; … He said the Lord Steward and he had confer'd upon it, and were of the same opinion with respect to that matter.
>
> I mentioned to him the great abuses and impositions which had prevailed in his Office, from the want of regular inspection, that the great object of these instructions was to correct them; he objected to several parts which he thought curtailed his power, and would lessen the dignity of his Office. I told him all those things were intended to be fully examined and considered.[44]

Gilbert's plan was presented in March 1783 after Shelburne had resigned. He recommended the abolition of all sinecure posts with the Treasury providing compensation for their occupants. In addition, he proposed that the sale of offices be abolished and offered detailed plans for the principal departments of the Household, along with lists of those who would be dismissed and details of their compensation. He recommended the appointment of a new official, a paymaster of the household, to have the authority to examine contracts for goods and work and who would pay the salaries and charges of court offices.[45] Gilbert's labours, however, failed to produce the desired reforms. He and Shelburne were attacked for penalising occupants of minor court posts while failing to check the main sources of influence, which was not their objective. Horace Walpole, a potential victim of Gilbert's pursuit of sinecures liable for elimination, complained that Shelburne set Gilbert to the task of eliminating sinecure positions which he did with great 'brutality'.[46]

The episode is emblematic of Gilbert's approach to public issues where he perceived inefficiency and the waste of public monies. It reveals his impatience to get on with the task, his tendency to be abrupt, even with the high and mighty, his mastery of detail and the fact that no item was too minor for his consideration. Because of the need for economy, he even asked Matthew Boulton to recommend a 'few good hands' capable of 'cleaning and repairing Lock keys', adding that 'the successful candidates would be employ'd constantly at a fix'd Monthly Wage'. The reason for this query was that the

---

[43] George Montague, Visct. Mandeville (1737–88), MP, Huntingdonshire, 1762; succ. father as 4th Duke of Manchester, 1762; collector of subsidies in port of London; 1762–88; Ld. of Bedchamber, 1762–70; Lord Chamberlain, 1782–83; Ambassador to France, 1783.
[44] BL, Bowood MS, Add. MS 88906, f. 114, Gilbert to Shelburne, 30 Dec. 1782.
[45] Reitan, *Politics, Finance and the People*, p. 118.
[46] Walpole, *Last Journals*, ii, 493. Walpole's father secured three sinecure posts for him. Their substantial proceeds supported him throughout his life.

king was being charged between '£4000 and £5000 in Smithy Bill[s], for cleaning & repairing Lock, Grate & such things at his several palaces'.[47] Finally, Gilbert was intrepid: he abolished the sinecure of the well-connected Henry Fane and went head to head in his battle with a Duke.

III: Poor Law Reforms

Within months of taking his seat in the Commons Gilbert was named to several select committees relating to local poor law issues. During the deliberations in one of them on the Gloucester petition the committee became involved in an extended debate over the merits of indoor and outdoor relief in which Gilbert took a peripheral part.[48]

The next year he went on to introduce the first of his major poor law bills. Its preface highlighted points that he reiterated over the next decades:

> Though we have many Laws, calculated for the Relief and Employment of the Poor; and though large Sums are annually raised for those Purposes; Yet, it is a Truth too fatally experienced, and too long lamented, that the Poor of this Kingdom, are in general greatly distressed, and frequently impelled by their Necessities to seek a present Supply in the public Streets and Highways, by means the most unjustifiable, the most fatal to themselves, and the most pernicious to Civil Society.[49]

Louise Ryland-Epton shows that in preparing 'A Scheme', Gilbert drew heavily on the ideas of established authorities and made no attempt to hide the fact that he was borrowing his points from others. Among his sources was Richard Burn, who argued for the use of hundreds, as opposed to the parish, as the basic unit for poor law administration. Other key ideas he borrowed were the restriction of the parish overseers,[50] and complaints regarding the miserable state of the poor despite the system's huge costs. Gilbert declared England's perverse settlement system, which drove the poor from their homes and forced them to wander until their only means of subsistence was begging, cried out for substantial and immediate remediation. Prior to drafting a bill, he sent copies of his pamphlet to the high sheriffs requesting that they inspect the plan during the summer and communicate it to local gentlemen,[51] a variant on a practice he was to adopt in subsequent efforts.

---

[47] Birmingham Archive, Matthew Boulton General Correspondence, 12/27 91, 12/27/99, Gilbert to Boulton, 26 Nov. 1782 and 24 Dec. 1782.

[48] The trustees of the Gloucester Workhouse petitioned for a bill to pay expenses they had incurred providing for the poor who could not be accommodated in the workhouse during the 1750s. After debate, the committee agreed that a bill should be brought in; *CJ*, xxix, 738, 850. See also Louise Ryland-Epton, 'The impact of back benchers in the creation of social reform: The indefatigable and honourable exertions of Mr Gilbert', *Parl. Hist.*, xxxix (2020), pp. 278–9.

[49] *A Scheme for the Better Relief and Employment of the Poor: Humbly Submitted to the Consideration of the Members of both Houses of Parliament. By a Member of Parliament* (1765), p. ii.

[50] Louise Ryland-Epton, 'Impact of back benchers', 279–80.

[51] Ryland-Epton, 'Impact of back benchers', 280–1.

His bill, which drew heavily on the ideas and responses of others, contained several provisions that formed a core of Gilbert's early measures. He proposed to divide each county into 'convenient Districts', because 'parochial Districts are generally too small for the Purposes of employing the Poor, and putting them under the proper regulations'.[52] The measure defined the process by which districts would identify directors,[53] who would, in turn, choose guardians to oversee the district's various institutions – hospitals for the sick, infirm and children, workhouses for those able to work, and houses of reformation for the idle, vagrants and disorderly – all to be established under the act.

Gilbert presented his bill on 1 February 1765. It had a relatively smooth passage through the lower chamber because it enjoyed the support of prominent MPs. As noted in Chapter 4, William Blackstone drafted the measure. Lord Orwell,[54] who had sponsored the Suffolk incorporation acts, was also an active supporter. On 18 March a motion to put off its third reading for three months was defeated by a vote of 155–9 with Orwell acting as teller for the majority. The measure was amended, and following its passage, Gilbert carried it to the House of Lords.[55]

On its arrival, the Earl of Egmont[56] launched fierce attacks against it at its first and second readings. He was joined by Lord Bute's associates who did their best to defeat the measure. It survived, however, thanks to the efforts of the Bedford party, including Gilbert's patron, Lord Gower. In the end, however, Gilbert's bill became a victim of the tortuous politics that convulsed the early years of George III's reign, as forces allied to the Duke of Newcastle and Lord Rockingham united with Bute's allies to defeat the measure in the upper chamber by a vote of 49 to 26.[57]

Gilbert did not make another attempt at poor law reform until 1775. In a speech in the Commons in March 1774 he reiterated the themes of 1765, namely that though immense sums were raised for the relief of the poor, they were 'in general, miserably accommodated'. He called for a committee to investigate the problems and eliminate chaos and waste.[58] Between 31 March and 3 May the committee adopted 32 resolutions, and on 24 May they were adopted by the House as the basis for new legislation and wiser, more humane poor law policy.

The plan appeared in a pamphlet published in 1775.[59] It retained the supervisory structure established in the 1765 bill. Among the new proposals was a resolution adopted

---

[52] *A Scheme*, p. 6.
[53] *A Scheme*, pp. 8–9, 11, 18.
[54] Francis Vernon, (c. 1715–83), MP, Ipswich, 1761–8; cr. Baron Orwell (I), 1762; Visct., 1776 and Earl of Shipbrook [I], 1777.
[55] *CJ*, xxx, 76, 259–60; *HPC, 1754–1790*, iii, 584.
[56] John Perceval (1710–70), 2nd Earl of Egmont (I), MP (I), 1731–43; MP, Westminster, 1741–7, Weobley, 1747–54 and Bridgwater, 1754–62; MP [I], 1731–48; cr. Baron Lovel and Holland (GB), 1762; Ld. of Bedchamber to Prince of Wales 1748–51; Jt. Postmaster Gen., 1762–3; First Ld. of Admiralty, 1763–6.
[57] Walpole, *Memoirs of George III*, ii, 101–2; *Additional Grenville Papers*, 252–3; *The Yale Edition of Horace Walpole's Correspondence*, ed. W.S. Lewis, et al. (48 vols, New Haven, CT, 1937–83), xxxviii, 528–9. Louise Ryland-Epton's corrected the division figure to 49–26, 'Impact of back benchers', p. 283 n. 51.
[58] *PH*, xviii, 541–6.
[59] Thomas Gilbert, *Observations of the Rules and Orders of the House of Commons with respect to the Poor, Vagrants and Houses of Correction* (1775).

by the committee that the Clerk of the House be ordered to secure an account of the number of parishes or districts in which a House of Industry or Workhouse had been established; money raised by parishes over the past three years to support such establishments; expenses for their buildings, and how and to what purposes their buildings were adapted; the number of poor in those facilities, in what labour they were employed and at what expense.[60] Data obtained from these surveys showing the prevalence of waste and mismanagement were supposed to have turned Gilbert against workhouses and more in favour of outdoor relief – views that formed a basis for his 1782 bill.[61]

Despite the resolutions and elaborate plans, the bill never made its way through the Commons, where members raised ancillary issues that clogged proceedings of a House already dealing with rebellious Americans. In any case, Gilbert's 1775 pamphlet engendered critical responses, and the provincial press indicated the bill had little chance of making its way through the House.[62]

In the aftermath, Joanna Innes suggests that Gilbert withdrew from the poor law debate for several years. Aside from an unsuccessful effort in 1777 to oblige the clergy and church wardens to make returns under oath of all charitable donations for the benefit of the poor, he took no steps to reform the poor laws until 1781.[63] Whether he was deterred by his failure in 1775 or by the reluctance of counties to assume additional costs during the American war is unclear.

On 22 May 1781, however, Gilbert moved to bring in a bill 'for the better relief and employment of the poor'. In effect, it was a draft for the famous 'Gilbert's Act', which finally reached the statute book in 1782. Several of the goals in 1781 coincided with those he outlined in 1775, but the measure, even more than its predecessors, was adapted 'to recurring themes in the current literature', including the more critical attitude of workhouses and overseers of the poor and an emphasis on economy.

> My Objects are to promote Industry..., to reform the dissolute, and refractory,... by a reasonable and prudent Oeconomy to guard against every Imposition and unnecessary Expence.[64]

He continued to press for more enlightened and effective poor law administration and the need to replace the existing local poor law officials.

> The Persons generally appointed to that Office (of overseer of the poor) are so unequal to the Trust. *A Great Part of the Distresses of the Poor, and the Profusion of Expence, arises from this Cause.* Some of the Parish Officers are apt to gratify themselves and their Favourites, and to neglect the more deserving Objects in the Application of the Parish Money.[65]

---

[60] Gilbert, *Observations*, pp. 6–7.
[61] A.W. Coats, 'Economic thought and poor law policy in the eighteenth century', *EcHR*, xiii (1960), 48
[62] Ryland-Epton, 'Impact of back benchers', pp. 283–4.
[63] Joanna Innes, 'Thomas Gilbert (c. 1720–98)', in *The Biographical Dictionary of British Economists*, ed. Donald Rutherford and Warren Samuels (2 vols, London, 2004), i, 1246–9.
[64] Gilbert, *A Plan for the Better Relief and Employment of the Poor*, p. 2.
[65] Gilbert, *Plan for the Better Relief and Employment of the Poor*, p. 9.

By 1781 Gilbert, like Burn, Blackstone and John Howard, had grown sceptical of the efficacy of the workhouse. 'For want of proper governors, suitable employment and good order, [they] frequently become odious to the poor People'. Instead, he proposed to restrict access to them to the 'vulnerable poor', the aged and infirm and young children. Able-bodied adults would be provided employment and, if employment was unavailable, they would receive outdoor relief. If an able-bodied labourer was temporarily unable to work, he and his family would be admitted on a short-term basis to a workhouse.[66]

The most familiar provision in Gilbert's Act permitted parishes to join together to establish a workhouse. Unions were not new. Local acts of Parliament had already established a number of them. Steven King notes, however, that Gilbert's act was the first to depart from the original poor law's dictate of 'local poverty – local relief' because it permitted that relief to extend beyond the boundaries of one parish.[67] It was also an example of permissive or enabling legislation in that it empowered local authorities to unite at their own initiative, without having to apply to Parliament to do so.

The fact that Gilbert waited until late May to introduce his bill highlights a distinctive aspect of his legislative practice. Gilbert's process was, as Joanna Innes has noted, consultative, or, as Ryland-Epton describes it, adaptive. He submitted his bills to the House in the late spring after responding to the ideas of a range of authorities, and carried the measures through two readings and their second reading committees where they were amended. After the committee reported the bills, if they reached that stage, they were printed. At this point Gilbert distributed them throughout the country to magistrates to review at Quarter Sessions or other meetings, and also to a range of philanthropists and other authorities. He sought their comments and corrections to incorporate in his bills before resubmitting them at the opening of the subsequent session. Thus, Gilbert's legislation reflected the views not only of his fellow MPs but tapped into the expertise of county magistrates and a host of other authorities. His tactics were later adopted by Jonas Hanway and other social reformers.[68]

Gilbert moved for leave to bring in what became 22 Geo III, c. 83 on 22 May, 1781 and presented the measure the next day. During the period the bill was under consideration in the House, Ryland-Epton shows, in the most original portion of her article, Gilbert mounted a national press campaign as part of his effort to secure its enactment. To this end, he published a supplement to his 1781 pamphlet, *A Plan for the Better Relief and Employment of the Poor*, which was widely advertised in the national and provincial press. As the debate continued, Gilbert amended his bill in response to objections as they arose.[69] The bill was reported from its second reading committee with amendments in late May, and the House ordered that the bill with amendments be printed with as many copies 'as shall be sufficient for the use of the Members of the

---

[66] *A Plan of Police*, p. 15.
[67] Steven King, *Poverty and Welfare in England, 1700–1850* (Manchester, 2000), p. 25.
[68] Joanna Innes, 'Parliament and the shaping of English social policy in the eighteenth century', *TRHS*, 5th ser., xl (1990), 88–9; Sarah Lloyd, *Charity and Poverty in England, c. 1680–1820: Wild and Visionary Schemes* (Manchester and New York, 2009), p. 157.
[69] Ryland-Epton, 'Impact of back benchers', pp. 284–6.

House'. In the interim, as was Gilbert's practice, the measure was distributed to magistrates and other local officials and an array of philanthropists. On 14 December 1781 the Commons gave leave to bring in two bills, the first for the relief and employment of the poor, which Gilbert presented on 17 December, and the second for leave to bring in a 'bill for amending and rendering more effectual the several laws in being relative to rogues, vagabonds, beggars and other disorderly persons', which Gilbert presented the same day. Both measures incorporated corrections and criticisms of those who had commented on Gilbert's distributed bill.[70]

The proceedings became complicated as Britain faced the loss of America and the collapse of the North administration. Amidst this confusion, Gilbert composed one last pamphlet,[71] that reflected another updating of his plan and a final appeal to public opinion. After a struggle with the Speaker over whether further amendments would be permitted, Gilbert's much amended bill received its third reading on 10 June and eventually the royal assent.

The Webbs called the 1782 Act 'the most carefully devised, the most elaborate and perhaps the most influential, for both good and evil, of ... poor law statutes between 1060 and 1834'. Paul Slack maintained that it was 'the first general reform act since the Workhouse Test Act of 1723, and ... it faced facts'.[72] In addition, Samantha Shave has demonstrated the act was more widely adopted than previously believed; she also evaluated how workhouse populations were accommodated in a variety of regimes and showed how the act stimulated the informal exchange of ideas and practices relating to poor relief by means of letters as well as in publications.[73]

The bill, however, did not represent the fulfilment of Gilbert's goals. Innes explains that it was no more than 'an unsatisfactory compromise, the most that he could get through a wartime parliament'.[74] In 1786 Gilbert passed two further measures. The first of which required English poor law overseers to make returns of their expenditures for the years 1783–85 (26 Geo. III, c. 56), thereby providing data for reformers to use in formulating subsequent plans for relief. Even Jeremy Bentham's disciples, who were scornful of Gilbert's efforts and capacities, condescendingly acknowledged that 'the information he has enabled the legislature to collect, may be useful to wiser heads'.[75] The second bill achieved a goal Gilbert had been trying to attain since 1775, but had earlier been thwarted by the House of Lords. It required parish clergy and church wardens to provide returns of all parochial charities for the benefit of the poor (26 Geo. III, c. 58). In 1787 he introduced another bill whose object was 'to employ the poor who are able to work, and to give Relief to the Impotent, by an equal tax upon the Inhabitants and Occupiers of lands, [and] Tenements'. The poor would be under the care of

---

[70] *CJ*, xxxviii, 482, 484, 624, 625.
[71] *Observations on the Bills for Amending and Rendering More Effectual the Laws* (1782).
[72] Quoted in *HPC, 1754–1790*, ii, p. 500; Paul Slack, *The English Poor Law, 1531–1782* (Cambridge, 1990), pp. 35–6.
[73] Samantha Shave, *Pauper Policies: Poor Law Practice in England 1780–1850* (Manchester, 2017), Chapter 2.
[74] Innes, 'Local acts of a national Parliament', in *Parliament and Locality*, p. 41
[75] *The Correspondence of Jeremy Bentham. Vol. III: January 1781 to October 1788*, ed. I.R. Christie (10 vols, 1971), p. 527.

guardians, and visitors who would also be responsible for placing children either in poor houses or with 'reputable people' to see that they were properly treated if the parents were unable or unwilling to care for them.

According to Gilbert the bill proceeded through the House of Commons 'in the most collaborative manner'. In its second reading committee, 'each member offered his opinion on every amendment and unless there was unanimity, the amendment was withdrawn and a new one offered'. With this procedure 'the bill made its way through the committee without a division being necessary'.[76] As usual Gilbert arranged for the bill to be reported and printed in order that it might be distributed to magistrates, to William Pitt and other interested parties, a point noted in the provincial press.[77] He acknowledged to the House on 10 December 1787 that recent setbacks had discouraged him but assured MPs that disappointments would not deter him, for:

> he saw the object so very important, and felt himself, after a long and severe application, so well acquainted with the subject, and the necessity of some reform, that as long as he had the honour of a seat in that House, and the health to do his duty, he should be inclined to exert the utmost of his endeavours to bring about some necessary regulations.[78]

Yet he made only one additional effort, this one in 1788, with a bill for the more effectual relief of the poor. It gave guardians a large measure of discretion on the size of the workhouses and encouraged voluntary charities to supplement public endeavours. The measure, however, never received a second reading.[79] With the exception of an enclosure, a road and the Staffordshire Gaol Bill, which he introduced between 1786 and 1788, the focus of Gilbert's legislative efforts during the late 1780s were tied to his work as Chairman of the Ways and Means, a demanding post he held from 1784–94.

By the time he submitted his final bill in 1788, opinion was shifting against the premises on which Gilbert's poor law proposals rested. As Innes notes, 'Gilbert's concern to enlarge and strengthen the powers of public authorities had a somewhat old-fashioned air'. That shift, she suggests, may account for why in his final proposal he gave his guardians the leeway to build smaller and fewer workhouses and also urged that future poor law reform be allied with voluntary charity and friendly societies.[80]

Yet Gilbert maintained a following among his colleagues in the House of Commons. When the House considered Edmund Burke's proposal to abolish the Board of Trade, several MPs wondered who would be left in its absence to tend to the needs of the poor. Thomas Pownall assured them that as he could not find that the lords of trade had

---

[76] Gilbert, *Observations on the Bills for Amending and Rendering More Effectual the Laws Relative to Houses of Correction* (1787), p. 3.
[77] TNA, PRO 30/8/ 138, f. 264, Pitt Papers, Gilbert to Pitt, 1 June, 1787; *Norfolk Chronicle*, 24 November, 1787.
[78] *PH*, xxvi, cc. 1279–80.
[79] Joanna Innes, '"The 'Mixed economy of welfare"', 163.
[80] Innes, 'The "mixed economy of welfare"', 163; and 'The state of the poor: Eighteenth-century England in European perspective', in *Rethinking the Leviathan: The Eighteenth-Century State in Britain and Germany*, ed. John Brewer and Eckhart Hellmuth (1999), pp. 249–62.

done anything, he naturally looked (as the public at large did) to the hon. Gentleman within a little distance of him (Mr. Gilbert) who upon that subject he considered as the only board of trade that he knew'. Similarly, Sir Gregory Page Turner[81] said of Gilbert during a 1788 debate that 'his name could be written in letters of Gold'. As Innes suggests, Gilbert, more than any other individual', set the agenda for *national* debate from the 1760s to the 1780s, on poor law questions.[82]

Page Turner's accolade came towards the end of Gilbert's active career. 1788 was the last year in which he introduced legislation relating to the poor law; not coincidentally, it was also when he gave up his responsibilities as chief agent of Lord Stafford's estates.

During his 31-year Parliamentary career, Thomas Gilbert was a notable legislator who compiled a long and varied list of legislative accomplishments – a list that is summarised at the end of this chapter. This list does not, however, cover the full extent of his legislative interests and causes. From 1773 he tried to put limits on the pervasiveness of alehouses, whose products he believed undermined the health and character of too many of their customers, a point he reiterated over the next decade.[83] He advocated on behalf of friendly societies and for an end to the practice of imprisoning those who were in debt for small sums. Hugh Malet also claims that in 1787 he secured the passage of a bill for the licensing of dogs, an important step in the control of rabies.[84]

Though a number of Gilbert's legislative proposals were useful, few were momentous. He was a believer in incremental change, and his overriding goal was to make systems work more honestly and efficiently in delivering services for those for whom they were intended, whether they were travellers on turnpikes, beneficiaries of poor law relief, or the denizens of the royal household.

His reforms were often cautious and practical. Eager to recruit a resident clergy to assist in overseeing his reformed poor law system, he took steps to ensure that even the poorest curate was housed in the parish he was assigned to lead. Like Burke he took delight in recommending the eradication of various court offices, but not because their occupants were pawns of the Crown in Parliament. Rather it was wasteful, he believed, to spend £5000 a year to repair locks and grates in the royal palaces, which is why he turned to Boulton to find smiths who could make the repairs for a good wage. Gilbert was a fixer: when he saw waste he worked to eradicate it and make systems operate more efficiently and humanely.

This attitude is a key to understanding Gilbert's motives behind more than 20 years of poor law reforms. Certainly, they owed much to mid-century reformers including Charles Gray, Lord Orwell and Richard Burn. Central to the goals in Gilbert's first three plans were the reorganisation of the structure of poor relief and the elimination of the

---

[81] Sir Gregory Page Turner, 3rd Bt. (1748–1805), MP, Thirsk, 1784–1805.
[82] *PH*, xxi, c. 250; Debrett, *Parl. Reg.*, n.s., xxii, p. 277.
[83] *PH*, xvii, 793; Innes, 'The mixed economy of welfare', 162.
[84] Hugh Malet, *Bridgewater, the Canal Duke, 1736–1803*, p. 37. Having gone through the *Journals of the House of Commons* for 1787, I found no indication that Gilbert initiated or carried such a bill through the House in the 1787 session. Malet, however, cites the *DNB* as his source, so I include the bill on my list of bills that Gilbert helped to enact.

worst vestiges of a settlement system which were costly to the rate payer and cruel to the poor. He looked also to replace parish overseers with guardians and visitors acting under the guidance of active magistrates. Again, the aim was an efficient structure, supervised by humane, educated officials who ensured that the poor received the services they required.

In all of this Gilbert looked not only for assistance from MPs but also from those who would implement the laws that Westminster enacted. He was collaborative, for he drew heavily upon the work and ideas of others. In presenting what became 'Gilbert's Act' in May 1781, he remarked on 'how unequal he was to the task he had undertaken' and how he relied upon 'the candor, good will and affection of the House'.[85] His chronicle of proceedings on the second reading committee on his 1787 bill highlights how much he relied upon his colleagues' review of his measure who then joined in proposing amendments. His practice of circulating printed copies of amended bills to magistrates and other informed parties reflected his recognition of the need to obtain comments from those who were knowledgeable and who would eventually implement his legislation.

Yet Gilbert was not a cipher. His legislation reflected his understanding of the relevant issues and his ideas on how to address the questions at hand. By the late 1770s he was unhesitating in presenting his views on topics ranging from poor law reform to the refurbishment of the royal court or the elimination of government waste. In each of these campaigns he displayed impatience.

That impatience was reinforced as he encountered the chaos of turnpike and highway legislation early in his career or, at its end, when he was thwarted in his attempts to lure country gentlemen into the magistracy to take up positions in poor law administration because they were intimidated by the 'Difficulty and Perplexity of the Laws'.[86] That morass led him to another crusade. To overcome the shortage of qualified candidates for the magistracy, Gilbert urged that efforts be made to make the laws 'as plain and intelligible as possible'. To this end, he recommended that one or two gentlemen at the bar be appointed by judges to inspect pending public bills during the Parliamentary session. During the intervals they should be employed:

> collecting and digesting the Statutes upon particular Heads when they are numerous, in order to their being reduced to one Act in a future Session; and if there should be a standing committee to superintend those Proceedings, it might be the Means of preventing many Inaccuracies in penning the new Acts and would soon render the rest easy and not illegible.[87]

---

[85] Debrett, *Parl Reg.*, n.s. i.i, p. 372.
[86] Gilbert, *A Plan for the Better Relief and Employment of the Poor and for Reforming and Amending the Laws Respecting Houses of Correction; and Vagrants; and for Improving the Police of the Country. Together with Bills Intended to Be Offered for These Purposes* (1781), p 28.
[87] Gilbert, *A Plan for the Better Relief and Employment of the Poor*, p. 29. For a good discussion of the confusing manner in which statute law was promulgated during the eighteenth century, see Sheila Lambert, *Bills and Acts*, Chapter 9.

While no committee was established to superintend the work of the learned gentlemen, it is clear in reviewing the totality of Gilbert's legislative work that his concern was to sort out and render coherent complex bodies of legislation. His campaigns to establish economical and coherently structured administration in national government, the poor law or the royal household represent the overriding goals of his career in public service. It is likely that these preoccupations derived from his training as a barrister, from his experience as the land agent of Earl Gower and the Duke of Bridgewater and finally from his partnership with his brother in establishing a series of profitable enterprises. These elements in Gilbert's background distinguished him from many of his fellow MPs. For more than 30 years he applied the insights he gained from his education and experiences to develop systems for the poor law, the court and the nation's transportation networks in the hope that they would operate more coherently and productively to better address the human needs of those they purportedly served.

Partial list of bills introduced by Thomas Gilbert, 1765–1788:

1. Better relief and employment of the poor bill: presented 1 Feb. 1765; failed in the House of Lords. *Additional Grenville Papers, 1763-65*, ed. John R.G. Tomlinson (Manchester, 1962, pp. 252-3); Louise Ryland-Epson, 'The impact of back benchers in the creation of social reform: *The Indefatigable and Honourable Exertions of Mr Gilbert*', Parl Hist., xxxix, 283, n. 51.
2. Bill to explain, amend and reduce to one Act of Parliament, the laws relating to the poor: presented 22 Feb. 1768; sent to the printer, Feb. 26, 1768.
3. Quaker tithes bill: presented, 30 Mar. 1772; withdrawn 8 Apr. 1772.
4. A bill enforcing several acts of Parliament for the recovery and payment of tythes, and other ecclesiastical dues, from people called Quakers, and for enlarging the powers thereby given: presented 13 Apr. 1772. Withdrawn after being amended in the House of Commons. G.M. Ditchfield, 'Parliament, the Quakers and the tithe question 1770-1835', *Parliamentary History*, iv (1985), 90.
5. Bill to reduce to one act statutes to preserve the public highways: presented 1 Apr. 1773; earlier versions presented on 13 February and 2 March, the latter being amended on 5 March (13 Geo. III, c. 78).
6. Bill to unite turnpike road acts into one Act: presented 5 Mar. 1773 (13 Geo. III, c. 84).
7. Bill to prevent the stealing of deer, & to repeal several statutes made for the like purpose: presented 24 May, 1775; sent to the printer, 25 May 1775.
8. Bill to prevent the stealing of deer (16 Geo. III, c. 30; probably for Earl Gower).
9. Bill to promote the residence of parochial clergy, by making provision for more speedy and effectual building, rebuilding, & repairing parsonage houses: presented 13 May 1776, sent to the printer, 21 May 1776. Hoppit, *Failed Legislation*, 440.
10. Bill to promote the residence of parochial clergy (Residence House Bill), by making provision for the more speedy and effective building, rebuilding, repairing, or purchasing, houses, and other necessary buildings and tenements for the use of these benefices: presented 21 Apr. 1777 (17 Geo. III, c. 52).

11. Bill to oblige the minister and church warden or other proper officers ... in England to make returns under oath of all charitable donations for the benefit of the poor: presented 21 Apr. 1777; defeated in the House of Lords, 3 June 1777. Hoppit, *Failed Legislation*, 444–5.
12. Bill for obviating a doubt touching the binding and receiving of poor children apprenticed, in pursuance of several acts of Parliament for the relief of the poor ... in England: presented 6 Mar. 1780 (20 Geo III, c. 36).
13. Bill for the relief and employment of the poor: presented 23 May 1781; sent to the printer, 25 May, 1781.
14. Residence Houses Bill (21 Geo. III, c. 66).
15. Bill to amend and render more effective, the laws relating Houses of Correction; presented 1 June 1781; sent to the printer, 11 June 1781. Hoppit, *Failed Legislation*, 460.
16. A Bill (with amendments) to amend and render more effective several laws regarding rogues, vagabonds, beggars and other idle and disorderly persons: presented 14 June 1781; amended 19 June 1781, sent to the printer 19 June 1781. Hoppit, *Failed Legislation*, 462.
17. A bill for the relief and employment of the poor; presented 16 December, 1781 (22 George III, c. 83).
18. Bill to amend and render more effective laws in being relative to Houses of Correction: presented 17 Dec. 1781 (22 Geo. III, c. 64).
19. A Bill for amending and rendering more effective the several laws relating to vagabonds, beggars, and other idle and disorderly persons: presented 12 Dec. 1781; rejected at third reading by a vote of 44 to 22, 10 June 1782. Hoppit, *Failed Legislation*, 462–3.
20. Bill to oblige overseers of the Poor in the several parishes and places within England to make Returns, upon Oaths, to certain Questions, to be specified in the Bill, relative to the State of the Poor, and Expenses on their Account, for each of the last three Years: presented 23 May, 1786 (26 Geo III, c. 56).
21. Bill for procuring, upon Oath, Returns of all Charitable Donations for the benefit of Poor Persons in ... England: presented 25 May 1786; passed 27 June 1786 (26 Geo III, c. 58).
22. Bill renewing the Newcastle-under-Lyme to Nantwich turnpike trust: presented 9 Mar. 1787 (27 Geo. III, c. 83).
23. Staffordshire Gaol Bill: presented 18 Apr. 1787 (27 Geo. III, c. 60).
24. Bill for the more effectual relief and employment of the poor: presented 28 May 1787; consideration of the report from the petition committee postponed, 28 May 1787. Hoppit, *Failed Legislation*, 494.
25. Bill for the more effectual employment of the poor: presented 11 Mar. 1788; second reading put off for three months, 44–10, 17 Apr. 1788. Hoppit, *Failed Legislation*, 496–7.

6

Essex Imbroglios

Up to this point the book has highlighted examples of MPs working for the most part harmoniously to advance legislative projects that promised to promote the well-being of their constituencies or their regions. Unified efforts of this sort were not always the norm, and local groups sometimes became mired in prolonged legislative battles stoked by personal animosities, political rivalries and contests occasioned by projects that impinged upon private property. Enclosure, turnpike and navigation bills from time to time gave rise to fierce contests that reached Westminster.[1] The issues that ignited those battles came into play in the legislative contests precipitated by the introduction of the Chelmer Navigation Bill in February 1766 and the more extended contest over the construction of a new Essex Gaol that extended from 1768 to 1771.

Though the battles involving these measures involved a variety of individuals both in Parliament and Essex, two figures emerged as the principal actors. Through the influence of his cousin, Lord Fitzwalter, Sir William Mildmay, Bt.[2] secured a position in the Office of Trade and Plantations in the 1750s and later a series of minor diplomatic posts, culminating in five years in Paris. Following Fitzwalter's death and the outbreak of war with France, Mildmay returned to Essex where he settled in, according to Hilda Grieve, as a member of the Essex county squirearchy, the county's bench, and as a preeminent figure in Chelmsford, the county town. Though he did not inherit Fitzwalter's peerage, he gained the family's seat, Moulsham Hall, and a much reduced estate.[3] Mildmay showed himself during proceedings on the Chelmer Navigation to be high-handed and occasionally duplicitous, while his primary concern during consideration of the Essex Gaol seems to have been to retain his hereditary right to collect a toll from those attending Chelmsford's market – a right which was threatened by the possibility that the gaol might be built on the market's site. His manoeuvrings were all the more controversial because he never was a member of the House.

Bamber Gascoyne was an aggressive, arrogant legislator who delighted in carrying points against numerous opponents and did not hesitate to denigrate the merits of his allies. For these reasons he was unpopular in the House and in Essex.[4] Qualities that

---

[1] For examples, see Langford, *Public Life*, 179–86.
[2] Sir William Mildmay (1705–71), Bt., Lord of the Manor of Bishop's Hall in Chelmsford and entitled to the tolls arising from the town's market.
[3] Hilda Grieve, *The Sleepers and the Shadows*, p. 143.
[4] *HPC, 1754–1790*, ii, pp. 487–8.

offended his fellow country gentlemen appealed, however, to Henry Fox,[5] who recognised him to be the sort of person who would 'treat any opponent roughly and coarsely who should deserve it'. For these reasons Fox arranged for him to come into Parliament for Midhurst in 1765.[6]

Gascoyne in his correspondence with John Strutt[7] proclaimed he was a legislative titan, who charged across the legislative stage singlehandedly vanquishing adversaries because his supposed allies were either supine, ill-informed or incompetent. He was, in short, an egoist and a braggart, but he was also a hardworking legislator who was often successful in securing his objectives, and his correspondence, despite its self-promotion, provides a vivid and engaging account of the workings of the eighteenth-century legislative machine.

Promoters of the Chelmer Navigation scheme, which became public early in 1765, promised that upon its completion that foodstuffs and fuel would be transported faster and at a lower cost than by land carriage, points contested by their opponents. The latter charged that to assure necessary water supplies for their project proprietors of the new navigation would reduce water available to mills along the Chelmer, especially those in the vicinity of Maldon.[8] They also complained that their property would be separated by cuts with the result that commons would be divided and lose value and be exposed to the 'intrusion of bargemen'.[9] The project, according to Gascoyne, originated from Chelmsford, for which it was designed. Opposition came from Maldon, whose wharves, warehouses and harbour dues would all suffer.[10]

To avoid an expensive contest, both sides met at Chelmsford in early December in order to settle the heads of the bill which the promoters proposed to bring in at the beginning of the 1766 session. According to a representative of the opposing landowners, the meeting did not go well: he reported to Lord Barrington that none of them understood the proposal and that Yeomans, their surveyor,[11] was 'unacquainted with the natural course of the River'. The one point on which the two sides agreed was that each would appoint two representatives to settle contentious points as they arose. If the referees could not agree, they would select a fifth party whose decision on the matter would be binding.[12] Despite continuing disagreements, this system remained in place and worked throughout proceedings on the measure until its final passage.

Promoters tentatively delivered printed proposals to the House of Commons on 31 January without informing their opponents, who included Strutt, Gascoyne and Lord

---

[5] Henry Fox (1705–74), MP, Hindon, 1735–41, New Windsor, 1741–61 and Dunwich, 1761–3; Surveyor Gen. of Works, 1737–43; Ld. of Treasury, 1743–6; Sec. at War, 1746–55; cabinet councillor, 1754; Sec. of state, south, 1755–6; paymaster general, 1757–65; cabinet councilor and minister in the House of Commons, 1762–3; cr. Baron Holland, 1763.
[6] *HPC, 1754–1790*, ii, 487.
[7] John Strutt (1727–1816), MP, Maldon, 1774–90.
[8] Essex Record Office [ERO], Strutt MSS, D/DRa o3. 'Objections to the present proposal' and 'John Strutt's Observations on the proposal' for the Chelmer Navigation. Strutt inherited mills from his father, and by 1781 owned an estate of 6,000 acres.
[9] ERO, Strutt MSS, D/DRa o3, 'Objections to the present proposal'.
[10] Quoted in *HPC, 1754–1790*, i, 488–9.
[11] Yeomans was the surveyor hired by the promoters of the plan to design and prepare the route for the proposed navigation. Despite Fychte's comments, he had a good reputation as an engineer.
[12] ERO, Strutt MSS, D/DRa o7, Thomas Fychte to Barrington, 6 December, 1765.

Barrington, who owned an Essex estate. Initially he had favoured the creation of a committee, including representatives of the projectors and opposing property owners, to meet at the upcoming assizes and to iron out their differences.

When it became apparent that the two sides would reach no agreeable accommodation at the local level, opponents of the plan prepared for the next phase of their campaign. Barrington, an experienced legislator, looked to recruit the 'experts' that opponents of the proposed navigation needed if a bill came before the Commons. After consulting with the noted engineer John Smeaton,[13] Barrington secured the services of Ferdinand Stratford, who for a guinea a day would come to Essex to survey the navigation's route and prepare an assessment of the projectors' plan in order to give evidence before a committee of the House. After his visit, he was critical of the proposal.[14] Barrington also warned that in order to mount an opposition, it was essential to hire a Parliamentary solicitor, for 'in all private business which I have carry'd thro' the two houses I have had no other assistance'. In the end, he hired Edward Barwell,[15] who he said 'understands the business of engineering as well as that of a Parliamentary agent, in which last respect he has no superior'.[16] Finally, with Strutt's help, Barrington set about canvassing landowners whose properties and mills might be injured by the navigation, to raise the funds for the campaign once the business came before the House. He estimated the cost would be between £300 and £400 to cover the fees of Stratford and Barwell, as well as those of the House.[17]

According to Langford, MPs were concerned that promoters of contested legislation should take every effort to consult local opinion before bringing their measures before the House.[18] On 10 October, John Strutt reported to landowners whose properties were likely to be affected by the navigation that its projectors had determined to bring in their bill without meeting to try to conciliate their critics.[19] Sir Anthony Abdy,[20] an Essex proprietor, though at this point uninvolved in the dispute, told Strutt that:

> the behaviour of the projectors seems to me very extraordinary. Sir Wm Mildmay, I understand, undertook to meet the Proprietors of the several estates through which the Cut is to pass & settle everything amicably ... The Projectors will not appear in a very good light in the House of Commons this Year, having not fulfilled what they under took. They will now have time to meet the Proprietors if they think proper, for no Business will be done in Parliament till after Christmas & as

---

[13] John Smeaton (1724–92), noted engineer, responsible for the design of harbours and canals, including the Calder and Hebble Canal, portions of the Forth and Clyde and the Birmingham and Fazeley Canals, and bridges at Aberdeen, Hexham and Perth.
[14] ERO, Strutt MSS, D/DRa o7, Barrington to Strutt, 15 July, 7 Sept. 1765.
[15] Edward Barwell (d. 1799) one of the Commons' principal committee clerks, whose career, according to D.R. Rydz, is 'illustrative of the advantages a clerkship ... had at the time for agent and client'. D.R. Rydz, *The Parliamentary Agents: A History* (1979), p. 40.
[16] ERO, Strutt MSS, D/DRa o7, Barrington to Fychte and H.L. Collins, 20 Sept. 1765 and Strutt to landowners, 21 Oct. 1765 and Barrington to Strutt, 7 Oct. 1765.
[17] ERO, Strutt MSS, D/DRa o7, Strutt to Barrington, 21 Oct. 1765 and Barrington to Strutt, 25 Oct. 1765.
[18] Langford, *Private Life*, pp. 170–2.
[19] ERO, Strutt MSS, D/DRa o7, John Strutt to landowners, 10 Oct. 1765.
[20] Sir Anthony Thomas Abdy, 6th Bt. (?1720–75), MP, Knareborough, 1763–75.

I should think it wd be right for you & Mr Fychte who live nearest to call upon him to fulfill his promise.[21]

In fact, in mid-November Mildmay wrote to Strutt, indicating that he would endeavour to get his group to meet with its opponents on 5 December, and at the end of the month he secured an attendance of his allies.[22] Parliament broke for the Christmas holidays on 20 December 1765 and resumed on 20 January 1766. Nevertheless, Barwell informed Strutt on 7 January that he had met with Thomas Yeomans, the engineer who devised the navigation, and Newdigate Poyntz,[23] the promoters' Parliamentary agent. The two were eager to meet with him to review a draft copy of a Chelmer bill and review clauses that Barwell might wish for; they also wished to move ahead as quickly as possible. The fact that a draft bill existed hints that the promoters had surreptitiously made their plans before 12 February 1766 when to the surprise of the landowner group, the Commons received a petition for leave to bring in a bill to make the River Chelmer navigable from the Port of Maldon to Chelmsford. The House moved that the petition be referred to a committee whose nominees included many who played a leading part in the contest that dragged on until 12 May.[24] On the day the petition was introduced, Mildmay made a vague offer of negotiation to Gascoyne. While emphasising that he was willing to adjust the affairs of the navigation 'in an amicable manner', he admitted that he had no authority to make any definitive agreement.[25]

Though Mildmay's approach at the outset of the Chelmer bill's Parliamentary journey may have represented a desire to avoid contentious contest, the measure's promoters were anything but conciliatory. On 18 March, Gascoyne reported that the committee on the measure's petition had sat on the 17th and gone half way through it. All of the promoters' friends attended along with Richard Rigby;[26] among the opponents only Barrington appeared. Despite being outnumbered, Gascoyne claimed he made favourable changes to the list of Commissioners.[27] The same day he informed Strutt that he learned from Sir Anthony Abdy, the independent referee, that Sir William Mildmay had sent cards for the Chelmer Committee to meet on 19 March. Upon hearing this, Gascoyne immediately confronted Newdigate Poyntz, who 'said he did it by Mildmay's order'. Gascoyne replied that since Mildmay was not an MP 'and as the Bill had not been delivered he might depend on it, I would alarm the House and the Country with this proceeding'. Poyntz replied that he had delivered the bill the previous evening to Barwell. Barrington, upon joining the group, informed Poyntz that the measure could not proceed until the issue to be settled by Abdy was resolved. Poyntz sent a message to countermand the notice. By trying to gain the upper hand Mildmay succeeded only in adding to the suspicion and ill-will which already divided the two

---

[21] ERO, Strutt MSS, D/DRa o7, Abdy to John Strutt, 26 Oct. 1765.
[22] ERO, Strutt MSS, D/DRa o7, Mildmay to Strutt, 13 Nov. 1765.
[23] Newdigate Poyntz (1715–72), Commons' clerk without doors, 1740–72.
[24] *CJ*, xxx, 534.
[25] ERO, Strutt MSS, D/DRa o7, Mildmay to Gascoyne, 12 Feb. 1766.
[26] Richard Rigby (1722–88), MP, Castle Rising, 1745–7; Sudbury, 1747–54 and Tavistock, 1754–88; Ld. of Trade, 1755–60; Sec. to Ld. Lt. [I] 1760; Jt. Vice Treasurer [I], 1759–1788; Paymaster Gen. 1768–82.
[27] ERO, Srutt MSS, T/B 251/07, Gascoyne to Strutt, 18 Mar. 1766.

sides, for Gascoyne ended his letter to Strutt by concluding that Mildmay was 'the most silly fellow' that ever existed.[28]

Nevertheless, the Chelmer's sponsors proceeded on 21 March to prove the arguments justifying their project in the committee on their petition. Gascoyne noted that:

> Sr Anthony Abdy attended and they drove him from the reference as they then declared it will cost them £4,000 to rail and fence the lands. They cannot proceed further till after the holydays. But I think a petition should be got up. Sr. Wm. [Mildmay] sent up to speak with me into the rooms above but I would not see him.[29]

Barrington reacted to the proceedings with indignation. On 22 March he told Strutt that the promoters had violated their treaty agreement. He had stipulated that until the referee had settled outstanding issues, nothing would be settled, as he had insisted several days earlier that the committee could not proceed until everything was determined by the referee.[30]

Nevertheless, the Chelmer Bill proceeded towards its passage. John Luther reported it from its second reading committee on 7 May, though Gascoyne claimed to have singlehandedly carried many points for the landowners' on the previous day. He gloated in a letter to Strutt on 7 May that:

> I have this moment finished your Chelmer bill, no Lord Barrington, no San[dy]s,[31] or friends for the land owners but Houblon[32] and Sir Brook Bridges[33] who knew nothing of the matter; however I have fought it out as well as I could.[34]

The bill's passage was relatively peaceful because on 26 April 'Sir John Turner[35] [Sir Anthony Abdy's replacement after Abdy joined the promoters], delivered his opinion on the issues submitted to him as the fifth referee'. Gascoyne saw his report as a draw; the landowners gained their point on the eligibility for those who would be commissioners, but Turner seemed to come down on the promoters' side on the issue of fences, though Gascoyne felt that landowners might later carry their points before juries.[36] As with many of the earlier contentious points, it was the referee who settled disputed questions.

The Chelmer Navigation Bill received the royal assent in late May 1766, about 16 months after the introduction of the initial proposal in January 1765. Yet the measure's

[28] ERO, Strutt MSS, T/B 251/07, Gascoyne to Strutt, 18 Feb. 1766.
[29] ERO, Strutt MSS, T/B 251/07, Gascoyne to Strutt, 22 Mar. 1766.
[30] ERO, Strutt MSS, D/DRa o7, Barrington to Strutt, 22 Mar. 1766.
[31] Hon. Edwin Sandys (1725–97), MP, Droitwich, 1747–54, Bossiney, 1754–61 and Westminster, 1762–70; Ld. of Admiralty, 1770; succ. as 2nd Baron Sandys, 1770.
[32] Jacob Houblon (1710–90), MP Colchester, 1735–41 and Hertfordshire, 1741–7 and 1761–8.
[33] Sir Brook Bridges, 3rd Bt. (1733–91), MP, Kent, 1763–74.
[34] ERO, Strutt MSS, T/B 251/07, Gascoyne to Strutt, 18 Mar. 1766.
[35] Sir John Turner, 3rd Bt. (1712–80), MP, King's Lynn, 1739–44; Ld. of Treasury, 1762–5.
[36] ERO, Strutt MSS, T/B 251/07, Gascoyne to Strutt, 28 Apr. 1766.

passage was something of an anti-climax. According to Hilda Grieve restrictive clauses in the act, which may have been introduced by Gascoyne, required that the navigation's commissioners raise £13,000 before proceeding with any work on the project.[37] They were unable to do so. Thus, the improvement of the Chelmer only followed on the passage of legislation introduced in 1792, and the struggle outlined above achieved no immediate result.[38]

Still, the episode is instructive for the historian of the legislative process for several reasons. It highlights the rarely cited role of the referee. While the two referees nominated by each side were unable to broker satisfactory compromises on crucial sticking points, and Sir Anthony Abdy's proposals on the issue of fencing were rejected by promoters of the navigation because their high costs, Sir John Turner's rulings regarding the power of commissioners and the fencing question broke the logjam that had held up the measure. It is a testament to his stature and the two sides' likely reluctance to continue a long and expensive battle that they accepted his decisions and allowed the measure to proceed to passage. The Strutt correspondence also sheds some interesting light on the position and activities of the Parliamentary solicitors: Newdigate Poyntz, the promoters' able agent, clearly recognised that part of his duties was to provide a check on Sir William Mildmay, whose waywardness got the promoters' side into several scrapes. On the other hand, Edward Barwell, in whom Lord Barrington had the greatest confidence, failed to impress opponents of the Chelmer Bill, including Fychte and Gascoyne, who were involved in the more detailed, day-to-day business of the committee work and opposition.

The case demonstrates the degree to which promoters of the navigation were prepared to expend time and money on a measure whose engineering was apparently faulty and whose promotion rested on assumptions that were overly optimistic. At the same time opponents made much out of the infringements upon properties abutting the navigation and elevated the possibility of bargemen walking across their lands into major assaults. Issues such as these were part and parcel of the debates that accompanied the navigation legislation of the period.

In April 1765 Gascoyne complained that his new office made him much more 'unuseful' because he was unable to attend until after two in the afternoon and it gave him little if any time to prepare.[39] Still his correspondence with Strutt shows that he was an active, aggressive legislator. Despite having to forward business that fell within the purview of the Board of Trade, he was able to devote time to secure small-scale legislative victories, for, as he told Strutt in 1766, he had been busy with the Staffordshire and Cheshire navigations which:

---

[37] Grieve, *The Sleepers and the Shadows*, p. 152. The act had specified that the necessary funds be raised within 12 months of its passage. John Boyes and Russell Ronald, *Canals of Eastern England* (Newton Abbot, 1977), pp. 63–5.

[38] I.E. Gray, 'Ferdinando Stratford of Gloucestershire', *Transactions of the Bristol and Gloucestershire Archaelogical Society* (1946, 7, 8), 412–5. The *VCH* erroneously states that the Chelmer Act received Parliamentary approval in 1765. It goes on to say, however, that work on the navigation was not completed until 1795 and that when done, it 'was of great advantage' to Chelmsford. *Victoria History of the Counties of England: A History of Essex*, II (1907), p. 334.

[39] ERO, Strutt MSS, T/B 251/7, Gascoyne to Strutt, 26 Apr. 1765.

have Both accepted of a clause by me to divide and separate the lands by ditch, hedge rail and other sufficient fence for keeping in sheep and other cattle and the proprietors are to keep repair and maintain the same and no proprietor is to be a commissioner so I flatter myself I shall succeed according to your wishes.[40]

Five weeks later he claimed he was 'deep in the Yorkshire Cloth Bill, the Staffordshire Navigation Bill on Monday, and the militia'.[41]

Gascoyne often found himself without allies in these battles. Both in Essex and in Liverpool, where his wife brought with her a large property, people regarded him as a difficult and disruptive force.[42] Despite his obvious abilities, the landowners opposing the Chelmer navigation were wary of taking him on as their leading spokesman in the House. Lord Barrington reluctantly accepted him as one of the group's referees, and others of the navigation's opponents regarded Barrington as their leader despite the fact that he absented himself from the committees in which Gascoyne took the leading and successful part.

I: Essex Gaol Bill

For Gascoyne and most Essex MPs, the crucial legislative business between 1769 and 1772 was the Essex Gaol Bill. In 1767 a grand jury condemned the existing gaol, a wooden structure erected in 1659, as 'too small, unwholesome, obnoxious and inconvenient' and 'frequently infected with gaol distemper'.[43] The result was the establishment of a committee that included many of those involved in the campaign for and against the Chelmer Navigation, including Sir William Mildmay, Bamber Gascoyne, John Strutt, Sir William Maynard, John Luther, Charles Gray as well as the Rev. John Tindal of Chelmsford. The committee appointed George Dance[44] to undertake surveys of potential sites for a new gaol – including the site of the existing gaol, and another in the town's marketplace on land owned by Mildmay along with other sites.[45] Dance favoured the site of the old gaol whereas Gascoyne and Strutt preferred the marketplace, but no site received the committee's unanimous endorsement. This lack of agreement complicated applications to Parliament. Thus, when the justices on 26 January 1769 petitioned Parliament for leave to bring in a bill for the new gaol in the marketplace, prospects for success were dim. The House referred the petition to a committee chaired by Sir William Maynard.[46] On 16 March Sir William

---

[40] ERO, Strutt MSS, T/B 251/7, Gascoyne to Strutt, 18 Mar. 1766.
[41] ERO, Strutt MSS, T/B 251/7, Gascoyne to Strutt, 11 Apr. 1766.
[42] See Sir William Meredith's letter to Charles Jenkinson in *Jenkinson Papers*, ed. Ninette S. Jucker (1949), pp. 208–9; and BL, Newcastle Papers, Add. MS 32936, ff. 116–17, Sir Evan Cunliffe to Newcastle, 25 Mar. 1762.
[43] Grieve, *The Sleepers and the Shadows*, p. 152.
[44] George Dance the younger (1741–1825), architect and surveyor; studied in Italy, 1759–65; selected when 27, to succeed his father as architect and surveyor to the Corporation of London, 1767; his first major work in this position was to rebuild Newgate Prison, 1770, and build the Guildhall.
[45] Grieve, *The Sleepers and the Shadows*, pp. 153–5.
[46] Sir William Maynard, 4th Bt. (1721–72), MP, Essex, 1759–72.

reported from the committee, and the House gave the petitioners leave to bring in a bill which Maynard and Sir Anthony Abdy – who acted as the solicitor for the bill – were to prepare with Charles Gray and Luther. Between 10 and 15 April, however, the House received five petitions against bill, with each group claiming that if passed, its implementation would impose heavy costs upon them.[47] Gascoyne reported that Maynard and Gray stood firm in the face of opposition, but the measure made no further progress in the 1769 session.[48]

In the meantime, a core group on the committee rallied around another site for the gaol on the Brickfields which offered ample space, fresh air and a safe distance from the market. Despite the fact that Gascoyne opposed the plan and Sir William Mildmay, who owned the site, was reluctant to part with it, a majority of the committee, after receiving Dance's report that the Brickfield was the proper site, favoured bringing in a new bill. Maynard presented the justices' petition on 26 January 1770. On 27 February he reported that the petition committee recommended bringing in the bill that he, Sir Anthony Abdy and John Luther were to prepare and present to the House. Once again, the bill provoked counter-petitions from Wallinger and the principal inhabitants of Chelmsford, who favoured locating the gaol on its original site and produced a series of witnesses to support their case. By contrast, no witnesses appeared in support of the bill with the result that the Commons' second reading committee amended the bill to relocate the proposed gaol to its original site rather than Brickfield. The amended bill subsequently passed the House of Lords without amendment on 11 April (10 Geo. III, c. 28).[49]

Bamber Gascoyne and his allies, Thomas Bramston,[50] Peregrine Bertie[51] and Strutt, were, like Gascoyne, Tories who refused to accept this legislative solution. With the assistance of Lord Rochford,[52] the county's Lord Lieutenant, they devised a plan to repeal the 1770 Act and locate the controversial gaol along with a new shire hall on the site of the White Hart Inn in the town centre, adjoining the marketplace. A majority of

---

[47] 10 Apr.: from the Mayor, etc., clergy and freeholders of Colchester and the principal inhabitants of Chelmsford, *CJ*, xxxii, 364; 11 Apr.: aldermen, etc. of Harwich, *CJ*, xxxii, 371; 12 Apr.: petition of J.A. Wallingham of Hare Hall, Essex, *CJ*, xxxii, 378; 15 Apr.: petition of Sir William Mildmay, Lord of the Manor of Bishops Hall, Chelmsford, *CJ*, xxxii, 386; petitioners from Colchester and Harwich noted they had been exempt from county levies 'from time immemorial' and complained that the sum to be raised to complete the gaol would impose a heavy burden on the finances of their towns. The Chelmsford inhabitants argued that the site chosen for the gaol, next to the market, would deter shoppers from coming to it for fear 'of malignant and pestilential distempers which the unhappy wretches under so close confinement are liable to', and would deprive farmers and others of their preferred lodging by removing the White Hart Inn. Wallingham's complaint was the obvious one that the new gaol would be 'detrimental' to his property, and Sir William Mildmay, who as Lord of the Manor collected tolls on all who came to market, was likely to lose substantial revenue if the gaol did, as was feared, cut into the market's weekly attendance.

[48] ERO, Strutt MSS, T/B 251/7, Gascoyne to Strutt, 19 April 1769; Hoppit, *Failed Legislation*, p. 404.

[49] *CJ*, xxxii, 837, 887; Grieve, *The Sleepers and the Shadows*, pp.155–8.

[50] Thomas Berney Bramston (1733–1813), MP, Essex, 1779–1802.

[51] Peregrine Bertie (1723–86), of Leyton, Essex, MP, Westbury, 1753–74.

[52] William Henry Nassau de Zuylestein, 4th Earl of Rochford (1717–81), Ld. of Bedchamber, 1738–55; Envoy to Turin, 1749–55; Groom of Stole, 1755–60; Ld. Lt. Essex, 1756–81; Ambassador to Madrid, 1763–6, to Paris, 1766–8; Secretary of State (North), 1768–70 and (South), 1770–5; Leader of the House of Lords, 1770–5.

the county's justices approved this controversial proposal at Quarter Sessions in October 1770, and in the face of strong opposition from Chelmsford and the county, they petitioned on 1 February 1771 for a new bill to enable:

> the Justices of the Peace of the County of Essex ... to erect a new Shire House, a Room for the Records, ... and for the repealing the said act passed in the last Session, for the rebuilding the Common Gaol of the said County; and for enabling the said Justices to purchase the *White Hart Inn* in Chelmsford ...; and upon the Scite [sic] of the same to rebuild the Common Gaol.[53]

As the chair of the petition committee, Sir William was directed to report to the House upon matters contained in five counter-petitions. This report provoked an unusual division with 71 members voting in support of the committee's recommendation to bring in the bill and 75 opposed.[54] The result of the vote was that the same committee, again with Sir William in the chair, heard testimony from witnesses on behalf of the five counter-petitioners (whose protests had been presented to the House on the same day as Maynard's report) as well as representatives of the justices of the county of Essex. The outcome of this prolonged scrutiny was a report of about 50,000 words which was presented by an ailing Maynard on 6 May.[55] The opponents reiterated their former points, and added a new complaint – that placing the gaol next to the marketplace meant that the county would jeopardise the town's fragile water supply. This prospect provoked a unanimous resolution opposing the bill at a parishioners' meeting in Chelmsford on 19 February 1771.[56]

Despite the strength of this group and the persuasiveness of the testimony of the counter-petitioners' witnesses, Gascoyne tried to stage a counter-coup.[57] He failed miserably. Proponents of the 1770 Act threatened in May 1771 to apply to the Court of King's Bench for a writ of *Mandamus* to compel the Essex Bench to demonstrate why the Act should not be implemented. Gascoyne and his supporters beat back motions introduced by John Luther to proceed with the 1770 Act at meetings of the Quarter Sessions in April and October, but on 10 October Essex supporters of the Act formally initiated proceedings for a writ of *Mandamus*.[58] In January 1772 the Court of King's Bench served notice on the Lord Lieutenant and justices of Essex to show why a writ of *Mandamus* should not be issued to instruct them to put the disputed Act into effect. The justices did not respond, and the Court went on to issue its *Mandamus*.

The obvious question is why the struggle lasted for so long and why Gascoyne and his allies persisted in promoting a site that was so obviously unpopular in Chelmsford and with large segments of the county. Gascoyne came from Barking in the southwest portion of the county. He had no immediate stake in where the gaol was placed in the town, but during the contest over the Chelmer Navigation he had formed an intense

---

[53] *CJ*, xxxiii, 124.
[54] *CJ*, xxxiii, 207–8.
[55] *CJ*, xxxiii, 368–98.
[56] Grieve, *The Sleepers and the Shadows*, pp. 160–1.
[57] ERO, Strutt MSS, T/B 251/7, Gascoyne to Strutt, 6 May 1771.
[58] Grieve, *The Sleepers and the Shadows*, p. 164.

dislike for Mildmay, a feeling that was mutual.[59] It is also clear from earlier discussion that most of those opposing the Chelmer Bill found Mildmay to be at best unreliable and sometimes ridiculous. Even Newdigate Poyntz, the measure's solicitor, found himself having to retract inappropriate decisions of his employer. The problem, however, extended beyond personalities in part because of political animosities that were exacerbated during and after the county election of 1768. Gascoyne and Strutt were part of what Namier described as 'a group of High Tories' who had recruited inexperienced candidates to run against Sir William Maynard and John Luther. These latter two had been selected at a county meeting to stand for the county that year and were returned without difficulty at the general election. Gascoyne, who had long aspired to represent the county, was embittered as a result of exclusion, particularly because he had hoped to receive the backing of the Tory group.[60] From a perspective of almost 40 years, Montague Burgoyne[61] remarked how these lingering partisan tensions had complicated the debates and proceedings on the gaol business:

> At that time, party disputes in this county were carried on with a considerable deal of animosity, and were not confined to the election of Members, but extended to the building of a new gaol, which in the year 1768 was in contemplation. The two parties could not agree as to the situation of the new building and appealed to Parliament and the courts of law for a decision of their disputes ... The provincial papers ... [were] filled with petitions and counter-petitions relative to this altercation, which lasted for some years.[62]

Yet, according to John Howard, the noted prison reformer, the struggle resulted in a gaol that was worth the effort. In his *State of the Prisons* he praised the new Essex Gaol as replacing a 'close prison, frequently infected with gaol distemper'. The new one, he wrote 'exceeds the old one in strength almost as much as in splendour. The county to their honour, have spared no cost'.[63] The cost was impressive. In comparison to 12 other counties building gaols between 1765 and 1780 listed in Christopher Chalklin's *Counties and Public Building*, the more than £20,600 that Essex lavished on its gaol far surpassed the expenditures of all the others, including Middlesex, Surrey and Sussex.[64] Yet James Neild, one of Howard's disciples, dismissed the plan of the new facility as being 'very defective because of a large chapel, large tap-room and kitchens and many domestic offices that prevented the circulation of air, essential to the preservation of health in prisons'. In fact, within ten years of its completion the gaol was in need of substantial refurbishment.[65]

[59] Grieve, *The Sleepers and the Shadows*, p. 152.
[60] *HPC, 1750–1790*, i, 276.
[61] Montague Burgoyne (1750–1836), Essex politician; appointed by Lord North, Chamberlain of the Till Office; Verderer of Epping Forest.
[62] Grieve, *The Sleepers and the Shadows*, pp. 156–7.
[63] Quoted in Christopher Chalklin, *English Counties and Public Building, 1650–1830* (London and Rio Grande, OH, 1998), p. 166.
[64] Chalklin, *Counties and Public Building*, p. 163, Table 9.1.
[65] Grieve, *The Sleepers and the Shadows*, pp. 165–6.

The faulty construction, according to Grieve, was the responsibility of the surveyor, William Hillyer, who was chosen by Gascoyne in 1770 to survey his parish church in Barking. While performing the work, Gascoyne discovered that Hillyer would take his instructions and held George Dance in low regard.[66] As Gascoyne's agent, Hillyer debunked the idea of building the new gaol on the site of the old one and recommended the White Horse Inn location as the most appropriate for the gaol and shire hall. Both surveyors at different times seem to have been swayed by pressure applied by their patrons or the weight of opinion on the bench. In an effort to make a political accommodation between the warring parties, Quarter Sessions in 1781 awarded the commission to build the new gaol to Hillyer, promising him five per cent of the final cost, which at the time was estimated at £15,000. The costs were notable, and the results of his work were unsatisfactory.[67]

The wrangling that accompanied the passage of the Chelmer navigation was hardly high minded, nor did the prolonged skirmish have a positive or productive outcome. The bill's proponents had carelessly put together their plan, and they failed to address the concerns of those whose properties might be harmed by its passage. Once they petitioned the House for leave to bring in a bill, they ignored the terms of an agreement they had reached with their adversaries as well as basic rules of Parliamentary practice. A principal author of these lapses was Sir William Mildmay, who seems, as Lord of the Manor of Chelmsford, to have had an outsized voice in devising the tactics of his camp. The suspicion his conduct engendered among the bill's opponents was fully justified.

Gascoyne permitted his personal and political resentments to dictate his conduct in selecting a site for the new county gaol. His proposal to locate it next to the marketplace had the advantage of thwarting proposals to place it on the site of the existing gaol; in addition it would cut into the fees Mildmay received from those attending market day, if attendance at the markets plummeted as opponents charged would be the case. In short, the personal pettiness of justices and MPs, which was reinforced by political rivalries, prolonged and disrupted deliberations on potentially useful measures. In the case of the Essex Gaol Bill, those rivalries resulted in an unsatisfactory and unnecessarily expensive building.

---

[66] Grieve, *The Sleepers and the Shadows*, pp. 158.
[67] Grieve, *The Sleepers and the Shadows*, p. 165.

7

Interest Groups: The West India Interest

This chapter and the one that follows focus on the legislative impact of interest groups and their members, especially the West India and Birmingham interests. Interest groups were not new to the Westminster political scene in the eighteenth century, but, following the revolution of 1688 and the establishment of a financial agreement with the Crown, Parliament met annually. As its legislative sessions became longer and the scope of legislation extended, Parliament's impact on the nation's life increased and interest groups proliferated.[1]

Moreover, they began to exert substantial influence on Parliament and the deliberations of government. Aware that the Commons spent much of its time dealing with the legislation presented by backbench MPs at the behest of their constituents, the landed elite that dominated the institution recognised, according to H.T. Dickinson, that in a commercial society such as Britain's, Parliament had to foster interest groups.[2]

The two chapters demonstrate that the lobbies discussed created different structures and approaches to government and the wider British public. As a result, their respective places within the British political framework in the second half of the eighteenth century differed. Each was successful up to a point, and the chapters will highlight the tactics each adopted and explain why they were adopted.

Though a number of authorities have acknowledged that its influence began to decline either from the late 1750s or with the outbreak of the American war, the West India interest remained a force as Wilberforce and other proponents of the slave trade's abolition discovered after 1788, when its leadership marshalled an influential body of support as issues of special importance to the islands came before Parliament. Nevertheless, forces that had supported the interest earlier in the century by the 1770s were beginning to turn against it, and during the 1780s the islands and their supporters in Parliament became increasingly alienated from an imperial government that they had previously relied upon for support and protection.

---

[1] For discussions of the types of interest groups and their tactics, see, John Brewer, *Sinews of Power: War, Money and the English State, 1688–1783* (Cambridge, MA, 1990), pp. 231–49; H.T. Dickinson, *The Politics of the People in the Eighteenth Century* (Basingstoke, 1995), pp. 56–89; Julian Hoppit, *Britain's Political Economies: Parliament and Economic Life, 1660–1800* (Cambridge, 2017), 150–62; Hoppit and Joanna Innes, 'Introduction', *Failed Legislation, 1660–1800. Extracted from the Commons and Lords Journals*, ed. Julian Hoppit (1997), pp. 18–22.

[2] H.T. Dickinson, *The Politics of the People in the Eighteenth Century* (Basingstoke and London, 1995), p. 57.

I: Lobbies – Background

Julian Hoppit has shown how once warfare regularised the need for regular Parliamentary sessions after 1688 and MPs began to familiarise themselves with the processes of making laws, different interests seized upon those processes for their own advantages.[3] Their prime mission was to represent the needs and concerns of their group. That involved monitoring the formulation of government policy and the flow of legislation to ensure that nothing hostile to the interest was adopted without having received its input. Representatives, however, had to make sure that their presentations linked the needs of the lobby to the broader ones of the nation in order to avoid being accused by MPs and opponents of being self-interested.

To make effective interventions it was essential for lobbies to be current on proceedings within government departments and at Westminster. At the very least key members had to scan each issue of the *Votes* in order to be aware of what had occurred in Parliament. That, however, was rarely sufficient to protect against surprises, so many interests retained agents to keep watch for them in London. The Protestant Dissenting Deputies, for example, employed Robert Yates, one of the Commons' clerks of ingrossments, to watch over issues of relevance to the interest, for which he received a retainer of 10 guineas a year.[4] Alternatively, interests sent groups of members to work with agents for the passage of their legislation or to organise the case against business which was potentially damaging to their cause. Liverpool's slave traders sent a delegation to London to organise a campaign to defeat Sir William Dolben's Slave Trade Regulation Bill in May and June 1788 on the grounds that the measure was 'too great for so hasty a decision; within a few Days of the prorogation of Parliament'[5] The ultimate tool, however, were the solicitor-agents, many of whom were clerks in the Commons. They drafted petitions for bills as well as the bills themselves, found an MP to present the petition and sponsor the bill, helped to secure attendances in each House and especially at meetings of the committees on the bills. In this they were sometimes assisted by the measure's sponsors if they had good connections at Westminster or, as we shall see, had influence with local MPs and peers.[6]

II: Early Development of the West India Interest: Structure and Composition

Until the 1760s the interest found that an informal structure adequately met its needs. According to Andrew O'Shaughnessy this was possible because of 'the coincidence of

---

[3] Julian Hoppit, 'Patterns of Parliamentary legislation, 1660–1800', *Historical Journal*, xxxix (1996), 113–114, 121–123.

[4] D.L. Rydz, *The Parliamentary Agent: A History* (1979), p. 34.

[5] BL, Liverpool Papers, Add. MS 38416, ff. 90–91, Samuel Green to John Tarleton, May 1788 (copy) enclosed in letter of John Tarleton to Lord Hawkesbury, 25 May 1788; cf. John Brewer, *Sinews of Power: War, Money and the English State* (Cambridge, MA, 1976), p. 238; and Langford, *Public Life*, p. 174.

[6] For a good discussion of the services of the solicitor-agent, see D.R. Rydz, *The Parliamentary Agent: A History* (1979), pp. 31–5.

the islands' interests with those of Britain'. In his view, the islands conformed perfectly to the principles of the Trade and Navigation Acts.[7]

Those acts were an outgrowth of mercantilists' conviction that national power depended upon wealth To this end, legislation enacted in 1651 and 1660, along with the tariff of 1660, restricted the export of colonial produce to the mother country; the laws also banned colonies from selling their produce to foreign nations and prohibited them from manufacturing finished goods from their raw materials or purchasing manufactured goods or produce from foreign nations or their colonies. Finally, all colonial imports and exports had to be carried on British shipping.[8]

The results of this system were more or less advantageous for both parties. West Indian exports made up 21 per cent of Britain's total imports in 1748, a figure that rose to 28 per cent by 1800. The islands' appetite for the mother country's exports grew from 5 per cent of her total in 1748 to 12 per cent by the end of the century. Planters, however, paid a price for their prosperity, as Britain continued to raise the duty on imported sugar in order to pay a portion of the cost of its wars. In 1750, the duty on a hundredweight of muscovado was 4s 10d; by 1815 it had risen to 30s. per hundredweight.[9]

Sugar was the West Indies' principal export, stoked by the British populace's ravenous appetite for the product: Britain's per capita consumption grew from ten pounds a person in 1748 to twenty in 1800. Yet, sugar and its by-products formed only a portion of the islands' exports, which included coffee, indigo, cocoa and cotton.

III: The Interest's Structure

The first major changes in the structure of the West India interest occurred at the end of the Seven Years War in 1763. Perhaps the most momentous was Jamaica's appointment of Stephen Fuller as its agent in 1764, a post he retained for over 30 years, during which time he assumed direction of the interest's component groups. Edward Long[10] maintained that Jamaica preferred merchants 'of good experience' for the post because their commercial experience gave them the knowledge that would be useful in assessing legislation and pending policies and their potential consequences. Other desirable attributes he cited included friendships among the London communities of planters and merchants, 'a polite and engaging address' that would enable him to make an impression at public events and before official boards, and the ability to gather

---

[7] O'Shaughnessy, 'The formation of a commercial lobby: The West India interest and British commercial policy and the American Revolution', *HJ*, xl (1997), 76.
[8] Richard B. Sheridan, *Sugar and Slavery*, pp. 41–9.
[9] B.R. Mitchell, *British Historical Statistics* (Cambridge, 1988), pp. 492–3; J.R. Ward, 'The British West Indies, 1748–1815', in *The Oxford History of the British Empire. Vol. II: The Eighteenth Century*, ed. P.J. Marshall (Oxford, 1998), pp. 422–4.
[10] Edward Long (1734–1813), member of a prominent Jamaican family and owner through his wife of the Springvale plantation; Gray's Inn, 1757–69; London resident from 1769; active member of the West India Society; author of *History of Jamaica or, General Survey of the Antient and Modern State of the Island* (3 vols, 1774); Judge, Vice Admiralty Court [sinecure].

information and present compelling, coherent arguments without alienating listeners. Ironically, these are the qualities which scholars such as O'Shaughnessy highlighted in characterising Fuller.[11]

The interest's second component was the group of London merchants trading with the islands who began to meet at the end of the century at the Jamaica Coffee House at St. Michael's Alley in the City's Cornhill Ward. The group created a more formal organisation – the Society of West Indian Merchants – as the result of the growth in their trade, competition with the French, and Britain's annexation of the Ceded Islands in 1763. Shortly after the creation of the Society, its leaders began to take steps that led to the creation over time of a permanent organisational structure: for example, beginning in 1769 the Society began to preserve minutes of its meetings, and it employed James Allen as its secretary.[12]

From the late seventeenth century, the colonial agents, selected either by the islands' assemblies or by the governors of the islands, formed a key element of the interest. Resident in London, they were instrumental in sustaining links between the islands and the metropole, especially as the wars of the late seventeenth and eighteenth centuries put pressure on the islands.

White populations on the British Caribbean islands were transient residents. After 1730, absenteeism on the Leeward Islands – according to O'Shaughnessy – became chronic; by 1745 absentees owned half the property on St. Kitts. Absenteeism was prevalent as well on the Windward Islands (Grenada, St. Lucia, St. Vincent and Tobago), and by 1740 over one-third of Jamaican planters were absentees. While a small portion of the migrants left for North America, the majority returned to Britain; by mid-century as many as 150 Caribbean planters had settled in Britain, and they soon came to form the interest's third and most numerous component.[13]

Like the merchants who assembled at the Jamaica Coffee House, the planters formed their own Planter's Club. William Beckford, the most powerful of Jamaica's absentees, believed it was useful for a number of gentlemen to gather together to consider what might promote the well-being of their country because out of many voices 'wisdom might come'.[14] The group met regularly at the Thatched House Tavern on St. James Street.

Once settled in Britain, absentees were pressed by their Caribbean relatives to enter the House of Commons in order to uphold the islands' interests, especially in the midst of wars. A sustained rise in sugar prices after the 1740s enabled many of the new

---

[11] Edward Long, *The History of Jamaica, or General Survey of the Antient and Modern State of that Island: With reflections on its Situation, Settlements, Inhabitants, Climate, Products, Commerce, Laws and Government* (3 vols, 1970), i, 119–21; O'Shaughnessy, 'Formation of commercial lobby', xl, 77–8; David Beck Ryden, 'Spokesman for opposition: Stephen Fuller, the Jamaica Assembly, and the London West India interest during popular abolitionism, 1788-1795', *The Jamaican Historical Review*, xxvi (2013), 9–11, 13–15.

[12] Lillian Penson, 'The London West India interest', *EHR*, xxxvi (1921), pp. 381–2, 390; O'Shaughnessy, 'Formation of a commercial lobby', *HJ*, xl, 79.

[13] Andrew Jackson O'Shaughnessy, *An Empire Divided: The American Revolution and the British Caribbean* (Philadelphia, PA, 2000), pp. 4–5.

[14] Perry Gauci, 'Learning the ropes of sand: The West India lobby, 1714–1760', in *Regulating the British Economy, 1660–1850*, ed. P. Gauci (Farnham and Burlington, VT, 2011), pp. 112–13.

arrivals to establish themselves as owners of estates.[15] Armed with the traditional accoutrements of the landed classes, portions of the West Indian planter elite formed the fourth branch of the West India interest by securing election to the House of Commons. The process began in earnest in 1754 when 13 West Indians were returned to the House. The moving force behind this wave was Beckford: he returned for the City of London, where he was joined by his brothers Julines[16] and Richard,[17] and later by his nephew Peter.[18] This infusion of West Indians gave rise to a reaction as the election of 1761 approached. West Indians tried to blunt the hostility blending in culturally and purchasing estates. They refused to emulate the nabobs,[19] who bought their way into the House by standing for closed boroughs. Instead they cultivated contacts in the countryside and the outports, sent their sons to public schools and the universities, cultivated Westminster's grandees and, in Beckford's case, adopted some of the more moderate items on the agenda of metropolitan radicals. In the eyes of many, however, their rise was too sudden and their wealth and their display too profuse. In the fury that engulfed England as it lurched its way towards war on the continent and in North America, efforts at assimilation could not protect some from the popular wrath against candidates with Caribbean links.[20]

IV: West Indians in the Commons

Different authorities have used a variety of criteria to identify MPs whom they include as part of the West Indian contingent in the House of Commons. For the most part they agree on including the islands' agents as well as merchants engaged in the West Indian trade in London, Liverpool and Bristol and bankers who financed their trade and provided credit for West Indian planters. A number of planters resided in Britain while continuing to own Caribbean estates. They comprised the largest contingent within the Parliamentary contingent, which also contained former civil officials and naval and military officers who had served in the islands. Finally, I have included members for London, Bristol and Liverpool, cities whose economies were closely tied to those of the islands, whose bankers financed and whose merchants carried on the slave trade which provided the islands with their labour. Except in the case of members from the three major ports, I made a point of identifying at least two of the sources cited in the notes to Table 7.1 to confirm inclusion in the West Indian Parliamentary

---

[15] For West Indians' land purchases, see John Habakkuk, *Marriage, Debt and the Estates System: English Landownership 1650-1950* (Oxford, 1994), pp. 453-61; O'Shaughnessy, *An Empire Divided*, pp. 12-13.
[16] Julines Beckford (?1717-64), MP, Salisbury, 1754-64.
[17] Richard Beckford (1712-56), MP, Bristol, 1754-6; alderman of London, 1754.
[18] Peter Beckford (?1739-1811), MP, Morpeth, 1768-74.
[19] For the reaction against nabobs, see Philip Lawson and Jim Phillips '"Our Execrable Banditti": Perceptions of nabobs in mid-eighteenth-century Britain', *Albion*, xvi (1984), pp. 225-41.
[20] This paragraph is based on material in Gauci, 'Learning the ropes of sand: The West India lobby' and 'The attack of the Creolian powers West Indians at the Parliamentary elections of mid-Georgian Britain, 1754-1774', in *Parliament, Politics and Policy in Britain and Ireland, c. 1680-1832: Essays in Honour of D.W. Hayton*, ed. Clyve Jones and James Kelly (Chichester, 2014), pp. 201-22.

contingent. In a few instances I have included an individual while leaving a question mark in the 'category' column. This is because Stephen Fuller included Sir Richard Hill and Joseph Gulston on his list 'Colony members of Parliament 1781 resident in Great Britain'. I have been unable to trace the connection of either man to the West Indies. Sir Richard was an evangelical who during the 1780s became an adherent of William Wilberforce. He was a fairly active member, but much of that activity seems often to have been on behalf of questions that were contrary to those which concerned Fuller. Joseph Gulston inherited a fortune from his father, the head of a mercantile house in Lisbon and a City merchant. The son, however, focused his attention on the embellishment of an Italian villa at Ealing Grove and on assembling a collection of books and engravings. By 1784 he was ruined financially. These projects rather than the needs of the West Indian islands seem to have consumed his attention.[21]

Table 7.1 MPs with West Indian connections sitting for English constituencies, 1754–1790

	Dates[22]	Category	Sources[23]
Sir Edmund Affleck	1782–88	navy	i
Benjamin Allen	1768–81	Jamaica plantations	i, v, ix
Sir George Amyand	1754–66	banker, Grenada plantations	i, v
John Amyand	1774–80	merchant/WIC	i, v
Richard Atkinson	1784–85	WI merchant	i, v
Chaloner Arcedeckne	1780–86	Jamaica plantations	i, iii, v
Anthony Bacon	1764–84	slave trader	i, iii
James Baillie	1792–1803	Grenada plantations; agent for Grenada	ii, iv, ix
William Baker	1747–68	banker	i
William Baker	1768–74, 1777–84, 1790–1802, 1805–07	merchant	iii

[21] HPC, 1754–1790, ii, 560.
[22] Dates are for total service in the House, save for members who were returned at each election between 1745 and 1790 for Bristol, Liverpool or London. In their cases, the dates indicate service only for those constituencies.
[23] I identified most of the MPs returned to the House before by going through biographies in Namier and Brooke (ed.), *The History of Parliament: The House of Commons, 1754–1790* (3 vols, 1964) (i); for members returned by 1790–1820 I relied primarily upon R.G. Thorne (ed.), *The History of Parliament: The House of Commons, 1790–1820* (5 vols, 1986) (ii). Other sources cited below enabled me to identify additional members or confirmed my inclusion of them in it. These include: Boston College, Burns Lib., Stephen Fuller MSS, 1766–85, MS 265, f. 181, 'Members of the House of Commons with an interest in Jamaica' (iii); M.W. McCahill (ed.), *The Correspondence of Stephen Fuller, 1788–95: Jamaica, the West India Interest at Westminster and the Campaign to Preserve the Slave Trade* (Malden, MA, and Chichester, 2014) (iv); Richard B. Sheridan, *Sugar and Slavery: An Economic History of the British West Indies, 1623–1775* (Kingston, Jamaica, 1974) (v); John Habakkuk, *Marriage, Debate and the Estates, English Landownership, 1650–1950* (Oxford, 1994) (vi); Andrew Jackson O'Shaughnessy, 'The formation of the colonial lobby: The West India interest, British colonial policy and the American Revolution', HJ, xl (1997) (vii); Lillian M. Penson, *The Colonial Agents of the British West Indies: A Study in Colonial Administration, Mainly in the Eighteenth Century* (1971) (viii); David Beck Ryden, *West Indian Slavery and British Abolition, 1783–1807* (Cambridge and New York, 2009) (ix); Gerritt P. Judd, *Members of Parliament, 1734–1832* (New Haven, CT, 1955) (x); Roger Anstey, *The Atlantic Slave Trade and British Abolition, 1760–1810* (Atlantic Highlands, NJ, 1975) (xi).

Sir Charles Warwick Bampfylde	1774–90, 1796–1812	PL	iii
Sir John Barnard	1721–66	merchant, insurance, London	i
Sir Charles Barrow	1751–89	merchant, WIC	i, v
Nathaniel Bayly	1770–9	Jamaica plantations	i, iii, v
Julienes Beckford	1754–64	Jamaica plantations	i, v, vi
Peter Beckford	1768–74	Jamaica plantations	i, v
Richard Beckford	1754–6	Jamaica plantations, Bristol	i, v
Richard Beckford	1780–96	merchant	i, iii, x
William Beckford	1754–70	Jamaica plantations, London, WI merchant	i, v, vi, x
William Beckford, II	1784–94, 1806–20	Jamaica plantations	i, iii, v
Slingsby Bethell	1747–58	WI merchant; Antigua plantations; London	i, v, x
John Blackburne	1784–1830	Lancashire	i, ii
Patrick Blake	1768–84	St. Kitts and Monserrat plantations	i, iii, v
John Bond	1780–1801	landowner	i, iii
Hon. William Bouverie	1776–1802	?	iii
John Boyd	1780–4	Jamaica plantations[24]	i, iii, v
Matthew Brickdale	1768–74, 1780–90	WI plantations, Bristol	i, iii
Hon. Thomas Bromley	1754–5	Barbados plantation	i, v, vi
Frederick Bull	1773–84	merchant, London	i
Sir Thomas Charles Bunbury	1761–84, 1790–1812	Grenada plantations	i, iii, iv
Edmund Burke	1774–80	Bristol	i
William Matthew Burt	1761–8, 1776–80	St. Kitts plantations, Governor	i, iii, v
Sir Philip Jennings Clerke	1768–88	WIC	i, iv
Sir William Codrington	1747–92	Antigua and Barbados plantations	i, iii, v
Sir Geoge Colebrooke	1754–74	Antigua and Grenada plantations; agent for Dominica	i, iii, v, viii
J.E. Colleton	1747–68, 1772–4	Barbados plantation	i, v
Sir George Cornewall[25]	1774–96, 1802–7	Grenada plantation	i, iv
John Crewe[26]	1765–1802	some WI property	i, iii, iv
Henry Cruger[27]	1774–80 1784–90	merchant, Bristol; Jamaica and St. Croix plantations	i, iv
Ellis Cunliffe	1755–67	merchant and shipper, Liverpool	i
George Daubeney	1781–4	WI merchant, Bristol	i, x

(continued)

---

[24] David Hancock, *Citizens of the World: London Merchants and the Integration of the British Atlantic Community, 1735–1785* (Cambridge, 1994), p. 145.

[25] S. Seymour, S. Daniels and C. Watkins, 'Estate and empire: Sir George Cornewall's management of Moccas, Herefordshire and La Taste, Grenada, 1771–1819', *Journal of Historical Geography*, xxiv (1998), 313–51.

[26] Abel Smith, trustee of Crewe's marriage settlement, was responsible for seeing that Crewe's heirs received compensation following the abolition of slavery in 1834. Nicholas Draper, *The Price of Emancipation: Slave Ownership, Compensation and British Society at the End of Slavery* (Cambridge, 2010), Appendix 1.

[27] Dresser, *Slavery Obscured*, p. 115.

Table 7.1 Continued

	Dates	Category	Sources
Sir Charles Davers	1768–1802	WIC; sugar refiner WIC/ Barbados	i, iii, v, x
John Dawes	1780–90	banker	iii
Henry Dawkins	1760–74, 1776–84	Jamaica plantations, WI merchant	iii, v
James Dawkins	1754–7	Jamaica plantations	i, iii, v, vi
James Dawkins, II	1784–1826, 1831–32	Jamaica plantations	i, ii, v, vi, xi
Philip Dehany	1774–80	Jamaica plantations	i, v, ix
William Devaynes	1784–1806	Commr. of Africa Co.	i, ii
Samuel Dicker	1754–60	Jamaica merchant and planter	i
William Dickinson	1768–74, 1777–90, 1796–1806	Jamaican planter, WI merchant; Jamaica	i, iii, v, vi
William Dickinson II	1796–1831	Jamaica plantations	i, v
John St. Leger Douglas	1768–83	St. Kitts	i, v
Thomas Erle Drax	1744–8, 1761–8	Barbados plantations	i, v, vi
Edward Hyde East	1792–3, 1823–31	Jamaica plantations	ii, x
George Durant	1768–74	WI merchant	i, x
Samuel Estwick	1779–95	Barbados plantations; agent for Barbados	i, iii, vii
Francis Eyre	1774–5, 1780–4	Jamaica plantations	i, iii
William Fitzherbert[28]	1761–72	WIC, Barbados plantation	i
Thomas Foster	1741–7, 1761–5	Jamaica plantations	i, v
Sambrooke Freeman	1754–61, 1768–74	St. Kitts plantations	i
Jeffrey French	1741–7, 1754	Jamaica plantations	i, iii, v
John Fuller	1754–55	Jamaica plantations	i, v
John Fuller II	1780–4, 1801–12	Jamaica plantations	i, ii, iii
Rose Fuller	1756–77	Jamaica plantations, WI merchant	i, v
Richard Grace Gamon	1784–12	St. Kitts plantations	i, iii, xi
Alan Gardner	1790–1806	navy, WIC (Jamaica)	i, ii
Bamber Gascoyne	1780–96	Liverpool	i, ii
Sir John Gibbons	1754–68	Barbados plantations	i, v, vii
Sir Richard Glyn	1758–68, 1768–73	banker, London	i
James Gordon	1785–96, 1808–12	Antigua plantations	i, ii, x
Sir William Gordon	1777–83	WI merchant and Jamaican plantations	i, iii
Samuel Greatheed	1747–61	St. Kitts plantations	i, v
Richard Erle Drax Grosvenor	1786–8, 1794–6, 1802–7, 1818–19	WIC/PL	i, v, vi
Thomas Grosvenor	1755–95	WIC	i
Joseph Gulston	1765–8, 1780–4	?	i, iii
Hon. Thomas Harley	1761–74	merchant, WI contractor London	i
George Hayley	1774–81	London, WI merchant	i, x
John Hardman	1754–55	Liverpool, merchant	i
James Modyford Heywood	1768–74	Jamaica plantations	i, v
Richard Hill	1780–6	?	i, ii, iii
William Innes	1774–5	West Indian merchant; banker	i, ix

[28] *Additional Grenville Papers, 1763–1765*, ed. John R.G. Tomlinson (Manchester, 1962).

Charles Jenkinson	1761–86	PL	i, iv
Sir James Johnstone	1784–90, 1791–4	Grenada plantations	i, ii, v, ix
John Kirkman	1780	London	i
Sir Robert Ladbroke	1754–73	London, banker	i
Robert Ladbroke	1780–96, 1802–7	West India merchant	i, iii, iv
James Laroche	1768–80	slaving agent; Antigua plantations	iv
Daniel Lascelles	1752–80	WIC; WI merchant	i, iv
Edward Lascelles[29]	1761–74, 1790–6	Barbados plantations and other WI islands	i, ii, v, vi, x
Edwin Lascelles	1744–90	Barbados plantations and other WI islands; WI merchant	i, iii, v, vi
Benjamin Lethieullier	1768–97	banker	i, xi
Sir Watkin Lewes	1781–96	London	i, ii
Sir Henry Lippincott	1780	WI merchant, Bristol	i
Charles Long	1789–1826	WIC	i, ii, xi
Dudley Long	1780–1821	WIC	i, ii, iii
Sir James Lowther	1757–84	Barbados plantations	i, iii
Thomas Lucas	1780–4	WI merchant	i, iii
Hon. George Fulke Lyttleton	1790–6	WIC	ii, x
Lauchlin Macleane	1768–71	Grenada plantations	i, v
Robert Mackreth	1774–90	Grenada plantations	i, v, xi
Henry Martin	1790–4	WIC	ii, x
Charles Martin	1747–74	Antigua/Nevis plantations	i, v
Samuel Martin	1754–74	WIC/Antigua	i, v
Charles Marsham	1768–90	St. Kitts plantations	i, ii, iii, iv, v
Sir William Meredith	1761–80	Liverpool	i, v
David Robert Michel	1780–4	WIC	i, iii, v
Crisp Molineux	1771–90	St. Kitts plantations	i, v
Robert Monckton	1751–4, 1774, 1778–82	St. Vincent plantations	i, v
Daniel Moore	1754–61	merchant; Jamaica PL	i
Edward Morant	1761–8, 1774–87	Jamaica plantations	i, iii
Richard Muilman Trench-Chiswell	1790–7	WI merchant	i, x
William Needham	1774–90	Jamaica plantations	i, iii, v
Arnold Nesbitt	1753–79	WI merchant	i, v, x
John Nesbitt	1780–1802	WI merchant	i, ii, iii, v, x
Nathaniel Newnham	1780–90	banker, London	i, ii
Robert Nugent, Ld. Clare	1754–74	Bristol	i
Richard Oliver	1770–80	West India agent and WI merchant; Antigua plantations	i, v, x
George Onslow	1754–74	WIC	i
Col. George Onslow	1760–84	WIC	i, iii
Thomas Onslow	1775–185	WIC	i, ii, iii
Sir Peter Parker	1784–90	navy/PL	i
Ralph Payne	1769–71, 1776–84, 1795–9	Gov., Leeward Is.; St. Kitts plantations	i, iii, v, x

(continued)

---

[29] For the Lascelles and their West Indies empire, see S.D. Smith, *Slavery, Family, and Gentry Capitalism in the British Atlantic: The World of the Lascelles, 1648-1834* (Cambridge, 2000).

Table 7.1 Continued

	Dates	Category	Sources
Richard Pennant	1767–80, 1784–90	Jamaica plantations Liverpool	i, iii, v, vi, ix
James Farrell Phipps	1780–6	St Kitts plantations	i, iii, v
John Frederick Pinney	1747–61	Nevis and Antigua plantations	i, v, vi
Charles Pole	1756–61	merchant; Liverpool Commr. Africa Co.	i
Sir William Pulteney	1775–1805	inherited Grenada estate of Sir James Johnstone; Tobago plantations	i, ii, v, x
Henry Rawlinson	1780–4	WI property, Liverpool merchant	i, v
George Rodney	1751–4, 1759–82	C.-in-C. Leeward Is., '61–'63, and Leeward Is. and Barbados, '79; C.-in-C., Jamaica '71–'74	i
Denys Rolle[30]	1761–74	Bahamas plantations	i
John Rolle	1780–96	Bahamas plantations	i
George Rose	1784–1818	Caribbean agent, wife's Dominica plantation	i
Thomas Salusbury	1724–9, 1734–56	Liverpool	i
John Sawbridge	1774–95	London	i, ii
John Sharpe	1754–6	St. Kitts plantations; 'agent to several West India Islands'	i, v
Fane William Sharpe	1756–71	St. Kitts plantations	i
Jarrit Smith	1756–68	Bristol	i
Henry Somerset, Marquess of Worcester	1790–6	Bristol	i
Hans Sloane Stanley	1768–84, 1788–1806	Jamaica plantations, WIC	i, x
Hans Stanley	1743–7, 1754–80	WIC	i, v, x
Thomas Stanley	1780–1812	Lancashire	i, ii, iv
Lovell Stanhope	1774–83	agent for Jamaica	i, viii, x
Sir Thomas Stapleton	1759–68	Monserrat and Nevis plantations	i, v, x
Anthony Storer	1774–84	Jamaica plantations	i, ii
Anthony Lagley Swymmer	1747–60	Caribbean agent, Jamaican plantation	i, v, x
Col. Banastre Tarleton	1790–1812	Liverpool	i, ii
John Tarleton	1792–6	slave trader	ii
Sir George Thomas	1790–7	Antigua plantations	ii, x
John Tomlinson	1761–7	Antigua plantations; WI merchant	i, v, x
Samuel Touchet	1761–8	WI merchant	i, v
John Townson	1780–7	merchant	i, iii
Barlow Trecothick	1768–74	WI merchant Caribbean properties	i, v, x
John Trevanion	1747–67	merchant	i, iii
Charles Tudway	1754–61	Antigua plantations	i, v, x
Clement Tudway	1761–1815	Antigua plantations	i, iii, v, x

[30] Michael Craton, 'Hobbesian or Panglossian? The two extremes of slave conditions in the British West Indies, 1783 to 1834', *WMQ*, 3rd ser., xxxv (1978), 324–56.

Benjamin Vaughan	1792–6	WI merchant and Jamaica plantations	ii, v, ix, x
John Ward	1754–74	PL	i, iv
William Ward	1780–8	PL	i, iii, iv
Brooke Watson	1784–93	merchant, London	i
Nathaniel Webb	1768–80	Monserrat and Antigua plantations	i, v
Sir Godfrey Vassall Webster	1786–90, 1796–1800	WIC	i, ii
Paul Wentworth	1780	Surinam plantation and WI merchant	i, x
George White Thomas	1784–1812	Monserrat and St. Kitts plantations	i, x
Jacob Wilkinson	1774–84	merchant and banker	i, iii
John Williams	1772	West Indian who bribed the Corporation and was unseated	i
William Woodley	1761–6, 1780–4	St. Kitts plantation; Gov. Leeward Islands, 66–71, 91–3	i, iii, x
Sir William Young	1784–1807	Gov. of Tobago; agent for St. Vincent; lands in Antigua, St. Vincent and Tobago	i, ii, viii, xi

Abbreviations: WIC/West Indian connection; WI/West Indian; C.-in-C./Commander-in-Chief; PL/planter

V: Extent of the Interest's Influence

While Lillian Penson and other scholars believed that the influence of the West India lobby began to decline by the early 1760s,[31] contemporary English or colonial observers did not share that assessment. In 1764, Boston merchants declared that West Indians were to blame for the Sugar Act[32] 'with no other view than to enrich themselves, by obliging the northern Colonies to take their whole supply from them; and they still endeavor the continuance of it under a pretence, that they can supply Great Britain and all her Colonies with West Indian goods, which is perfectly chimerical'. John Adams added that the northern colonies had been sacrificed to 'the superior interest of the West Indies in Parliament'.[33] As late as 1788 Edmund Burke was still lamenting that it was not worth bringing abolition bills before the House of Commons because planters and merchants had retained the power to wreck a politician's career and his party. He was, however, being overly dramatic.[34]

---

[31] Penson, 'London West India interest', 124; Thomas, *British Politics and the Stamp Act Crisis*, pp. 31–33.
[32] The Sugar Act forbade the import of foreign rum to the British Isles and the Empire, reduced the duty on foreign molasses from 6d to 3d a gallon and increased the tax on sugar imports to one pound seven shillings per cwt. The colonial customs service in North America was reorganised and enlarged; likewise, the North American naval squadron was enlarged and assigned responsibility for enforcing the legislation O'Shaughnessy, *Empire Divided*, p. 65.
[33] Quoted in O'Shaughnessy, *Empire Divided*, p. 66.
[34] Reginald Copeland, *The British Anti-Slavery Movement* (New York, 1964), p. 62.

Throughout the 1760s the islands generally refused to join the North American colonies in raising constitutional objections to the imperial government's right to levy taxes upon them. They remained quiet even during the Stamp Act crisis, though they would pay more under the new levy, and they already sent London large amounts to cover the costs of the imperial government.[35] Open resistance to the measure was limited to St. Kitts, Nevis and Monserrat where riots occurred. These may have been stoked by external pressure from North America, on which the islands were dependent for provisions. Other West Indians followed the North American patriots in rejecting the British claim that colonies were virtually represented in Parliament, with the exception of St. Kitts and Nevis, who complied with the act, for which they were condemned in the North American press and boycotted by North American merchants.[36] Indeed, as colonial assemblies in North America moved towards rebellion, Jamaica passed votes of loyalty to the British Crown. Even the once obstreperous Leeward Islanders rejected a motion that was critical of its popular governor's[37] praise for Lord North and his policies.[38]

In London, however, a few West Indian MPs mounted an opposition to the Stamp Act. Paul Langford highlighted the central role of Barlow Trecothick,[39] a North American merchant, in mobilising the British merchant communities against the Act and encouraging them to petition Parliament in support of repeal. According to Langford, the outpouring of petitions and accompanying propaganda had the effect of turning British opinion in favour of repeal.[40] William Beckford and Rose Fuller also made notable contributions. During the first substantial debate on the preliminary resolutions on 6 February 1765 Beckford was the sole MP to question the wisdom of imposing an internal tax on the colonies, noting that 'the North Americans do not think an internal and an external duty the same'. While acknowledging the right of Parliament to tax, Rose Fuller doubted its 'propriety' and rejected George Grenville's assertion that the existence of the Post Office in North America legitimised his subsequent imposition of an internal tax.[41] Stephen Fuller wrote that the 'the major part' of the 49 members who had opposed the duty on the 6th were 'Gentlemen of the Colonies'.[42]

---

[35] O'Shaughnessy, *Empire Divided*, p. 86.
[36] O'Shaughnessy, *An Empire Divided*, pp. 81–101.
[37] Sir Ralph Payne (1739–1807), Gov. Leeward Islands, 1771–5, 1799–1807.
[38] Michael Craton and James Walvin, *A Jamaican Plantation: The History of Worthy Park, 1670–1970* (1970), p. 76.
[39] Barlow Trecothick (?1718–1775), MP, London, 1768–1775; alderman of London, 1764–1774; sheriff, 1766; Ld. Mayor, 1770; provincial agent for New Hampshire, 1766–1774; sometime resident of Boston, Massachusetts and the West Indies where he owned plantations in Grenada and Jamaica.
[40] Paul Langford, 'The first Rockingham administration and the repeal of the Stamp Act: The role of the commercial lobby and economic pressures', in *Resistance, Politics, and the American Struggle for Independence, 1765–1775*, ed. Walter H. Conser, Jr, Ronald M. McCarthy, David J. Toscano, Gene Sharpe (Boulder, CO, 1986), pp. 97–105.
[41] *Parliamentary Diaries of Nathaniel Ryder, 1764–1767*, ed. P.D.G. Thomas. Camden Miscellany, Vol. xxiii, Camden, 4th ser. Vol. vii (Royal Historical Society, 1969), pp. 257, 259.
[42] John J. Burns Library, Boston College, Stephen Fuller Letter Books, Joseph J. Williams, SJ ethnological collection, MS.2009.030, Fuller to Committee, 7 Feb. 1765.

Nevertheless, he subsequently exhibited little urgency in marshalling West Indian forces against the Stamp Act. After some hesitation West Indians decided on 10 February 1765 that they needed to petition the House: Fuller drafted the document, which raised doubts about the wisdom of the tax, had it signed by the planters and merchants and enlisted Rose Fuller to present it. Then, to avoid giving offence, he showed it to George Grenville before having it presented to the House. Grenville saw no problem with Fuller's petition and preferred to leave it to the House to decide whether it should be accepted.[43] He was primarily concerned to get Fuller's thoughts as to how to contain smuggling, which the latter promised to submit in writing.[44] Fuller's petition was finally presented on 11 February 1765, and following a motion by Sir William Meredith, witnesses were examined by the American committee regarding the consequences of the Act. Trecothick testified to the losses that British merchants had incurred since the imposition of the tax.[45]

Attempts at accommodation with a minister whose policies were likely to have a damaging effect on Jamaica and the other islands had pragmatic goals. As Fuller explained to the Jamaican committee on 18 March, there was little chance of securing the elimination of the duty on rum, Jamaica's second most valuable export, and an increase of the one on brandy, the principal competitor to rum, unless smuggling could be contained. Thus, he believed it was best for him 'to turn my thoughts that way, and more particularly as Mr. Grenville had desired my sentiments upon that Subject'. His brother Rose had already raised the issue in the House of Commons, and Stephen was naively confident that steps could be taken 'to root out smuggling completely!'[46] Fuller's belief that co-operation with the ministry could prove mutually advantageous was to be an on-going theme of his agency.

That co-operation was extended to the next administration by Rose Fuller and William Beckford as the Rockingham ministry, in reaction to widespread agitation in America and pressure from Britain's merchant communities, moved to repeal Grenville's Stamp Act. Important proceedings on the question in the Commons took place in a committee of the whole House on American affairs, chaired by Rose Fuller.

In this capacity Fuller tried to ensure that witnesses and speakers buttressed the case for repeal. On 17 February he allowed little scope for opponents, instead opening the proceedings with two witnesses who addressed issues raised in his brother's Jamaican petition. Even Beeston Long,[47] the first of the witnesses put forward by those who opposed repeal, indicated that islands such as Antigua faced the possibility of starvation because of the cessation of American trade. According to Horace Walpole, committee members became impatient with Fuller's favouritism. The result was an assault on his evenhandedness:

---

[43] The rules of the House prevented it from receiving petitions against taxes except from the City of London.
[44] *Proceedings and Debates of the British Parliament Respecting North America. Vol. II: 1765-1768*, ed. Richard G. Simmons and Peter D.G. Thomas (Millwood, NY, 1983), p. 26.
[45] *Proceedings and Debates*, ii, 134. Thomas, *The Stamp Act Crisis*, pp. 217–19.
[46] Boston College, Burns Library, Fuller MSS 256, ff. 87–8, Fuller to Committee, 18 March, 1765.
[47] Beeston Long (1711–1785), partner in the West Indian trading house of Long, Drake and Long; sometime Chair of the Society of West India Merchants; Governor of the Royal Exchange Assurance Co.

before he [Fuller] could make his report Mr. Shiffner ironically proposed to thank the chairman for his impartiality: Onslow[48] defended, and moved to thank him seriously. This provoked so much, that Fuller was accused of not doing his duty by suppressing the riots and insults offered to several members who voted against repeal.[49]

Undaunted by the criticisms, Rose Fuller continued his whole-hearted defence of the repeal effort. When William Blackstone proposed in the American committee on 24 February to limit the repeal to colonies that had deleted resolutions challenging the right of Parliament to tax, Fuller objected, arguing that the bill of repeal should be separate from 'any other consideration', and that 'a separate bill ought to be brought in upon the first resolution in relation to the right'.[50] William Beckford continued throughout the proceedings to question Britain's right to tax the colonies, thus earning their accolades.[51]

The role played by Beckford and Fuller during proceedings on the Stamp Act stood out among the West India contingent in the House of Commons. Only seven other members of the interest appear in Ryder's accounts of proceedings on the Act. Two of them, Lord Nugent and Hans Stanley spoke in favour of the Stamp Act. Others listed in Ryder's reports including Sir John Gibbons,[52] George Onslow, Sir William Baker and Sir William Meredith supported repeal. Among the core group of West Indian MPs at least ten, or about a third of the total, voted against repeal according to O'Shaughnessy.[53] On this issue and on other British responses to American resistance the West Indian Commons contingent remained divided down to the end of the war.

The tenuous partnership some West Indians had established with the North Americans during the early months of 1766 barely survived the passage of the repeal of the Stamp Act. West Indians continued to oppose their trade with the Dutch and

---

[48] George Onslow (1731-1814), MP, Rye, 1754-61 and Surrey, 1761-74; Out Ranger, Windsor Great Park, 1754-63; Surveyor of King's Gdns, 1761-3; Ld. of Treasury, 1765-77; Ld. Lieut., Surrey, 1776-1814; Comptroller of Household, 1777-9; Treasurer, 1779-80; Ld. of Bedchamber, 1780-1814; succ. as 4th Baron Onslow, 1776; cr. Earl of Onslow, 1801.

[49] Walpole, *Memoirs*, iii, pp. 30-1. Fuller remained a fierce partisan. When Alexander Wedderburn and Jeremiah Dyson moved in a subsequent debate to add a clause declaring that any person calling into question the Stamp Act or abusing it in any manner should be guilty of praemunire, 'Fuller, with severe invectives on the Tories said that such a motion would have been well timed in the reigns of Henry VIII or Charles II'. For other concerns regarding Fuller's partiality, see Thomas, *Stamp Act Crisis*, p. 233.

[50] *Ryder Parliamentary Diaries*, p. 314; *CJ*, xxx, 602.

[51] *Ryder Parliamentary Diaries*, pp. 256-7, 267; Perry Gauci, *William Beckford: First Prime Minister of the London Empire* (New Haven, CT and London, 2013), pp. 120-2.

[52] Sir John Gibbons (c. 1717-76), MP Stockbridge, 1754-61 and Wallingford, 1761-8; cr. K.B., 1761; Member of the Barbados Assembly, 1745-68. Ryder noted that he spoke on 6 Feb. 1765, but did not include his remarks. According to his biography in *HPC, 1754-1790*, ii, 498, he spoke against the Stamp Act on 6 Feb. and voted for its repeal in 1766.

[53] Sir Charles Bunbury, W.M. Burt, J.E. Colleton, T.E. Drax, Sir Alexander Grant,* Sir James Lowther, Samuel Martin, William Sharpe, Hans Stanley and Sir Thomas Stapleton. I do not include Grant on my list of members of the interest because he sat for a Scots constituency, but do include Nugent who sat for Bristol. He opposed repeal. Andrew J. O'Shaughnessy, 'The West India interest and the crisis of American independence', in *West Indies Accounts: Essays on the History of the British Caribbean and the Atlantic Economy in Honour of Richard Sheridan*, ed. Roderick A. McDonald (Kingston, Jamaica, 1996), pp. 129, 143, n. 21.

French Caribbean islands, while the North American merchants complained that the duties on sugar and molasses remained too high because of the Sugar Act. The issue of duties remained a major point of contention between the two sides. Fuller informed Governor Lyttleton of Jamaica that 'the Sugar Colonies however disposed to cooperate with [the [North Americans] ... in a repeal of the [Stamp Act] ... are & will be very tenacious in the former [Sugar] Act ... This has hitherto hindered a conjuncture, and will in my opinion *prevent any future Conjunction between the Continental Proprietors to the Island Proprietors residing in England*'.[54]

While the Rockingham administration arranged the final details of the repeal of the Stamp Act, it encouraged the West Indians and North Americans to settle between themselves the issues relating to molasses duties and a more open trade. During those proceedings Bristol's Society of Merchant Venturers petitioned for the establishment of a free port in Dominica. The petition, which was presented on 7 April by Nugent, argued that the establishment of free ports to receive foreign produce would be a means of increasing manufacturers and extending the commerce of Britain.[55] The proposal was subsequently supported by petitions from the merchants of Lancaster and Manchester cotton manufacturers, while sugar refiners of London and Bristol petitioned to register their usual complaints.[56]

These interventions intensified the struggle between the West Indians and the North Americans and opened fissures within the West Indian interest in London. Beckford joined with West Indian merchants in opposing the free port proposal which he claimed would aid the islands' competitors. On the other hand, Rose and Stephen Fuller, acting in concert with the Rockingham administration and its Chancellor of the Exchequer, William Dowdeswell,[57] supported the proposal as did the merchant and manufacturing communities in the major British and North American ports.

Beckford insisted that the West Indians had a 'right' to be heard on matters that so directly affected their well-being and eventually 'flooded' the House with papers to back his arguments, and reinforced that evidence in May 1766 with witnesses who testified before the American Committee. His presentations were seen by members to be self-interested and did little more than drag out the proceedings.[58]

In the end the West India interest made a number of concessions in order to reach an agreement. The Free Ports Act, according to Richard Sheridan, established two different systems of trade. Dominica's ports were to capture the trade of Martinique and Guadeloupe. They were allowed to re-export British and colonial goods that had legally entered the island as well as slaves from Africa, so long as an import duty of 30s a head was paid. They could also re-export products from foreign colonies, including sugar and molasses, so long as the imported staples were not shipped to a British island.

---

[54] Quoted in O'Shaughnessy, *Empire Divided*, p. 67.
[55] *CJ*, xxx, 704; Minchinton, *Politics and the Port of Bristol*, pp. 105–6; *Proceedings and Debates*, ii, pp. 366, 373.
[56] *CJ*, xxx, 705, 759.
[57] William Dowdeswell (1721–75), MP, Tewkesbury, 1747–54 and Worcestershire, 1761–75; Chancellor of the Exchequer, 1765–6.
[58] *CJ*, xxx, 778, 790, 797, 801; Gauci, *William Beckford*, pp. 123–4; Thomas; *Stamp Act Crisis*, pp. 267–8.

The act made Dominica a trading colony of some importance, one where French and Spanish traders purchased large numbers of slaves and British manufactured goods.

Jamaica's free ports differed from Dominica's as a result of the safeguards included to protect its planters. Provisions relating to the re-export of slaves and manufacturers were the same as Dominica's. Four ports were opened in Jamaica: Kingston, Savannah-la-Mar, Montego Bay and Santa Lucea.[59] The Act contributed to the revival of Jamaica's slave trade and increased its annual inflow of bullion by substantial amounts.

Though the West India interest surrendered on many points, it made some key gains. Its sugar retained its monopoly in the metropolitan market. Secondly there was no longer a duty on West Indian sugar entering North America, while that on foreign sugar remained, and sugar exported from the northern colonies would be considered foreign sugar.[60] Francis Armytage assigns much of the credit for securing the final compromise that led to the agreement to Rose and Stephen Fuller. He emphasises that they only agreed to allow the importation of French sugar so long as the monopoly of the West Indian islands in Great Britain was maintained.[61]

Because they were alarmed by the North Americans' moves towards independence, neither the islands' assemblies nor the West Indian lobby at Westminster took any decisive steps to oppose British policy during the late 1760s and the first several years of the next decade.[62] Rose Fuller, for example, was so outraged by the Boston Tea Party that he recommended imposing a fine of £20,000 to compensate the East India Company.[63] At the same time, the interests' leaders, including Beeston Long, Fuller and Beckford, managed to relieve the islands from some of the strictures that Britain imposed on America. For example, they were able to exempt them from the jurisdiction of the Board of Customs in Boston and the Vice Admiralty Courts, and Lord Hillsborough, Secretary of State for the Colonies, exempted Virginia and the West Indies from the Townshend duties. Members were inactive or divided in response to the Coercive Acts in 1774 and stood by passively as the House passed the Massachusetts Regulating Act (14 Geo. III, c. 45) and the Quebec Act (14 Geo. III, c. 83).

VI: The Interest and the American War of Independence

It was not until the end of 1774 that the islands and their representatives in London began to face the implications of Britain's North American policies and endeavour to alter them. In December 1774 Jamaica's Assembly dispatched an address to George III protesting that all colonists enjoyed the rights of Englishmen. The Jamaicans went on

---

[59] Sheridan, *Sugar and Slavery*, pp. 461–2.
[60] Thomas, *Stamp Act Crisis*, pp. 271–2.
[61] Francis Armytage, *The Free Port System in the British West Indies: A Study in Commercial Policy, 1766–1822* (London, 1953), p. 43. For a brief discussion of the role of Lord Nugent in securing the Free Port Act, see Chapter 3.
[62] O'Shaughnessy, *Empire Divided*, pp. 127–34.
[63] O'Shaughnessy, *Empire Divided*, p. 129.

to challenge the notion that Parliament was sovereign over a colony's internal affairs and called upon the King to prevent the enslavement of the colonies.[64]

The first sign of life among the London contingent occurred when 23 planters, alarmed by the prospect of war and its potential impact on the islands, approached Beeston Long on 3 January 1775 and noted that:

> The very alarming Situation in which the West Indies are placed, by the late American proceedings, induced us to apply to you as Chairman of the Society of the West India Merchants, to request, that they will not come by any Resolutions, as a separate Body at their meeting, but that they will join with us, in calling a General Meeting of the whole body of Planters, and West India Merchants, to deliberate on the Steps to be taken by us jointly on the present important crisis.[65]

The result of the planters' initiative was the formation of the Society of West India Planters and Merchants, which henceforth became the focal point of the interest's organisation. Following a meeting on 18 January, the group never disintegrated into two separate organisations as had existed earlier in the century. The Society's permanence resulted from shared interests and from an on-going series of crises that endangered the entire interest. In the short term, the American non-importation agreements, which led to a ban on its trade with Britain and its colonies, disrupted the traditional pattern of the West Indian island's commerce with the North American colonies.

That trade was crucial as it had provided the islands with foodstuffs and estate supplies in return for rum, sugar and molasses; likewise, the war led to the appearance of privateers who harassed Caribbean shipping, blocking the movement of goods to and from the islands. Nor did the islands' provision crisis cease with the end of hostilities. From 1783 Americans as foreigners could not send their ships to British colonies, thus perpetuating the provisioning problems. In addition, planters and merchants by the late 1780s had to deal with the abolitionists' campaign first to regulate and then abolish the slave trade, and by the 1790s the islands faced the uprising in Hispaniola, the renewal of war in the Caribbean and the threat of slave revolts inspired by the doctrines of the French Revolution and the example of the upheaval in Haiti.

On 18 January 1775 members of the interest in London debated whether to petition Parliament in the face of the North American colonies' non-importation agreements and the ministry's determination to declare New England in rebellion. Faced with this prospect and the need to warn oficials of the likely impact war would have on the West Indies, Rose Fuller urged his colleagues to petition the House. As usual, many hesitated for fear of offending ministers. After prolonged debate Richard Oliver was delegated to

---

[64] O'Shaughnessy, *Empire Divided*, p. 138; *Journal of the Assembly of Jamaica [JAJ]*, 22 Dec. 1774, Address of the Assembly of Jamaica.

[65] Douglas Hall, *A Brief History of the West India Committee* (St. Lawrence, Barbados, 1971), pp. 1–10. David Beck Ryden estimated that 1500 members attended general meetings of the society between 1785 and 1807; the great majority did so only at three or fewer meetings over the 22-year period. *West India Slavery and British Abolition*, p. 52.

present the petition to the House, which he did on 2 February.[66] Despite the initial hesitation the petition was a forceful statement of the islands' situation and an accurate forecast of the impact the loss of American provisions and supplies would have on the plantation economies.

A second West Indian petition provoked by the administration's Prohibitory Bill, which would cut off all trade with the rebellious colonies, reiterated many of the points of the 2 February document. It emphasised the islands' economic importance to Britain and the degree to which they would be threatened with ruin by war and the loss of American trade. Both petitions were referred to a committee of the whole House.[67] The West Indians selected Richard Glover[68] to make their case before the committee. Acting as the agent for the petitioners, Glover examined the witnesses on their behalf. Like the petitioners, Glover's eventual report, which he delivered on 16 March, emphasised the economic importance of the islands to the British economy and the likelihood that a war would have a ruinous impact on their economies. His report along with the supporting evidence was published and distributed to members of Parliament. Neither, however, slowed the implementation of the administration's policy.[69]

Nathaniel Bayly,[70] who served as the chair of the new Society during the 1770s, was more forceful than Glover or the West India Society's petition in issuing Cassandra-like warnings in speeches over three weeks culminating in one on 1 Dec. 1775 when he condemned the dangerous and foolhardy, even wanton nature of the North administration's policies and warned that:

> He was well informed, nay he was fully convinced, that the inhabitants of those islands must be starved; and though they should not; their crops must be left, as they had not lumber enough to save the present; that such being the case, the proprietors must be ruined, and the consequences would in the end reach the

---

[66] *CJ*, xxxv, 912; *PH*, xviii, 219–20; Almon, *Parl. Register*, i, 131; O'Shaughnessy, 'The West India interest', p. 132. The petitioners expressed their concern that the North Americans non-importation agreements of the previous autumn would have a devastating impact on the West Indian islands, which they reminded the members contained British property amounting 'to upwards of thirty millions Sterling; and further Property of many millions more is employed in the Commerce comprehending *Africa*, the *East Indies* and *Europe*; and that the whole Profits and Produce of those capitals ultimately centre in *Great Britain* and add to the National Wealth, while the Navigation necessary to all its Branches establishes a strength which Wealth can neither purchase nor balance'. They also stressed that 'the sugar plantations in the West Indies are subject to a greater variety of contingencies than other species of property, from the necessary dependence on external support, and that therefore should any interruption happen in the general system of their commerce, the great national stock thus vested and employed must become unprofitable and precarious'. *CJ*, xxxv, 91.

[67] *CJ*, xxxv, 7 Dec. 1775; Almon, *Parl. Register*, iii, 272–3.

[68] Richard Glover (?1712–85), MP, Weymouth and Melcombe Regis, 1761–8; Hamburg merchant. *CJ*, xxxv, 202; *PH*, xviii, cc. 462–78.

[69] *The Evidence Delivered on the Petition Presented by the West-India Planters and Merchants to the Hon. House of Commons, as it Was Introduc'd at the Bar, and Summ'd Up by Mr. Glover* (1775); Almon, *Parl. Register*, i, pp. 327, 347–60; O'Shaughnessy, *Empire Divided*, p. 141.

[70] Nathaniel Bayly (c. 1726–98), MP, Abingdon, 1770–4 and Westbury, 1774–9. Returned to Jamaica, 1779.

merchants, so as ... to bring on a general bankruptcy among those in any manner concerned ... in the West India trade.[71]

Despite Bayly's condemnation of the Prohibitory Bill, nine members of the West India interest supported the North administration after the outbreak of war.[72] Moreover islands which had asserted their rights against Parliament in 1775, during the early months of 1776 saw their assemblies proclaiming their loyalty to the Crown.[73] At the same time the priority of their advocates in London was to enlarge the market for the islands' produce and to secure for them the supplies they required. A committee of the West India planters and merchants dispatched a memorial to North and Lord George Germain[74] arguing that because the islands had lost their North American markets for sugar and its by-products, ministers should take steps by way of compensation to stop the distillation of grain in Great Britain and Ireland in order to stimulate demand for West Indian rum, thereby enabling planters to purchase the lumber and provisions that they urgently needed.[75] The planters' difficulties were so severe that even a surge in the sale of rum would do little to alleviate their situation, for American privateers had successfully disrupted what remained of the West India trade. *Aris's Birmingham Gazette* reported in January 1777:

> Another Capital House in the West India Trade stopped Payment last Week, which makes the fourth, and it is imagined that others must follow. All this is the natural Consequence of American Captures; upwards of 180 ships from the West India Islands having been taken by their privateers in the Course of last year.[76]

[71] For 1 and 21 Dec., see, *PH*, xviii, 37–8, 1106; and *HPC, 1754–1790*, ii, 68. Anthony Storer, who supported the ministers until the late 1770s, told Lord Carlisle that if the Prohibitory Bill lasted for more than a year 'it seems even to moderate W. Indians to be totally ruinous to them. What seems to affect them most by the passing of this Bill is not the fear of starving, which they have they apprehensions of, but the danger there is of there being taken on false pretenses by men of war that are to protect them, or by the Americans, on whose coast they are always obliged to pass very near. In short, every West Indian, except Jack Douglas is in the utmost consternation'. *HMC, Carlisle MSS*, p. 311.
[72] William Dickinson, St. Leger Douglas, John Fuller, Sir William Gordon, Daniel and Edwin Lascelles, Samuel Martin, Sir Ralph Payne, A.M. Storer. O'Shaughnessy, 'The West India interest', 135.
[73] O'Shaughnessy, *Empire Divided*, pp. 149–51; *JAJ*, 22 Dec. 1775.
[74] Lord George Sackville (1716–85), MP Dover, 1741–61, Hythe, 1761–8 and East Grinstead, 1768–82; MP [I], 1733–62; Capt. 3rd Horse; Lt. Col. 28 Ft. 1740; Col. Army 1745; Col. 20 Ft. 1746–49; 12 Drag. 1749–50; 3rd Horse 1750–7; Maj. Gen. 1755; Col. 2nd Drag. Gds. 1757–9; Lt. Gen. 1758; Lt.-Gen. of Ordnance 1758–9; C.-in-C. British forces, Germany, Oct. 1758; dismissed the service, 1759; Ranger of Phoenix Park, 1751; Clerk of the Council [I], 1737–85; Chief Secretary [I], 1751–5; Jt. Vice-Treasurer [I], 1765–6; First Ld. of Trade, 1775–9; Sec. of State for America, Nov. 1775–Feb. 1782; took name of Germain, 1769; cr. Viscount Sackville, 1782.
[75] *Gentleman's Magazine*, xlvi (Mar. 1776), part 1, p. 63.
[76] *Aris's Birmingham Gazette*, 13 Jan. 1777. The same newspaper provided an additional report of the impact of the privateers, based on testimony of three West India merchants before a committee in the House of Lords on 6 or 7 Feb. 1778. According to Alderman Wooldridge, Beeston Long and William Creighton, there were as many as 170 American privateer ships, manned by up to 20,000 sailors. The three estimated that the losses of British merchants due to the activities of the privateers amounted to £1.8 million. As a result of their depredations, insurance rates which before the war had been two per cent had risen to four or five per cent for ships sailing in convoys; ships not sailing in convoys were unable to obtain insurance. According to their testimony privateers had seized 559 British ships. *Birmingham Gazette*, 9 Feb. 1778.

The result of these depredations was a serious shortage both of food and supplies, thus fulfilling Bayly's earlier dire predictions. A second more powerful reason for the West Indians' hesitation to support the American upheaval was the outbreak of a slave revolt in Jamaica in 1776. The seriousness of the revolt and fear it might lead to risings on other islands made the leaders of the various assemblies unwilling to take any steps that might hint at any sympathy for ideas that could encourage their enslaved populations to follow the example of their rebellious Jamaican counterparts. Even with these precautions, one report indicated that slaves in Barbados were in 'a state of rebellion'.[77]

The depredations of American privateers and rebellious slaves highlighted for white settlers their dependence on the British for supplies and protection. In February 1776 the admiralty revived the convoy system as a means of protecting the West Indian trade against the privateers. The following January Fuller reported that the Admiralty had denied a request to support four convoys a year from Jamaica, but after the Society of West India Merchants sent a request for convoys in May, June and August, the Admiralty agreed.[78]

Nevertheless, on 2 February 1778 Bayly moved that a copy of the address and petition of the council and assembly of Jamaica be laid before the House respecting the distresses that the island suffered at the hands of the privateers. The Jamaicans noted that Britain went to vast expense to send out a squadron to its colonies, but:

> gets little benefit from it, for admirals cruise for prizes to enrich them-selves, without paying the least regard to the complaints from the inhabitants, of the damage they daily receive on the coast, and in their very ports, from privateers.[79]

As if this corruption was not bad enough, worse was to come as a result of the outbreak of war with France in 1778, with Spain the next year and with the Netherlands in 1781. The effect was to leave the islands vulnerable to attack and takeover. Dominica fell to the French in September 1778, St. Vincent in June of the next year and Grenada nine days later. Faced with the prospect of a French invasion of Britain itself and under heavy military pressure in North America following the loss at Saratoga in the autumn of 1777, Britain was in no position to reinforce its garrisons or fleets in the Caribbean. Nevertheless, the islands cried out for protection as Barbados and the Leeward Islands came under threat from the fleet of Admiral D'Estaing in July 1779.

In its dire situation the West India interest turned to Stephen Fuller to press the islands' case with the government. He was well-situated to undertake the task: he enjoyed access to the leading members of the ministry, and in particular to Lord George Germain, who, according to Fuller, 'embraces every proposition for the benefit of the colonies'.[80] On 7 Feb. 1778 Fuller was able to report to the Jamaican committee

---

[77] For the 1776 revolt, see Michael Craton, *Testing the Chains: Resistance to Slavery in the British West Indies* (1982), pp. 125–39.
[78] Boston College, Burns Library, Fuller MSS 256, ff. 14, Fuller to Committee, 22 Jan. and 4 June, 1777.
[79] Almon, *Parl. Reg.*, x, 326–7.
[80] Quoted in O'Shaughnessy, *Empire Divided*, p. 206.

that he met at the Admiralty with representatives of the Society of Merchants regarding the defence of the coasts of Jamaica and that the Admiralty had agreed to add six ships to the 23 already on the Jamaican station. Following the French conquest of Dominica in September, Fuller on behalf of the West India Society urged that an additional squadron be sent out to the West Indies. After the Admiralty refused the request, he appealed to Germain who replied that if the Society could make a case, he would do what he could to get additional troops and ships. A month later the Society dispatched its case, and soon thereafter received news that reinforcements had sailed to the Leeward Islands.[81]

Yet, the interest also endured many brush-offs. Walpole records an incident in which West Indian merchants, afraid of offending the ministers, prepared 'a very warm Remonstrance to the King ..., which after, being a little softened ... the King received on his return from Chapel, and gave it to the Lord of the bedchamber ... without reading it, and with no more distinction than he gives to the petition of a begging gentlewoman that sues for a pension'.[82] Likewise, in a letter to the committee Fuller reported that North on March 1781 had proposed an increase in the duty on sugar of 4s 3d per cwt in the committee of supply and that it was accepted without any opposition. A delegation consisting of Fuller, Neave[83] and Pennant called upon the minister to protest but received no concessions.[84]

Still, the North administration was willing to lend its assistance to the West Indies. Following major hurricanes that caused extensive damage in Barbados and Jamaica in September and October 1780 Samuel Estwick,[85] in his maiden speech, issued a plea for financial assistance that was reinforced by petitions from the Assembly of Barbados and the Society of West India Planters and Merchants in a petition, drafted by Fuller.[86] Though Estwick was an opponent of the war, North recommended the 'consideration of the petitions'. Two days later, the committee of supply reported in favour of a grant of £80,000 for Barbados and £40,000 for Jamaica.[87] Moreover, when in 1780 the London sugar refiners and sugar bakers challenged the West Indians' monopoly by demanding the right to refine foreign prize sugars and sell them in Britain, North supported the planters and upheld their sole right to provide the British market with unrefined sugar. A second effort to breach that monopoly in 1781 met with no success.[88]

---

[81] Boston College, Burns Library, Fuller MSS 256, Fuller to Committee, ff. 88, 102, 145–6., 1 May 1778, 7 Nov. 1778, 7 Dec. 1778.

[82] Walpole, *Memoirs*, ii, 231–2.

[83] Sir Richard Neave, Bt. (1731–1814), chair of Society of West India Merchants and of London Dock Co.; dir., Hudson's Bay Co., Fellow Royal Society, 1785.

[84] Sheridan, *Sugar and Slavery*, pp. 459–62; Boston College, Burns Library, Fuller MSS, 546, f. 237, 23 Mar. 1781.

[85] Samuel Estwick (?1736–1795), MP, Westbury, 1779–1795; assistant agent for Barbados, 1763–1778 and agent, 1778–1792; dep. paymaster gen, 1782–83; registrar of Chelsea Hospital and searcher of the customs of Barbados, 1783; 1784–1795.

[86] Boston College, Burns Library, Fuller MSS 256, ii, f. 244–5, Fuller to committee, 13 Jan. 1781.

[87] *HPC, 1754–1790*, ii, 406; *CJ*, xxxviii, 101, 120.

[88] Boston College, Burns Library, Fuller MSS 256, f. 246, Fuller to Committee, 29 May 1781. During a debate on another petition from the London sugar refiners, North defended the islands' monopoly, claiming that Parliament could not 'break through it without violating the public faith of the Kingdom'. Though he valued the refiners and was aware of their hardships, he concluded 'it is not wise policy to break the colony laws by which the West India islands had so long prospered'. Debrett, *Parl. Reg.*, iii, 423–4.

VII: The Interest in Decline

Eric Williams argued in *Capitalism and Slavery* that the American revolt was the beginning of the sugar colonies' 'uninterrupted decline'. Cut off from the northern colonies and later the United States as a result of the Revolutionary War and American independence, the plantations profitability declined, which according to Williams was a primary cause for the abolition of the slave trade in 1807 and the Emancipation Act in 1833.[89]

In May 1780 the cotton manufacturers of Manchester, suffering from a shortage of their raw material because of the disruption of trade due to the war, petitioned for a bill to allow the free import of cotton because a 'shipping monopoly' deprived them of the supplies that they required. They urged that imports temporarily be carried by the ships of any neutral power from any part of Europe, free of duty.[90]

Because the proposal represented a breach of the Navigation Act of 1660, it provoked counter-petitions. Henry Rawlinson, a Liverpool MP, presented a petition on behalf of the merchants both of Liverpool and Lancaster who feared the Manchester bill would be 'immediately attended with fatal consequences to the Navigation of this Kingdom, prove greatly injurious to the Merchant, the Planter, and every Person dependent upon, or interested in the Trade to *the West Indies*'. John Spottiswood, agent of the assembly of Tobago, also presented a petition on behalf of the 'raisers' of cotton in the West Indies who feared the proposal would be 'destructive to the islands' which depended on the British market. Tobago petitioners feared that under the act, the manufacturers would purchase cotton produced on the Dutch and French islands at a far lower price than their own because of lower insurance and freight costs.[91] In support of their proposal Manchester manufacturers argued that they had lost access to Grenada, their primary source of cotton, with the result that prices for raw cotton had risen sharply. Finally, the Tallow chandlers of London and Westminster argued in favour of the proposal because they relied upon £500,000 of Turkish cotton each year for their wicks and believed that passage of the bill would reduce the current high price of their product.[92] Eventually the government threw its support behind the Manchester proposal, and the bill passed through both Houses and received the royal sanction on 23 June.[93]

The Manchester episode highlighted the vulnerability of the West India interest as it entered the 1780s. The interest's reiterated demands for more naval and military protection during the late 1770s and early 1780s left it in a poor position to resist the North administration when it raised the duty on muscovado as a means of securing additional revenue. Once the war was over a heavily indebted government turned its attention to consolidating its Empire. As it did so, long-time friends of the West Indies moved to reinforce the Navigation system to foster that consolidation. They did so in 1783 by issuing an order in council which closed the ports of the British West Indies to

---

[89] Eric Williams, *Capitalism and Slavery* (New York, 1961), pp. 120–53.
[90] W. Bowden, 'English manufacturers and the commercial treaty of 1786', *American Historical Review* [AHR], xxv (1919), 26; *CJ*, xxxvii, 718.
[91] *CJ*, xxxvii, 763–4, 772–3.
[92] *CJ*, xxxvii, 795, 853.
[93] *CJ*, xxxvii, 919.

the ships of the United States over the fierce objections of the West Indians and their allies in London. Underlying the order of 1783 was the desire to promote British shipping at the expense of the North Americans.

The war also left planter society on the defensive in the face of slave populations who far outnumbered white settlers. Those populations were strengthened by the arrival of free populations of colour; they were also empowered by their military, militia and naval service during the later phases of the American war, by the arrival of freed slaves from North America and by the wider propagation of the 'rights of man'. All of these contributed to a greater assertiveness among communities of colour on the British islands at a time when the loss of the southern slave owning colonies of North America meant that the West Indian islands stood almost alone as slave-owning societies within the Empire as the first rumblings in support of abolition began to be heard.

Finally forces which before 1775 had served as allies for the West Indian interest in Britain began to join the sugar refiners in challenging the interest. British merchants wanted to control the West Indian trade, which meant excluding the North Americans. The Royal Navy supported the British merchants' claims, believing that a vibrant British Merchant marine would form the 'nursery of seamen' on which the navy traditionally depended in time of war. The powerful East India Company also began to look for access to the British market for its sugar, thus posing a challenge to the West Indian monopoly. Finally, the free trade arguments of Adam Smith and others began to gain adherents: Smith himself wrote in a letter to William Eden that he 'felt little anxiety about what becomes of American commerce because he saw the prospect of better markets elsewhere'.[94]

Confronted by these challenges the West India interest upgraded and modernised its organisation. As already noted, the organisations of the planters and merchants had already merged to form the Society of West India Planters and Merchants in January 1775. By April 1779 the Society had created a Standing Committee which monitored pending business between general meetings, and to cover expenses it imposed charges of 1d upon each hogshead of sugar and puncheon of rum unloaded at London. It also employed Joseph Allen as a full-time secretary. The Society also improved its efforts to spread its publicity, by planting paragraphs in the press to buttress its case on behalf of policies it supported. Throughout the 1780s and 1790s it commissioned writers to produce pamphlets on its behalf as it engaged in battles with the government on a variety of issues and with the abolitionists. In short, it took on the trappings of an effective lobby though it was never able to mobilise mass support in a way that its abolitionist opponents did in 1788 and 1792. By comparison, its efforts were limited, tentative and elitist.[95]

---

[94] Quoted in O'Shaughnessy, *Empire Divided*, pp. 241–2. For Smith, see John Ehrman, *The Younger Pitt: The Years of Acclaim*, p. 159. For the East India Company's campaign and the West Indians' reaction, see *Correspondence of Stephen Fuller*, pp. 148–9, 159, 209–210, 223.

[95] Between Dec. 1787 and the following June, the Abolitionist Society was able to mobilise its supporters to send 102 petitions to the House of Commons, signed by between 60,000 and 75,000 people. The culmination of its campaign came in 1792 when between 350,000 and 400,000 men and women signed over 500 petitions. The extent of this petitioning was without precedent in British history to that point. Seymour Drescher, *Capitalism and Antislavery: British Mobilization in Comparative Perspective* (New York, 1987), pp. 69–80; and *Abolition: A History of Slavery and Antislavery* (Cambridge, 2009), pp. 213–18; James Walvin, 'The public campaign in England against slavery, 1787–1835', in *The Abolition of the Atlantic Slave Trade*, ed. David Eltis and James Walvin (Edinburgh, 2007), 48–9.

Responsibility for coordinating the West Indian interest's campaign in this difficult environment fell to Fuller. By general agreement he was well-equipped for the task. As agent for the largest of the British islands he enjoyed a natural pre-eminence, and his family not only possessed extensive Jamaican estates, but Fuller himself was connected with prominent absentee families including the Pennants, the Sloanes and the Dickinsons. With his brother Thomas he had conducted a successful West Indian agency and merchant house. With these connections Fuller moved easily among London's West Indian community. He enjoyed access to the highest levels of government not only during the 1760s and 1770s but during the 1780s when he met and corresponded with the younger Pitt and with various members of his cabinet, including his first Home Secretary, Lord Sydney, the President of the revived Board of Trade, Lord Hawkesbury and Henry Dundas,[96] all of whom resisted the abolition of the slave trade. Fuller was notable too for his graciousness, for he rarely attacked his opponents harshly and made a point of sharing credit with those with whom he worked, including Lord Penrhyn and Edward Long. His connections, personality and adeptness as a lobbyist enabled him for 30 years to coordinate the varied elements of the interest and marshal its forces as it became apparent that the interests of the West Indies no longer coincided as they once had so closely with those of Britain.[97]

Following the end of the American war, the interest's primary mission was to establish commercial ties with the United States. On 31 March 1783 it adopted a series of resolutions, the first of which was to authorise the importation to the islands of goods from the United States either by British or American ships and also the export of the 'growth and produce of the islands' by the same means. At a second meeting on 4 April, they further urged the removal of additional duties on sugar and rum. None of these resolutions produced the desired effect. To the contrary, the Coalition government on 2 July 1783 issued an order-in-council that permitted the British West Indies to import American specified provisions and supplies, including flour, grain, vegetables and livestock, and export to the United States rum, sugar, molasses, coffee, ginger and pimento. All trade, however, was confined to British shipping, as British shippers argued that aliens and former rebels should not enjoy so lucrative a branch of British trade, particularly as an estimated 60,000 British sailors had been demobilised following the peace.[98]

The interest refused to relent in the face of this embargo. The Society bombarded first the Coalition and then the new Pitt administration with representations demanding that American ships be admitted to the West India trade. Lord Penrhyn was charged by the West India Society to call upon the embattled William Pitt which

---

[96] Henry Dundas (1742–1811), MP, Edinburghshire, 1774–82; Newton I.o.W., Sept.–Dec. 1782; Edinburghshire 1783–90 and Edinburgh, 1790–1802; Solicitor-Gen. [S], June 1779; Sole Keeper, 1779–80; Treasurer of the Navy, 1782–3; Ld. of Trade, 1784–6; Commr. of Board of Control, 1784–93; Home Sec., 1791–4; Pres. of Board of Control, 1793–1801; Sec. for War and Colonies, 1794–1801; Privy Seal [S], 1801–1811; 1st Ld. of Admiralty, 1805–1805; cr. Visct. Melville, 1802.

[97] For other evaluations of Fuller as leader of the lobby, see O'Shaughnessy, 'Formation of a colonial lobby', *HJ*, xl, 77–8; David Beck Ryden, 'Spokesman for oppression', 5–15; and *The Correspondence of Stephen Fuller, 1788–1795*, pp. 29–39.

[98] Herbert C. Brill, 'British colonial policy in the West Indies, 1783–1793', *EHR*, xxxi (1916), 443–4.

he did frequently.⁹⁹ The new minister was not unsympathetic to the islands' needs. After an abortive attempt at compromise, which would have permitted American vessels of under 80 tons (too small to make transatlantic journeys) to enter West Indian ports, produced a storm of protest from British chambers of commerce, Pitt ordered the committee on trade to investigate the question and make a report. After three months during which it gathered evidence and took testimony, the committee concluded that the West Indian islands were able to supply most of their own lumber and provisions and would within three years supply the whole. Likewise, it seemed unlikely to its members that the Americans would retaliate if the restrictions on their shipping remained. In short, the West Indian economy would remain prosperous under the current system, the American market would not be lost and British navigation would receive the support it needed if the order-in-council remained in place.¹⁰⁰

The issue gained further pertinence in February 1786 when Charles Jenkinson moved for leave to bring in a bill to reinforce the ban on American shipping. During his presentation, however, Jenkinson declared that he had intended to bring the bill to make the ban permanent until he learned of a petition being planned by the Assembly of Jamaica. Because of the pending petition, he announced he would postpone the presentation of his bill until the petition arrived.¹⁰¹ In fact, he presented it on 13 April, and it was read a second time on the 25th. The House went into committee on the measure on 1 May and spent several days over the next several weeks reviewing its details. The Assembly's petition only reached London in late April. On 19 May Fuller petitioned the House of Commons in his own name setting forth the grievances of the Jamaican Assembly and its desire for:

> a partial Intercourse with the *American* State in *American* Bottoms, and also in respect to the high Duty upon Sugar and Rum; and that the Petitioner hath it in Charge ...; to represent, that the Condition of the Planters is now even more deplorable than it was last year; they complain that, by Reason of the Restrictions upon their Trade with the *American* State, a Monopoly is carried on in Lumber and Flour, by a few Houses on the Island, who, having those Articles exclusively in their Hands, are enabled not only to fix what Prices they please upon them, but to regulate those Prices exclusively by their Calamities.¹⁰²

---

[99] Though summoned to office by George III following the House of Lords' rejection of the Coalition's controversial India Bill in Dec. 1783, Pitt's new government lacked a majority in the House of Commons until after elections in March and April 1784.

[100] Brill, 'British colonial policy', 438–9; Ehrman, *The Younger Pitt: The Years of Acclaim*, pp. 334–5. Ehrman noted that Pitt accepted this proposal despite the fact that it contradicted the details of the bill he had introduced a year earlier. He did so in part because of the evidence the committee assembled and primarily to ensure the provision of sailors for the fleet.

[101] Duke University [DU], David M. Rubenstein Rare Book and Manuscript Library, Fuller MSS, 5462, ff. 6–7, Fuller to committee, 28 Feb. 1786. Jenkinson was given leave to bring in his bill on 11 Apr. *CJ*, xli, 562: *PH*, xxv, cc. 1372–5.

[102] *CJ*, xli, 562, 598, 610, 661, 764, 767, 828; DU, David M. Rubenstein Rare Book and Manuscript Library, Fuller MSS, 5462, ff. 34–5, Fuller to committee, 27 Apr. 1786.

Nevertheless, Jenkinson's bill, which passed though both Houses largely without opposition, declared that no foreign built ship could qualify for British ownership, even if owned by a British subject, nor could a British subject qualify unless he belonged to a commercial house trading in Britain. It finally declared that vessels built in America or owned by a US citizen could not secure British registration.[103]

In addition, William Eden's recently concluded commercial treaty with France threatened to undermine the economic position of the islands by giving an advantage to French brandy over West Indian rum. The result was a further round of petitions, mainly on Fuller's part,[104] followed by negotiations between Pitt and Lord Hawkesbury particularly as the terms of the treaty related to the import of French brandy. In this case the interests' lobbying was successful, for on the day that Fuller dispatched his petition, Pitt told Lord Penhryn in the House that he intended 'to further reduce the duty on rum from 5s to 4s' but 'that he could go no lower on rum, without bringing the Brewery & home distillery upon him and hazarding the production of the revenue'.[105] Securing the interest's point was a complicated business that was accomplished by means of Fuller's petitions, by memoranda dispatched by the West India Society and by negotiations conducted by Penhryn and Fuller.[106]

An unexpected and more serious challenge to the islands appeared at the end of 1787. In a brief letter to the committee, Fuller reported that 'the Slave Trade is to be brought forward in the House this Sessions, but I cannot find at present by what mode'. Over the next two months, he sent additional news, including the determination of the Society for the Abolition of the Slave Trade to end the trade, and the Society's initiation of a petitioning campaign to influence the House of Commons in favour of that goal. Fearing the impact of such a campaign on Jamaica's large and volatile slave population, Fuller urged Lord Sydney to encourage the King to instruct the West Indian governors to prevent any mischiefs. He also informed the committee of Pitt's determination to support William Wilberforce's plan to move for the abolition of the trade, but only after an inquiry into the trade itself. Thus, Fuller set out to gather the evidence and witnesses the interest needed to counter the arguments of the abolitionists.[107] He identified witnesses who could testify to the manner in which Jamaican planters treated their slaves and the conditions on slave ships and went to the extent of submitting questions to the Privy Council which might be asked of these witnesses. He also made an

---

[103] 26 Geo. III, c. 60; Ehrman, *Younger Pitt: Years of Acclaim*, p. 340. DU, David M. Rubenstein Rare Book and Manuscript Library, Fuller MSS, 5462, f. 61, 27 June, 1786.

[104] *CJ*, xlii, 399–400, 21 Feb. 1787.

[105] DU, David M. Rubenstein Rare Book and Manuscript Library, Fuller MSS, 5462, ff. 101–103, Fuller to committee, 20 Feb. 1787.

[106] *PH*, xxvi, cc. 378–469; the copy of a memorial of the general meeting of the West India Planters and Merchants to the Lords of HM's Treasury, delivered on 26 Dec. 1786 regarding the Treaty and duties on brandy and rum, is printed in the *Annual Register*, xxviii (1786), 286–8.

[107] *Stephen Fuller Correspondence*, pp. 67–71; DU, David M. Rubenstein Rare Book and Manuscripts Library, Fuller MSS 5462, ff. 141, 149, 159–61, 152, 157–8. Pitt entrusted the inquiry to a committee of the Privy Council, to be chaired by Hawkesbury. For examples of the material that Fuller collected, see *Fuller Correspondence*, pp. 73–5; DU, David M. Rubenstein Rare Book and Manuscripts Library, Fuller MSS 5462, ff. 167–70, 165–6, Fuller to Committee, 20 Feb. 1788, Estimates of number of slaves shipped to Jamaica, 1702–1775, of number of sugar estates and sugar output [1787] and of total value to planters' property [1788].

extended visit to France to report on the plans of French slave traders to extend their operations with the active support of the French government.[108]

MPs were more active in upholding the West Indian positions once the question of abolishing the slave trade came before the House in 1788 than they had been on business relating to the order-in-council or the commercial treaty. This was especially the case following Sir William Dolben's introduction of the first of his Slave Trade Regulation Bills (28 Geo. III, c. 54) on 26 May. The 1788 Act was succeeded by a series of others, all of them introduced by Dolben, though not as an alternative to abolition.[109] Despite its moderation the measure produced a furious opposition in the Commons and stubborn obstruction from Lord Chancellor Thurlow, Lord Sydney and other peers in the House of Lords.[110] Not surprisingly the first opposition came from the ports. On 28 May Penryn presented a petition from the merchants and traders of Liverpool who protested that the charges against the trade were untrue and asked to be heard. Likewise, William Ewer[111] introduced a petition on behalf of London merchants setting out the benefits of the trade. The petitioners were concerned that the reforms would increase their costs and thus work to the advantage of the French, their principal competitors. Despite protests from London and the outports, the measure passed because of the compelling evidence that Dolben and his supporters assembled on behalf of the bill and because William Pitt threw the full weight of his influence behind the bill in both houses.

Following William Wilberforce's introduction of his 12 resolutions regarding the slave trade on 12 May 1789,[112] the interest altered its tactics. Once supporters began to appreciate their opponents' strength and the degree of their public support, they sought to draw out proceedings even as they warned those proceedings tended to stir up the passions of the islands enslaved populations,[113] thus contradicting their demands that the deliberations be concluded as quickly as possible. As they considered the Privy Council's report, which was hostile to the Trade, defenders of the trade demanded that the House conduct its own investigation and in a committee of the whole House where proceedings were bound to be interrupted because of the pressure of other business.[114]

---

[108] *Fuller Correspondence*, pp. 81–2, 82–4, 101–2; The National Archives [TNA], Colonial Office Papers, CO 137/87, ff. 266–7, Fuller to Sydney, 24 Aug. 1788.

[109] PH, xxvii, c. 576. The subsequent Acts included 30 Geo III, c. 33, 34 Geo. III, c. 80 and 39 Geo. II, c. 80 which respectively safeguarded the lives of seamen, made it illegal to jettison ill or unruly slaves and made earlier regulations permanent. The acts helped to reduce mortality rates on the Middle Passage substantially by as much as 50 per cent. *Fuller Correspondence*, p. 62, n. 9.

[110] For the Lords' opposition, spearheaded by Hawkesbury and Thurlow, see McCahill, *House of Lords in the Age of George III*, pp. 269–70, 356–8.

[111] William Ewer (c. 1720–89), MP Dorchester, 1765–89; Director, Bank of England, 1763–89; Dep. Gov. 1779–82; Gov., 1782–3.

[112] PH, xxviii cc. 63–7.

[113] The issue of potentially unruly slaves became a recurring theme in letters addressed to Stephen Fuller and others, and in letters Fuller dispatched to government officials especially in relation to Dolben's bill. See *Correspondence of Stephen Fuller*, pp. 90–3.

[114] *Parl. Reg.*, 2nd ser., xxvi, 177–9, 181, 208, 213–14, 217. Supporters of abolition successfully moved that the inquiry be undertaken by a select committee in committee rooms 'above stairs' to prevent the proceedings in a committee of the whole House from being drawn out as a result of interruptions from other legislative business as subsequently happened in the House of Lords. For those delays, see 'Introduction', in *Correspondence of Stephen Fuller*, pp. 57–9.

Moreover, after opposing the bill to regulate the slave trade in 1788, when confronted with Wilberforce's determination to abolish the trade in 1789, members of the West Indian group, including John Sawbridge and Charles Marsham, discovered that regulation was a palatable alternative to abolition and proclaimed their support for what their colleagues had opposed only a year before.[115] By the early 1790s absentee planters and their Parliamentary allies as well as many of the island's assemblies discovered that regulation offered a desirable alternative to abolition.

Overall, there was a sense among the West Indian MPs that the discussion of abolition was not only dangerous, but the possibility of its realisation was potentially fatal to the well-being of the islands. Henry Cruger, himself a slave owner, considered abolition 'ruinous in the extreme', and Crisp Molineux told the House that abolition 'will destroy the West Indies'.[116] Nor were these the isolated sentiments of a few individuals.

Few better embodied this sense of alienation than Simon Taylor,[117] Jamaica's wealthiest planter. Prior to his death, Taylor had amassed among the greatest assets in the British Empire. Over the years he maintained a correspondence with Chaloner Arcedeckne,[118] an absentee Jamaican planter who was active in the business of the West India Society. On 17 Jan. 1791, an indignant Taylor wrote that:

> I consider the British Minister [Pitt] to be a more inveterate enemy to us than the French or Spanish nation. I see the miscreant Wilberforce has begun upon the Slave business again.[119]

Six months earlier his outlook was gloomier and more belligerent:

> Where is faith to be put in a Nation that gave Charters and passed Acts of Parliament to encourage the African trade for Negroes & Proclamations for people to settle the Islands, & to embark their all in those undertakings and then to abuse the people they have deluded and wish to stop the trade by which only they can carry on their settlements ... Can Mr Pitt or his Friends think all will risk our lives to remain under the jurisdiction of those people, who have these last 2 or 3 years past been abusing us as merciless Tyrants, Diabolical Murderers, Men who not having any mercy ourselves, are entitled to no justice from others, and for that reason it is meritorious to rob us of our properties or bury us in the Sea.[120]

---

[115] *Parl. Reg.*, 2nd ser., xxvi, 177–8, 198.
[116] *Parl. Reg.*, 2nd ser., xxvi, 199, 200.
[117] For a brief overview of Taylor's career, the extent of his wealth and his place in eighteenth- and early nineteenth-century Jamaica, see R.B. Sheridan, 'Simon Taylor, sugar tycoon of Jamaica, 1740–1813' *Agricultural History*, xlv (1971), 285–96.
[118] Chaloner Arcedeckne (?1743–1809), MP, Wallingford, 1780–4 and Westbury, 1784–6; active member of the West India Society.
[119] Cambridge University Library, Vanneck-Arcedeckne Papers, 3A/1791/1, Taylor to Arcedeckne, 17 Jan. 1791.
[120] CUL, Vanneck-Arcedeckne Papers, 3A/1790/9, Taylor to Arcedeckne, 7 June 1790.

On 10 Dec. 1790 the Council and Assembly of Jamaica adopted a Remonstrance to be sent to George III after earlier resolutions the two bodies dispatched to the Commons had elicited no response. The resolutions were a response to Wilberforce's resolutions of 2 May 1789 which, according to the Jamaicans, were 'founded on imperfect information and prejudice, or on alleged grievances, which ... are remediable without so violent, so impolitic a sacrifice [as abolition]'.

The Remonstrance maintained that Britain was obligated to provide for the security of her colonies on the basis of charters and acts dating back to the reigns of Charles II and William and Mary. It concluded by making a series of constitutional assertions regarding the rights of British colonists, which they claimed were:

> as inviolable as those of their fellow-citizens within any part of the British dominions: they are interwoven with the fundamental constitutions of the empire, and which constitutions do not give omnipotence to a British parliament. The British Parliament is not competent to destroy, nor partially mutually mutilate private properties. We apprehend, such a violation of the property of any subject of the British realm (not under legal forfeiture) without *our* consent, or without full compensation, would be an unconstitutional assumption of power, subversive of all public faith and confidence as applied to the Colonists; and must ultimately tend to alienate their affections from the Parent State.[121]

It is interesting that members the Assembly define their rights exclusively in terms of their right to enslave Africans. Because of the assault on their so-called right after 1787 and throughout the 1790s and early years of the nineteenth century, West Indians and their London allies, once regarded as privileged favourites, came to see themselves as the injured and betrayed victims of duplicitous ministers, an unfaithful polity and a vengeful, ignorant public who did not share the conviction that the islands had a right to carry on the slave trade. In short, the interests of the islands no longer seemed to coincide with those of the nation – a dangerous position for an interest group.

The West Indies and its interest had always suffered from a fundamental weakness – their complete dependence upon Great Britain. That situation arose from three vulnerabilities: first, the high cost of their sugar, which forced planters to exert their energies on maintaining their right to provide the British market; second, the white settler population relied upon Britain to provide the forces to protect them from their own restive slaves who outnumbered them by a factor of ten to one; and finally the islands were dependent upon British naval and military protection to defend against the French, the Spanish, the Dutch and, between 1775 and 1783, the depredations of American privateers.

As a result of their dependence the West Indians for the most part played an insiders' game, and during the second half of the century they had ample tools to do so, including

---

[121] *Report, Resolutions, and Remonstrations of the Honourable the Council and Assembly of Jamaica, at a Joint Committee, on the Subject of the Slave Trade* (1790), *JAJ*, 22–3; TNA, Pitt Papers, 30/8/350, ff. 369–375. For the full text of the Remonstrance, see *Correspondence of Stephen Fuller*, pp. 236–7.

the most skilled lobbyists of the age, a numerous, wealthy and well-connected Parliamentary contingent and a sense among the British political elite that the well-being of the West Indian islands was crucial to Britain's own prosperity.[122]

The strength of the interest had probably become a source of its weakness by the last years of the century as it found its traditional props less than reliable. After 1780 not even Lord North could be counted upon as an ally, and West Indians in the House of Commons and in the Caribbean regarded the younger Pitt as an enemy. Without a minister on whom they could count, the West Indians lacked a reliable prop. After his illness in 1788–89 George III was weakened, and Lord Grenville demonstrated in 1806 and 1807 that the House of Lords, despite its prolonged obstruction of the abolitionists, could be subdued. The interest made intermittent and tentative efforts to arouse the public, but their efforts paled in comparison to those of the abolitionists, and in any case the public to which they appealed was an elite group. They were suspicious of the mass petitions.

That suspicion was reflected in the reactions of the interest to the mass of petitions that flooded the halls of Westminster in 1788 and again in 1792. The Assembly of Jamaica in its petition to the Crown in 1792 described the 1792 petitions as 'the dreadful Effects of these wild and enthusiastic Doctrines, prevalent among certain mistaken and ill-informed Persons in Europe'.[123] The interest had made intermittent and tentative efforts to arouse the public. As a group of insiders, it distrusted and feared the public to which the abolitionists appealed with such effect and had focused its message on the propertied elite. So Stephen Fuller dismissed the petitions in support of abolition as irregular and in violation of the norms of the House and established precedents. The whole thing, he concluded, was nothing more than 'the practice of Enthusiasts & Fanaticks'.

---

[122] As the West Indian islands and Britain itself were threatened by the French in 1779, George III informed the Earl of Sandwich that 'our [Caribbean] islands must be defended even at the risk of an invasion of this Island. If we lose our Sugar Islands it will be impossible to raise money to continue the [American] war'. *The Private Papers of John, Earl of Sandwich*, ed. G.R. Barnes and J.H. Owen (3 vols, Naval Records Soc., 1932–8), lxxv, 163–4.

[123] *Correspondence of Stephen Fuller*, pp. 73, 185.

8

Lobbies: Birmingham, The Chamber of Manufacturers and the Fisheries

By the last quarter of the eighteenth century Birmingham had emerged as the third largest city in England and Wales – after London and Bristol. It gained access to a wider world after 1760 as a result of Warwickshire becoming what John Money calls 'the nodal point in a new system of communications and transport'. That network, composed of turnpikes and canals, established the interdependence of the various parts of the West Midlands and made the region better aware of its ties with other areas of England. The result was an interchange, not just of goods, but of news and of more viewpoints. Over the long term, the result of the broader exchanges was a new appreciation of the need to co-operate and reach out to far-off places for the sake of their mutual advantage.[1]

Opened to this larger world, Birmingham grew from a population of 23,600 in 1750 to 73,670 by 1801 and 182,922 in 1841.[2] Unlike Manchester and its surrounding towns in Lancashire, the Birmingham economy was based on the workshop, not factory production. It was famous for its Soho metal working shops, which produced everything from silver plate to components for Watt's steam engine. Small foundries with their skilled labour became Birmingham's hallmark.

As a growing region, Birmingham and its hinterland had an extensive legislative agenda which the town's and region's leaders pursued with a variety of allies. Their goals were to promote improved transportation, expand trade and sometimes counter ministerial policies they regarded as hostile to manufacturing. Initially, Birmingham's leaders relied upon traditional sources of power to secure their goals. Over time, however, they became impatient with a system dominated by landed gentlemen who, they believed, neither understood nor gave priority to manufacturers' needs. Instead they turned to the Chamber of Manufacturers in the 1780s to provide a voice by which the manufacturing interest could speak directly to the administration and Parliament on issues of importance to a growing sector of the national economy. Despite the

---

[1] John Money, *Experience and Identity: Birmingham and the West Midlands, 1760–1800* (Manchester, 1977), p. 24.
[2] Gordon E. Cherry, *Birmingham: A Study in Geography, History, and Planning* (Chichester, 1994), pp. 33–5; Eric Hopkins, *Birmingham: The First Manufacturing Town in the World, 1750–1840* (1989), pp. 28–9.

Chamber's collapse in 1787, many still clung to the hope either of finding a powerful voice for the manufacturing sector or, like Josiah Wedgwood, of securing genuine political reform.³

Birmingham was not a Parliamentary borough. Instead, those qualified voted for members for Warwickshire. The system satisfied many Birmingham merchants and manufacturers because they could rely upon MPs from the region as well as neighbouring peers to promote their needs with ministers and in Parliament. Two of the town's leading citizens, Matthew Boulton and Samuel Garbett,⁴ were adept at cultivating local MPs and grandees⁵ on behalf of Birmingham's interests. In a frequently cited letter, Garbett informed William Burke:⁶

> I have an old acquaintance with Sir Charles Mordaunt and Mr. Bromley,⁷ the Member[s] for this county and must thro' them and some of their friends who I have the honour to know and who would be offended if in my own name I should petition Parliament thro' any other hands, viz: Sir Roger Newdigate, Mr Bagot,⁸ and Lord Grey:⁹ and these old country families look upon themselves as the patrons of the neighbourhood and really have great inclination to serve us when they distinctly understand the subject.¹⁰

The problem for Garbett was that the 'old country Families' did not always influence government in ways that Birmingham manufacturers wished. He early recognised that the patronage system would not always meet the manufacturers' needs and complained that 'the little ... attention given by Administration to support our manufacturers afford a very mortifying prospect to such as himself who see the ground which is being lost daily'. What Garbett wanted was 'a committee of warm-hearted men being formed to take into consideration the state of British manufactures for exportation ... Surely a set of gentlemen could be found in Parliament who would give some attention to a point of such importance'.¹¹

By 1765 these concerns became secondary for Birmingham merchants alarmed by the impact of George Grenville's Stamp Act on their enterprises. On 23 December 1765

---

³ *The Selected Letters of Josiah* Wedgwood, ed. Ann Finer and George Savage (New York, 1965), pp. 25–7.
⁴ Samuel Garbett (1717–1803) made a fortune as a merchant before founding Samuel Garbett & Co. in partnership with Dr. John Roebuck in Prestonpans and Birmingham and established Carron Company, iron works in Scotland; prominent in the development of canals.
⁵ For their ability to enlist peers in support of their various projects, see McCahill, 'Peers, patronage and the Industrial Revolution', *Journal of British Studies*, xvi (1976), 84–107.
⁶ William Burke (1729–98), MP, Great Bedwyn, 1766–74; Sec. and Registrar of Guadeloupe, 1759–63; Dep. Paymaster of forces in India, 1782–93.
⁷ William Throckmorton Bromley (?1726–69), MP, Warwickshire, 1765–9.
⁸ William Bagot (1728–1798), MP, Staffordshire, 1754–80; succ. fa. as 6th Bt.1768; cr. Baron Bagot, 1780.
⁹ Grey, Charles Harry, Lord, (1737–1819), MP, Staffordshire, 1761–8; Ld. Lt. Staffordshire 1783–1819; succ. fa. as 5th Earl of Stamford; cr. Earl of Warrington, 1796.
¹⁰ Quoted in J.M. Norris, 'Samuel Garbett and the early development of industrial lobbying in Great Britain', *EcHR*, 2nd ser., x (1958), 451, n. 1.
¹¹ John Norris, 'Garbett and early industrial lobbying', *EcHR*, 451–2; *Calendar of Home Office Papers of the Reign of George III, 1766–1769*, 2 vols, ed. Joseph Redington and R.A. Roberts (1979), p. 90.

they met to inform Parliament of 'the Inconvenience this Neighbourhood suffers from the want of Remittances, and the stop that is put to the sending of goods to America'.[12] The meeting was organised by Garbett and 19 others who raised a petition to the Commons and a letter soliciting the assistance of the nobility and gentry in securing repeal of the Stamp Act.[13] Their reliance upon connections to well-placed patrons such as the 2nd Earl of Dartmouth was crucial. Dartmouth, who operated iron foundries, had long-standing ties to the town. As First Lord of Trade in the Rockingham administration, he was well-positioned to understand Birmingham's needs and see they were addressed. The Birmingham merchants dispatched their petition to him for his approval on 4 January, warning of extensive local unemployment if the Act was not repealed. Garbett encouraged Dartmouth to 'make such use of the facts relative to the stagnation of trade with America as may prevent the frightful consequences which must ensue from so many necessitous workmen being suddenly unemployed'. Dartmouth later warned the House of Lords that 'fifty thousand men in this kingdom were at this time ripe for rebellion for want of work from the uneasy situation in the colonies'. The messages provided by the Birmingham community thus helped to shape the views their ally presented in the cabinet and the Lords as he participated in formulating and defending the ministry's policy regarding the Stamp Act.[14]

I: Indirect Representation

Sir Charles Holte's[15] return for Warwickshire in 1774 marked the point at which Birmingham could claim one of the county seats for itself, though the MPs returned down to the 1830s were drawn from county families. Nevertheless, the principle that Birmingham would select at least one member held. In 1780 Lord Craven[16] tried to put up Lord Guernsey[17] for the county but was rebuffed at a county meeting that nominated Sir Robert Lawley who was returned with Sir George Shuckburgh and was henceforth recognised as Birmingham's representative. Thomas Gem explained Lawley's selection to Dartmouth in this way:

> The various commercial regulations so frequently made by the Legislature affect the trade and manufactures of this place very much and render it an object of great importance to its inhabitants, that gentlemen may, if possible, be chosen for the

---

[12] John Alfred Langford, *A Century of Birmingham Life; or A Chronicle of Local Events from 1741 to 1781* (2 vols, Birmingham, 1868), i. p. 117. *Aris's Birmingham Gazette* reported in Oct. 1765 that the value of orders from America had fallen by £600,000 over the previous 18 months. Money, *Experience and Identity*, p. 162.

[13] Among the nobility and gentry were: the Earls of Huntingdon and Denbigh, Earl Gower and Lord Craven, as well as Morcaunt and Bromley. Money, *Experience and Identity*, p. 182, n. 21.

[14] Money, *Experience and Identity*, p. 164; HMC, Dartmouth MSS, 14th R, Part 10, ii, 32.

[15] Sir Charles Holte, 6th Bt. (?1721–82), MP, Warwickshire, 1774–80.

[16] William Craven (1738–91), succ. as 6th Baron Craven, 1769.

[17] Heneage Finch, Lord Guernsey (1751–1812), MP, Castle Rising, 1772–4 and Maidstone, 1774–7; succ. as 4th Earl of Aylesford, 1777; Ld. of Bedchamber, 1777–83; Capt. of the Yeomen of the Guard, 1783–1804; Ld. Steward, 1804–12.

County who are connected with the people and not entirely uninformed of the particulars in which their interest consists. While, therefore, we lament the loss of our former members, it concerns us to exert ourselves in the choice of at least one proper person to succeed them. We have applied to Sir Robt. Lawley for this purpose, who has consented to stand forth as a candidate on the day of nomination at Warwick on Friday next. As he is a gentleman of affluent fortune and truly independent principles we flatter ourselves he will meet with your approbation and support. The freeholders in this place and its environs are almost unanimous in his favour. We have reason to believe that the sentiments of the gentlemen in the neighbourhood agree with ours.[18]

II: Canals

During the 1770s Birmingham's lobbying focused on the Birmingham Canal, which, as initially designed, was to run from the town to Aldersley, north of Wolverhampton and from there, ultimately, to the Trent and Mersey[19] and the Severn, via the Staffordshire and Worcestershire Canal. It finally opened in April 1772. After hiring John Lane as agent 'to conduct the intended application to Parliament', a core group of the canal's proprietors waited upon Lords Gower and Grey, Sir Walter Bagot and Thomas Anson[20] to secure their support. They also gained a promise of assistance from Thomas Gilbert, the Commons' leading authority on canal legislation. A committee of proprietors then directed Lane to prepare a bill in September 1767. The House received a petition for leave to bring in a bill which was referred to a committee on 1 December 1767. Mordaunt reported from the committee to bring in the bill which eventually received royal approval on 24 February 1768 (8 George III, c. 38).

Within 11 months, however, the proprietors of the Company went back to Parliament to get an act to amend the one of the previous session – a not unusual circumstance.[21] As noted in Chapter 5, Matthew Boulton and the company's chairman again enlisted Gilbert, who 'offered his services to the proprietors ... to consider and settle the Petition to be sent up to him by the Committee'. Gilbert reviewed it with George White,[22] a Commons' clerk and the Company's agent. The committee then reviewed the draft and ordered its clerk to write 'to the members for the County, ... and such Lords, and Members as are likely to assist us in the undertaking, requesting their

---

[18] *HMC, Dartmouth MSS*, 15th R, iii, pp. 252–3, Gem to Dartmouth, 14 Sept. 1780.
[19] Authorised by an act of 1766, the Trent and Mersey represented the first phase of James Brindley's plan to link England's main rivers (Trent, Mersey, Severn and Thames) and London by inland waterway to Birmingham, Bristol, Liverpool and Hull. It was completed in 1777.
[20] Thomas Anson (?1695–1773), MP, Lichfield, 1747–70.
[21] For the reasons for the application, see the petition for the bill, *CJ*, xxxii, 159.
[22] George White (d. 1789), Clerk of the Journals, 1756–70; Clerk without Doors, 1771; Clerk on the Secret East Indian Committees, 1772–1781; White was the first of the Commons' clerks to establish a large business as a Parliamentary agent. O. Cyprian Williams, *The Clerical Organization of the House of Commons, 1661–1850* (Oxford, 1954), p. 77.

Patronage and support'.[23] Lord Beauchamp reported from the committee on the petition on 9 February.[24]

It prepared 'fresh Clauses' to alter the measure which a general meeting of proprietors reviewed on 16 February. All apparently went well, for at a meeting on 10 March, the Committee ordered that letters of thanks be sent to Lord Beauchamp, who conducted the measure in the Commons, to Gilbert, and to Lord Dartmouth, who oversaw its passage in the Lords, 'for their assistance in conducting our amended Bill through both houses of Parliament'.[25]

The canal, vital to Birmingham's commerce and industry, was completed in three phases: first from the Wednesbury coal fields to Birmingham; then after difficulties and litigation to the terminus in Birmingham; and finally to the Staffordshire and Worcestershire Canal.[26] That process was slow, partly because of the physical difficulties that had to be overcome.

There were contentions problems involved in completing the terminus at the Birmingham end. The initial plan had been to build wharves at New Hall Ring, which belonged to William Colmore. The Company, however, changed its plans upon discovering that the ground there leaked. After pursuing various legal options, Colmore on 26 November 1770 petitioned for leave to bring in a bill to compel the Company to complete its New Hall Terminus.[27] This was granted on 6 December:[28] attempts to reach an accommodation outside of Parliament failed, because Colmore's bill provoked significant opposition. The Birmingham Canal Company submitted its counter-petition in January 1771 contending that Colmore ignored the fact that the Birmingham proprietors had endeavoured to complete the connection 'but were thwarted by the nature of the land'. Owners and occupiers on Colmore's property and nearby manufacturers also petitioned against his measure.[29] Despite intense opposition Colmore's bill received the royal assent in late February.[30]

Beyond these difficulties, the original Act authorising the Birmingham Canal specified that if that the canal company failed to complete the connection to the Staffordshire and Worcestershire Canal within six months of its connection to Birmingham, the Staffordshire and Worcestershire would be entitled to complete the link itself. Thus, on 31 January 1771, seven months after the Birmingham Company

---

[23] TNA, RAIL, 810/1, Birmingham Canal Minute Book, ff. 16, 67.
[24] *CJ*, xxxi, 193.
[25] TNA, RAIL 810/1, Birmingham Canal Minute Book, ff. 73, 77.
[26] S.R. Broadbridge, *The Birmingham Canal Navigations. Vol. 1: 1768–1846* (Newton Abbot, 1974), p. 18.
[27] *CJ*, xxxiii, p. 24. Colmore argued that his consent to the canal's original proposal was contingent upon the proprietors completing the canal to the Newhall Ring, as specified in the Act, and that if it did not fulfil that commitment, he would 'be very materially injured in his Property'.
[28] *CJ*, xxxiii, 44.
[29] At issue were competing property rights: the owners and occupiers worried that the extension of the canal to Newhall Ring would reduce the value of their properties, and manufacturers feared it would threaten their water supplies, given the leakage. *CJ*, xxxiii, 93–4.
[30] 11 George III, c. 67; Broadbridge, *Birmingham Canal Navigations*, pp. 22–3; Birmingham Archives, Matthew Boulton General Correspondence, MS 3782/12/195, Gilbert to Boulton, 16 Feb. 1771. Boulton was surreptitiously opposed to the extension because it threatened his water supplies. Jenny Uglow, *Lunar Men*, p. 119.

was supposed to have made the link, the Staffordshire and Worcestershire delivered a petition for leave to bring in a bill to make the connection. The Birmingham Canal counter-petitioned on 20 February,[31] but because of other disputes both sides agreed to accept Lord Dartmouth as an umpire. The upshot was that an agreement between the two companies was reached quickly.[32]

Before 1785 the Birmingham Canal Company faced a final Parliamentary battle. From its opening neighbours feared it aspired to create a monopoly. To forestall that possibility, different groups drew up plans to complete the link to the Trent and Mersey. The decisive step came in August 1781 when at a meeting in Warwick, a canal was planned from Bilston and Wednesbury via Fazeley to Atherstone at the end of the Coventry Canal with a branch to Birmingham. Garbett described the project as a 'Parallel Cut that would cause much injury to his Birmingham Canal friends';[33] indeed, it provoked those friends to develop their plan to extend the canal to the Trent and Mersey. The rival group presented its petition on 6 December 1782. *Aris's Birmingham Gazette* noted on 13 January 1783 that the contest involved 'the entire region's connection with the rest of the country'. The result was a battle that is vividly described in Hutton's *History of Birmingham*:

> Both parties beat up for volunteers in the town to strengthen their forces; from words of acrimony, they came to those of virulence; then the powerful batteries of hand-bills, and newspapers were opened: every town within fifty miles, interested on either side, was moved to petition, confident of victory... Each party possessed that activity for which Birmingham is famous, and seemed to divide between them the legislative strength of the nation; every corner of the two houses was ransacked for a vote: the throne was the only power unsolicited. Perhaps at the reading... there was the fullest House of Commons ever remembered on a private bill.[34]

Broadbridge noted that during proceedings on the two bills members of the Birmingham canal committee remained permanently in London, lobbying members in each House and arranging petitions and clauses. The rival company's bill received its second reading on 3 February; counsel were scheduled to be heard on the 6th, but proceedings were postponed eight times. Nevertheless, the rival group's bill made its way through the Commons, was passed in the House of Lords and received the royal assent to become law (25 George III, c. 92).

The new act provided for the construction of Fazeley Line as well as six additional cuts in addition to creating a new company – the Birmingham and Fazeley Canal

---

[31] *CJ*, xxxiii, 107, 184. The proprietors of the Birmingham company contended they had already expended £204,000 – more than was authorised by the 1768 Act, and that they were 'desirous of completing the tie' agreeable to their assurances to the Staffordshire and Worcestershire 'with all dispatch'.
[32] For details of the agreement, see Staffordshire Record Office, Dartmouth MSS, D564/12/4, Sir Edward Littleton to Lord Dartmouth, 27 Feb. 1771.
[33] BL, Bowood MS, Add. MS 88906/01/011, f. 33, Garbett to Shelburne, 30 Jan. 1782.
[34] Hadfield, *The Canals of the West Midlands* (Newton Abbot, 1966), p. 71, from William Hutton, *The History of Birmingham* (2nd edn, 1783).

Navigation.³⁵ In the following year the two formerly contending companies were united under the original Birmingham Company by another act into the awkwardly named Birmingham & Birmingham & Fazeley Canal Company. The battle had been fought on a grand scale by the proprietors of the competing companies, each side bolstered by petitioners for and against one or the other of the two bills. Sir Robert Lawley and Lord Lewisham³⁶ bore most of the burden of shepherding the various bills through the House.

III: The Birmingham Assay Office

The initiative for seeking an assay office at Birmingham came from Matthew Boulton. As the Earl of Shelburne explained to his wife during a visit to Birmingham:

> they [many in the town] are in great way of an assay master which is allowed at Chester and York; but it is very hard on a manufacturer to be obliged to send every piece of plate to Chester to be marked ... It would be of infinite public advantage if silver plate came to be manufactured here as watches lately are, and that it should be taken off of the imposing monopoly of London.³⁷

Boulton obviously had coached his visitor on the needs of Birmingham silversmiths who had embarked on the production of silver plate. Moreover, the Earl in 1771 received a direct example of the need for such an office. He had ordered two sets of candlesticks from Boulton which the latter sent to Chester for marking. Not only did it take 12 days to receive their mark, but because of 'careless packing, ... the chasing was entirely destroyed'. Boulton, as a result, had to make many repairs, and lamented:

> that altho' I am very desirous of becoming a great Silversmith, yet I am determined never to take up that branch in the Large Way I intended unless powers can be obtained to have a Marking Hall at Birmingham. This is not the first time by several that I have been served so.³⁸

The result of Boulton's frustrations was that he applied to Parliament. Before he dispatched his petition, Gilbert Dixon, solicitor for the 'artificers of silver' in Sheffield, informed him of his clients' intention to make a similar application. Upon learning of Birmingham's plan he was instructed to inquire whether Birmingham would:

---

[35] Broadbridge, *Birmingham Canal Navigations*, pp. 40–1.
[36] Legge, George, Ld. Lewisham (1755–1810), MP, Plymouth, 1778–80 and Staffordshire, 1780–4; Ld. of Bedchamber to Pr. of Wales, 1782–3; Ld. Warden of Stanneries, 1783–98; President of India Board, 1801–2; Ld. Steward, 1802–4; Ld. Chamberlain, 1804–10; succ. as 3rd Earl of Dartmouth, 1801; K.G. 1805.
[37] Quoted in H.W. Dickinson, *Matthew Boulton* (Cambridge, 1937), p. 64.
[38] Dickinson, *Boulton*, p. 65.

take the Workers in Plate at Sheffield into the Scheme, so as to go hand in hand with you in parliament and to be both comprehended in the same act..., only to be separate Companies and separate Offices – and upon terms and Conditions you wou'd be willing to receive them into your Scheme.[39]

According to Dixon, the Duke of Norfolk,[40] Lord Rockingham, Sir George Savile, Edwin Lascelles, as well as the members for York[41] supported the plan.

The two groups' petitions challenged the long-established pre-eminence of the London Goldsmiths who disputed their applications on the grounds that the:

Power of trying, touching assaying and marking, . . . is a very great and important Trust, and ought to be committed to such Persons, and in such Places, only, where the same is likely to be discharged with the greatest Care and Fidelity. [The] Mystery of Goldsmiths have been a Guild . . . Time out of Mind.[42]

Prior to submitting his petition, Boulton had enlisted Lord Dartmouth, who in turn had secured the support of John Robinson. Robinson assisted a Mr. Chamberlain, solicitor to the Mint, in drafting Birmingham's bill. In addition, Boulton applied to Lord North for his support[43] and in December informed Dixon he had had a conference with the King on the matter, and also with 'many of the nobility, particularly some of the present Ministry all of whom seem persuaded of the justness & propriety of the establishing such an office at Birmingham and have promised their assistance'.[44] On 11 May 1773, he informed his partner, John Fothergill: 'as to the House of Lords I have twice the interest in that House than in ye Lower House . . . Lord Denbeigh [sic] took me about with him yesterday in his Chariot to several ministerial Members pressing them to serve us. He says he has talked much to the King in my fav[ou]r'.[45] Ten days later he informed Fothergill, he was lobbying on behalf of his Sheffield allies: 'I see but little of ye Sheffield folks & have the whole of their business upon my hands so that for another week I shall be closely engaged in waiting upon all ye Lords Spiritual & Temporal that I shall have little time to attend to our own business'.[46]

In the Commons the burden of carrying the two bills fell upon Thomas Gilbert and Thomas Skipwith.[47] Gilbert had a longstanding connection with Boulton. His brother

---

[39] BA, Matthew Boulton Papers, General Correspondence, 3782/12/23/253, Gilbert Dixon to Boulton, 2 December 1772.
[40] Edward Howard (1682–1777), succ. brother as 8th Duke of Norfolk, 1732.
[41] Lord John Cavendish (1732–96), MP, Weymouth and Melcombe Regis, 1754–61 and Knaresborough, 1761–8, York, 1768–84 and Derbyshire, 1794–6; Ld. of Treasury, 1765–6; Chancellor of Exchequer, 1782, Apr.–Dec. 1783; Charles Turner (?1727–83), MP, York, 1768–83.
[42] Petition of the Warders and assistants of the Company of the Mystery of Goldsmiths of the City of London, 17 Feb. 1773, *CJ*, xxxiv, 134–5.
[43] Eric Robinson, 'Matthew Boulton and the art of Parliamentary lobbying', *HJ*, vii (1964), 210.
[44] Quoted in Arthur Westwood, *The Assay Office at Birmingham. Part I: The Foundation* (Birmingham, 1936), p. 9.
[45] Quoted in Dickinson, *Matthew Boulton*, p. 69.
[46] Quoted in Westwood, *Assay Office*.
[47] Sir Thomas George Skipwith (?1735–90), MP, Warwickshire, 1769–80 and for Steyning, 1780–4; succ. as 4th Bt., 1778.

John had been apprenticed to Boulton's father. Gilbert sought Matthew's support when he stood for Lichfield in 1768, and the two worked to secure funding for the Trent and Mersey Canal. Gilbert, as already noted, played an important part in guiding the Birmingham Canal bills through the House of Commons while Boulton was one of the canal's original projectors.

Skipwith chaired the committee on the petitions from Sheffield and Birmingham, reporting them from committee and summarising the testimony of the witnesses from both cities.[48] The Birmingham bill was read a second time on 6 April, and Skipwith chaired its second reading committee. As the bills moved through the House, petitions poured in for and against, from Sheffield, Birmingham, London and elsewhere.

As the contest intensified, an additional committee was established with Gilbert as its chair. Its mission was to inquire into any irregularities in the Assay Offices at London and seven other offices. The new committee met for the first time on 8 March and subsequently sat concurrently with Skipwith's. A total of 71 MPs attended the two committees, 63 appearing once or twice; three attended three times; Skipwith and Gilbert attended a total of 18 times; Sir John Wrottesley,[49] 12 times; Thomas Harley, member for the City of London, 11; Thomas Pownall, nine; and Lord Guernsey appeared eight times.[50] Skipwith and Gilbert delivered the reports of their committees on April 29.

Of the two, Gilbert's was the more sensational and important. Apparently on the advice of Boulton, his committee secretly purchased 22 pieces of London-assayed plate. After referring them to the Mint for testing, it was found that the silver content of 21 of the 22 pieces was below standard, thus undermining the London Goldsmith's claim that their centuries of experience in 'touching, marking and assaying' gave them an indisputable right to maintain their monopoly.[51] Gilbert's committee concluded 'from the Manner in which the said several Assay Offices have been and are now conducted, that they are liable to many abuses and Impositions, & that various Frauds have been committed upon Silver Plate, contrary to the Legal Standards established in this Kingdom'.[52]

The report, also, contained summaries of testimonies of witnesses from London indicating not only lapses from established procedures but also of innumerable frauds. Only offices in Chester and Newcastle were judged to be sound.[53] With these revelations, the Assay Office Bill received the Commons' approval on 18 May. It passed the Lords ten days later, when it also received the royal assent (13 George III, c. 52). Birmingham's Assay Office opened on 31 August 1773.

---

[48] *CJ*, xxxiv, 190–3.
[49] Sir John Wrottesley, 8th Bt., (1744–87), MP, Newcastle-under-Lyme, Mar.–June, 1768 and Staffordshire, 1768–87; army, 1761, Capt. 85 Ft 1762; Capt. 1 Ft. Gds; and Lt.-Col. 1770; Col. Army 1779; Maj. Gen. 1782; Col. 45 Ft. 1784–7.
[50] Robinson, 'Boulton and Parliamentary lobbying', 219–21.
[51] Jenny Uglow, *The Lunar Men*, p. 204; *House of Commons Sessional Papers*, xxv, 327–8.
[52] *House of Commons Sessional Papers*, xxv, 334
[53] *House of Commons Sessional Papers*, xxv, 305–11, 334.

IV: Other Birmingham Issues, 1770s: America, Patents and Theatres

In January 1775 Matthew Boulton described for Lord Dartmouth a split among Birmingham merchants and manufacturers. During a meeting, manufacturers set 'forth their distress and determination to petition Parliament for redress, notwithstanding remonstrances offered by Doctor Roebuck and himself [Boulton] against such unwise action'. The more moderate doctor along with Boulton tried to show that the commercial inconveniences were not so great as the manufacturers represented.[54] Though unable to prevent their colleagues from petitioning, they and others in the town promoted their own petition 'which tended 1st to take off that stigma theirs [manufacturers'] would carry with it, and 2dly to promote Permanince [sic] in the execution of our Laws and consequently better security of their American Debts'.[55]

Soon after performing this service in support of a government of which Dartmouth was a member, Boulton asked the Earl for a favour for James Watt and himself: he requested that Dartmouth support Watt's application to extend the existing patent on his steam engine for 14 years and, in addition, enlist Lord North to do the same, for the prime minister's 'concurrence would make us happy as it would put us out of all suspense'.[56] He stressed not only the utility of Watt's invention, but the time and expense to which he had gone in perfecting it. Boulton added that he stood to lose a good deal unless the patent was extended because he had financed Watt's trials and experiments over the last year at Soho.[57]

In addition to soliciting the support of Dartmouth and Lord North, Boulton enlisted Lord Guernsey to present the petition in the Commons and carry the measure through the House. Guernsey managed to steer the bill through each of its stages despite the fact that on 20 March 1775 William Pengree petitioned against the bill on behalf of William Blakey, who in 1766 had obtained a 14-year patent to make and sell an engine. Blakey claimed to have received no notice of Watt's 1769 patent, and Pengree claimed that Watt's 1769 machine was an imitation of Blakey's.

---

[54] *HMC, Dartmouth MSS*, 14th R., ii, pp. 257–8. In a follow-up letter on 15 Jan. Boulton assured Dartmouth that no branch of manufacturing would be so affected by the turmoil in America as the nail trade, in the Earl's own parish of Bromwich. p. 259.

[55] *HMC, Dartmouth MSS*, 14th R., ii, 17 Jan. 1775, pp. 257–8. The petition stated that 'The inhabitants of the Town of Birmingham and Neigbourhood are apprehensive that any Relaxation in the Execution of the Laws respecting the Colonies of *Great Britain* will ultimately tend to the Injury of the Commerce of the said Town and Neighbourhood'. It was presented to the House on 25 January 1775. *CJ*, xxxv, 77–8.

[56] BA, Matthew Boulton General Correspondence, Box 228/130, Boulton to Dartmouth, 21 Feb. On 16 Jan. Dartmouth replied that he appreciated Boulton's efforts to 'stop the misguided & misinformed zeal of your friends in Birmingham from petitioning' and also for the counter-petition he was organising. He wondered 'whether it would not be right to confine y[ou]rs in general terms to the support of Authority of the Laws of the Kingdom over all the Dominions of the Crown', a recommendation which Boulton and his allies adopted. BA, Matthew Boulton General Correspondence, Dartmouth to Boulton, 16 Jan. 1775.

[57] *HMC, Dartmouth MSS*, iii, 15th R., 213.

Applicants for patents had to submit written specifications of their inventions, defining their uniqueness. Patentees complained it was impossible in writing to specify the uniqueness of an invention in a manner that would satisfy the courts, because it had never been laid down what a specification should do. This lack of specificity provided the basis for Blakey's claim, but Watt was partially protected against his charges because along with his written specifications in 1769, he had submitted detailed drawings of his engine.[58] Boulton's assiduous lobbying during which he approached more than 100 MPs also provided crucial reinforcements to the cause as Watt's bill made its way through both Houses on its way to receiving George III's approval.[59]

Boulton also featured prominently in the struggle to license the New Street Theatre, an issue that embroiled Birmingham during the middle years of the decade. At that time, theatrical performances were licensed by the Crown and regulated by local magistrates. With the appearance of the New Street Theatre under the direction of Richard Yates in 1774, a competitor emerged to the long-established King Street Theatre. Neither was licensed. According to a squib in the *Birmingham Gazette* from May 1773 Birmingham manufacturers regarded theatres as 'tending to promote Negligence, create Expense, and corrupt the Morals of the Industrious'.[60]

Nevertheless, Yates in February 1777 applied for a license for this theatre,[61] which was contested by the Reverend John Parsons, Rector of St Martin's, Birmingham. In two letters to Lord Dartmouth, Parsons argued that such a license would promote 'idleness and dissipation'. He also pointed to the results of a questionable poll in which ratepayers opposed the application.[62] Parsons believed that it was best to leave control of the theatres to the bench, a point on which Yates agreed. He regarded his application as a means by which the town would regain control of the two theatres.

Boulton reinforced this point in supporting Yates' application in his letter to Dartmouth. He stressed that:

> if we do not have one house established by authority, I know we shall continue to be pestered with two, which being more than the place can support, necessitates the losing party to have recourse to various stratagems for putting off their tickets at any rate, ... and from this result many evils to apprentices and the lower classes of people, ... Whereas, I am convinced that one licensed house opened for four months only of the year and under the direction of twenty inhabitants of respectable character in Birmingham would produce a quite contrary effect.

For Boulton the opportunity to attend a good play enhanced the taste and skill of his designers and painters. He also felt that a vibrant theatre would be a benefit for the town's businesses, for it would provide 'some inducement to prolonging' the visits of 'persons of fashion' to Birmingham.[63]

---

[58] Eric Robinson, 'James Watt and the law of patent', *Technology and Culture*, xiii (1972), 115–39.
[59] H.T. Dickinson, *Politics of the People*, p. 73.
[60] Quoted in Langford, *Century of Birmingham Life*, p. 273.
[61] *CJ*, xxxvi, 673.
[62] *HMC, Dartmouth MSS*, 14th R. iii, 232–4, 15, 17 Feb. 1777.
[63] *HMC, Dartmouth MSS*, 14th R, iii, 234–5.

Despite his lobbying, the bill was defeated in the Commons at its second reading on 29 April by a vote of 69 to 18.[64] In addition to the opposition of manufacturers and Parsons' evangelical allies, Edmund Burke, because of pressure from his Quaker constituents in Bristol and especially from Richard Champion, his foremost supporter, opposed the bill's second reading after initially supporting Yates.[65]

Despite this setback, another petition to licence the New Street Company was presented in January 1778 but languished unattended. Forces in the town, however, were able the following January to broker an arrangement between the competing theatres that established New Street as pre-eminent; in 1786, the King Street Theatre closed.[66]

V: Coal, Fustians and the Chamber

The 1780s marked a return to the broader national focus that Samuel Garbett had advocated 20 years earlier – one that culminated in the formation of the short-lived Chamber of Manufacturers. The Chamber's collapse followed on differences of opinion regarding Pitt's French commercial treaty in 1787, because of divisions that arose between the newer industries of the Midlands and Lancashire and the long-established manufacturing centres in London and the south.

Birmingham never ceased to be preoccupied with issues relating to its businesses, but a series of episodes occurred during the first years of the decade that highlighted the inadequacies of the government's support for manufacturers and, indeed, its lack of understanding of their needs. For example, in 1784 Birmingham learned that the Emperor Joseph II of Austria had closed his dominions to British goods, not from British officials but from a local firm. Worse still, the Pitt administration assumed that the edict would not be enforced and took no steps to try to counteract it.

More serious for Birmingham was the willingness of administrations to impose unwelcome taxes. The Coalition's Receipts Tax fell upon the nation's middling populations and led to vociferous campaigns for its repeal.[67] That controversial tax was succeeded by a series of levies that were offensive to manufacturers because they were imposed on the materials of manufacturing, including coal and fustians. Garbett told Sir George Shuckburgh that some of his neighbours believed the proposed Coal Tax 'borders upon lunacy to those who know the Manufactures in Iron Copper Brass &c &c &c'.[68] According to a petition from the cotton manufacturers the fustian tax was especially offensive because the excisemen who descended upon them to enforce it disturbed 'the harmony and arrangement of their manufacture, to deprive them of personal liberty and the free exercise of their property'.[69] The intrusions of excisemen

---

[64] Langford, *Century of Birmingham Life*, i, pp. 282–3.
[65] For a report of Burke's speech at the measure's second reading, see *Aris' Birmingham Gazette*, 5 May 1777.
[66] The previous discussion is based mainly on Money, *Experience and Identity*, pp. 88–91.
[67] For a debate on the motion for its repeal, see *PH*, xxiv, cc. 97–109, 4 Dec. 1783.
[68] BL, Bowood, Add MS. 88906/01/011, ff. 58–9, Garbett to Sir George Shuckburgh, 17 July 1784.
[69] *PH*, xxv, 362.

were, in fact, the main cause for opposition to the measure, and fear of similar intrusions caused potters and ironmasters of the West Country to join cotton masters in their opposition.[70]

By the summer of 1783 Birmingham had in its recently established Commercial Committee an organisation able to give voice to its concerns. Among the first of these was an effort by Bristol brass makers to secure a bill to repeal laws prohibiting the export of unwrought brass, a material much in demand among the Birmingham trades.[71] A Birmingham committee petitioned against the Bill on 14 June. According to Garbett the Bristol proposal was supported by Lord North in conjunction with Cornish and Bristol MPs. Against this large contingent was the small contingent of Warwickshire and Staffordshire members.[72] Fortunately, Garbett enlisted Lord Rawdon,[73] recently elevated to the House of Lords. In his first speech, he managed to convince his colleagues that the bill should go no further, and it was defeated.[74]

The brass question was only one of those on which Birmingham manufacturers found themselves involved in Parliamentary skirmishes with competitors from other regions. In the summer of 1784 Garbett became embroiled in a contest over the Sheffield Plate Bill. He reported to Boulton that he was able before the bill was reported from its committee to have a conference with Henry Duncombe, the measure's Sheffield agent and its Parliamentary solicitor. The Sheffield group agreed to recommit the bill and add 'something' that Garbett proposed. The committee met again on 13 July, attended by many Yorkshire members along with Shuckburgh, 'Sir Edward Littleton[75] and Mr. Hammet'.[76] They agreed to Garbett's motion to enlarge the privilege of marking within a radius of 100 miles of Sheffield and added his figure denoting the proportion of silver to copper for each piece. Garbett reported he had declared his opposition to the bill unless more effective restraints were included to maintain the integrity of this valuable trade. Though he managed to modify the legislation, he regretted that he had agreed to the passage of a bill that would have 'villainous Effects'.[77]

The Sheffield silversmiths and their supporters had only a decade earlier worked with Birmingham to obtain assay offices for their towns, yet during proceedings on their 1784 bill they were hostile and condescending. Lord Effingham[78] and the Sheffield agent dismissed the Birmingham silver trade as 'insignificant' and 'not worth

---

[70] Earl Reitan, *Politics, Finance and the People, Economical Reform in England in the Age of the American Revolution, 1770-92* (Basingstoke and New York, 2007), 211.
[71] Matthew Brickdale presented the bill on 13 June.
[72] There were two divisions on the bill in the Commons, carried by the measure's supporters by votes of 126-12 and 35-17. Hoppit, *Failed Legislation*, pp. 472-3.
[73] Francis Rawdon (1754-1826), MP [I], 1780-3; cr. Baron Rawdon [GB], 1783; succ. as Earl of Moira [I] 1793; Gen. 1803, Commander of Forces, Scotland, 1802-6; Master General of Ordnance, 1805-7; Ld. Lt., Tower Hamlets, 1806-1827; succ. mother as Baron Hastings, 1808; Gov. General and C.-in-C., India, 1813-22; cr. Marquess of Hastings, 1817.
[74] McCahill, 'Peers, patronage and the industrial revolution', 99-100.
[75] Sir Edward Littleton, 4th Bt. (?1725-1812), MP, Staffordshire, 1784-1812.
[76] Benjamin Hammet (?1736-1800), MP, Taunton, 1782-1800; alderman of London; sheriff, 1788-9.
[77] BL, Bowood MS, Add. MS. 88906/01/011, ff. 57-8, Garbett to Shelburne, 19 July, 1784; Add. MS 88906, 01/011, ff. 58-9, Garbett to Sir George Shuckburgh, 17 July 1784.
[78] Thomas Howard (1747-91), succ. as 3rd Earl of Effingham, 1763; Treasurer of Household, 1782-3; Master of Mint, 1784-9; Gov. Jamaica, 1789-90.

notice'.[79] Contending as he was with legislators of the stature of Wilberforce and Duncombe, Garbett was fortunate to have secured any modifications, though he remained dissatisfied with the Bill.

However, William Pitt's presentation of his plan for a new commercial relationship between Ireland and Britain in 1785 forced British manufacturers to set aside parochial disputes and form the sort of organisation that Garbett had envisaged in the 1760s. The Irish propositions were a primary catalyst behind the formation of the Chamber of Manufacturers, though the earlier tax issues were also an important factor.

The proposals which came before the House of Commons in February 1785 consisted of a series of resolutions. The second would have permitted Ireland to take part in colonial and foreign trade almost on the same terms as Britain. Resolutions three through six related to tariffs on manufactured goods of the two countries: duties were to be equal and reduced to the level of the kingdom that had the lowest. The plan finally required that Ireland would contribute a portion of its hereditary revenue in the event of a surplus towards the support of the imperial fleet; a controversial point in Ireland.[80]

While the government granted special favours in the resolutions to certain British interests including the East India Company, the landed and the woollen interests, many of the newer British industries saw the plan as being advantageous towards Ireland. On account of its low taxes, cheap labour and because the Irish government provided support to the country's nascent industries with loans, bounties and subsidies, English manufacturers believed Ireland enjoyed competitive advantages over themselves because they faced higher local taxation and labour costs. British manufacturers also charged that the Irish government encouraged their labourers to emigrate and bring with them their skills and trade secrets.[81]

VI: Chamber of Manufacturers

The proposals reconfirmed manufacturers' belief that the administration neither comprehended the impact of its earlier taxes nor appreciated the importance of their role in the nation's economic life. For these reasons Birmingham's Commercial Committee on 7 February 1785 adopted resolutions, including one that stated that:

> every tax on manufactures, or on the raw materials employed in them ... is impolitic, as it tends to depress or crush the ardour of invention, and those adventurous attempts after improvement and new discovery to which many of the new British manufactures owe that superiority they have attained ...
> ...

---

[79] Industrial Revolution: A documentary History, Papers from the Boulton-Watt Archive and the Matthew Boulton Papers: Series One: Birmingham Central Library, Box 30F, Samuel Garbett & Family, 1765–1785 (Box 73), www.ampltd.co.uk: Garbett to Boulton, 14, 19 July 1784.
[80] Witt Bowden, 'The influence of the manufacturers on some of the early policies of William Pitt', AHR, xxix (1924), 659–61.
[81] Bowden, 'Influence of manufacturers', AHR, pp. 660, 664–9.

Resolved, That in order ..., to counteract the opinion, which has prevailed, that manufactures are proper objects of taxation, it is become necessary to correspond with the Commercial Committees and eminent Merchants and Manufacturers in different parts of the kingdom, in order to represent such particulars to Government, respecting exports to foreign countries, and to the manufacturers which are established there .. , as may be most effectual for the protection of British Manufacturers in general.[82]

The impetus for the Chambers' formation came primarily from the cotton, woollen, iron and potteries industries. Representatives of Britain's manufacturers gathered in London where they selected a chairman who was directed to write to the main manufacturing centres requesting them to send deputies to London so that a collective sense 'of the trading interest of Great Britain could be collected ... not only relative to a commercial treaty with Ireland, but with other European states'.[83] As a follow-up, Garbett wrote on 22 February that he would have Boulton and Watt 'procure a meeting of as many of the principal traders now in London in consequence of the negotiations for a commercial intercourse with Ireland and to desire the Chairman to write to the principal manufacturing establishments requesting them to send deputies to London at this important crisis'.[84] He took care, however, to assure Shelburne that it 'will be necessary to keep some of us within moderate Bounds, & that being cool & deliberate will not impede but excite animated Conduct in others'.[85]

VII: Disillusionment

The Chamber was a loosely organised federation with the power resting in local committees. Over 60 petitions were dispatched from them to the House of Commons between March and 12 May with critiques of the commercial resolutions.[86] The organisation's structure meant, however, that it was subject to centrifugal forces. National leaders divided over how best to the make the organisation's case. While Wedgewood and Manchester cotton spinners allied themselves with the opposition Whig party in Parliament and joined William Eden and Lord Sheffield in attacking the propositions, Garbett and the iron masters preferred to negotiate with Pitt and his lieutenants. In May 1785, for example, Garbett, Sir Robert Lawley and Isaac Hawkins-Browne[87] met with the minister to discuss a possible bounty on iron in the event that the resolutions were adopted.[88] At the same time Lord Sheffield tried to enlist Boulton

---

[82] Langford, *Century of Birmingham Life*, pp. 321–2.
[83] Norris, 'Garbett and Parliamentary lobbying', *EcHR*, pp. 156–7; Money, *Experience and Identity*, pp. 36–7; Langford, *Century of Birmingham Life*, i, 322–3.
[84] Boulton-Watt Archive and the Matthew Boulton Papers: Series One: Birmingham Central Library, Box 30F, Samuel Garbett & Family, 1765–1785 (Box 73), www.ampltd.co.uk: Garbett to Boulton, 22 Feb. 1785.
[85] BL, Bowood MS, Add. MS 88906/G/011, ff. 43–4, Garbett to Shelburne, 18 Nov. 1784.
[86] Bowden, 'Influence of manufacturers', *AHR*, 671. Collections of petitions against the propositions are among the Pitt Papers. TNA, PRO, 320/8/145, f. 51; PR0 320/8/165, ff. 165–7 and throughout PRO 321/8.
[87] Isaac Hawkins-Browne (1745–1818), MP, Bridgnorth, 1784–1812.
[88] Money, *Experience and Identity*, p. 39.

to step forward; Sheffield informed him that 'several respectable Manufacturers' were to testify before a committee of the House; he recommended either Boulton or Watt should be in London, 'as men of intelligence were badly needed'.[89] Boulton, however, followed the example of Garbett and negotiated with the government, along with Richard Reynolds of Coalbrookdale and William Gibbons of Bristol, to ensure that their iron wares received a bounty that would equalise their products with those of the Irish in the event that the propositions became law.[90]

Regardless of the tactics they adopted, the different camps remained hostile to the Irish proposals, and their continuing criticisms, reinforced by the many petitions, forced the minister to modify his initial proposals. The alterations were so extensive that when the amended propositions were returned to Dublin, they were rejected by the Irish Parliament, so the Chamber of Manufacturers could claim a victory in its campaign to mobilise manufacturing opinion.

The unity of the Chamber was put to a more serious test, however, during the negotiations and the Parliamentary debates on the commercial treaty with France in 1786 and 1787. In the end the cotton, woollen, hardware and pottery industries provided the main manufacturing support for the treaty and were seen as its prime beneficiaries. On the other side were the older, specialised trades of the south and southeast, particularly those based on London. The latter took over the Chamber and declared their opposition to the agreement, to the disgust of Wedgwood, Watt and Garbett. Amidst this schism the Chamber disintegrated.

In the aftermath of the Chamber's collapse its former leaders went off in different political directions. Garbett and Boulton, with their experience of relying upon well-placed MPs and peers and Birmingham's system of 'indirect representation', saw no reason to abandon that practice. Birmingham's Commercial Chamber enjoyed such success selecting the nominees for two county seats prior to the 1784 general election that John Money notes the committee in 1784 engineered 'what amounted to Birmingham's pre-emptive nomination to the Warwickshire seats' for the second time in a row. During the 1784 Parliament, Lawley and Shuckburgh were especially attentive to the needs of the town, with the result that neither Garbett nor Boulton supported the reform movements of the period. Birmingham also declined to petition in support of Pitt's proposals for Parliamentary reform in 1785.[91]

Birmingham's system of 'particular representation', however, could not satisfy the town's manufacturers indefinitely. Even as Pitt was negotiating his commercial treaty with France, Garbett again signalled his discontent to Lord Lansdowne:[92]

> the eminent Manufacturers have looked with terror at Ministers, who they always found watching for opportunities to tax their Industry, & the Material or Instruments with which they were to acquire their Fortune, and we will have been & are now compelled to pay Taxes for <u>permission</u> to work for exportation.[93]

[89] BA, Matthew Boulton General Correspondence, MS 3782/12/30/23, Sheffield to Boulton, 12 Mar. 1785.
[90] Money, *Experience and Identity*, p. 39.
[91] Money, *Experience and Identity*, pp. 159, 213.
[92] The Earl of Shelburne received the Marquessate of Lansdowne in December 1784.
[93] BL, Bowood MS, Add. MS 88906/01/012. Ff. 2–3, Garbett to Lansdowne, 2 Oct. 1786.

The Impression is strongly in our Mind that Ministers from complacence to Members of Parliament will hear a Talk, but never seriously endeavor to remedy the evident Evils which are injurious to our Manufacturers, tho' it would cost not more than a few Hours attention.[94]

The aftermath of Birmingham's 'Priestley Riots' in July 1791 alienated Garbett from Warwickshire's ruling elite. He was outraged by their harsh response to the rioting and the spirit of repression that followed, and wrote to Lansdowne in 1792 on the case of Birmingham manufacturers who had raised £100,000 to check 'extravagances' practiced against them in mining and smelting. Having done so, they applied to Garbett for his patronage, who reported:

> it would be Rash at present to venture in the Bussle [sic] for they are accused of being Presbyterians, & the infernal Spirit under the name of Church & King is still alarmingly troublesome, & I have so much lost confidence in the execution of the Law that I durst not go about 14 Days since to a public Meeting upon the Slave Trade as at former meetings I had been Chairman and was threatened in consequence of it by the Gunsmiths.[95]

Garbett's disgust, however, was not limited to the local elite. As he beheld the spectacle of the Portland Whigs, recently allied with Pitt, lapping up peerages and other rewards, he wrote that his fellow manufacturers noted:

> with what eagerness sinecure Places are supported as Patronage and grasped as Emoluments, and with what Listlessness the real fundamental Interest & Happiness of the Country is regarded. They cannot be insensible that many Nobles are sharing the plunder produced by War, and that those who have not an Interest to support it suffer little in comparison with Traders.[96]

Still, their negativity and fear of repression did not lead Garbett or his colleagues to repudiate their allegiance to the system of 'particular representation'. Instead it was left to Birmingham's Society for Constitution Information to call upon the town's working men to sign a petition to the Commons, demanding equal representation for the people and the restoration of their ancient rights to speak forthrightly.[97]

Birmingham's artisans, however, did not join this call for radical reform. According to Money, they had assimilated the lessons of 1774 which were fairly conservative. Holte's victory in 1774 was used as an example of what people could achieve if they exerted themselves to exercise their liberties in a legal fashion. A pre-industrial sense of community persisted in Birmingham in ways it did not in the industrial towns of the north. Nor were Garbett's lamentations symptomatic of the views of the entire Birmingham manufacturing community. Boulton remained a defender of the

---

[94] BL, Bowood MS, Add MS. 88906/01/012, f. 107, Garbett to Lansdowne, 8 Nov. 1786.
[95] BL, Bowood MS, Add. MS. 88906/01/013, f. 132, 7 Feb. 1792.
[96] BL, Add. MS 88906/01/014, f. 38, Bowood MS, Garbett to Lansdowne, 18 Mar. 1794.
[97] Money, *Experience and Identity*, p. 214.

established order: he told Lord Stafford in December 1792 that he had endeavoured to win over the town's prominent Dissenters to the core ideas of 'a local Association for the Protection of Liberty and Property' and believed as a result that all would be quiet at Birmingham.[98]

VIII: –Birmingham Conclusions

The Birmingham interest is a useful example of an interest group because it was at once traditional and forward looking. Firmly rooted in the traditional patronage network, it relied for much of the second half of the eighteenth century upon skilled lobbyists and Birmingham's unique system of 'indirect representation' that evolved after 1774. With the help of both, it successfully challenged the monopoly of London's Company of the Mystery of Goldsmiths. Shortly thereafter, Lord Rawdon, nephew of their long-time patron, the 10th Earl of Huntington,[99] defeated Bristol's bill to repeal restrictions on the export of brass, a measure supported by the leaders of the Cornish copper industry and that county's numerous MPs.[100]

Nevertheless, the Birmingham interest in the 1760s and 1770s relied upon an ad hoc structure. Boulton and Garbett called upon members in both chambers to take up their projects, advocate on their behalf with ministers and steer their measures through Parliament. They had no official status and at points were at odds with the sentiments of many of their colleagues – in Boulton's case on the American war in the 1770s, in Garbett's on the organisation and directions pursued by the Birmingham Canal Company. The town did not establish its Commercial Committee until the early 1780s. Money emphasises the importance of the 1774 election that established Birmingham's right to nominate a candidate for at least one of the county seats. He maintains that this outcome was not as a coup organised by the manufacturers of the town to secure their own nominee. Rather the election took place amidst a political discussion that focused upon freeholder's rights and 'ancient Whiggery' – quite different from the priorities of Garbett and Boulton which focused at the time on ministerial connections and possession of a substantial bank balance.[101] By 1784, however, the town's Commercial Committee managed to nominate two candidates – Sir Robert Lawley and Sir George Augustus Shuckburgh. They were reliable and attentive to the town's needs as its merchants and manufacturers perceived them and made every effort to inform themselves of the city's business. In this respect they were probably unique. Dugdale Strafford Dugdale,[102] who held the Birmingham seat for the county after Shuckburgh, confessed in 1820 that he and his fellow Warwickshire MP, Francis Lawley, believed that their knowledge of 'the various subjects connected with the manufactures of the

---

[98] Money, *Experience and Identity*, pp. 213–14.
[99] Francis Hastings (1729–89), succ. as 10th Earl of Huntington, 1746; Master of the Horse, 1760–1; Groom of the Stole, 1761–70.
[100] McCahill, 'Peers, patronage and the industrial revolution', *JBS*, xvi (1976), 92–3.
[101] Money, *Empire and Identity*, pp. 179–80.
[102] Dugdale Strafford Dugdale (1737–1836), MP, Birmingham, 1802–31; Captain, Warwickshire Yeoman Cavalry, 1803.

place [Birmingham] was defective'.¹⁰³ The interest's reliance upon landed patrons also had obvious limitations. Dartmouth's influence diminished with the fall of North in 1782, and, in any case, his views were not always compatible with those of the Birmingham manufacturers, nor were those of Lord Gower.

After the collapse of the Chamber of Manufacturers Birmingham never completely reverted to earlier patterns of lobbying. Its leaders remained suspicious of Pitt and his cohort of MPs, and some like Garbett looked forward to the time when there would be a strong manufacturing voice at Westminster. The repression that followed the 'Priestley riots' did not extinguish these hopes. Despite the repression, manufacturers in 1791–92 raised £100,000 to check 'extravagances' against them in mining and smelting.

Somehow, Birmingham's leaders overcame the obstacles in that 'poisonous' environment. Their community sustained its potential despite the repression. The transportation network created during the 1760s and early 1770s had opened the West Midlands to the nation: in the process expanding the orbit of its business connections and its cultural and political awareness. The result was not only a wider market for the town's goods but a willingness to form partnerships with a variety of different communities. That, as Money suggests, was key to Birmingham's growth and progress. During the last decades of the century the city was laying the foundations which eventually transformed it into 'the workshop of the world'; its history of vigorous and effective lobbying was a part of that process.

Boulton was a master of the traditional art of lobbying which relied upon sympathetic patrons and reliable MPs. Garbett was also an adept lobbyist, but he had the broader vision which gave rise to the Chamber of Manufacturers. Though the Chamber collapsed, he regarded it as a living, vital vision. As a result of its formation, he told Lansdowne in 1785,

> there are three hundred gentlemen who are connected with that association that have more property and more knowledge of the state of general Commerce than 300 that might be named in the House of Commons. In this neighbourhood there are many who have transactions in every considerable town in Europe ... I rejoice they have met and united and that I have been a material instrument in occasioning it.¹⁰⁴

IX: The Fisheries

The fisheries and their proponents constituted a different sort of interest. Unlike Birmingham manufacturers, the fisheries were never a unified group: the various branches focused on different catches, fished on different coasts around Britain and around the globe. Insofar as there were linkages, the goals were to promote the prosperity of their bases. The other unifying elements were that they provided

---

[103] David Cannadine, *Lords and Landlords: The Aristocracy and the Towns, 1774–1976* (Atlantic Highlands, NJ, 1980), p 149.
[104] Quoted in Norris, 'Garbett and the early development of industrial lobbying', *HJ*, 460.

experienced seamen for the fleet in time of war and, to a greater extent than Birmingham or Leeds, relied upon government policy and protection. Bob Harris[105] and Anna Gambles stress that the motives behind Britain's promotion of fisheries were patriotic and nationalistic. By fostering regional development, policy makers and the interests behind the necessary legislation believed they would be encouraging commercial expansion, economic growth and, as the fisheries expanded, enlarging reserves of potential sailors and shipwrights for the fleet in time of war.

The fisheries relied upon a partnership with the state that encouraged their expansion by providing bounties, paid on the quantity of exported fish. The bounties were funded from customs fees (a system applied to a range of products, including corn). The first herring bounties were introduced in 1707; others on fish were enacted in 1719. According to Julian Hoppit there was no overall plan behind their introduction; instead the bounties were implemented in a piecemeal fashion. While it is unclear who initiated the various measures, Hoppit indicates that their passage required the Treasury's approval, for the outlay was significant. According to one study, over £600,000 in bounties on cod and herring were paid out between 1751 and 1782, with the majority going to Scotland. Another indicates that over £1 million went to the British herring fishery between 1765 and 1797, again with a substantial portion going to Scotland.[106] This data confirms Gambles' thesis that a principal goal of late eighteenth-century fishery acts was to stimulate regional economic development especially in remote, politically unstable and backward areas.[107]

My brief survey focuses on several diverse and unrelated achievements of the interest: Henry Beaufoy's[108] fisheries Acts of the mid-1780s, Jenkinson's Trade with America Act of 1785 and the British Fisheries Acts of 1786, the latter two relating to the Newfoundland fisheries.

Henry Beaufoy emerged in the 1780s as a force in the House of Commons. He was notable for his mastery of the details relating to foreign trade. Based on that mastery and their shared goals, Pitt drafted him on 12 February 1787 to chair the Commons' committee on the commercial treaty with France.[109] Beaufoy was also a proponent of religious toleration and in 1787 moved unsuccessfully for the repeal of the Test and Corporation Acts.[110]

An advocate for many reforms, including Parliamentary reform in 1783 and 1785 and later reform of the excise laws,[111] Beaufoy was moved to take up the cause of the fisheries by report of the Scottish economist, James Anderson, who focused on Scottish

---

[105] Bob Harris, 'Patriotic commerce and national revival: The free British Fishery Society and British policy, c. 1749–58', *EHR*, cxiv (1999), 285–313.

[106] Julian Hoppit, *Britain's Political Economies: Parliament and Economic Life, 1660–1800* (Cambridge and New York, 2017), pp. 251–4, 262–3.

[107] Anna Gambles, 'The political economy of fisheries policy in Britain and the United Kingdom circa 1780–1850', *JBS*, xxxix (2000), 292.

[108] Henry Beaufoy (1750–95), MP, Minehead, 1783–4 and Great Yarmouth, 1784–95; Sec. Bd. of Control, 1791–3.

[109] *PH*, xxvi, 469.

[110] For his speech in support of the bill for repeal in 1787, see *PH*, xxvi, 781–817 and for one of his attempts to limit the 'depredations' of excise officials, see *ibid.*, xxvi, 118–19.

[111] *HPC, 1754–90*, ii, 72–3.

fisheries.[112] In March 1785 Henry Dundas, Scotland's political manager, moved for the appointment of a committee to examine the state of British fisheries. The committee, which Beaufoy chaired, produced four reports over four months. As the session dragged on, Pitt proposed that the business be deferred to the following session since attendance in the House was diminishing. George Dempster,[113] an influential Scottish MP, protested that the business was so important that it should be done, even in a House of two MPs.[114] Because of his pleading and Beaufoy's pressure, Pitt relented, and Beaufoy delivered the committee's recommendations. Among them were proposals for the simplification of the Salt Tax, which, as it currently existed, inhibited the work of fishermen trying to cure their catch. The prosperity of the industry also depended upon the removal of certain restrictions as well as the simplification and reduction of duties. Pitt, though initially hesitant, eventually consented to their adoption so long as restrictions were placed on curers in order to prevent frauds.[115] The result was the Fisheries Act of 1785 (25 Geo, III, c. 65), the first of a series of measures to emerge from the House over two sessions.

In addition to his interventions in 1785, Dempster joined Beaufoy in support of his efforts while also promoting Scottish fisheries. To assure safe navigation on Scotland's north coast Dempster introduced a motion in 1786 to bring in a bill to erect lighthouses on the coasts of Aberdeenshire and Orkney, reported it from its petition committee in April and carried the bill to the House of Lords on 20 June; during the same session, he also presented the Highland Society's bill to build towns and fishing stations in the highlands and on the islands and reported it from its petition committee on 2 June.[116]

During the same session, Beaufoy, with the support of Dempster and a majority of the House, forced the administration to accept resolutions relating to the east coast's turbot fishery. These resolutions in turn led to the establishment of a committee on the state of British fisheries, again chaired by Beaufoy. He reported from the committee on 27 February, 3 May and again on 8 June when he presented the committee's recommendation that there be a shilling bounty on British caught herring. In March he presented another British fisheries bill based on the reports from the committee. The eventual act settled premiums and bounties which were gradually shifted from tonnage bounties to barrel bounties, payable by the fisherman or curer who produced the barrel of fish. In addition, the Act (26 Geo. III, c. 58) reduced the excise on domestic consumption and provided grants to landlords willing to undertake the settlement of the poor with secure tenure in fishing villages where they would be provided with boats and equipment. Finally, the statute incorporated the British Society for Extending

---

[112] 'Third report from the committee appointed to enquire into the state of the British fisheries, and into the most effectual means for their improvement and extension', *Commons Sessional Papers*, 53 (1785), 93–116. For discussions of the report, see Gambles, 'The political economy of fisheries policy in Britain', *JBS*, 295–9; and Salim Rashid, 'James Anderson and regional economic development in Scotland', *History of Economic Ideas*, xvii (2009), 21–5.

[113] George Dempster (1732–1818), MP, Perth Burghs, 1761–8, 1769–70; Sec. to Order of the Thistle, 1765–1818; Director, E I. Co, 1769 1772–3.

[114] Andrew Munro Lang, *A Life of George Dempster, Scottish MP of Dunnichen (1732–1818)* (Lewiston, NY, Queenstown, ON, Lampeter, 1998), p. 151.

[115] Ehrman, *The Younger Pitt: The Years of Acclaim*, pp. 351–2.

[116] Lang, *Life of George Dempster*, pp. 148, 153; *CJ*, xli, 839, 878, 918, 952.

British Fisheries, & Improving the Sea Coast of the Kingdom. Its mission was to provide employment and prevent depopulation in the highlands by forming towns and establishing communications systems between them. The Society was a private body, dependent upon contributions (its governor was the Duke of Argyll and among its 12 directors were Beaufoy, Dempster and William Wilberforce). Beaufoy's work did not end with the 1786 Act. An act of 1787 (27 Geo. III, c. 10), which he also carried, removed ambiguities from the previous legislation and provided for additional duties on fish caught by British seamen to be sold in the home market.

The status of Newfoundland fisheries became a matter of concern after the American war – especially to two small Parliamentary boroughs, Dartmouth in Devon and Poole in Dorset, both of which had long-established ties to the Newfoundland trade. There were by the 1780s growing settlements of Americans and Canadians in Newfoundland who were importing provisions from New England, which was outside the orbit of the navigation system, so Britain faced challenges to its monopoly in the carrying trade that had mandated cargoes be shipped in British vessels. That requirement in turn raised the issue of how to sustain the Newfoundland trade as a key nursery of seamen for the fleets.

Charles Jenkinson drafted a plan for the Pitt administration that was similar to an earlier one he had devised for the West Indian islands which had faced somewhat similar issues. While British shipping interests demanded that Newfoundland be supplied exclusively from Britain and Canada, Jenkinson recognised that goods would seep in from New England and that an embargo would cause the price of provisions in the fisheries to soar. Thus, American bread, flour and livestock were allowed entry but only on British ships under provisions in his Trade Act of 1785 (25 Geo. III, c. 1).[117] A subsequent Newfoundland Fisheries Act (26 Geo III, c. 26) followed on a report of a Commons' select committee, chaired by Michael Angelo Taylor,[118] and tightened the registration of British shipping and, to stimulate the British trade, introduced bounties for large ships delivering turbots to the port of London.

According to his biography in the *History of Parliament* volumes, Arthur Holdsworth,[119] took a prominent part in debates on the 1785 trade bill with the United States and helped to orchestrate the compromise between competing parties that lead to the bill. He attributed his efforts to the fact that 'it was to the Newfoundland trade carried on from Dartmouth, that he stood indebted for his seat in that assembly'.[120] Edmund Bastard,[121] the other Dartmouth MP, pressed Lord Hawkesbury[122] four years later on the state of the Newfoundland catch. In August 1789 he negotiated with Hawkesbury regarding a clause in a bill to regulate that trade because it caused alarm among his constituents; in the end he gained enough so that in his speech, which

---

[117] Ehrman, *The Younger Pitt*, pp. 341–4.
[118] Michael Angelo Taylor (?1757–1834), MP, Poole 1784–90, 1791–6, 1812–18; Heytesbury, 1790–1; Aldeburgh, 1796–1800; Durham, 1800–2, 1818–31; Rye, 1806–7; Ilchester, 1807–12; Sudbury, 1832–4.
[119] Arthur Holdsworth (c. 1757–87), MP, Dartmouth, 1780–7; Gov. Dartmouth Castle, 1777–87.
[120] *HPC, 1754–1790*, ii, 631.
[121] Edmund Bastard (1738–1816), MP, Dartmouth, 1787–1812.
[122] Jenkinson was elevated to the peerage as Baron Hawkesbury in the summer of 1786.

Stockdale's Debates described as 'a masterly detail of the nature of the fisheries at Newfoundland', even as he reiterated his constituents' concern that the bill would 'materially affect the trade of the country', he could acknowledge that they 'had nevertheless great confidence in the care and prudence of his Majesty's ministers'.[123]

These groups stand in contrast to the West India interest in a variety of ways. In the first place, they lacked a large contingent of their own MPs in either House of Parliament or well-placed sympathisers in a succession of cabinets during the second half of the century. Their success instead depended on their capacity to tap into what Paul Langford called 'landlord representation', the effectiveness of their advocates and the fact that their causes, to a greater degree than those of the West India interest, seemed to legislators to speak to the needs of the nation. For these reasons the Birmingham and Fisheries interests made the more positive impact on British public policy during the final decades of the eighteenth century. Thus, it is appropriate to conclude the chapter with an assessment of interest groups that appeared in a recent article by Julian Hoppit. Noting their centrality in the life of eighteenth-century Britain, he emphasised that:

> Within a political system that was formally rigid and exclusive, the creation and efforts of tens of thousands of interest groups provided a much-needed means of ensuring the system did not ossify. Across the period, such groups bear witness to the vitality of Britain's economy and an important openness in its polity. They were, indeed, a characteristic expression of several key features of 18th-century Britain: of the importance of the local and the specific; of lines of attachment via statutes from the present to the past; of the difficulties of collective action for many, and of relative ease for other; and of the importance of negotiation to authority. It was essential to Britain's economic performance that Parliament be pressured in such ways.[124]

---

[123] *HPC, 1754–1790*, ii, 64, from Stockdale's *Debates*, xv, 135–6.
[124] Hoppit, 'Petitions, economic legislation and interest groups in Britain', in *Pressure and Parliament from Civil War to Civil Society*, ed. Richard Huzzey (Chichester and Medford, MA, 2020), p. 71.

9

Parliamentary Reform: Instructions and Representation

I: Context

This chapter examines the movement for Parliamentary reform that emerged in and around London in the 1760s and 1770s and spread to Yorkshire amidst discontent engendered by high taxes, debacles in America, the entry of France, Spain and the Netherlands into the war against Britain and, finally, the rise of the Volunteers in Ireland. Reformers produced a range of proposals but were unable to unite behind one programme, while the various plans introduced by John Sawbridge and John Wilkes in the 1770s and the Younger Pitt in the 1780s were overwhelmingly rejected in the Commons. Indeed, new manufacturing centres, including Leeds, Stockport Manchester and Birmingham, did not bother to dispatch petitions in support of Pitt's 1785 reform bill.

There are many reasons for these failures. The proposals of the 1770s were too radical for the great majority of MPs, who in any case distrusted Wilkes and, to a lesser extent, Sawbridge. Many were suspicious of the idea of a national Association, formed to put pressure on an elected Parliament to enact various sorts of electoral or economical reforms; indeed, a number saw it as an unconstitutional intrusion on Parliament's authority to make laws. At the time that Pasi Ihalainen argues a greater appreciation of democracy began to permeate the House of Commons, Pitt's 1785 reform bill went down to ignominious defeat. In part this was due to the measure's shortcomings, which will be discussed below. More fundamentally it reflected Pitt's inability to marshal broad public support for his bill.

That failure reflects a long-standing lack of urgency for Parliamentary reform that characterised eighteenth-century England. David Hayton examined its causes in his introductory survey for the 1690–1715 volumes of the *History of Parliament*.[1] Other explanations, however, are offered throughout this book. As Julian Hoppit noted, interest groups were vital to maintaining the vitality of Britain's eighteenth-century order; the means by which many of those interests gained access to a landlord-dominated Parliament was through what Paul Langord called 'landlord representation'.

---

[1] www.historyofparliamentonline.org/volume/1690-1715/surve/constituencies-and-elections

The system provided towns such as Manchester or Birmingham prior to 1774 access to Parliament, as discussed in Chapter 8. In addition, I argue throughout this chapter and throughout the book that large numbers of MPs were effective in tending the legions of specific and local legislative projects of their constituents, and that in the course of overseeing their passage year after year, they and their constituents formed tight bonds. In many instances, the MP became an implicit representative who by the mid-1780s was willing to follow constituents' instructions, not just on issues relating to specific or local legislation but on matters of national consequence. As these ties between member and constituents expanded to include harmonious communication and action on a broader range of issues, constituents saw little need to press for reform, for Parliament was already meeting many of their legislative needs.

II: State of Parliamentary Representation

In his book on Parliamentary reform, John Cannon began his section on the eighteenth century by demonstrating the degree to which the hotly contested political arena of Queen Anne's reign all but atrophied in the 50 years following her death. During the middle decades of the century the great aristocracy reached the height of its power. By 1761 almost two-thirds of England's boroughs were dominated by patrons. The consolidation of great estates meant that the lesser gentry could no longer compete at elections with landed magnates, even as the ranks of the latter were also reduced. In the election of 1761 only 4 of 40 English counties and 42 of 203 boroughs were contested. One grandee, Sir James Lowther, enjoyed total electoral control of Westmorland and Cumberland, while supporters of Ambrose Goddard,[2] who was eventually returned as a member for Wiltshire at a by-election in 1772, marvelled that county contests there were controlled by dukes, earls and lords. Their dominion was made all the easier because the electorate grew at a slower rate than the overall population.[3]

Between the mid-1760s and the last years of the 1770s the principal centres of discontent with such a system were London and its environs and later Yorkshire. Both drew to a degree from the country programme of the 1730s and 1740s which had reacted to the corruption of the Walpole regime by trying to reduce the number of pensioners and placemen in the House of Commons and increase accountability of MPs by repealing the Septennial Act and restoring triennial Parliaments. Organisers of the country campaigns encouraged electors to bombard their MPs with instructions to advance their issues in Parliament. In pursuit of these goals 100 sets of instructions were dispatched by 74 separate bodies to MPs between October 1739 and November 1742.[4]

---

[2] Ambrose Goddard (?1727–1815), MP, Wiltshire, 1772–1806; agent at Lisbon for the Post Office until he succeeded to his family's Wiltshire estates in 1772.
[3] John Cannon, *Parliamentary Reform* (Cambridge, 1973), pp. 49–51.
[4] Nicholas Rogers, *Whigs and Cities: Popular Politics in the Age of Walpole and Pitt* (Oxford and New York, 1989), pp. 240–1.

III: Reform Movements

What was different about the radical reformers who emerged in and around London in the 1760s and early 1770s, according to H.T. Dickinson, was not only that theirs was an extra-Parliamentary movement, not one attached to Parliamentary opposition groups, but also that its leaders recognised that Parliament had become too corrupted to reform itself. The radicals accepted that ministers had undermined the integrity of the Commons through the distribution of patronage. For this reason the traditional country remedy of removing placemen and pensioners from the House was insufficient to resolve the problem of a corrupted House because it was so severe. Instead, only the concerted activity of the people could secure a reform of the constitution, of which 'economical reform' would be but a part. By energising the electorate and forcing MPs to listen to their constituents, the House of Commons became more truly representative of the people.[5]

Though the roots of London radicalism reached back to discontents that emerged in the 1730s and 1740s, it was John Wilkes who rallied the City's small merchants, craftsmen and manufacturers, along with the journeymen, wage earners and apprentices who revelled in his capacity to harass authority and make life difficult for the elite. According to Lucy Sutherland, Wilkes' adherents resented the subordination of City politics to the needs and interests of the opposition and the government.[6] Though Wilkes never espoused a coherent political programme and lacked a political organisation, there were among his sometime supporters men committed to a reasoned programme of reform. Among them were MPs for London, Southwark and Middlesex who served between 1761 and 1784.[7] Together these MPs along with other radicals joined to form the Society for the Support of the Bill of Right (SSBR) in the wake of the infamous Middlesex elections of 1768-9. The SSBR espoused the traditional country prescriptions of shorter Parliaments and place bills along with the more novel proposal of 'a more fair and equal representation of the people'. The latter included enfranchising mercantile and manufacturing centres that sent no members to Parliament.[8] At a public meeting in the City on 10 February 1769 William Beckford spoke on behalf of the Common Hall's reform programme, adding his strong support for measures against bribery at elections. In addition, he called for the elimination of rotten boroughs which he said allowed 'little pitiful boroughs equal representation with great cities'. He denounced the influence of the aristocracy and concluded by noting that while the

---

[5] H.T. Dickinson, *Liberty and Property: Political Ideology in Eighteenth-Century Britain* (London, 1977), pp. 195-6.
[6] Lucy Sutherland, 'The City of London in eighteenth-century politics' in *Politics and Finance in the Eighteenth Century*, ed. Aubrey Newman (London, 1984), p. 63.
[7] Members for London included William Beckford (1761), Richard Oliver (returned 1770), Frederick Bull (returned 1773), John Sawbridge (1774); Sir Watkin Lewes (1781) and Barlow Trecothick (1768); Middlesex: John Glynn (1768), John Wilkes (1774) and Sir Cecil Wray (1782). Southwark: Sir Joseph Mawbey (1761).
[8] Brewer, *Party Ideology and Popular Politics at the Accession of George III* (Cambridge, 1981), p. 206; John Cannon, *Parliamentary Reform*, pp. 45-6; Ian R. Christie, *Wilkes, Wyvill and Reform: The Parliamentary Reform Movement in British Politics, 1760-1785* (1962), pp. 36-7.

City favoured the introduction of triennial Parliaments, he preferred that they be annual.⁹

Three times voters returned John Wilkes for Middlesex in 1768 and 1769, only to have the House of Commons turn him aside despite the fact his outlawry had been quashed. The Commons then went on to seat his defeated opponent, Henry Lawes Luttrell.¹⁰ The administration and the House acted on questionable legal grounds in expelling Wilkes since the law provided that a criminal, convicted and under sentence for his crimes, could not be removed from the House. Moreover, its actions armed him with the constitutional issues that he and his adherents reiterated over the next months and years. As Beckford charged during a debate in the House on 10 February 1769:

> the House of Commons alone, cannot make a law, binding anybody but themselves – If they, by a vote, can disqualify one person, they may go and disqualify whom they please; the consequence of which must the getting into their own hands the power of the whole government.¹¹

In short, the episode raised the question as to whether the administration was usurping the power as to who could and could not represent a constituency.¹²

The SSBR was crucial in raising these points not only because it presented comprehensible statements of political and constitutional issues, but because it extended the movement and its message beyond London with a steady flow of pamphlets and local branches to co-ordinate the campaign. In 1771, however, pressures within the SSBR and Wilkes' use of its funds for personal purposes led to a split and the formation of the rival Society for Constitutional Information. According to John Brewer the split came about between groups that 'were radical in method' (Wilkes), and those who were 'radical in ideology and purpose' (Horne Tooke, Sawbridge, et al.).¹³ Among the prominent members of the SSBR were Thomas Brand Hollis,¹⁴ and radical ideologues including John Jebb¹⁵ and John Cartwright.¹⁶ Cartwright set a tone for break-away

---

⁹ Gauci, *William Beckford*, pp. 169–70; Cannon, *Parliamentary Reform*, pp. 51–2, 61–2; Christie, *Wilkes, Wyvill and Reform*, p. 36.
¹⁰ Hon. Henry Lawes Luttrell (?1737–1821), MP, Bossiney, 1768–9, 1774–84; Middlesex, 1769–74; Plympton Erle, 1790–4 and Ludgershall, 1817–21; MP [I], 1783–7; Ensign, 48 Ft. 1757; Capt. 16 Lt. Drag. 1759, Maj., 1762; Dep. Adjutant-Gen. in Portugal and Local Lt. Col. 1762; Lt.-Col. 1 Horse 1765; Adjutant-Gen. [I], 1770–83; Maj. Gen. 1782; Lt.-Gen. of Ordnance [I], 1787–97; Col. 6 Drg. Gds. 1788–1821; Lt.-Gen; 1793; C.-in-C. [I], 1796–7; Master-Gen. of Ordnance [I], 1797–1800; Gen., 1798; succ. fa. as 2nd Earl of Carhampton [I], 1787.
¹¹ *PH*, xviii, c. 586–7.
¹² Christie, *Wilkes, Wyvill and Reform*, p. 31, paraphrasing *The Public Advertiser*, 4, 8 Feb. 1769.
¹³ Brewer, *Party Ideology*, p. 199.
¹⁴ Thomas Brand Hollis (1719–1804), MP, Hindon, 1774–5 when unseated on petition for bribery and fined one thousand marks; succ. to estates of his friend Thomas Hollis and took name Hollis, 1774; Unitarian and pro-American; friend of Joseph Priestley and Richard Price.
¹⁵ John Jebb (1736–86); fellow of Peterhouse, 1761; FRS, 1779.
¹⁶ Maj. John Cartwright (1740–1826), RN, 1758–70; Chief Magistrate, Newfoundland Station, 1766–70; Major, Notts. militia, to 1782; author, *Take Your Choice* (1776) the 2nd edition of which (1777), *The Legislative Rights of the Commonality*, advocated annual Parliaments, the secret ballot and universal suffrage; strongly pro-American during their disputes with Britain and an early supporter of the London Corresponding Society, est. 1792.

society by pressing for the need to disseminate the ideas of the society and educate the public on the issue of constitutional reform by means of pamphlets and public lectures.

By these means the reformers set out to extend their support beyond the metropolis. They contested the election of 1774 in a range of constituencies. The results, as Ian Christie showed in his 1970 article, were modest as few electors had the appetite for the agenda presented by radical candidates.[17] In addition, the SSBR on 11 June 1771 issued a resolution that enlarged the Common Hall's earlier recommendation, instructing that persons intending to stand as candidates for Parliament would be required to sign a declaration that, if elected, they would do all in their power to shorten the duration of Parliaments, reduce the number of placemen and pensioners in the Commons, work to promote a more equal representation of the people and enquire into the causes of discontents which have disrupted the nation during the current reign.[18] The election brought no radical sweep, but reformers managed to extend their support beyond the metropolis and emerged in 1775 with 12 MPs who could be counted upon to vote for proposals that would change the way in which the House was constituted.[19]

Unfortunately for this small contingent, their colleagues in the House had little or no interest in pursuing the topic. On 26 Apr. 1771 John Sawbridge introduced the first of his annual, unsuccessful motions for the shortening of Parliaments. He justified his motion by arguing that 'the length of Parliaments gave up that power which the constituents ought to have over their representatives, that of frequent examination into their conduct and rejection of them if they are thought unworthy'.[20]

Sawbridge's motion was defeated by a vote of 105–54. That rejection did not deter him from reintroducing the motion annually year after year into the mid-1780s. In 1775, he managed to gain 100 supporters, a high water mark in terms of his support. As the American crisis worsened and finally resulted in war, the issue of Parliamentary reform fell victim to the backlash against the Americans and those who opposed the war. In 1776 John Wilkes introduced his proposals for the reform to an audience of suspicious, hostile MPs Towards the end of his remarks he took the opportunity to:

> throw out general ideas, that every free agent in this Kingdom should…, be represented in parliament; that the metropolis, which contains in itself a 9th part of the people, and the counties of Middlesex, York and the others, which so greatly abound with inhabitants, should receive increase in their representation; that the mean, and insignificant boroughs, so emphatically styled 'the rotten part of our constitution', should be lopped off, and the electors then thrown into the counties; and the rich, populous towns, Birmingham, Manchester, Sheffield, Leeds, and the others, be permitted to send deputies to the great council of the nation.

---

[17] See Christie, *Wilkes, Wyvill and Reform* for short summaries of the ideas of Cartwright, pp. 62–3 and John Jebb, pp. 78–9; Christie, 'The Wilkites and the general elections of 1774', in *Myth and Reality in Eighteenth-Century British Politics and Other Papers* (1970), pp. 244–60.

[18] Christie, *Wilkes, Wyvill and Reform*, p. 48 from the Public Advertiser, 13 June, 1771; see also, Christie, 'Wilkites and election of 1774', p. 245.

[19] Christie, 'Wilkites and the election of 1774', p. 259.

[20] Quoted in *HPC, 1754–1790*, iii, 410.

Lord North, according to reports of the proceedings, 'jokingly supposed that honourable gentleman was not serious, nor ever meant his proposition should get to a committee'. An indifferent House did not bother to take up his motion. Instead, after it was seconded by Frederick Bull, members turned aside Wilkes' motion 'to bring in a bill for a just and equal Representation of the people of England in Parliament' without a vote.[21]

The inability of the London reformers to attract a significant body of support in the House of Commons, the deteriorating situation of British forces in America after the disaster at Saratoga in October 1777, followed by the outbreak of war first with France and later with Spain and the Netherlands, raised questions in Parliament about the administration's conduct of affairs, which faced increasing criticism, especially directed at Lord George Germain, the Secretary of State for America, and Lord Sandwich, the First Lord of the Admiralty. Tied to these frustrations and grievances were others, including the Irish demands for greater legislative independence and outcries against the cost of war and the burden of high taxation.

Patrick O'Brien and Peter Mathias highlighted the economic burden of the wars on the nation and the British taxpayer over the course of the eighteenth century. Summarising their conclusions, Brewer showed that taxes accounted for about 3.5 per cent of the national income in 1670, rising to over 9 per cent by the end of the War of the Spanish Succession in 1714 and to between 11 and 12 per cent at the end of the American war. Seen in another, more immediate way for the taxpayer, the share of British per capita income taken for taxes increased from 16 per cent in 1716, to 20 per cent near the end of the Seven Years War in 1760, to 23 per cent at the end of the American war, which concluded with the loss of the colonies and severe upheavals in the British West Indies.[22]

In fact, the crisis of the war and its related costs led to an outburst of calls for an end to its prosecution in America as well as demands of 'economical reform'. Among the first to take up the cry for the latter was Thomas Gilbert, hitherto a supporter of the Crown, who as noted in Chapter 5, rose in the House on 2 March 1778 out of concern at the 'expenditure of public money, particularly the exorbitant contracts and abuses of office...' and proposed a tax of one fourth on the incomes of all placemen. He claimed that he took the step 'the better to enable his Majesty to vindicate the honour and dignity of his Crown and the dominions thereunto belonging'.[23] His initial motion carried in the committee of supply, but the administration marshalled its forces and defeated it when the committee made its report.[24] Other efforts followed, including Sir Philip Jennings-Clerke's first attempt to remove government contractors from the House on 13 April 1778, John Crewe's measure to disenfranchise revenue officers, introduced in 1780 and, most famously, Edmund Burke's measure for economical

---

[21] *PH*, xvii, cc. 1295–8.
[22] Brewer, *The Sinews of Power*, p. 91 from P. Mathias and P. O'Brien, 'Taxation in England and France, 1715–1810: A comparison of the social and economic incidence of taxes collected for the central governments', *Journal of European Economic History*, v (1976), Table 6.
[23] *HPC, 1754–1790*, ii, 500.
[24] For an earlier account of Gilbert's protest, see below, Chapter 5, p. 150.

reform which he introduced in a speech on 11 February 1780, a proposal that resulted in several bills. Neither his measures nor those of Jennings-Clerke or Crewe reached the statute book until 1782 during the second Rockingham administration. Designed to undercut the Crown's ability to corrupt the House of Commons, Cannon, Christie and John Ehrman agree that their measures, though much trumpeted, accomplished little.[25] Ironically, it was North who made the most substantive contribution by proposing the creation of a Commission of Public Accounts, to be composed of seven members, not MPs, who would inform the House annually of the true state of the nation's accounts, expose deficiencies in the management of the public's money and offer proposals to prevent large accumulations in certain notorious accounts, particularly those of the paymaster of the forces and the treasurer of the navy. Though the plan was attacked by Burke, Shelburne and other reformers, the commissioners became a body of experts whose reports subsequently served as the basis for theirs and many others' reforms over the next decades.[26]

In the short term, however, the focus for reform moved to Yorkshire where the Reverend Christopher Wyvill, a North Riding landowner, in 1779 launched a movement that responded to the upsurge of discontent among the Yorkshire gentry with the government's handling of the American crisis. His first step was to organise a petition in support of economical reform which was ultimately signed by about 8,000 freeholders and gentlemen. Among this group were a significant number of the higher, well-educated gentry of the county who came forward to lead the county over the next several years in support of a campaign not only for economical but also for constitutional reform.[27] Two hundred prominent gentlemen permitted their names to be used on a public notice calling for a county meeting in Yorkshire on 30 December 1779; their public support proved to be crucial in enlisting leaders from the commercial and manufacturing communities to support the movement.[28] The meeting attacked the alleged waste of public money and urged that the House should act to 'inquire into and correct the gross abuses in the expenditure of public money, reduce all exorbitant emoluments', abolish sinecures and unworthy pensions 'and appropriate the produce to the necessities of the state, in such a manner as to the wisdom of parliament shall seem meet'.

The economical reform movement awakened a broad popular response. Between February and April 1780, the Commons received 41 petitions, 26 of them from English

---

[25] Cannon, *Parliamentary Reform*, pp. 85–6; Christie, *Wilkes, Wyvill and Reform*, pp. 151–4; Ehrman, *The Younger Pitt: Years of Acclaim*, p. 90.
[26] Reitan, *Politics, Finance and the People*, pp. 64–7 and *passim*.
[27] Sir George Savile, member for the county, presented the petition produced by the meeting on 8 February 1780.
[28] Ian Christie, 'The Yorkshire Association, 1780–4: A study in political organization', in *Myth and Reality*, pp. 261–5. Gamaliel Lloyd, a prominent Leeds businessman, claimed that one of the factors that made the Association appealing to his friends was that it was sponsored by so many gentlemen of large independent fortunes, who because of their education and other circumstances were better informed in politics than merchants and other businessmen. Christie, 'The Yorkshire Association, 1780–4', p. 265. For the disparity between The Association's goals for economic reform and Burke's initial proposals, see *Wilkes, Wyvill and Reform*, pp. 87–9.

counties, including Yorkshire, three more from Wales, and others from Westminster and London.[29] Yorkshire's full political programme of 1780 included triennial Parliaments and the addition of 100 county members in addition to economical reform.

Wyvill also proposed a Plan of Association in February. Each corresponding committee would send three deputies to a meeting in London, scheduled for 11 March. He proposed barring politicians from serving as deputies because he saw them as instruments of party politics, but he later modified this standard. Nevertheless, he refused to take part in proceedings of the assemblies with a party leader.

In a sign of the nation's unease with the idea of 'association', only 12 counties and four cities and boroughs[30] sent deputies to the London assembly. Moreover, the assembly which met at St. Albans Tavern came up with proposals that alienated moderate attendees. Aside from the demands for economy and reduction of the Crown's influence, the programme it offered included annual Parliaments and a provision that electors were to vote at the next election only for candidates who would sign the Association platform. The meeting finally resolved that a law should be secured to reduce the expense and influence at elections, a favourite goal of Lord Mahon, member for Chipping Wycombe.[31]

Because of the internal divisions, Wyvill refused to summon a congress of the Association in 1780, leaving the way open for the Westminster Committee and the radical influence of Brand Hollis, who in the summer of 1780 published a plan that proposed universal male suffrage, payment of members, exclusion of all placemen, election by secret ballot and the elimination of the property qualification.[32] The Westminster Committee, impatient with the moderation and hesitation of their provincial partners, voted to circulate its proposals at a meeting on July 11, shortly after London was enveloped in the chaos of the anti-Catholic Gordon riots.

Following the collapse of North in 1782, Wyvill vainly endeavoured to win over Lord Rockingham and his prominent followers in Yorkshire despite their opposition to Parliamentary reform, for Rockingham's was still Yorkshire's pre-eminent party. In the meantime, several of the committees that had initially responded to Yorkshire's original initiative wavered or withdrew from the Association movement. Cheshire, for example, proclaimed that 'it was the opinion of most of the gentlemen present, that the late proceedings of the associating deputies assembled in London, were big with the most fatal consequences' and resolved to wind up its county committee. Gloucestershire

---

[29] Reitan, *Politics, Finance, and the People*, p. 52.
[30] Bucks, Devon, Dorset, Essex, Glos., Herts., Hunts., Kent, Middlesex, Surrey, Sussex, Yorks, Westminster, London, Newcastle, Nottingham.
[31] Bucks., Devon, Gloucestershire and Sussex recommended amendments to this programme that would eliminate annual Parliaments and favoured only proposals for economical reform. The Rockingham Whigs would support only economical reform and opposed all other aspects. Christie, *Wilkes, Wyvill and Reform*, pp. 92–3, 100–1.
[32] Cannon, *Parliamentary Reform*, p. 82; Christie, *Wilkes, Wyvill and Reform*, pp. 107–8. Hertfordshire limited its support to economical reform. Devon, Essex, Somerset and Surrey accepted plans of association that included only the main points of the Yorkshire programme – more equal representation, triennial Parliaments and economical reform.

concluded that the business of national reform should be left to a Parliament elected by the people and that it was not a suitable topic for an association.

In short, metropolitan radicalism, the conservative reaction to the Gordon riots and the nation's preoccupation with the failures of the British campaign in American made a broad popular campaign for Parliamentary reform during the early years of the 1780s unlikely. Prospects were further reduced by the political convulsions that accompanied the completion of the Fox-North Coalition and its eventual installation as a Coalition administration in 1783, since Lord North and his allies remained steadfast in their opposition to reform.

Nevertheless, in May 1783 William Pitt the younger introduced a garbled plan that he patched together with Wyvill's assistance. In presenting it, he stressed 'that his object was not to innovate, but rather to renew and invigorate the spirit of the constitution'. To do this Pitt took aim at rotten boroughs which he proposed to disenfranchise, but only after they were convicted of bribery at elections by select committees of the Commons. In that case, voters would be transferred to the counties and an 'addition' would be made of 100 knights of the shire. The plan generated little enthusiasm and was defeated by a vote of 293 to 149.[33] Two years later he met with a similar lack of success when he introduced his second reform bill on 19 April 1785. The proposal had many similarities to its predecessor. With the consent of their electors Pitt proposed to purchase 36 small boroughs, using funds from a special fund of £1 million under the management of a committee of the House. The 72 affected seats would be distributed between the counties and the metropolis. In addition, the electorate was to be enlarged to include the 40 shilling copyholders and some leaseholders. Pitt proposed to include some of Lord Mahon's proposals for the improved regulation of county elections, but his plan was again defeated, this time by a vote of 174 to 248.[34]

This succession of defeats highlights the political nation's lack of enthusiasm for Parliamentary reform and the shortcomings of Pitt's two efforts. Despite the efforts of reform groups over 15 years, the supporters of reform were unable to raise more than 24 petitions on behalf one of Pitt's proposals – hardly manifestations of broad national enthusiasm – and quite in contrast to the hundreds that poured into Westminster on behalf of abolition of the slave trade in 1788 and 1792.

Pitt began as a committed reformer working against great odds. In 1783 he was a young man with only two years of Parliamentary experience and without a party of his own. The King was hostile. Pushed by his allies in the Association, he opted for compromises to secure a measure that engendered little excitement and had slim chances of success. According to Eugene Black, the Coalition had split the extra-Parliamentary reform movement at a time when it was on the verge of gaining sufficient support among the elite to carry the day.[35] John Cannon justifiably refuted that claim,

---

[33] *PH*, xxiii, 829; Christie, *Wilkes, Wyvill and Reform*, pp. 180-2; Ehrman, *The Younger Pitt*, pp. 74-6.
[34] See Ehrman, *The Younger Pitt*, pp. 226-7; and Cannon, *Parliamentary Reform*, p. 213; *PH*, xxv, cc. 450-70; 469-70.
[35] E.C. Black, *The Association: British Extra-Parliamentary Organization, 1769-1793* (Cambridge, MA, 1963), pp. 104, 108.

noting that the movement was already split by 1771 and that the county movement on behalf of economic reform began to wane with the winding down of the American war. For Cannon, the real problems were that Pitt ignored the northern industrial and trading towns in his first proposal, favouring instead the counties and the metropolis. The result was that neither in 1783 nor in 1785 did Birmingham, Manchester, Leeds or Sheffield petition on behalf of reform. Indeed, in the latter instance only two counties and a motley array of ten towns and boroughs sent petitions supporting his reform measure. Finally, he notes that opponents were effective in highlighting divisions among reformers, playing upon the public's suspicions of democracy by reminding them of election brawls and drunken orgies. More to the point was the failure of Wyvill and his followers to explain the practical advantages that might follow from a reform of Parliament.[36]

IV: Petitions

The fact that reformers were never able to gain a 'more fair and equal representation' during the 1770s and 1780s did not mean that 'the people' lacked a voice at elections or within the eighteenth-century political system. Frank O'Gorman showed 30 years ago that even in the smallest boroughs, patrons had to attend to the needs and opinions of their constituents and could not take them for granted.[37] Likewise Dickinson, John Phillips, Susan Mitchell Sommers and Kathleen Wilson have celebrated voters' independence and increasing partisan loyalties. Voters were able to take on and even defeat local elites in Newcastle-upon-Tyne, and at least challenge them in Maidstone, where an election for control of the corporation 'radiated political vitality'. Challenges likewise occurred in Norwich, Northampton and the county and various boroughs of Suffolk.[38] Moreover, as David Eastwood stresses, the interaction between candidate and constituents did not end on the hustings. 'Petitions, instructions, and resolutions of county meetings were part of a formal political vocabulary which enabled constituencies, or elements within constituencies, to communicate with their members'.[39] This they did

---

[36] Cannon, *Parliamentary Reform*, pp. 94–7. North offered especially effective criticisms of Pitt's measure, *PH*, xxiii, cc. 849–51, 853. The petitions came from Nottinghamshire and Yorkshire as well as from boroughs including York, Great Yarmouth, Scarborough, Newcastle-upon-Tyne, Norwich, Hull, Morpeth, King's Lynn, Launceston and Lyme Regis. The last two were small freemen boroughs. For an overview of the reform movements and their long-term consequences, see H.T Dickinson's excellent 'Radicals and reformers in the age of Wilkes and Wyvill', in *British Politics and Society from Walpole to Pitt, 1742–1789*, ed. Jeremy Back (Basingstoke and London, 1990), pp. 123–46.

[37] O'Gorman, *Voters, Patrons and Parties*, pp. 9–10.

[38] H.T. Dickinson, 'Radical politics in the north-east of England', 1–11; John A. Phillips, *Electoral Behavior*, pp. 18, 28–9, 34, 79–83, 88–92, 250–1, 304–10; and 'From Municipal matters to Parliamentary principle: Eighteenth-century borough politics in Maidstone', *JBS*, xxvii (1988), 327–51; Kathleen Wilson, *The Sense of the People*, pp. 343, 354–72; 425–8; Susan Mitchell Sommers, *Parliamentary Politics of a County and its Town: General Elections in Suffolk and Ipswich in the Eighteenth Century* (Westport, CT, 2002), pp. 38, 189–90.

[39] David Eastwood, 'Parliament and locality: Representation and responsibility in late-Hanoverian England', in *Parliament and Locality, 1660–1939*, ed. David Dean and Clyve Jones (Parliamentary History Yearbook Trust, Edinburgh, 1998), p. 76.

frequently, so that there was an on-going relationship between the two in which constituents in many instances shaped the conduct of their members, not only on business of immediate relevance to the constituency, which even Edmund Burke would have admitted as legitimate, but also on matters of national interest.

In his article on public petitioning[40] Peter Fraser maintained that an act of Charles II (13 Car. II, c. 5) 'operated as an effective check on all public petitioning far into the eighteenth century. There were innumerable private petitions prior to 1779, but they did not try to teach MPs 'wisdom'. Until the 1770s, Fraser maintains petitioners did so on their own behalf and could be represented at the bar by counsel while the House was in committee. In the wake of the Middlesex elections, however, a number of counties and towns sent addresses to the King protesting the expulsion of Wilkes after he was returned by Middlesex voters, asking that the King dissolve Parliament due to what the petitioners regarded as the Commons' unconstitutional actions.[41] Among the most notable of these protests was the City of London's Remonstrance, which like the others addressed demanded a dissolution. When challenged following Sir Thomas Clavering's[42] hostile motion as to why he chose to present the controversial Remonstrance, William Beckford responded that he took this step after the Crown was:

> advised to take no notice of the many petitions presented by numerous and respectable bodies of men from almost every quarter of the kingdom. I therefore, was of opinion, that a measure striking as this Remonstrance is, might awaken an attention to enquire into and to remove the causes of public discontent.[43]

Criticising Sir Thomas' motion, Edmund Burke provided further justification for the Remonstrance and public petitioning that speaks directly to Fraser's points. After opposing the motion in the first instance because it besmirched the City, Burke urged his colleagues:

> not to condemn the public virtue in the citizens of London which should actually excite our admiration: nor treat that candour in their Remonstrance, which is highly meritorious, as if it was the effusions of disloyalty; it is the right of the British subject to petition, let us not deprive him of that right. The right of

---

[40] Peter Fraser, 'Public petitioning and Parliament before 1832', *History*, xlvi (1961), 195–211.
[41] Despite Fraser's claim, Philip Loft shows that the greatest number of petitions to Parliament in the eighteenth century coincided with the 'rage of party' from the mid-1690s to 1722, though petitioners were motivated by clashes of interest rather than party politics. According to Loft's data, the average number of petitions presented each session during those years surpassed the average even for the 1780s and early 1790s. Moreover, Mark Knight's tables show that many of those petitions and addresses dealt with major topics of national interest before the 1770s. Philip Loft, 'Petitions and petitioners to the Westminster Parliament, 1660-1788', *Parl. Hist.*, xxxviii (2019), 342–61; Mark Knights, 'Participation and representation before democracy: Petitions and addresses in premodern Britain', in *Political Representation*, ed. Ian Shapiro, Susan S. Stokes, Elizabeth Jean Wood and Alexander S. Kirshner (Cambridge and New York, 2009), pp. 45–6.
[42] Sir Thomas Clavering, 7th Bt. (1719–94), MP, St. Mawes, 1753-4; Shaftesbury, 1754–60 and Durham Co. 1768–90.
[43] *PH*, xvi, cc. 875–6.

election has been already violated; let us not do aggravated injuries to the constitution.[44]

It is further notable, according to James Bradley, that the addresses that were sent to the Crown in 1765, 1770 and 1775 in favour of conciliating the rebellious Americans came principally from the southwest where patronage was most prevalent, not from counties or populous boroughs. Bradley argues that 'agitation with respect to America in 1765 and again in 1775, regarding Wilkes in 1770, economic reform in 1780, and Parliamentary reform in 1782 implies that instead of stifling popular activity, patronage may have actually stimulated it by encouraging popular reaction'.[45] He attributes the high degree of agitation during the period of the American upheaval in the southwest partly to the concentration of Parliamentary seats in the region and with them, more electoral contests which might have heightened political awareness. Even at a time when patrons were tightening their grip over Hampshire's constituencies, he notes that the greatest number of conciliatory addresses came from the county in which the Crown exercised the greatest influence. He also points out that petitions and addresses on behalf of conciliation usually came in response to those in favour of coercion and contained many more signatures than those advocating coercion.[46] In short, the prevalence of patron-dominated constituencies was not a deterrent to the expression of public sentiment on major national issues.

Though large portions of the public could signal their views by means of petitions, there were limits to the impact those petitions might have on MPs. In the first place there was no guarantee that a member would agree to present a petition or that the House would take it into consideration. This was the case, for example, with many of the conciliatory petitions in 1774 and 1775. After one from the merchants of London trading with America was admitted on 23 January 1775, Edmund Burke pointed to Lord North and condemned the conduct of the administration for admitting the petition 'yet determined that it will never be heard'. He continued by explaining that he had a petition from the merchants of Bristol trading with America, yet 'as he found there were two committees now, the one for hearing evidence, the other for burying petitions, he plainly saw his petition would share the fate of the other, and be buried in oblivion'.[47]

---

[44] *PH*, xvi, c. 876–80. Clavering's motion carried on 19 March by a vote of 284 to 127. Burke did, however, force Lord North to admit that he had 'advised' the king on his controversial response to the Remonstrance which included the statement that the Remonstrance was 'irreconcilable to the constitution'. *PH*, xvi, 880–1.

[45] James E. Bradley, *Popular Politics and the American Revolution in England: Petitions, the Crown and Public Opinion* (Macon, GA, 1986), p. 128.

[46] Bradley, *Popular Politics*, pp. 128–9, 66–7. On the ability of the disenfranchised to sign petitions see also, John A. Phillips, 'Popular politics in unreformed England', *Journal of Modern History*, lii (1980), 599–625. Loft challenged Phillips' claim that the ability of the disenfranchised to sign petitions enlarged the political nation in 'Petitions and petitioners', p. 350.

[47] Almon, *Parl. Reg.*, i. p. 106.

V: Instructions

Given these limitations, constituencies as well as county meetings and individuals resorted to sending instructions to their MPs on issues that ranged from business relating to the particular constituency or county, to taxes or other impositions and other matters of the broadest national concern. Issuing instructions between elections began in the eighteenth century and was initially seen as likely to 'debase' the status of the MP according to Clive Emden. Whether they debased an MP or not did not undercut the effectiveness of such instructions. They were used on 'a massive scale' and with great effect in 1733 against Walpole's excise scheme and again with more limited success in the mid-1760s against the Cider Tax.[48] Advocates of instructions during the excise crisis made grandiose claims on their binding quality because of their number and extent. Indeed, the *Craftsman* argued:

> tho' the instructions of a particular county, city or town ought not to prevail against the instructions of the rest of the Kingdom, or against the common good of the Kingdom; yet when the nation in general concurs in one and the same thing, as they have done against any further extension of the excise laws, this voice of the whole people, by whom all the House of Commons are elected, from whom the whole House derives its authority, may and ought to be considered as of very great weight.[49]

The argument is notable in its claim that the Commons derived its authority from the electors. What made the excise crisis exceptional, however, was that it was the instructors' unanimity of sentiment which in turn endowed their instructions with their legitimacy. The *Craftsman's* statement did not claim that members were obligated to obey the individual instructions of their constituents. That was left to a later Wilkite generation and, in particular, to William Beckford, who upheld the right of the City of London to instruct its members in 1769. When challenged as to how he could support the City's Remonstrance, Beckford asked his fellow MPs how he could 'oppose my judgment to 6,000 of my fellow citizens?'[50]

By contrast, Edmund Burke, when confronted with the prospect that, as a potential candidate for Westminster in 1774, he would have to 'take the test' promising to support electoral reform, more frequent elections and the exclusion of placemen, and accept

---

[48] Paul Kelly, 'Constituents' instructions to members of Parliament in the eighteenth century', in *Party Management in Parliament, 1660–1784*, ed. Clyve Jones (Leicester and New York, 1984), pp. 170–1; Patrick Woodland, 'Extra-Parliamentary political organization in the making: Benjamin Heath and the opposition to the Cider Excise'. *Parl. Hist.*, iv, 115–36.
[49] Quoted from the *Craftsman*, x, 186–7 in Kelly, 'Constituents' instructions', 171
[50] Quoted in Parry Gauci *William Beckford*, p. 169.

Figure 9.1 William Beckford, James Townshend and John Sawbridge gathered at a table and conversing, engraving, 1830. From the New York Public Library. Photo by Smith Collection/Gado/Getty Images.

the instructions of his constituents, he withdrew and turned instead to Bristol where, shortly after his election, he told his new constituents:

> Parliament is not a Congress of Ambassadors from different and hostile interests, which interests each must maintain, as an Agent and Advocate, against other Agents and Advocates; but Parliament is a deliberative Assembly of one Nation, with one Interest, that of the whole; where, not local Purposes, not local Prejudices ought to guide, but the general Good, resulting from the general Reason of the whole. You chuse a Member, indeed; but when you have chosen him, he is not a member of Bristol, but he is a Member of Parliament. If the local Constituent should have an Interest, or should form an hasty Opinion, evidently opposite to the real good of the rest of the Community, the Member for that place ought to be as far, as any other from any endeavour to give it Effect.[51]

In short, he demanded the right to make his own reasoned determination as to what was in the nation's best interests after hearing his fellow MPs debate the great national questions that came before the House. Though it was the right of all men to deliver an opinion, he would:

---

[51] *Writings and Speeches*, iii, 'Speech at the conclusion of the poll', iii, pp. 69–70.

always rejoice to hear... authoritative instructions; Mandates issued, which the Member is bound blindly and implicitly to obey, to vote, and to argue for, though contrary to the clearest conviction of his judgement and conscience; these are things unknown to the laws of this land, and which arise from a fundamental Mistake of the whole order and tenour of our Constitution.[52]

The radical Catherine Macaulay,[53] in reaction to the Middlesex elections and the expulsion of Wilkes, in 1775 published a pamphlet in defence of the Westminster instructions in which she maintained:

though the obeying every mandate of constituents may, in some very extraordinary conjunction of opinions and circumstances, be wrong, yet at a time when the representatives had affected an entire independence, or rather an absolute sovereignty, over their constituents, this might be a worthy sufficient reason for many worthy men, as a far lesser evil, to submit to an indefinite obligation of obedience.[54]

There were, however, several instances while serving as member for Bristol when Burke bowed to his members' instructions, though it meant reversing his position on business already pending in the House. As noted above in Chapter 3, he reversed his support for the Birmingham Theatre Bill in 1777 after a group of his Bristol supporters, including the Quaker Richard Champion, urged him to oppose the measure's second reading.

It was one thing for Burke to relent on a matter of local business when pressed by his closest Bristol ally, but quite another when he agreed to work with administration officials and Lord North to secure the alterations in offensive legislation for Bristol allies. In 1775, Paul Farr, one of his principal Bristol supporters, called upon Burke to secure amendments to the administration's Prohibitory Bill which banned all commerce with the rebellious American colonies. To secure these revisions, Farr instructed Burke to work with Henry Cruger and two other local MPs. In the end, Burke secured the amendments without any assistance from those three, but he found the entire exercise to be a disagreeable one.

The debate on instructions did not exist only in the realms of theory. Horace Walpole was indignant in 1761 when the City of London instructed its MPs to oppose certain details in the peace preliminaries, protesting that they infringed upon the authority of Parliament to advise the administration on foreign policy. More often observers ridiculed members, in particular those from the City, when they claimed to act upon the instructions from their constituents. Walpole recorded episodes arising as

---

[52] *Writings and Speeches*, iii, 'Speech at the conclusion of the poll', p. 69. Ten years later, he was even more emphatic on the point. On 20 March 1784 he told the freeholders of Buckingham, who were about to petition in support of the new Pitt government, that Parliament was the proper forum to discuss the India Bill: the people, he said, had approved of the American war and then disapproved of the India Bill which showed to him that they lacked the capacity to comprehend great issues. F.D. Loch, *Edmund Burke*, i. p. 538.

[53] Catherine Macaulay (1731–91), author of *History of England from the Accession of James I to the Accession of the Brunswick Line* (1763–83) and political pamphlets including *Observations on Reflections on a Pamphlet Entitled Thoughts on the Cause of Present Discontents* (1770) and *Observations on the Rt. Hon. Edmund Burke, on the Revolution in France* (1790).

[54] Quoted in Kelly, 'Constituents' instructions', 180, from *Address to the People of England, Scotland, and Ireland on the Present Crisis of Affairs* (1775).

a result of the City's instructions in great detail, sometimes with disapproval, sometimes with glee, depending upon whether the instruction resulted in embarrassment to administrations or members whom he disliked.[55] Likewise, James Harris took delight in the difficulties that Richard Oliver encountered as a result of moving an address to the King 'in obedience to the hot and heavy instructions of his constituents... to know who were the advisers of the measures (established you will observe by Act of Parliament) regarding the Courts of Admiralty in America, about Popery and Despotism in Canada, &c'. Faced with a possible rout, Oliver relied upon friends to extricate him from disaster by moving the previous question and the order of the day. Their efforts failed, and Oliver's motion was defeated overwhelmingly, 163 to 10, while 'Rigby[56] treated the Livery with the contempt they deserved'.[57]

Not surprisingly, debates regarding the legitimacy of instructions extended to the floor of the House of Commons. On 14 March 1781 Sir Henry Hoghton expressed surprise that John Sawbridge, the London radical, 'should talk of the commands of his constituents'; Sir Henry added that:

> if he was implicitly to follow the inclinations of those who sent him thither, he could not be said to be a free man;... and could not come under the description of giving his countenance to any measure with that freedom which it behooved every member of that House to do. He called it an abject state for any gentleman, and such a one as no member of that House ought to accede to.

Sawbridge's answer to this outburst was pointed: he replied:

> that he came there to do the business of his constituents, not his own; he scorned the idea of being in an abject situation. He received no favours from ministers; and he believed his conduct in Parliament would be found as steady, uninterested, and unimpeached as any in the House.[58]

Sawbridge and his fellow radicals were unique in the 1770s and 1780s in maintaining the obligation of MPs to follow the instructions of their constituents. In so doing they were drawing on a practice that dated from the country opponents of Sir Robert Walpole in the 1730s and 1740s.[59] Nevertheless, they went far beyond the country movement in citing the absolute primacy of the constituent instructions and the requirement that the candidate standing for election take a pledge to honour those instructions on all occasions.

---

[55] *Last Journals*, i, 437–8; iv, 68, 77, 154, 197.
[56] Richard Rigby (1722–88), MP, Castle Rising, 1745–7, Sudbury, 1747–54 and Tavistock, 1754–88; Ld. of Trade, 1755–60; Sec. to Ld. Lt. [I], 1757–61; Master of the rolls [I], 1759–88; Jt. Vice-Treas. [I], 1762–5, Jan.–June, 1768; Paymaster Gen., 1768–82.
[57] *A Series of Letters of the First Earl of Malmesbury*, i, 333–4.
[58] Debrett, *Parl. Reg.*, n.s., ii, 258–9.
[59] Nicholas Rogers, *Whigs and Cities*, pp. 98–104, 120–1, 240–5, 286.

Beyond most of the members for the City after 1770, the London radicals found allies, including Wilkes, Sir John Glynn and later Richard Mainwaring, members for Middlesex, Sir Cecil Wray as Member for Westminster and Sir Joseph Mawbey, so long as he sat for Southwark or Surrey.⁶⁰ Henry Cruger, who was something of an imposter, told his Bristol constituents in 1774 that:

> it has ever been my opinion that electors have a right to instruct their Members. For my part I shall always think it my duty in Parliament to be guided by your counsels and instructions.⁶¹

VI: A House More Open to Democracy?

By the mid-1780s, according to Pasi Ihalainen, democracy as a term had come to be regarded as a part of the constitution which could be 'referred to by almost any Parliamentary speaker, and in most cases, in a neutral or positive sense'.⁶² In this environment MPs were able more openly to declare when they were following constituents' instructions without encountering the sort of harassment that their more radical colleagues routinely endured from other MPs as late as 1781, when Sir Henry Hoghton attacked John Sawbridge for following the 'commands' of his constituents, which left him, according to Hoghton, without the freedom to make up his own mind. Like Sawbridge, several of those who opposed citing their constituents' wishes when opposing the new taxes were active reformers including James Martin,⁶³ Lord Galway⁶⁴ and Joshua Grigby.⁶⁵

In this more open environment an agitated Hans Sloan Stanley⁶⁶ wrote to an associate that:

> you will see the Constitution verging towards a Democracy, by the Posts, and Subscriptions, which Members of the New Parliament have submitted to Sign; by which Act, I say, they instantly give up every Idea of a member of the House of Commons, and are little above the situation of the Distributor of letters, who are transmitting the sentiments of others, and not their own. A Member of Parliament is properly instructed when he is instructed as to a point, which locally affects the

---

⁶⁰ Brook Watson, though a member for London, said in June 1784 he would obey instructions only if a 'clear decided sense could be collected'. By June 1789 he announced, however, he did not believe MPs should always follow them. *HPC, 1754–1790*, iii, 611.

⁶¹ *HPC, 1754–1790*, ii, 280.

⁶² Pasi Ihalainen, *Agents of the People: Democracy and Popular Sovereignty in British and Swedish Parliamentary Debates, 1734–1800* (Leiden and Boston, MA, 2010), 309.

⁶³ James Martin (1738–1810), MP, Tewkesbury, 1776–1807; *HPC, 1754–1790*, iii, 113–14.

⁶⁴ Robert Monckton Arundell, 4th Viscount Galway [I] (1752–1810), MP, Pontefract, 1780–3, 1796–1802 and York, 1783–90; Comptroller of the Household, 1784–7; *HPC 1754–1790*, iii, 151.

⁶⁵ Joshua Grigby (?1731–98), MP, Suffolk, 1784–90; *HPC, 1754–1790*, ii, 556.

⁶⁶ Hans Sloan Stanley (1739–27), MP Newport I.o.W. 1768–80, Southampton, 1780–4, Christchurch, 1788–90 and Lostwithiel, 1796–1806; Dep. Cofferer of Household, 1780–2; Ld. of Trade, 1780–2.

place he represents, as if for example, a Member for South[amp]t[o]n, was instructed as to wine, or a Lymington Representative, as to Salt, but whenever the time comes, that a Majority of the House acknowledge themselves bound to obey Instructions on general Topics, either in regard to [a] Foreign situation of the state, or in regard to Taxes, and do obey them, Adieu! to the excellence of this hitherto well composed Fabrick of Liberty![67]

Sloan Stanley was correct in identifying taxation as a question on which MPs were attentive to their constituents' instructions. With the new consensus regarding democracy that had been achieved by the mid-1780s, over 20 MPs indicated in speeches in the Commons that they opposed the unpopular Receipts and Shop Taxes, the Coal Tax or, in one instance, the Post Horse Duties Bill because of constituents' instructions.[68] Members from London, Middlesex, Westminster and Southwark stood out in the group because, as they repeatedly noted, their constituents paid the bulk of the assessments under the Receipts and the Shop Taxes due to the area's wealth. Pressure, however, came from smaller towns, including Stamford, Taunton and Pontefract. Its member, John Smyth, after noting he had received instructions from the borough to oppose, remarked that 'though he thought the paying a blind and implicit obedience to constituents was not only to admit a doctrine dangerous to the independence of that House, but to sacrifice his own judgment, yet he was of opinion, that the utmost deference should on every occasion be paid to the wishes of those who were to be materially and personally affected by measures of government'.[69] He was not alone in offering that sort of justification for his conduct. A number of MPs were attentive to the appeals of constituents during the 1780s when they questioned unpopular taxes, probably because of the fury that had accompanied the financing of a long and disastrous war. For this reason, they were willing, as Smyth and others such as Sir George Yonge were, to overcome their reservations regarding instructions.

Indeed, the impact that constituents' instructions had on moderate MPs has been underestimated. For the most part constituents dispatched instructions to inform their representatives of their views regarding petitions for leave to bring in specific or local bills. What is remarkable is that by the 1780s members, even conservative members such as John Rolle or General Sir George Howard, were willing to attend to instructions on general legislation which they might earlier have ignored. These were men who had supported North to the end of the war and were unsympathetic to the programmes of London or the Yorkshire reformers, unlike Lord Galway, who after supporting North's

---

[67] Hampshire Archives, Hans Sloane Stanley MSS, 28 M57/54, Sloane to J. Ridding, 19 Apr. 1784.
[68] D.P. Coke (Nottingham), C.J. Fox (Westminster), 4th Viscount Galway (York), Joshua Grigby (Suffolk), Benjamin Hammet (Taunton), Sir Richard Hotham (Southwark), Gen. Sir George Howard (Stamford), William Henry Lambton (Co. Durham), Paul LeMesurier (Southwark), Sir Watkin Lewes (London), William Mainwaring (Middlesex), John Martin (Tewkesbury), Nathaniel Newnham (London), Col. George Onslow (Guildford), John Rolle (Devon), John Sawbridge (London), John Smyth (Pontefract), Henry Thornton (Southwark), James Townsend (Calne), Sir Gregory Page Turner, Bt. (Thirsk), William Windham (Norwich), Sir Cecil Wray, Bt. (Westminster), and Sir George Yonge, Bt. (Honiton).
[69] *PH*, xxv, 791, 30 May 1791.

administration from 1780 until its collapse two years later, became active in the Association movement.[70] By contrast, Rolle disapproved of committees without doors that aimed to 'watch and control Parliament'. He believed such groups were 'neither legal nor constitutional'. Yet, more than most of his colleagues, his constituents' views seem to have formed Rolle's views on a wide range of questions. He cited their instructions in 1787 to justify his introducing a bill for the relief of Exeter's poor, and again in May 1790 when they demanded that he oppose Wilberforce's propositions relating to the abolition of the slave trade.[71]

Rolle is an example of a member who, though suspicious, even hostile to the Association movement, was willing to receive and act upon the instructions of his constituents. In this respect he was similar to John Smyth of Pontefract, who though part of the petitioning movement, was not an associator and certainly not prepared to give a 'blind and implicit obedience' to instructions. Similarly, Colonel George Onslow had taken a lead in attacking the press for publishing accounts of the Commons' proceedings in the early 1770s. One of his motions led to the Brass Crosby case whose outcome enabled the press to report on the Commons' debates. Onslow claimed that in introducing his motion against the press he was only defending 'the honour and dignity of the House of Commons'. In introducing the motion he was, of course, showing his antipathy to London's Wilkites. Yet he reversed himself on 11 June 1783, after initially supporting the Receipts Tax, and told the House that his constituents' instructions 'had wrought a very wonderful conversion on his mind' and that he would 'vote the sense his constituents entertained of the tax';[72] John Sawbridge would have approved of his conduct.

Kelly maligns General Sir George Howard[73] whom he describes 'as a notable courtier who was certainly no radical and was simply playing to his Stamford constituents'[74] when he told the House that he always considered it as his duty to comply with the instructions of his constituents.[75] The General was no toady, though his legislative record prior to the 1780s was generally unremarkable. Prior to his vote against the Shop Tax, he had adhered to government. Between 1765 and 1767 he presented a Yorkshire enclosure bill, but by the 1770s he emerged as something of an expert in the intricacies of estate legislation.[76] More importantly, in March 1786 he was willing to embrace controversial issues, taking up the petition of the property owners on the Caribbean island of St. Eustatius for a bill to vest in trustees the bullion, stores and effects captured in 1781 by a force commanded by Lord Rodney and General John Vaughan on that island and St. Martin where the British commanders, according to

---

[70] *HPC, 1754–1790*, iii, 150.
[71] *HPC, 1754–1790*, iii, 150; *PH*, xxvii, c. 82.
[72] *HPC, 1754–1790*, iii, 227–8; *PH*, xxiii, cc. 1011–12.
[73] General Sir George Howard (1718–96), MP, Lostwithiel, 1761–6 and Stamford, 1768–96; army, 1725; Capt. 3 Ft. 1739; Lt.-Col. 1744; Col. 1749; Maj.-Gen. 1750; Lt. Gen. 1760; Col. 7 Drag., 1763–79; Gen. 1777; Col. 1 Drag. Gds. 1779–96; f.m. 1793; Gov. Minorca, 1766–8; Chelsea Hospital, 1768–95; Jersey, 1796.
[74] Kelly, 'Constituents' instructions', 83.
[75] *PH*, xxxiii, c. 1003.
[76] See *CJ*, xxxiii, 238; xxxiv, 538, 669, 692, 736, 734.

Andrew O'Shaughnessy, had engaged in 'indiscriminate plunder'.[77] On 19 May Howard presented a bill to this effect after the House gave leave for its introduction. The bill was part of the reaction to the rape of St. Eustatius that was orchestrated by Burke and others. Beyond this effort, Howard tended to traditional military issues, including his oversight of the passage of a bill 'to amend and render more effectual an act of George III regarding the bounty to be paid to garrison officers and officers on the King's ships at Gibraltar for taking enemy ships', which he carried to the Lords after it passed the House.[78] If Howard was not an exciting legislator, he was by 1786 at least an active one, capable of handling complex business and responsive both to constituents, members of his profession and to the mistreated settlers of the empire. He was not just the sort of member to 'play' to his constituents.

Another MP who welcomed instructions but had moderate political inclinations was Sir William Dolben. As member for Northamptonshire in the 1768 Parliament he performed the usual legislative chores of a knight of the shire: in 1772 he oversaw the passage of four enclosure bills and another to incorporate the Marine Society, which became a leading charitable organisation. The following session he was busier, overseeing the passage of seven enclosure, four estate and four road bills along with a measure for the 'better cultivations of open fields, wastes and commons', which he reported from its second reading committee. In 1781, as member for Oxford University, he carried a bill through the Commons to allow married men to serve as the heads of colleges at the Universities of Oxford and Cambridge, only to see it fail in the Lords. He also spoke on behalf 'instructions, which came from his county because he was persuaded nothing could be more conducive to the great objects of the war than an oeconomical and faithful expenditure of public money'.[79] Nevertheless, he opposed Burke's bill for regulating the civil list revenue, because:

> if it were right to destroy the influence by which Members were returned to that House, it did not go far enough, for it ought to have destroyed the influence of the aristocracy and of wealthy individuals as well as the influence of the Crown; and he said he should have no objection to a general and fair plan of reform that went to the reduction of influence on both sides.[80]

Dolben went on to support Pitt's reform bills in 1783 and 1785.

By no means all MPs responded to instructions with Dolben's enthusiasm. Having received the instructions of the bailiffs, aldermen and burgesses of East Retford, Wharton Amcotts[81] wrote to the Duke of Portland because he found himself 'obliged to comply with the wishes of my constituents and vote for the repeal of the receipts tax in

---

[77] O'Shaughnessy, *Empire Divided*, p. 217. He has an extensive discussion of the assault on St. Eustatius and, in particular, its impact on the island's Jewish community, as well as the reaction in Britain and the innumerable lawsuits brought against the perpetrators – Lord Rodney in particular, pp. 214–30.
[78] *CJ*, xlii, 369–71, 749, 816, 828, 935, 941, 946–7, 955–6.
[79] Debrett, *Parl. Reg.*, n.s. iii, 243.
[80] Quoted in *HPC, 1754–1790*, ii, 328, from Debrett, *Parl. Reg.*, ii, 41.
[81] Wharton Amcotts (1740–1807), MP East Retford, 1780–90, 1796–1807; cr. Bt., 1796.

1783'. He explained that 'it gave me great concern to oppose Government..., being determined to support your Grace's administration upon every question whenever your Grace is pleased to call upon me'.[82] Others also found they could not resist constituents. In May 1784 Henry Thornton[83] supported Pitt's Shop Tax against the wishes of his Southwark constituents. The latter were persistent, forceful instructors, and Thornton was unable to withstand their pressure. By 2 March 1786 he informed the House that the manner in which he had previously conducted himself on the question 'had been misrepresented to his constituents, and had drawn upon himself a degree of unpopularity greater perhaps than had ever fallen upon a representative of any place before'.[84] Others were more forthright than Thornton. Robert Smith,[85] in introducing a petition from Nottingham against Pitt's Irish commercial resolutions in 1785, highlighted his disagreement with points raised in it.[86] Lord Sheffield was even more direct, telling William Eden that 'my constituents took the trouble of sending me a petition against the [receipts] tax, accompanied by several most strenuous letters, but... I voted for it'.[87]

Sir Walter Blackett,[88] however, delivered the most dramatic repudiation of instructions during the period. In February and April 1769 and again in January 1770 he had voted in support of Wilkes on the Middlesex election as he was pressed to do by his Newcastle constituents. Blackett spent the summer of 1770 abroad with his wife to restore his health and returned to the House in November where on the 15th he surprised his colleagues by rising to repent having followed his constituents' instructions:

> upon a point which for some months hath greatly disturbed me...: and the only apology I can offer for thus disturbing the House... is, that I am conscientiously compelled to it. Diffident of myself, forsaking my own judgment, and adopting the opinion of others, I voted last sessions that Mr. Wilkes was not incapacitated from sitting in Parliament. Reconsidering that vote the night I had given it, and indeed ever since, hath occasioned the greatest uneasiness to me: and whilst I was abroad this summer ruminating upon what I had done, it appeared to me that the only satisfaction I could give to my mind, was, to acknowledge here the error, as I conceive, I had committed, and return to my own opinion, as I now do; – That Mr. Wilkes is incapacitated, constitutionally incapacitated, from sitting in this House during this Parliament.[89]

---

[82] *HPC, 1754–1790*, ii, 19.
[83] Henry Thornton (1760–1815) MP, Southwark, 1760–1815; evangelical colleague of Wilberforce.
[84] *HPC, 1754–1790*, iii, 525.
[85] Robert Smith (1752–1838), MP, Nottingham, 1779–97; partner in family bank; cr. Baron Carrington, 1797.
[86] *PH*, xxv, cc. 703–4.
[87] *The Journal and Correspondence of William, Lord Auckland*, ed. Robert John Eden, Bishop of Bath and Wells (2 vols, 1861), i, 52–3.
[88] Sir Walter Blackett, 2nd Bt. (1707–77), MP, Newcastle-upon-Tyne, 1734–77; alderman of Newcastle, 1729; Mayor, 1735, 1743, 1756, 1764, 1771; sheriff, Northumberland, 1731–2.
[89] Quoted in *HPC, 1754–1790*, ii, 95. See also, Walpole, *Memoirs*, iv, p. 197 for his comments on the episode.

As Paul Langford pointed out, MPs 'were perfectly used to being instructed by their constituents', particularly on local business, a point earlier highlighted by Sloan Stanley.[90] Lord Brownlow Bertie stood out in the 1760s and 1770s for the substantial volume of Lincolnshire legislation which he guided through the House of Commons, and Philip Yorke grew from a tentative novice usually legislating at the behest of his uncles into one who by the mid-1780s attended to his Cambridgeshire constituents on national as well as local business. Lord Barrington carried several controversial Plymouth paving bills for proponents there despite the protests of residents of the town's outlying parishes. Similarly, Lord Clare, Jarrit Smith, Matthew Brickdale and Edmund Burke worked with considerable success for more than two decades to secure the legislation sought by the merchants and manufacturers of Bristol and the Society of Merchant Venturers. These are only a few examples, and others can be found in Chapters 2, 3, 4 and 8.

The Corporation of Nottingham made regular demands upon its members. Its burgesses even told the town's MPs in 1768 that they possessed 'an undoubted right as your constituents to give you instructions'.[91] In November 1783 the Mayor and burgesses instructed Daniel Parker Coke[92] and Robert Smith to support the City of London's motion for the repeal of the Receipt's Tax and sent a similar request on 28 May 1784.[93] In 1785 the Corporation instructed both members to oppose the Coventry Canal Bill because it would harm Sir Thomas White's Charity Estate in Nottingham. In addition, it is likely, according to John Beckett, that the town's MPs were involved in the passing of a series of turnpike acts, along with the Nottingham Canal Bill.[94]

VII: Other Modes of Communication

Several MPs relied on distinctive means to secure the information they needed from constituents both on local and national issues. Bamber Gascoyne,[95] the son of the member who featured prominently in Chapter 6, told the House when presenting a petition from his Liverpool constituents against Pitt's Irish propositions that he had written to his Liverpool friends 'to depute a few of the best informed of them to come

---

[90] Paul Langford, *Public Life*, pp. 189–90. Langford, however, failed to note the degree to which they were used to being instructed on national questions.
[91] *Records of the Borough of Nottingham, Being a Series of Extracts from the Archives of the Corporation of Nottingham. Vol. VII: 1760–1800*, ed. Duncan Gray and V.W. Walker (Nottingham, 1947), pp. 204, 206; J.V. Beckett, 'Parliament and the localities: The borough of Nottingham', in *Parliament and Locality, 1660–1939*, ed. David Dean and Clyve Jones (Parliamentary Yearbook Trust, Edinburgh, 1998), pp. 61–2, 64–5.
[92] Daniel Parker Coke (1745–1825), MP, Derby, 1776–80 and Nottingham, 1780–1802, 1803–12; Commr. for Settling American Claims, 1782–5.
[93] Since there are no lists for either division, it is impossible to tell if the members followed their constituents' instructions. On 30 May 1785 Coke acknowledged that he had received instructions from his constituents to oppose Pitt's unpopular Shop Tax and made a point of noting 'that their instructions were perfectly consistent with his own sentiments'. *PH*, xxv, c. 794.
[94] J.V. Beckett, 'Parliament and the localities: The borough of Nottingham', pp. 61–2, 64–5.
[95] Bamber Gascoyne (1758–1824), MP, Liverpool, 1780–96.

to town to assist him in a matter in which they must necessarily be so much more conversant than himself'.[96]

John Tucker had a quite different relationship with his constituents, according to a study by Bob Tucker and Jeremy Black.[97] Despite his dependence on government funding, to support his various construction projects, including a dockyard, he became a moderate supporter of the country programme of reform during the middle years of the century. Most important, however, Tucker and Black show that his views both on local and national issues were formed in part as a result of an on-going dialogue, facilitated by his brother, Richard, with a group of supporters, including friends and business associates at Weymouth. Some of the latter formed an informal debating society, for which Tucker provided a flow of printed material, including newspapers, essays, pamphlets, copies of the votes and of the Lords' protests, all of which stoked the local group's interest and understanding of broader national issues and, in turn, Tucker's appreciation of their views.[98]

Larger groups were inventive in discovering ways to influence MPs between elections. Paul Langford demonstrated in a 1973 article that the elder Pitt owed his rise to power in 1757 to an outpouring of 'gold boxes', by which means the City of London and a succession of boroughs across Britain conferred their freedom upon him.[99] According to Langford, they adopted this method of expressing their disapproval of the dismissal of the short-lived Devonshire Administration of which Pitt had been a part and their demand that he be restored to office. They resorted to this tactic because petitions, the alternative, were traditionally the means by which the political nation expressed grievances, and in this case their aim was positive – to restore Pitt to power. Langford judged that in this instance their tactic was effective, because:

> in creating an atmosphere intensely favourable to Pitt, and in influencing the judgments and attitudes of the other actors in the drama – of the king and Fox who appear to have lost their nerve..., of Newcastle who had previously failed to come to terms with Pitt, and of the many courtiers, placemen, and M.P.s who at the critical moment in June 1757 vetoed a Waldegrave-Fox Ministry, and made inevitable a combination of Newcastle and Pitt.[100]

The success of this effort was due not just to the volume of 'boxes', but because their output reflected the views of the propertied – 'the landed gentry of the counties and the mercantile elites of the cities, and the base among the small freeholders of the countryside and the petite-bourgeoisie of the towns'.[101] Langford acknowledged that in the mid-

---

[96] *PH*, xxv, cc. 342–3.
[97] Tucker and Black, 'John Tucker, MP, and mid-eighteenth-century British politics', *Albion*, xxix (1997), 15–35.
[98] Tucker and Black, 'John Tucker, MP', pp. 21–2, 31–3, 35–6.
[99] Notices of the City and later the corporations of smaller cities and towns came for the most part in gold or silver boxes.
[100] Paul Langford, 'William Pitt and public opinion, 1757', *EHR*, lxxxviii, (1957), 54.
[101] Langford, 'Pitt and public opinion', *EHR*, 55.

eighteenth century, most members of the political nation would have agreed with the point made in Fox's newspaper, the *Test*, that 'the people taken in their gross are very improper and inadequate judges of their own interest'.[102] Thus it was crucial that the boxes come from the propertied. The rival *Con-Test* responded to the *Test*'s dismissal of the outpouring as reflecting 'the passions of the multitude', by noting that among the so called 'multitude' were 'the lord mayor and court of aldermen of the city of London, and the several great corporations, men who have an extensive property, and consequently, a real interest in the welfare of the Kingdom and the honour of the crown'.[103]

The practice that Langford celebrated was a one of a kind effort. Over the long term petitions and addresses proved to be a more potent political tool, one that was open to a far wider segment of the population. John Cannon and Paul Kelly have highlighted the outpouring and impact of addresses and instructions in support of the younger Pitt following George III's dismissal of the Coalition government in December, 1783. According to Cannon the 200 addresses sent to the King in the early months of 1784 exceeded the combined total of petitions sent in opposition to the Jewish Naturalization Bill in 1753, against the Cider Tax in 1763, in favour of the Society in Support of the Bill of Right's petition in 1768, as well as those supporting Lord George Gordon's petition for the repeal of the Roman Catholic Relief Act and later the Association petitions in 1780.[104]

Moreover, the addresses in support of Pitt and George III had notable effects on the political conduct of several MPs. Bristol's two sitting members were coalitionists who had supported the India Bill and initially opposed Pitt. When a poorly attended meeting in early February 1784 issued a statement backing Pitt, the two MPs, Matthew Brickdale and George Daubeney,[105] refused to present it, but three weeks later another better-attended session unanimously adopted a resolution thanking the king 'for dismissing ministers who had been desperate enough to sacrifice every public good which stood in the way of their unbounded ambition'. Brickdale and Daubeney, according to John Cannon, played it safe, and Daubeney told his constituents that the two MPs would put 'the most favourable construction on our conduct'.[106] Shukburgh Ashby,[107] returned at a by-election on 14 February at Leicester, voted with the Coalition on 27th to the disgust of the town's Corporation. He immediately explained that his vote was on a matter of no importance and swore that he would never again oppose Pitt. According to Cannon, he lost his seat at the subsequent election; according to his very brief biography in the *History of Parliament* volumes, Ashby declined to stand for re-election despite the fact that he was popular in the town.[108]

---

[102] Langford, 'Pitt and public opinion', *EHR*, 55. The date of the passage from the *Test* is 7 May 1757.
[103] Quoted in Langford, 'Pitt and public opinion', 58, from the *Con-Test*, 14 May 1757.
[104] Cannon, *The Fox-North Coalition*, pp. 186-7. See also Paul Kelly, 'Radicalism and public opinion in the general election of 1784', *BIHR*, xlv (1972), 72-88.
[105] George Daubeney (1742-1806), MP, Bristol, 1781-4, merchant, sugar refiner and partner in a firm of glass manufacturers.
[106] Quoted in Cannon, *Fox-North Coalition*, p.189. According to the author of Brickdale's biography in *HPC, 1754-1790*, ii, 115-16, 'he followed his own independent line, influenced only by the instructions and the interest of his constituents'.
[107] Shukburgh Ashby (1724-92), MP, Leicester, 15 Feb.-25 Mar. 1784; sheriff, Leics., 1758-9.
[108] Cannon, *Fox-North Coalition*, pp. 189-90; *HPC, 1754-1790*, ii, 29.

While in the House, John Hussey, Lord Delaval,[109] received innumerable requests from his Berwick constituents to promote their projects, including the controversial Tweed Fisheries Bill of 1771. He dutifully attended to these, but when he supported the Coalition in 1784, after his constituents had voted Pitt the freedom of the borough and directed the members to give his government 'every constitutional support', he was criticised.[110]

Yet his constituents' annoyance did not prevent them from returning Delaval at the 1784 election. They gave him some leeway, perhaps because of his previous attention to all those local matters. In any case, following the election Delaval told the House on 24 May:

> he voted with the majority of the present Parliament because he was sure they spoke the sense of the people... If the people of Great Britain were at any time, which he did not believe would be the case, to change their opinion concerning the right honourable gentleman [Pitt], he should think it incumbent upon him, as one of their representatives, to alter his.[111]

It may be stretching the significance of Delaval's re-election, but his case highlights the importance of constituent service over a period of time and the bond that developed out of the extended service. All over England there were communities during the last decades of the eighteenth century that benefitted from those connections and did not, as a result, press for the reform of Parliament.

The fact that individual MPs began openly to acknowledge that they took a position on a national issue in response to their constituents' instructions or petitions did not mean that they followed those instructions in all instances. Often the member made a point of noting it was easy to follow his constituents' directions because their views coincided with his own. Moreover, MPs were not afraid, as already noted, of taking positions that contradicted instructions. Though the Corporation of Nottingham asserted its right to instruct its MPs, Daniel Parker Coke was, by his own admission, wary of taking a position that went against his own opinions, and Robert Smith noted when about to vote that his was cast in opposition to the views of his constituents.

The singular achievement of the late eighteenth-century House of Commons lay in its capacity to open itself to a dynamic world. That it did so was not, as we have seen, the result of political reform. Instead the achievement was that of the members themselves, chosen by an unreformed electoral system, who were in many instances fortunately attuned to the needs of the communities they represented. Though they did not always display the ardour that Samuel Garbett would have wished, many of the

---

[109] Sir John Hussey Delaval (1728–1803), MP, Berwick-upon-Tweed, 1754–61, 1765–74, 1780–6; cr. Bt. 1761; Baron Delaval [I], 1783 and [GB], 1786.

[110] Langford, *Public Life*, pp. 189–90. In fact, the two members delivered the borough's freedom to Pitt and returned his expressions of appreciation to appease their constituents, according the *Public Advertiser*, 16 Mar. 1784; Kelly, 'Radicalism and public opinion', 85.

[111] Quoted in *HPC, 1754–1790*, ii, 312. Paul Kelly maintained that 'it would be unwise to write off the pressure of public opinion in the constituency as a cause of Delaval's conversion, especially since he avowed it [in his speech quoted above]'. Kelly, 'Radicalism and public opinion', 86.

MPs discussed in these chapters were attentive and professional in their dealings with their constituents and in their mastery of the systems of the House. Though some were not above advancing their own projects and those of their families, they were loyal to their constituents, and as time went on, they were more and more open to listening to their opinions on national as well as constituency matters. This did not mean that they were prepared in all cases to espouse their views or sacrifice their opinions to advance those of constituents and neighbours. But the willingness of a number of MPs who were not radicals to acknowledge that they were open to the influence of those with whom they had worked closely on legislation over time reflected the democratic spirit which, according to Pasi Ihalainen, began to permeate the House of Commons in the 1780s.

As noted earlier, the connection between MPs and constituents was reinforced by English MPs' growing acknowledgment of democratic principles. It was manifested in the willingness of a large cadre of moderate and conservative MPs to act upon the instructions of constituents, not just on local and specific bills, but on questions relating to taxation and commercial policy and other national issues. By the 1780s a broader segment of MPs responded to, indeed welcomed, the instructions of constituents. They did so, however, without surrendering their right to retain their independent judgment; they never went to the extremes of London radicals who maintained it was their duty to act upon all such instructions. Equally important was the fact that they could acknowledge their obligation without fear of attack in ways that were impossible in earlier decades.

The greater appreciation of democracy that Ihalainen describes as permeating the House in the mid-1780s enabled MPs to express themselves more openly, especially in terms of their relations with constituents. It did not result, however, in their espousing the reform of Parliament. Two decades later MPs took a stronger line, focusing their attack on an obstructive House of Lords because it refused to pass a series of their Reversion Bills which enjoyed broad popular support. Their response to the Lords' obstruction was notable because of the range of MPs who absorbed the spirit of the 'members from various political groups' who in 1799 'defined the British political order as based on the principle of the sovereignty of the people'.[112] Inspired by their principles, moderate and more radical MPs challenged the right of the Lords repeatedly to turn aside measures which enjoyed the broad support of the public and overwhelming majorities in the House of Commons. In so doing they challenged the legitimacy of the House of Lords as a legislative institution. It took them, however, more than 20 years to take up the issue of Parliamentary reform.

Indeed, one of the themes that runs through this period is the lack of urgency among MPs and many of their constituents for reform itself. David Hayton emphasised the point in his survey of the House at the outset of the century:

> A general lack of concern with enfranchising prosperous but unrepresented towns is not difficult to understand. For one thing, they might already enjoy an effective

---

[112] Pasi Ihalainen, *Agents of the People*, p. 499.

'virtual' representation, through knights of the shire, or sympathetic Members for neighbouring enfranchised boroughs, as was the case with Manchester; or could bring economic influence of their own to bear upon the electors in some smaller parliamentary borough, as the clothiers of Newbury did at Great Bedwyn. Second, it was by no means clear which particular boroughs should be enfranchised, what the criteria should be for selection, and how the process should be undertaken.[113]

Similarly, Paul Langford wrote that in 1783, while the younger Pitt was trying to reform Parliament, 16 parishes in outer London, along with 'large population centres', ranging from Leeds, Doncaster, Halifax, Manchester and Stockport in the North, to Birmingham and Brighton, had at least five bills pending in Parliament though they lacked direct representation. Yet neither Birmingham, Manchester, Sheffield nor Leeds petitioned in support of Pitt's bill.[114]

They may have failed to do so for any number of reasons. A number could rely, as did Manchester more than 70 years earlier, upon the 'landlord representation' system Langford described, or on the willingness of boroughs such as Great Bedwyn to take up the projects of neighbouring craftsmen. As demonstrated in Chapters 7 and 8, interest groups exerted a powerful influence on local landed grandees as well on the national administration when they could make a case that their goals coincided with regional needs or those of the nation. Another factor, of course, was the success of large numbers of MPs over 30 years or more in advancing the legislative projects put forward by a broad range of constituents, neighbours and interest groups. Much of this legislation MPs promoted was specific – turnpike, navigation, enclosure, estate bills or local. The same MPs, a Gilbert, a Bunbury, a Savile, Bastard, John Rolle who advanced those bills, and even so obscure a member as Peniston Powney,[115] authored general acts on their own initiative that usually avoided becoming matters of political debate in the House of Commons. They drew upon their knowledge and experience, and the expertise of the Crown's legal officers and Parliamentary agents whom they consulted in preparing their measures. As some stepped into the national arena, they encountered controversy: Gilbert did so as he manoeuvred his poor law bills through the House or when as Chairman of Ways and Means he was entrusted with the task of guiding the passage of Pitt's finance bills. Rose Fuller faced pressures when he was chosen by the Rockingham administration to chair the committee of the whole House that would make the case for the repeal of the Stamp Act, and Wilberforce and his abolition bills provoked storms, partly because they inspired massive popular support but mainly because the West India interest was able to enlist powerful allies in the City, at Court and the principal outports to join it in opposing the proposals. Individual members were advancing larger numbers of controversial projects by the 1780s, and at the same

---

[113] www.historyofparliamentonline.org/volume/1690-1715/surve/constituencies-and-elections
[114] Langford, *Public Life*, p 206.
[115] Peniston Powney (?1743–94), MP, New Windsor, 1780–94; Ranger, Windsor Little Park, 1788–94. In 1782 Powney introduced a bill to prevent the 'vexatious removal of paupers'. Following his death the *Reading Mercury* noted that 'his public and private virtues will make him long remembered with respect'. *HPC, 1754–1790*, iii, 317–18.

time they more openly acknowledged their willingness to follow the instructions of constituents in shaping their conduct on the national questions that came before the House. The latter was not a new phenomenon, but it involved a wider portion of the Commons' membership and provoked less critical response than in earlier years. It represented the closer bond between member and constituent, but did not mean that the member was completely surrendering his independent judgment.

What matters is that there were large numbers of MPs who dealt effectively with their constituent's legislative proposals – not only those that came from residents of counties and the larger boroughs. Small boroughs such as Tiverton and Dartmouth could secure their needs. More than that, they were authors of important legislation in their own right and active participants in the business of the nation, both on behalf of their constituents and acting according to their own best judgments. In these variety of ways as legislators, late eighteenth-century MPs 'enhanced the usefulness of the Commons'[116] as their predecessors who had chaired T.K. Moore's and Henry Horwitz's second reading committees had done in the early 1690s – though on a broader scale.

---

[116] T.K. Moore and Henry Horwitz, 'Who runs the House? Aspects of Parliamentary organization in the later seventeenth century', *Journal of Modern History*, xliii (1971), 226–7.

10

The Commons and the Lords: A Legislative Partnership?

In 2009 I argued that the upper House 'functioned for the most part as a co-operative partner of the Commons in the legislative process', and that it 'was a useful chamber,... that [under the leadership of the law lords] took a lead in correcting poorly drafted measures and in rendering others more suitable for their declared intent'. I claimed that before the 1790s the Lords' disposal of reform bills was 'often uncontroversial... and did not damage relations between the chambers for more than a few weeks'. While the Lords over time became a more efficient legislative body during the King's reign, this study shows that it disposed of useful, sometimes important legislation introduced by MPs. I did not in 2009 appreciate the utility and importance of much of what the peers rejected.

If one goal of this chapter is to reassess the impact of Lords' veto on legislation initiated by individual MPs, the broader goal is to provide a detailed picture of how the two chambers interacted on legislative business. To do so will involve providing an examination of the constraints under which both branches operated, examples showing the degree to which they co-operated on contentious business, cases in which they disagreed, the repercussions of those disagreements, and finally an assessment of the Lords' impact on the Commons' legislation along with a discussion of the two groups, the judges and the bench of bishops, groups that were most likely to thwart measures sent up from the Commons.

I: Constraints: Peers' Electoral Interests

Though a standing order of the Commons forbade peers from interfering in the election of its members, the nobility's electoral interests grew between 1754 and 1790. Different authorities have offered varying estimates of peerage's interests in English and/or English and Welsh boroughs. Namier calculated that 55 peers returned MPs from borough seats at the general election in 1761,[1] while John Cannon estimated that 60 English peers returned 156 MPs from English and Welsh borough and county seats

---

[1] Namier, *Structure of Politics*, i (1957), pp. 48–9.

at the same election.² At the general election of 1780, Ian Christie cited 52 English peers returning 123 MPs,³ and at the 1784 election Cannon identified 58 English peers who returned 138 MPs from English and Welsh seats.⁴

The MPs returned under these circumstances were rarely free agents. In 1790, for example, the 1st Marquess of Buckingham, who intended to bring in Admiral Sir Alexander Hood⁵ once again for Buckingham, wrote to say:

> I feel that all explanations between honourable minds are unnecessary, but that you may not suppose any difficulties can be annexed to your situation, I wish you to understand that I shall have no arrangement to propose to you for vacating your seat or for changing its representation during the present parliament unless we should unfortunately differ essentially in our publick opinions, & in that case (the least likely to happen of any I can state) I am persuaded that the same fair & honourable impulse which has hitherto guided you would induce you to surrender your seat, & to preserve the same private regards with which you have honoured me.⁶

While Hood retained his seat until he received his British peerage, Robert Lowther⁷ was less fortunate: he was ousted by his brother, Sir James Lowther,⁸ after voting against the Bute administration on a question relating to John Wilkes. Robert insisted 'that he had always voted according to his reason and conscience; that he scorned to be dictated', and would therefore vacate the seat'.⁹ Sir James was similarly outraged when William Lowther,¹⁰ another of his members, failed to attend the opening of Parliament in November 1781, and so sent off a blast, stating that situations of that sort had not happened before, and if William could not attend constantly, he should resign his seat, so Lowther could select a more reliable member.¹¹

Among eighteenth-century patrons Sir James was notorious for his intolerance of any hint of independent behaviour. His contemporaries described him as 'tyrannical, overbearing, and frequently under no restraint of temper or reason'.¹² After his appointment as a Lord of the Treasury, John Robinson, who sat for Lowther's seat at

---

² John Cannon, *Aristocratic Century: The Peerage of Eighteenth-Century England* (Cambridge, 1984), p. 109.
³ Ian R. Christie, *The End of Lord North's Ministry, 1780–1782* (1958), pp. 49–50.
⁴ Cannon, *Aristocratic Century*, p. 109. I excluded from his list two patrons who were Scottish peers.
⁵ Alexander Hood (1726–1814), MP, Bridgwater, 1784–90, and Buckingham, 1784–96; R.N, 1741; Capt. 1756; R.-Adm. 1780; V.-Adm., 1787; Adm., 1794; cr. K.B., 1788; cr. Baron Bridport [I], 1794; and Baron Bridport [G.B.], 1796.
⁶ BL, Bridport Papers, Add. MSS 35202, ff. 154, Buckingham to Hood, 6 Dec. 1790.
⁷ Robert Lowther (1741–77), MP, Westmorland, 1759–61 and Mar.–Dec. 1763.
⁸ Sir James Lowther, 5th Bt. (1736–1802). MP, Cumberland, 1757–61, Dec. 1762–Dec. 1768, 1774–84; Westmorland, 1761–2; Cockermouth, Mar. 1769–74; Ld. Lt. Westmorland, 1758–1802 and Cumberland, 1759–1802; cr. Earl of Lonsdale, 1784 and Viscount Lonsdale, 1797.
⁹ *HPC, 1754–1790*, iii, 60–1.
¹⁰ William Lowther (1757–1844), MP, Carlisle, 1780–4, Cumberland, 1784–90 and Rutland, 1796–1802; Ld. Lt., Cumb. and Westmld, 1802–44; cr. Earl of Lonsdale, 1807 and K.G.
¹¹ Hugh Owen, *The Lowther Family* (Chichester, 1990), p. 385.
¹² *HPC, 1754–1790*, iii, 56; ii, 80.

Cockermouth, discovered that his patron expected him to put his interests before those of George Grenville, who had appointed him to the post. When the two finally quarrelled over a patronage question, Robinson found himself a more comfortable haven at Harwich at the election of 1774. It was impossible for members who held office under the Crown to remain for long under Lowther's thrall.[13]

Not all MPs who sat for seats controlled by peers endured such bondage. For example, Lord Chancellor Thurlow secured a seat for John Scott[14] at Weobley with the promise that he could take it in the confidence that, for the most part, he would be free to pursue his own course in the House.[15]

This, however, was an exceptional case. By and large peers' members were not only at the beck and call of their patrons, but authorities ranging from George III to the prime minister and a variety of the patron's noble friends called upon him to make sure that his member(s) were present at upcoming divisions in the Commons on business of special interest and importance to the applicant. For the King it was Alderman Newnham's[16] motion concerning the Prince of Wales' debts;[17] the Prince himself called on Lord Hertford to enlist his members' support on that business.[18] Lord North in April 1776 urged Lord Pelham[19] to make sure Sir Thomas Miller[20] attended the next day when John Wilkes moved for the reform of Parliament.[21] Requests from political leaders were numerous. Lord Rockingham, as party leader, dispatched a peremptory summons to the 3rd Duke of Portland to the effect that 'Lord E Bentinck, Capt. Bentinck,[22] Mr. Curwen,[23] Ld. Grey & multis aliis – their Company is much wished for in the House of Commons on Wednesday next, & that they are desired to stay the evening or all Night if agreeable'.[24] Many of these requests related to the more mundane business of the House. The autocratic Lord Buckingham insisted that his members in 1797 'not be provoked to say one word' in response to George Tierney's[25] motion

---

[13] Owen, *Lowther Family*, p. 285.
[14] John Scott (1751–1838): MP, Weobley, 1783–96 and Boroughbridge, 1796–9; Chancellor of Durham, 1787–99; Solicitor-Gen., 1788–93; Attorney-Gen., 1793–9; L.C.J. of Common Pleas, 1799–1801; Lord Chancellor, 1801–6 and 1807–27; cr. Baron Eldon, 1799 and Earl of Eldon, 1821.
[15] HMC, *Kenyon MSS*, p. 516.
[16] Nathaniel Newnham (c.1741–1809), MP, London, 1780–90 and Ludgershall, 1793–6; Alderman of London, 1774; sheriff, 1775–6; Ld. Mayor, 1783–4.
[17] HMC, *Ailesbury MSS*, p. 280.
[18] BL, Egerton MSS, 3262, Hertford MSS, Prince of Wales to Lord Hertford.
[19] Thomas Pelham (1728–1805), MP, Eye, 1749–54 and Sussex, 1754–68; Ld. of Trade, 1754–61 and of Admiralty, 1761–2; Comptroller of Household, 1765–74; Surveyor Gen. of Customs of London, 1773–1805; C.J. in Eyre North of Trent, 1774–5; Keeper of the Great Wardrobe, 1775–82; succ. Duke of Newcastle as Baron Pelham, 1768; cr. Earl of Chichester, 1801.
[20] Sir Thomas Miller, 5th Bt. (1731–1816), MP, Lewes, 1774–80 and Portsmouth, 1806–16.
[21] BL, Chichester MSS, Add. MS. 33090, f. 136, North to Pelham, 29 Apr 1776.
[22] John Albert Bentinck (1737–75), MP, Rye, 1761–8; R.N., 1757; Capt., 1758.
[23] Henry Curwen (1728–78), MP, Carlisle, 1761–8 and Cumberland, 1768–74.
[24] University of Nottingham, Manuscripts and Special Collections, PwF 9003, Rockingham to Portland, 13 Feb. 1768.
[25] George Tierney (1761–1830), MP Colchester, 1789–90, Southwark, 1796–1806, Athlone, 1806–7, Bandon Bridge, 1807–12, Appleby, 1812–18, and Knaresborough, 1818–30; Treasurer of Navy, 1803–4; Pres., Board of Control, 1086–7; Master of the Mint, 1827–8.

regarding the Marquess' lucrative sinecure office in the Exchequer, 'as it will be enough for me to decide upon my line (if any) as soon as I know what the attack is'.[26]

Another indication that their members were regarded as extensions of the patron was that he received plaudits when his member particularly distinguished himself. In 1781 the 4th Duke of Rutland[27] congratulated Sir James Lowther 'on the success' of the younger Pitt's maiden speech in the Commons. The Duke added that 'the satisfaction I have felt in his having fulfilled all the encomiums of him is very great, and I trust, Sir, yours will not be less in the thoughts of having placed him in that situation where his abilities may operate with utility to his country'.[28]

Finally, an analysis of how peers' MPs voted at important divisions shows that as a block they reinforced the strength of a succession of ministries. For example, only 35 members returned by peers voted against Charles Fox's India Bill at its second reading on 17 Nov. 1783 while 70 supported it. By the following March, however, Stockdale, who compiled a list of government and opposition forces in the lower house, assigned 77 MPs to Pitt's camp and only 60 to Fox. According to Edmund Burke 54 of the MPs who had previously adhered to Lord North, a partner in the Coalition government with Fox, joined Pitt by the following spring. Of these, 24 owed their seats to one of 14 noble patrons who, in the interim, had rallied to Pitt.[29]

In short, MPs returned by those patrons were, often, bound men. They entered the House on the understanding they would vote according to the wishes of their patron, the majority of whom were allied to the governments of the day. Failure to do so could put their seats in jeopardy. That penalty was imposed on brothers and other relatives as well as those who had no personal or family connection to the patron. The member was expected to attend and vote as instructed upon receiving instructions from the patron, both on important public issues as well as on the range of specific and local bills that made up the bulk of the legislation that came before the House. No matter how prominent he might become, he had at least to share the accolades he earned with the man who returned him. It is not surprising that William Pitt, the triumphant young Prime Minister, transferred from Lowther's borough at Appleby and instead stood for Cambridge University at the election of 1784.

II: Constraints: Lords' and Commons' Privileges

The House of Commons established its right to grant funds to the Crown by the late seventeenth century. Thereafter it was watchful in preventing the Lords from impinging upon its privileges. The upper House was barred not only from introducing money bills, but from amending provisions in finance legislation. The latter point became a

---

[26] *HMC, Fortescue MSS*, iii, 402, Buckingham to Lord Grenville, 8 Dec. 1797.
[27] Charles Manners, Marquess of Granby (1754-87), MP, Cambridge Univ., 1774-9; succ. gd. fa. as 4th Duke of Rutland, 1779; Ld. Lt., Leicestershire, 1778-87; Ld. Steward of Household, Feb.-Apr. 1783; Ld. Privy Seal, Dec. 1783-Feb. 1784; Ld. Lt. (I), 1784-7.
[28] *HMC, Lonsdale MSS*, p. 139.
[29] McCahill, *House of Lords*, pp. 309-11.

source of contention on which there were continuing disputes between the two Houses. The Commons invariably rejected bills when the Lords altered financial details – sometimes with some violence. On 11 June 1779, for example, Speaker Norton threw an amended bill over the table onto the floor of the chamber (a routine gesture) after which Richard Whitworth[30] kicked it to the door of the House.[31]

Peter Thomas claimed that the Lords 'never seriously challenged the principle that the Commons had control over money bills'.[32] If the Lords accepted the principle, individual peers continued throughout the period to protest that the Commons' privileges impinged upon those of the upper House and left it to some degree toothless.

Because the issue remained contentious. Lord North arranged in July 1779 for a narrower definition of the Commons' privileges and a more precise definition of the Lords' rights. The occasion to test the new formulation was provided when the Lords returned a Militia Bill to the Commons 'materially altered', provoking a protest from Sir Adam Fergusson,[33] who asserted that the measure was a money bill, and the Lords could not alter 'a title of it'. Sir Grey Cooper, a Treasury official, set out the new formulation:

> that in money bills. . ., which contain a grant of money by the Commons, to the crown, and which are founded on resolutions come to in a committee of supply, or a committee of the whole House, the Lords by established parliamentary usage, have no right to make any. . . alteration. . . whatever, except verbal errors and literal mistakes; and even in those cases, a particular entry is ordered to be made in the Journals of the Commons, why they agree to such an amendment.

He proceeded:

> that in all Bills which be free of grant money to the crown, but contain impositions or tolls on the people, as road and navigations bills, and bills relative to the customs and excise, it has been resolved,. . . that the Lords have no right to alter any matter by annexing condition or qualification to them relating to the toll or duties, either by augmenting or diminishing them, or by exempting any person from any part of such tolls or duties or varying in any respect the application, collection or appropriation of them; but that [in other] matters in such bills, the Lords are competent to make alterations and amendments.[34]

Though opposition MPs continued to maintain the Lords had infringed upon the Commons' privileges, when appealed to, Speaker Norton left it to the Commons to resolve the question, which it did in support of Cooper's statement.[35]

---

[30] Richard Whitworth (?1734–1811). MP Stafford, 1768–1780; sheriff, Staffs. 1758–9.
[31] Thomas, *House of Commons*, p. 66.
[32] Thomas, *House of Commons*, p. 68.
[33] Sir Adam Fergusson (1733–1813), MP, Ayrshire, 1774–80, 1781–1784, 1790–1796 and Edinburgh, 1784–1790; Ld. of Trade, 1781–82
[34] *PH*, xx, 1008–11; Thomas, *House of Commons*, p. 68.
[35] *PH*, xx, cc. 1008–11, 1018; *Morning Chronicle*, 6 Aug. 1803; Thomas, *House of Commons*, p. 68.

Despite the new formulation, individual peers protested against the restrictions under which they operated when considering money bills for the reminder of the century. One complained the rule meant that peers had to adopt financial measures 'as a matter of course, without being at liberty to judge whether they were proper or equitable'. It was degrading, another maintained, to be told that the House could not alter bills of supply, and others protested that the lower House assumed as a matter of course that the Lords would consent to their impositions.[36] For the most part these were protestations of members who ignored of realities of Parliamentary procedure because they had no responsibility. On the other hand, Shelburne, a former minister, was disingenuous when he complained that the Commons' propensity to encroach on the Lords' legislative integrity 'must materially impact, if not totally destroy the constitution'. He was not alone in regarding the Commons' preoccupation on this issue with concern: Charles James Fox protested in June 1783 that 'the order of the House, respecting money bills, was too strictly construed' by his colleagues.[37]

The Lords took various steps to limit the impact of the Commons' authority over financial matters. At the beginning of the century the upper House had protected itself by adopting a standing order (no. 25) against tacks – the adding of unrelated but potentially contentious items to bills of supply in order to ensure their passage. Because of restrictions on altering money bills, the Lords could not remove these extraneous items. This was a point on which the peers were especially attentive. After being prompted by Thurlow, the Duke of Leeds,[38] in his role as leader of the House, moved to throw out the Cocoa Nut Duty Bill in 1790 as a tack because it covered a range of topics.[39]

Yet, the issue of amended money bills was less complicated or contentious than it might seem. By the latter part of the century the two Houses had worked out an accommodation described by George Bramwell in his *Manner of Proceeding*. According to him, the Commons often, after rejecting a bill in which the Lords had amended a clause in violation of its orders on money bills, introduced a new one incorporating the offending clause. Lord Mansfield went so far as to maintain that the practice was routine. The Commons rejected the amended money bill, he noted, but 'they would introduce another with their lordships' amendment'.[40]

III: Other Sources of Institutional Conflict

The upper House was jealous of the privacy of its proceedings and assertive of its right to fine, even imprison those who reported its deliberations, maligned its members or

---

[36] Debrett, *Parl. Reg.*, ii, 236–7, 308; and *Parl. Reg.*, 2nd ser., lxiv, 252.
[37] McCahill, *House of Lords*, pp. 287; *PH*, xxxiii, cc. 808, 894.
[38] Francis Godolphin-Osborne (1751–99), summoned to Lords as Marquess of Carmarthen, 1776; Ld. of Bedchamber, 1776–7; Ld. Chamberlain to Queen, 1777–80; Ld. Lt. East Riding, 1778–80, 1782–99; Ambassador to France, 1783; Sec. of State Foreign Affairs, 1783–9; succ. as 5th Duke of Leeds, 1789; K.G. 1790.
[39] BL, Leeds Papers, Add. MS 28064, f. 198, Thurlow to Leeds, undated; *Parl. Debs.*, viii, c. 427.
[40] Bramwell, *The Manner of Proceeding on Bills in the House of Lords* (1831), p. 75; *PH*, xxiii, 1029. See also, *Correspondence of George III*, ed. Sir John Fortescue, vi, no. 4344, p. 380.

called into question its good standing. Throughout the 1760s and 1770s the 3rd Earl of Marchmont[41] avidly pursued offenders, many of whom were supporters of John Wilkes. The contests became intense during the Middlesex elections of the late 1760s. The issue came to a head, however, on 10 December 1770 during a tense discussion of the Falkland Islands crisis. As the Duke of Manchester moved an address to reinforce the British garrison at Gibraltar, he was interrupted by Earl Gower who demanded that the chamber be cleared in case a Spanish agent was present. Chaos ensued. According to Walpole, 'members of the Commons went down in a fury to their House following the outbreak in the Lords'. The volatile George Onslow 'made a complaint of the injurious manner in which they [MPs] had been thrust out by force... Lord North, to humour the Commons, joined in the blame, but dissuaded the motion. It was battled, however, for two hours, and some Lords who had come hither were turned out'.[42]

The episode of December 1770 created tensions that endured for four years during which no MP entered the upper chamber. The result was that the business of the Parliament was disrupted, and in a frenzied atmosphere, members' tempers flared when either House committed trivial infringements of established practices. An example occurred on 1 April 1772 when the Lords sent a master in chancery and a clerk assistant[43] to deliver several bills it had passed to the lower House. An observant MP, noting that the bills were not delivered by the usual messengers, moved first that the speaker not report the message and second that the House appoint a committee with respect to messengers.

William Burke reported from the committee that the usual pattern was for one of the judges (sometimes including the chief justice of the king's bench), or 'at least... two master(s) in chancery'[44] deliver bills from the Lords. He added that on the first day of the current session, the speaker had got into difficulty there and that:

> as he was leaving the chamber but before he got to the bar, some persons called out, Clear the House, Go out, withdraw, or to that effect, in a manner that he thought indecent... An MP added that the Lords' officers treated MPs 'as they did the mob'; another reported that while the King was passing bills, a door keeper took several MPs by their arms and pushed them out of the chamber.[45]

Fuelled by these reports the House turned aside several conciliatory motions. Jeremiah Dyson,[46] the expert on procedure, offered a compromise that would restore the

---

[41] Hugh Hume-Campbell (1693-1794), MP, Berwick-on-Tweed, 1734-40; succ. as 3rd Earl of Marchmont, 1740; 1st Commr. of Police [S], 1747-64; Rep. Peer [S], 1750-1784; Keeper of Great Seal [S], 1764-94.
[42] Walpole, *Memoirs*, iv, 145-6.
[43] According to Walpole, the clerk assistant 'was dressed like another master', *Memoirs*, iv, 77.
[44] The House of Commons established in the mid-seventeenth century that if one of the judges did not carry bills from the Lords, the task should be performed by two masters in chancery. *PH*, xvii, c. 425.
[45] *PH*, xvii, cc. 426-8. BL, Hardwicke Papers, Add. MS 35610, f. 183, Hardwicke Papers, James Harris to Hardwicke, 2 Apr. 1772.
[46] Jeremiah Dyson (?1722-76), MP, Yarmouth I.o.W., 1762-8, Weymouth and Melcombe Regis, 1768-74 and Horsham, 1774-6; Clerk of the House of Commons, 1748-62; Sec. to Treasury; 1762-May, 1764; Ld. of Trade, 1764-8 and of Treasury, 1768-74; Cofferer of Household, 1774-6.

legislative process. He moved that the Commons receive the message of the master of chancery and clerk, that the Commons 'take notice of the unusual method of sending messages to the House and desire the same may not hereafter be drawn into precedent'. His message was sent to the upper House after initially being defeated. The Lords responded that one of the masters being ill on the 9th, they had sent the clerk assistant in his place. In short, the fracas amounted to nothing but occurred amidst tensions that were intense as a result of the Lords' exclusions and because the two chambers were struggling to cope with Wilkite radicalism, the aftermath of the Middlesex elections, Dissenters' applications for relief from subscription to the 39 articles and the emerging crisis in the American colonies.[47]

Two months later a routine act by the Lords again provoked another silly outburst from the Commons. The occasion was an amendment which the peers added to Thomas Pownall's Corn Bill, which all admitted was a money bill.[48] The Commons' response on 18 June was notable for Edmund Burke's diatribe. He opened by expressing his desire for the restoration of good understanding between the two Houses and warning of the dangers of the current stalemated situation:

> when there is not easy intercourse between the two Houses, when their doors are shut upon members of each other, it is impossible to impart those mutual lights which are frequently necessary in the progress of a Bill. For want of this communication and this knowledge, I aver, that three Bills were lately lost in that House… The Lords do not know what is going forward in this House; and what is worse, they do not understand the principles of the constitution.

After this sensible introduction, Burke turned to the issue at hand. As he did, his measured speech turned into a rant in which he accused the Lords of

> invading a known and avowed right, inherent in this House as the representatives of the people. For what do the Lords say when they attempt to invade this privilege? Why, Sir, they plainly say to us and to the people, you shall no longer tax yourselves… Can liberty exist a moment, if we allow them to lay their sacrilegious hands upon this holy of holies, this palladium of the constitution?[49]

The Commons subsequently rejected the amended bill. Nevertheless, a new measure was introduced and passed in the following session. Reason was restored, despite Burke.

The Lords' doors remained closed to strangers for four years while reports of the Commons' proceedings continued to appear in the press. In 1771, Lord North permitted MPs to introduce motions to prosecute printers who published those materials. The famous 'printers' case' of 1771 followed on this decision. John Wilkes and Robert

---

[47] *PH*, xvii, cc. 430–1.
[48] The Lords added an amendment to the effect that 'no bounty should be paid upon exported corn'. *PH*, xvii, c. 512.
[49] *PH*, xvii, cc. 513–14.

Morris, Secretary of the Society of the Supporters of the Bill of Rights, convinced three printers to decline to appear before the House when summoned for violating the Commons' order against printing its proceedings. When William Whittam, the Commons' messenger, tried to arrest one of them, a City constable instead arrested Whittam for assault and false arrest. Though he was released after giving bail before Lord Mayor Crosby,[50] Alderman Oliver and Wilkes, the Commons subsequently committed Oliver and Crosby, both of them MPs, to the Tower. The episode made clear, however, that the Commons had no jurisdiction in the City, so it found itself unable to punish the printers. From this point publication of its proceedings became the norm.[51] The Lords, however, continued the fight – barring not only the press, but all 'strangers', including MPs. Their resistance did little to contain the press, but further aggravated relations with the Commons which in 1774 banned peers from their House.

The dispute between was resolved in 1774 when the Lords finally opened their doors to 'strangers'. The administration could no longer tolerate the perpetuation of squabbles that disrupted the business of legislation. The 2nd Lord Lyttleton[52] made an initial attempt to resolve the differences on 6 December. Though supported by Viscount Weymouth, the government's leader in the Lords, he failed.[53] Lyttleton was persistent: he moved again on the 18th to open the doors of the House to MPs and 'so many of the public at large as should be introduced by English peers'. Lord Chancellor Apsley[54] supported the motion which was accepted without debate.[55] Thereafter reports of proceedings in the Lords were published in the press.

IV: Co-ordination

It was to the interest of governments, individual sponsors of public bills and sponsors of specific and local legislation to co-ordinate the progress of their measures as they moved from one house to another. Key to success was bringing together parties who

---

[50] Brass Crosby (1725–93), MP, Honiton, 1768–74; London common council, 1758; purchased office of City Remembrancer, 1760; sheriff, London and Mdsx. 1764–5; alderman, London, 1764; Ld. Mayor, 1770–1.

[51] This discussion is based largely on John Brewer, 'The Wilkites and the law, 1763–74: A study of radical notions of governance', in *An Ungovernable People: The English and their Law in the Seventeenth and Eighteenth Centuries*, ed. John Brewer and John Styles (New Brunswick, NJ, 1780), pp. 128–71.

[52] Hon. Thomas Lyttleton (1744–79), MP, Bewdley, 1768–9; succ. fa. as 6th Bt., and as 2nd Baron Lyttleton, 1773; Chief Justice in Eyre North of Trent, 1775–9.

[53] Lord Marchmont described the views of the 28 Lords who voted to open the House as 'most monstrously repugnant to every Constitutional principle of the communication between the two Houses, & totally subversive to the rules of proceeding sanctioned by the uniform practice of men, who knew how to make themselves important without ever fetching sense from the Commons, & diverting the Mob by throwing abuse & dirt at one another'. National Library of Scotland, Rose MS, MS 3528, f. 7.

[54] Henry Bathurst (1714–94), MP, Cirencester, 1735–54; justice of the common pleas, 1754–78; Lord Chancellor, 1771–8; cr Baron Apsley, 1771; succ. fa. as 2nd Earl Bathurst, 1779; Lord President, 1779–82.

[55] Almon, *Parl. Reg.*, ii, 4–5; *PH*, xviii cc. 47–8; Walpole, *Last Journals*, i, 413.

had a potential interest in the legislation to create the widest possible agreement. A good example is the case of Thomas Gilbert's 1777 bill to enable patrons of livings to tap Queen Anne's Bounty for loans to build glebe houses to provide residences for poor curates (17 Geo. III, c. 52). Being a careful legislator, Gilbert submitted his measure in advance to the bishops, who according to Bishop Porteus[56] of Chester:

> made several useful alterations in it. The most material one was striking out the Clause which gave a power to the Incumbent with the consent of the Diocesan and Patron to raise money by letting Leases of 21 years of the Glebe or part of the Tithes. It was thought this was liable to great Abuse especially the leasing the glebe.[57]

Especially on any matters relating to the church or the law, it was essential to follow either Gilbert's example or for the authors of legislation to submit their bills to one or more of the judges. While doing so would not ensure success, failure was bound to provoke diatribes from one or more of those authorities and the likelihood that the delinquent measure would be thrown out in the upper House.

It was also routine for the sponsors of specific and local bills to recruit supporters in each House and begin to co-ordinate strategies even prior to arranging the introduction of their measure in the House of Commons. As noted in Chapter 5, even before they had finalised a draft of the petition for their bill, the committee of proprietors of the future Birmingham Canal ordered their clerk to write to the members for Warwickshire 'and such Lords and Members as are likely to assist us in the undertaking, requesting their Patronage and support'.[58]

While the proprietors of the Birmingham Canal may have been better organised than the typical proponents of specific or local bills, many of those who were interested in the outcome of these measures enlisted neighbours, and other allies in either House to support (or, depending on the circumstances – to oppose) the whole range of specific or local bills, especially if they were contested. To attend under these circumstances became a routine part of a member's or peer's duties.

In cases where differences arose on amendments made by the Lords to measures initiated in the Commons, representatives – members appointed by each House – met in conference. For the Commons' participants the goal was to point out which of the Lords' amendments their House found objectionable and refused to accept. Following the conference, the Lords' representatives returned to their chamber and presented a report listing the controversial amendments and, in some cases, explaining the reasons for the Commons' refusal to accept the Lords' alterations. Conferences were formal sessions in which information was exchanged. No negotiation occurred, nor did resolution of disputes take place. After the Lords had had time to deliberate on their members' report, the House dispatched another delegation to the Commons to report

---

[56] Dr. Beilby Porteus (1731–1808), Chaplain to Archbishop Secker, 1762, and to the King, 1769; Bishop of Chester, 1776; tr. to London, 1787.
[57] LPL, Porteus Notebooks, MSS 2098, f. 7. The bill passed without difficulty through each House.
[58] TNA, Rail, 810/1, Birmingham Canal Minute Book, ff. 16, 67.

whether they would insist upon any of their amendments or, as they did more frequently, bow to the Commons' demands.

A more substantive innovation occurred in the 1790s following the appointment of the 2nd Baron Walsingham[59] to the post of the Lords' Chairman of the Committees. Within two years of his installation, Walsingham established his right to receive specific and local bills while still under consideration in the Commons in order to make alterations he deemed necessary. This was a significant concession which permitted him to recommend amendments even to financial clauses before the measures had passed the Commons. The lower House seems to have accepted most of his recommendations – changes, which if made in the Lords, would have jeopardised a measure if they infringed upon the Commons' rights regarding money clauses.[60]

V: Legislative Friction

The Commons' legislation encountered a variety of obstacles when it reached the upper chamber. It was a standing and sometimes legitimate grievance in the Lords that so many bills arrived from the lower House during the final weeks of the session after many of the bishops had departed to undertake diocesan visitations and their lay colleagues had returned to their estates.

The consequence of this situation was either that government measures received cursory scrutiny before being returned, often unamended, by disgruntled peers, or that peers found excuses to throw out bills they claimed were too complicated to scrutinise in the short time left to them before Parliament was prorogued. Sometimes their motives in such instances were political. On 26 June 1788 Lord Sydney, who became more hostile to the tamest of reforms the longer he remained the Lords' leader, reacted to the motion to read the 3rd Earl of Stanhope's[61] bill for a reform of county elections by moving that its commitment be put for three months. He did so on the grounds that due to the importance of the bill,

> the multitude of clauses which it contained, and their extensive and complicated nature; and compared with the late period of the session, he felt himself under the necessity of their lordships opposing proceeding any further in a business which necessarily demanded so much consideration.[62]

Contrary to Sydney's prognosis, however, the bill made its way through the Lords before being thrown out at its third reading on 5 July.[63]

---

[59] Thomas De Grey (1748–1818), MP, Wareham, 1774; Tamworth, 1774–80 and Lostwithiel, 1780–1; succ. as 2nd Baron Walsingham, 1781; Groom of the Bedchamber, 1771–7; Ld. of Trade, 1777–81; Under-Sec. of State for American Dept., 1778–80; Vice-Treas. [I], 1784–7; Jt. Postmaster Gen., 1787–94; Chairman of Committees, House of Lords, 1794–1814.

[60] BL, Liverpool Papers, Add. MS 38231, f. 31, Walsingham to Liverpool 5 May 1796.

[61] Charles Stanhope, Viscount Mahon (1753–1816), MP Chipping Wycombe, 1780–6; succ. fa. as 3rd Earl Stanhope, 1786.

[62] PH, xxvi, c. 178.

[63] PH, xxvi, c. 179. Sydney was not an unbiased source: in a letter to Lord Hawkesbury on 12 June, he described Stanhope as 'that insufferable madman'. BL, Add. MS, 38223, f. 87, Sydney to Hawkesbury, 12 June 1788.

Another of the peers' grievances was the poor quality of measures that came up from the lower House. The judges repeatedly complained of this problem. During a debate on George Townshend's Militia Bill of 1757, Chancellor Hardwicke[64] charged that MPs 'being destitute of the advice and assertions of the judges, are apt to pass laws which are either unnecessary or ridiculous, and almost every law they pass stands in need of some new law for explaining and amending it'.[65] Nor were claims of this sort restricted to the law lords. In 1785 Lord Stormont[66] attributed the extensive amendments the Lords made to the government's Public Offices Bill as a justification for the upper chamber's existence and a tribute to the peers' vigilance in

> not suffering it to pass as it had been presented by the Lower House for their concurrence was... an instance of the regard and jealousy of that honourable station which they possess in the Government of their country. The sending the bill back to the other House with amendments would convince the authors of this bill that their [sic] existed in their Lordships not only a power but a disposition to correct either their negligence or their ignorance, in whatever bills they might thus produce for their acquiescence. This he therefore trusted, would cause them to be more careful and circumspect in the future.[67]

These remarks were not designed to contribute legislative harmony between the two Houses but were an inevitable by-product of the Lords' status as Parliament's revising chamber.

A prime example of lordly arrogance and condescension occurred in 1786 when Lord Loughborough convinced his colleagues to throw out Wilberforce's bill to regulate the disposal of the bodies of executed criminals. Loughborough believed it was a 'Bill of so serious a nature, so important in its consequences' that he had to call upon the lords to put an end to it. The bill affected 'the criminal justice of the country by altering it in mode and execution' and imposed hardships upon the judges. According to Loughborough, holding out for criminals the prospect of public dissection was a deterrent for those who might commit similar crimes and as such had been 'of advantage to the community'. He also criticised the fact that the bill made dissection and the loss of burial rights the result of crimes of very different magnitudes ranging from murder to robbery of a few shillings.[68]

Finally, he complained that Wilberforce had not submitted the measure to the judges before bringing it into the House, suggesting:

---

[64] Philip Yorke (1690-1764), MP, Lewes, 1719-22 and Seaford, 1722-33; Solicitor Gen., 1720-4; Attorney-Gen., 1724-33; C.J., King's Bench, 1733-7; Ld. Chancellor, 1737-56; cr. Baron Hardwicke, 1733 and Earl of Hardwicke, 1754.
[65] *PH*, xv, c.724.
[66] David Murray (1727-96), succ. as 7th Viscount Stormont [S], 1748; representative peer, Scotland, 1754-96; Minister to Saxony, 1755-64; Ambassador to France, 1772-8; Sec. of State, (North); Leader of the House of Lords, 1779-82; Lord President, 1783, 1794-6; succ. as 2nd Earl of Mansfield, 1794.
[67] *The Times*, 13 Apr. 1785.
[68] Peter King, *Punishing the Criminal Corpse, 1700-1840: Aggravated Forms of the Death Penalty in England* (1988), p. 142.

that it would have been natural... that any gentleman, who thought of a project for altering the criminal law, & its mode of execution, would at least have asked the opinion some one of more of the judges, & shewn his intended Bill to him.

And he took up the old charge that the bill was drafted in a 'loose manner', which led in turn to a lecture on the impropriety of

men not conversant with law, turning projects in respect to it, & in moments of vivacity coming forward with raw, jejune, ill-advised, and impracticable schemes for the mode of distributing and carrying into execution the criminal justice of the country.

While conceding that Wilberforce may have had the best of intentions, Loughborough dismissed his effort, informing his listeners that the author of the bill was 'not aware that the criminal justice of the country was too weighty to be lightly handled, or rendered the subject of a speculative project'. He concluded by moving that the bill be reported from its committee in three months, a motion the House adopted.[69]

When they wrote their father's biography, his sons contradicted Loughborough's condescending narrative of events surrounding the bill. The measure was not, they maintained, created by laymen. The Solicitor General, Archibald Macdonald,[70] drew up the bill, and Richard Pepper Arden, the Attorney General, corrected it. Once drafted, it 'was put into the hands of one of the most active of judges who undertook to communicate upon the subject with the rest of the bench at a general meeting'. According to his sons, Wilberforce encouraged 'some of the principal lawyers to speak... with any of the judges over whom they possessed influence'. The bill was returned to him with amendments, and though he disliked them, 'yet on the grounds of policy, [he] submitted to them'.[71] In fact the measure that Loughborough criticises had been redrafted by the government's law officers and reintroduced in 1786 as a government measure with the support of William Pitt.[72]

Wilberforce's experience was not unique. Charles Abbot,[73] for a time the speaker of the House of Commons, recorded an instance in which Loughborough, by then the Lord Chancellor, objected to his Copyright Bill in 1801 – not to the principle, but to some of its phrases. When shown that previous acts justified them, he still opposed. Two days after the initial encounter Loughborough admitted that had he known Abbot was sponsoring the measure 'he would have taken as much care of it as if it had been

---

[69] *PH*, xxvi, cc. 195–9, 200–1, 5 July 1786.
[70] Archibald Macdonald (1747–1826) MP, Hindon, 1777–80 and Newcastle-under-Lyme, 1780–93; Solicitor Gen. 1784–8; Attorney Gen. 1788–93; Ld. Chief Baron of the Exchequer, 1793–1813.
[71] R.I. and Samuel Wilberforce, *Life of Wilberforce*, i, pp. 114–15.
[72] For a discussion of Pitt's motives in taking up this measure, see Simon Devereux, 'Inexperienced humanitarians? William Wilberforce and William Pitt and the execution crisis of the 1780s', *Law and History Review*, xxxiii (2015), 839–85.
[73] Charles Abbot (1757–1829), MP, Helston, 1795–1802, New Woodstock, 1802–6 and Oxford University, 1806–17; Clerk of Rules, 1794–1801; Chief Sec. to Ld. Lt. [I], 1801–2; Sec. of State, [I], 1801–2; Keeper of Privy Seal [I], 1801–29; Speaker of House of Commons, 1802–17; cr. Baron Colchester, 1817.

his own'. Accordingly, the Bill passed, 'though not without some difficulty in the Commons, as a result of some of the alterations made in the Lords'.[74]

As Lord Chancellor for almost 14 years, Lord Thurlow established himself as even more of a martinet than Loughborough. It was not uncommon for him to greet a bill upon its arrival by dismissing it as 'a MASS of NONSENSE put together by some person who pretended to know law'.[75] Thurlow was at odds with Pitt and some of his cabinet colleagues by the late 1780s and early 1790s, so he would even tie up government measures in the Lords. For example, at the end of July 1789 he blamed the solicitor general for the Tobacco Bill's faulty drafting, which he said 'arose from want of due attention in those whose business it was to draw up and superintend the clauses'. This was typical', he added, 'of the slovenly manner in which Bills were framed'. The next year he attacked a clause in another Tobacco Bill. Having moved for the removal of the offensive clause and carried his point with the support of other ministers at odds with Pitt, Thurlow announced that he wished to amend the bill further. Though the Duke of Leeds countered that the amendments would complicate the measure's passage, Thurlow added his alterations to what was a money bill. Leeds eventually staged a counter coup and passed the bill without any of the Lords' amendments, returning it to the Commons in the same state as it had arrived.[76]

Usually, Thurlow, however, carried his points in the House of Lords where he enjoyed an extensive following. The Earl of Pembroke[77] records an incident in 1781 when the House initially beat back his attempt to throw out a divorce bill at its first reading. Not to be thwarted, he patched together a majority when, according to Pembroke, 'nobody expected any further debate, and threw out the bill'.[78] In a similar vein, Bishop Warren of Bangor reported that after passing the Commons without opposition, a bill to relieve the bishops of the Scottish Episcopal Church of the penalties under which they had laboured, the measure was postponed in the Lords without any word being spoken, 'it being privately understood that the Chancellor [Thurlow] disapproved of its present shape'.[79]

Not all judges were as obstructive or hostile to innovation as Thurlow or Loughborough. Though detested by Wilkite radicals,[80] Lord Mansfield, according to some current authorities, was the 'founder of the commercial law', and his decision in the Sommerset Case in 1770 was a decisive blow against slavery in England. By discharging Sommerset and declaring that the powers of a slave owner over a slave were not known to English law, he effectively ended slavery there, although that was not the intent of his decision.[81] One of Lloyd Kenyon's first acts as Attorney General in

---

[74] TNA, PRO, 30/9/33, Colchester Papers, 29 June 1801.
[75] *The Times*, 7 June 1791, referring to the Popery Bill.
[76] *The Times*, 30, 31 July, 7 Aug. 1789. For the circumstances surrounding Thurlow's dismissal, see G.M. Ditchfield, 'Lord Thurlow', in *Lords of Parliament. Studies: 1714–1914* (Stanford, CA, 1995), pp. 72–6.
[77] Henry Herbert (1734–94), succ. as 10th Earl of Pembroke, 1750; General, 1782; Ld. of Bedchamber to Prince of Wales, 1756 and to King, 1760–3, 1770–80; Gov. Portsmouth, 1782–94.
[78] Lord Herbert, ed., *Pembroke Papers (1780–1794): Letters and Diaries of Henry, Tenth Earl of Pembroke and his Circle* (1950).
[79] BL, Berkeley MSS, Add MS 39312, ff. 99–100, Warren to Berkeley, 7 July 1789.
[80] See Brewer, 'The Wilkites and the law', 140, 155–9.
[81] Edmund Herward, *Lord Mansfield* (Chichester and London, 1979), pp. 105, 144–7.

the second Rockingham administration was to introduce legislation requiring holders of offices including the treasurer of the navy and the paymaster general of the forces to account for the huge gains they often made from the public money they held until it was disbursed for public purposes. Though he was a member of a reforming administration, his proposal failed because of opposition from his colleagues, including Charles James Fox.[82] When in 1788 Lord Stanhope's bill for the reform of county elections was ready for presentation to the House of Commons, Pitt called upon Kenyon to present it to the Commons which he did.[83]

The law lords' substantial influence in the upper House meant that useful or humane bills failed to reach the statute books. A number of peers also found that their presence stifled legislative proceedings. In 1780, at the end of proceedings on the Cricklade Election Bill, Lord Fortescue[84] protested that:

> the dignity of that House would be lowered and tarnished by the profusion of lawyers which time might occasionally introduce into it. It was no longer a House of Peers; it was converted into a mere court of law, where all solid and honorable principles of truth and justice were shamefully sacrificed to low, pettifogging chicanery and quibbles used in Westminster Hall. That once venerable, dignified, and august assembly, resembled more a meeting of attornies than a House of Parliament.[85]

The judges were not alone in preventing legislative innovation. As already discussed in Chapter 4, the bishops took an active part in turning aside efforts to end the requirement that Anglican clergy, undergraduates at Oxford and Cambridge Universities and Dissenting ministers and teachers subscribe to the 39 articles. They along with Oxford dons proposed restrictions before agreeing to relaxations of the Test and Corporations Acts as they affected Dissenters in 1779. Nor were these their only interventions. The same year Shute Barrington[86] responded to the increase in the number of applications for divorce bills by bringing in a bill 'to degrade the Adultress from her Rank when she has any, to limit the allowance to be made to her & to prevent her from marrying at all for a certain time, & then not to marry the Adulterer'. Prior to presenting his bill, he had consulted with Thurlow and Blackstone on its formulation. The measure was generally well received in the Lords, though Lord Effingham and the Dukes of Manchester and Richmond argued that it was 'idle to enforce Morality by Penal Laws' and that men were generally the most culpable. The Lords approved the measure, but it failed in the Commons.[87]

---

[82] Fox's speech is found in *PH*, xxxii, 1128–37; Hon. George T. Kenyon, *The Life of Lloyd, First Lord Kenyon, Lord Chief Justice of England* (1873), pp. 90–3.
[83] HMC, *Kenyon MSS*, p. 525.
[84] Matthew Fortescue (1719–85), succ. as 2nd Baron Fortescue, 1751.
[85] *PH*, xxiii, 1387.
[86] Shute Barrington (1734–1826), Chaplain to the King, 1760; Bishop of Llandaff, 1769; tr. to Salisbury, 1782 and to Durham, 1792.
[87] Lambeth Palace Library, Porteus Notebooks, MSS 2098, f. 91.

VI: Commons' Bills Lost in the Lords, 1754–90

Julian Hoppit's *Failed Legislation* shows that 126 bills introduced by 78 MPs sitting for English constituencies failed in the upper House between 1754 and 1790.[88] Among the most numerous group of measures that lapsed in the upper chamber were those relating to the relief of the poor (c. 12 measures). Many were introduced by backbench MPs who had established records of legislating in this area. Among them are Dowdeswell's bill allowing parish annuities for the poor in 1777, Thomas Gilbert's Rogues and Vagabonds Bill, part of his poor law programme of 1781,[89] and John Rolle's unsuccessful Poor Bill of 1789, one of several such measures he introduced in the late 1780s, most of which failed before they reached the Lords. Closely related to these defeated measures were a series of unsuccessful bills introduced by Lord Maitland[90] in 1784 and John Sawbridge between 1785 and 1789 for the relief of insolvent debtors, which fell prey to the judges. James Bland Burges'[91] potentially useful Debtors and Creditors Bill secured the Commons' approval but proceeded no further after reaching the Lords. Among other categories of measures passed by the Commons that failed in the Lords were 11 enclosure bills, eight road or streets bills and Sir Henry Hoghton's measures for the relief of Dissenters in 1772 and 1773.

There were other potentially useful reforms that failed in the upper House. These included several bills to prevent bribery at elections, proposed by Lord Mahon, two in 1783 and one in 1784. In addition to his bribery bills, Mahon presented legislation in 1785 and 1786 to better secure the rights of electors at county elections. In the latter instance, the measure provoked exasperated comments from Lord Sydney, who tried to set it aside because of the lateness of the session before it was rejected by his colleagues.[92] In addition to these thwarted reforms, the Lords rejected several notable social reforms, including Sir Charles Bunbury's Criminal Laws Bill of 1772, one part of his crusade to reduce the multitude of laws imposing the death penalty.[93] Another of Bunbury's measures, this one to repeal 21 Jac. I, c. 27, also failed in the Lords. The purpose of this terrible act was to prevent the murder of bastard children by imposing the death sentence on mothers who concealed the deaths of their infant bastard children. The statute presumed that by concealing those deaths the mother was guilty of their murder. Bunbury introduced his bill on 21 February 1776: Burke, Fox and Sir William Meredith also argued for the act's repeal, and the Commons passed it by 5 March.[94] Despite the fact that the act was rarely enforced, the Lords' second reading committee in March put off its report for six months.[95]

---

[88] Hoppit's list does not include Thomas Gilbert's 1765 Poor Bill which failed in the House of Lords due to political machinations.
[89] See Chapter 5, p. 110.
[90] James Maitland, Lord Maitland (1759–1839), MP Newport, 1780–4 and Malmesbury, 1784–9; succ. as 8th Earl of Lauderdale (S), 1789; representative peer of Scotland, 1790–6; Keeper of Great Seal of Scotland, 1806–7; Commr. to France, 1806–7; cr. Baron Lauderdale [UK], 1806; K.T., 1821.
[91] James Bland Burges (1752–1824), MP, Helston, 1787–90; Bankruptcy Commr., 1777–83; Under-Sec. of State, Foreign Affairs, 1789–95; Night Marshal of the Household, 1795–1824.
[92] Ghita Stanhope and G.P. Gooch, *The Life of Charles, Third Earl Stanhope* (1914), pp. 64–5.
[93] *LJ*, xxxiii, 434.
[94] Radzinowicz, *Criminal Law*, i, pp. 431–5.
[95] Hoppit, *Failed Legislation*, pp. 438–9.

The upper chamber also rejected Blackstone's second creditors' relief bill of 1767, later celebrated by Sir William Holdsworth, and 15 years later it rejected Sir William Dolben's bill to enable men to remain heads of colleges at Oxford and Cambridge Universities after they married.[96]

All of these bills were apolitical, and their defeat had few long-term repercussions. That was not the case with the Lords' rejection of Charles Fox's controversial India Bill on 15 and 17 December 1783. The circumstances behind these well-chronicled events date back to the formation of the Coalition between Fox and Lord North the previous March, if not before. After a prolonged delay George III unwillingly allowed the former political opponents to form an administration which he detested as being imposed upon him. The Coalition caused shocks among the political elite. Some authorities[97] have claimed that the disapproval had largely dissipated by the summer, though evidence shows it continued to alienate individuals across the political spectrum.[98]

The India Bill certainly undermined support for the coalition government. Crafted by Edmund Burke as a key part of his campaign to cleanse the government of India, the measure followed on efforts of previous administrations to control the East India Company and its employees. To do so, Burke set aside its Court of Directors and Proprietors. In their place, he granted seven commissioners, appointed by Parliament at the recommendation of the ministers, the authority to select India's rulers. The commissioners could be removed only by a vote of the Commons. Also, nine deputy commissioners, subject to the seven commissioners, were to monitor the company's trade. The bill provoked strong opposition because of its assault on the company's privileges specified in its charter, and because by granting India's patronage to commissioners nominated by Parliament, it would, according to Lord North, enable critics to mount the cry of 'influence of party against the Crown & People'. Since all the commissioners were aligned politically with the Coalition, it was easy to regard the effort as a political power grab. Loughborough, the Coalition's leader in the Lords, worried that the 'Curse of India will be the Ruin first of the Administration & then of the Country'.[99] The bill cruised through the House of Commons, but opposition to it mounted in the Lords, though ministers made ineffectual efforts to enlist support there.

Early in December Thurlow and Earl Temple[100] presented the King with a memo recommending that he inform peers and bishops through an intermediary that he opposed the India Bill. This was only part of a wider scheme which would lead to the dismissal of the Coalition ministry following the Lords' rejection of the India Bill in the Lords and the appointment of a new Minister. For this post the conspirators settled on

---

[96] Hoppit, *Failed Legislation*, pp. 466–7; *LJ*, xxxvi, 612.
[97] John Cannon, *The Fox-North Coalition: The Crisis of the Constitution, 1782–1784* (Cambridge, 1969), pp. 61–3; Leslie G. Mitchell, *Charles James Fox and the Disintegration of the Whig Party, 1782–1794* (1971), p. 61.
[98] McCahill, *House of Lords*, pp. 182–4.
[99] BL, Auckland MSS, Add. MS 34413, f. 296, W. Eden to Morton Eden, 21 Nov. 1783 and ff. 305–6, Loughborough to Eden, Thursday evening [Dec. 1783].
[100] George Nugent Temple Grenville (1753–1813), MP, Buckinghamshire, 1774–9; succ. as 3rd Earl Temple, 1779; cr. Marquess of Buckingham, 1784; Sec. of State, Foreign Affairs, 19–22 Dec. 1783; Ld. Lt [I], 1782–3, 1787–9; Ld. Lt., Bucks., 1782–1813.

William Pitt. They entered into the plot, according to Cannon, in which the King relied upon the Earl of Clarendon[101] and the Hanoverian minister to act as intermediaries to Pitt. These two were to secure Pitt's promise to take office in the event the Lords rejected the Bill and the King dismissed the Coalition. In the meantime, John Robinson was preparing a state of the Lords to determine the likelihood of the peers rejecting the Bill once the King's views were made known. His survey indicated defeat was likely in that case.

Because the details of the plot remained secret, the Coalition's leaders remained confident of victory: Fox predicted in the early hours of 15 December that he would have a majority of 30, even after Lord Temple had revealed on 13 December that the King would look upon those peers who supported the measure as his enemies.[102] In fact, the Lords rejected the bill at its second reading on the 15th by a vote of 87–79, and two days later it was thrown out by 95 to 76. George III then dismissed the Coalition ministry on 18 December and called Pitt to form a new administration.[103]

What followed was a stalemate that immobilised British government for several months. On 17 December William Baker introduced two resolutions in the Commons. The first declared that any report of the King's opinion on a pending measure with the intention of influencing the conduct of members was 'a high crime and misdemeanor, derogatory to the honour of the Crown, a breach of the fundamental privileges of Parliament, and subversive of the fundamental privileges of the constitution'. The second called for the House to resolve itself into a committee of the whole House to consider the state of the nation. Both were agreed on by a vote of 225 to 153.[104] The committee remained in session for much of the next month, as Fox and his colleagues inveighed against the new government, charging that it lacked legitimacy because of the questionable circumstances of its appointment and lacked a majority in the House of Commons. On 19 January, Fox claimed that Pitt came into office 'upon unconstitutional grounds, and upon such principles as were disgraceful to himself,... & as must necessarily deprive him and his coadjutors of the confidence of that House'.[105] For the next six weeks the Commons refused to ratify the new minister's revenue measures or renew the Mutiny Bill.

The House of Lords, however, on 4 February adopted resolutions condemning what a majority regarded as the Commons' unconstitutional actions. Lords Thurlow and Gower denounced the Commons' obstruction of the executive, setting the stage for the 3rd Duke of Richmond to offer a classic statement of the Lords' role as the constitution's equipoise. He reminded peers that it was their 'duty as hereditary counsel of the Crown, to interfere whenever the Commons or the Crown, in the exercise of their respective functions, clash with each other'. In such circumstances, they were called upon to

---

[101] Hon. Thomas Villiers (1709–86), MP, Tamworth, 1747–56; Envoy to Poland, 1738–41, 44–6; Minister to Austria, 1742–3; Envoy to Prussia, 1746; Ld. of Admiralty, 1748–56; cr. Baron Hyde, 1756; Jt. Paymaster Gen. 1763–5, 1786; Chancellor of Duchy of Lancaster, 1771–82; 1783–6; cr. Earl of Clarendon, 1776.
[102] McCahill, *House of Lords*, p. 185.
[103] *PH*, xxiv, 160; *LJ*, xxxvii, 37; *Later Correspondence*, i, xxvi.
[104] *PH*, xxiv, 199.
[105] *PH*, xxiv, 199, 312.

censure the extreme claims of the Commons and uphold the right of the King to select his own ministers, which the Lords did by a vote of 100–53.[106]

Pitt's determination to persist eventually wore down his opponents. Fox and his followers after more than six weeks of opposition finally provided the votes to grant supplies and pass the Mutiny Act. Once they did, the King dissolved Parliament, and at the subsequent elections Pitt secured a substantial majority.[107]

The electoral victory was accompanied by an outpouring of loyal addresses dispatched to the King. Their profusion and vehemence shocked former coalitionists. William Eden complained to Lord Sheffield that 'the Country is utterly mad for Prerogative;... but his Majesty seems to be placing his Crown upon the back of a Runaway Horse. It was offensive enough when Fox used to talk of the Majesty of the People, but I never expected to see the Court of St. James enter into that Copartnership'.[108]

The India Bill and its aftermath had a profound impact on the politics of Westminster over the next decade. Fox and his allies were unable to see in Pitt any semblance of integrity. It took the French Revolution, the advance of revolutionary armies and the threat of domestic radicals for conservative Whigs to reconcile themselves to Pitt and finally break with Fox.

VII: Conclusion

Because I knew less than I now know about the House of Commons at the time I wrote the book on the Lords, this chapter presents a more negative picture of the relations between the two Houses than the earlier work. Based on the narratives presented in this and previous chapters, it is apparent that relations between the two were more contentious than I had acknowledged in my earlier work.

Nevertheless, there were factors that contributed to the harmony of eighteenth-century Parliaments. The most notable was that between 25 and 29 per cent of English MPs returned at elections between 1761 and 1784 owed their seats to peers, with the result that both on legislative and political questions they acted as their noble masters instructed. The Lords was also successful in setting some limits on the Commons privileges relating to money by establishing its right to reject tacks and later to amend enclosure bills. As Lord Mansfield noted, the Commons also incorporated the Lords' amendments to money bills into new legislation which they passed and sent back to the upper House. In short, the two Houses could reach accommodations on contentions procedural issues.

Still, peers were disdainful in their criticisms of bills which came up from the Commons. The judges were the main culprits, but they were not alone. These sorts of reactions were an inevitable consequence of the Lords' role as Parliament's revising chamber, but they engendered ill will, especially when the charges, as in the case of

---

[106] *PH*, xxix, 507.
[107] *HPC, 1754–1790*, i, 87–96; Ehrman, *The Younger Pitt: The Years of Acclaim*, pp. 142–9.
[108] BL, Auckland MSS, Add. MS 45728, ff. 75–6, Eden to Sheffield, 10 Apr. 1784.

Lord Loughborough's assault on Wilberforce's bill allowing for the burial of executed criminals, seem to have been unjustified.

Sloppy drafting of measures initiated in the Commons was a problem. It increased the costs of legislating, often forcing proponents of imperfectly drafted measures passed in one session to introduce corrected versions later. The hasty revision of William Dolben's Slave Trade Regulation Bill in 1788 unnecessarily extended the length of the Parliamentary session and led to a confusing back and forth as the two Houses rushed to pass the measure. The same incident showed that the Lords' capacity to make revisions was also inhibited by the Commons' practice of sending up controversial bills towards the end of the session. Complaints of this sort became increasingly common in the late 1780s as Parliament dealt with a wider array of financial and colonial legislation, some of which only arrived in the Lords in late June and July.[109]

Moreover, it is notable that as more backbench MPs were initiating legislation on a range of penal, penitentiary, poor law questions or those relating to imprisoned debtors, the Lords became increasingly aggressive in rejecting those measures. Many of the measures were the work of knights of the shire who had long experience in the affairs of local government and the militia as a result of their service as justices of the peace. Joanna Innes, David Eastwood and Richard Connors have made particular note of the degree to which these MPs drew upon their experience in local government to frame national legislation that addressed questions ranging from prison and legal reform to the poor law and the militia. While some of their efforts sometimes lapsed in the Commons, they more frequently failed in the upper House where they sometimes faced peremptory dismissal.

Political radicals, including London's John Sawbridge and Lord Mahon, also introduced political reforms. Sawbridge's attempts to shorten the life of Parliaments annually foundered in the Commons, but several of Mahon's efforts, as noted above, were lost in the Lords.

As I noted in my book on the Lords, the peers' consistent obstruction of the abolition question in the 1790s and its refusal in the early nineteenth century to weaken 'Old Corruption' by eliminating reversions provoked sustained outcries.[110] In 1792 supporters of abolition bombarded Parliament with 509 petitions in support of their project. Nevertheless, the Lords delayed progress on the measure by undertaking a so-called investigation into the trade whose leisurely proceedings dragged on to 1795. *The Times* and the *Annual Register* both criticised the upper chamber for its dilatory proceedings, the latter charging they were 'met with the general disapprobation of all mankind'.[111] In fact, obstructive tactics of this sort called into question the legitimacy of the House of Lords

---

[109] The House of Lords did not adjourn in 1788 until 11 July, in part because of the prolonged proceedings on Dolben's Slave Trade Regulation Bill and in 1789 until 11 August because of the disruptions caused as the result of the King's temporary incapacity. For a brief discussion of imperial legislation during this period see Julian Hoppit, *Britain's Political Economies: Parliament and Economic Life, 1660–1800* (Cambridge, 2017), especially pp. 124–9.

[110] A reversion granted to the recipient the right to succession to an office or some other emolument under the Crown upon the death of the occupant. It was a much sought after form of patronage. McCahill, *The House of Lords in the Age of George III* (London, 2009), 229–31 and 264–71.

[111] *Annual Register* (1792), p. 115; *The Times*, 23 June 1788.

among the supporters of the abolition question. Thus, when he moved the second reading of the bill to abolish the trade in February 1807, Lord Grenville addressed the issue of the Lords' obstruction and the impact it had had on the public standing of the House:

> In calling your attention to this great measure, let me entreat you to consider that the whole country looks to the Parliament to wipe away the stigma attached to its character in continuing this detestable traffic; that it looks not merely to Parliament but to your lordships' house. Twice has this measure failed in this house, and if this iniquitous traffic is not now abolished, the guilt will rest with your lordships.[112]

The failure of the relatively minor reversion bills, which were introduced by the backbench reformer Henry Bankes,[113] with the support of other independent MPs, including Henry Thornton and J.P. Bastard between 1807 and 1810, provoked strong protests from the public and many MPs. Moderate MPs including J.W. Ward[114] lamented that the behaviour of the House of Lords in 1807 showed it refused 'to assist the house of commons in redeeming the pledge which the Commons had a few years ago given the people to enquire into and reform public abuses',[115] while Samuel Whitbread declared that obstruction would only provoke further public agitation. In succeeding debates several speakers stressed that their primary obligation was to the public: George Tierney announced that 'it was his first, his chief, and almost his only duty to attend to the interests of the people, regardless of the impact that conduct might have on the House of Lords'.[116] Given the Lords' obstruction, the Commons had to uphold the rights of the people. It was their paramount duty, Tierney maintained, to adhere to those rights as petitions poured in in support of reversion bills. As he reintroduced a renewed bill after it had faced a series of defeats in the upper House in April 1809, Lord Porchester[117] emphasised that his measure:

> was the first practical act recommended by two successive committees appointed by that house... In that house it had been received without a dissentient voice; even the King's ministers did not feel it justifiable or politic to interfere with it in its passage through that house. But an opposition formidable in its means and personnel and persevering in its hostility appeared in another branch of the

---

[112] *Parl. Debs.*, viii, c. 663.
[113] Henry Bankes (1756–1834), MP, Corfe Castle, 1780–1826 and Dorset, 1826–31.
[114] Hon. John William Ward (1781–1833), MP, Downton, 1802–July 1803, Worcestershire, 1803–6, Petersfield, 1806–7, Wareham, 1807–12, Ilchester, 1812–18 and Bossiney, 1818–23; succ. fa. as 4th Visc. Dudley and Ward 1823; cr. Earl of Dudley, 1827; Sec. of State, Foreign affairs, Apr. 1827–May 1828.
[115] *Parl. Debs.*, x, 1260–2.
[116] *Parl. Debs.*, x, cc. 1262–4, 1266, 1339, 1342; xiv, 12, 19. According to Philip Harling, Bankes did not favour political reform. He saw the elimination of reversions and other measures of 'public economy as an effective way of stifling radicals'. 'Parliament, the state and "Old Corruption": Conceptualizing reform, c. 1790–1832', in *Rethinking the Age of Reform: Britain 1780–1850*, ed. Arthur Burns and Joanna Innes (Cambridge, 2003), p. 2006.
[117] Henry George Herbert, Lord Porchester (1772–1833), MP, Cricklade, 1794–1811; Maj. W. Som. Yeoman Cav., 1798; Lt. Col., 1798; Col. 1803; succ. fa. as 2nd Earl of Carnarvon, 1811.

legislature, and was for a time successful, not only against the unanimous feeling of that house, but also against the general and expressive voice of the country.[118]

Such was the extent of public pressure that even Lord Sidmouth, a reactionary politician, supported a bill which renewed the Reversion Bill annually between 1808 and 1810. He told his brother:

> Considering how it [the bill] has been opposed in Parliament & what is felt about it out of Doors, I am satisfied that the Rejection of it would tend to produce all those Consequences which it is the professed & real object of those who resist it to avert. I believe this so strongly that I shall certainly vote for the Bill, altho' I do not think that any great public Interest is involv'd in it, except that which is created by public Feeling & Opinion.[119]

Unnerved by the public furore and annoyed by the persistent opposition of two of the King's sons who encouraged courtiers and bishops, normally a mainstay of government support in the Lords, to continue resisting the bill, Spencer Perceval and the 2nd Earl of Liverpool[120] marshalled the government's forces and succeeded in forcing through annual renewals of the Reversion Bill.[121]

'The expressive voice of the people' had, with the support of their representatives in the Commons, forced the diehard lords to relent in the face of more serious challenges to the legitimacy of their House. Members of the groups who in 1799 had 'defined the British political order as based on the principle of the sovereignty of the people'[122] must not only have taken some satisfaction in seeing their ideas result in this modest triumph, but also have been heartened by the passion and energy of the public and the tenacity of MPs in upholding the views of those they represented.

During the 1770s and 1780s the Lords rejected the reform measures of MPs without incurring sustained criticism from the press or members of the Commons. That was not true by the 1790s and the early nineteenth century, especially when the measures involved related to abolition or curtailing 'Old Corruption'. Proceedings on these bills testify to the impact that the provincial and national press and petitioning campaigns had on the conduct of MPs. To a far greater degree than during earlier decades, a fairly wide array of members cited public attitudes, not just in shaping their views of the House of Lords, but, as we saw in an earlier chapter, in shaping their attitudes on pending legislation relating to local and national questions.

---

[118] *Parl. Debs.*, xiv, c. 19. Motion def. 121–106.
[119] Devon Record Office, Sidmouth Papers, 152n/c 1808/OZ: Sidmouth to Hiley Addington, 4 Apr. 1808. See also Harling, *The Waning of 'Old Corruption': The Politics of Economical Reform in Britain, 1779–1846* (Oxford, 1996), p. 116.
[120] Robert Banks Jenkinson (1770–1827), MP Rye, 1790–1803; summoned to House of Lords as Baron Hawkesbury, 1803; Commr. Bd. of Control, 1793–9; Ld. of Trade, 1799; Master of Mint, 1799–1801; Sec. of State, Foreign Affairs, 1801–4; for Home Affairs, 1804–Jan. 1806; Mar. 1807–9; for War and Colonies, 1809–12; First Lord of Treasury, 1812–27; succ. as 2nd Earl of Liverpool, 1808.
[121] See McCahill, *House of Lords*, pp. 229–30.
[122] Pasi Ihalainen, *Agents of the People*, p. 499.

11

Conclusion

This book has shown that English MPs in the latter half of the eighteenth century were often diligent and active legislators who were attentive to the needs of their constituents, especially in attending to their proposals for the specific and local legislation that formed much of Parliament's legislative agenda between 1754 and 1800. As time went on county members were more often assisted by their respective county's borough members and its 'landlord representatives' in these tasks. Knights of the shire continued to serve as invaluable allies for interest groups, as Thomas Stanley was for Manchester cotton manufacturers who required allies to secure the repeal of the fustian excise or as Frederick Montagu proved when he guided legislation through the House which established the cotton industry on the same legal basis as its woollen and linen competitors.

Borough members were not to be outdone by county MPs as they achieved notable legislative accomplishments of their own. After decades of frustrating struggle between competing factions at Hull, Walter Spencer Stanhope and Samuel Thornton, working with Yorkshire's MPs, were able to impose a plan for an enlarged dock that would meet the needs of the town's port. Sir Roger Newdigate, an otherwise polarising figure in the House, carried as a result of timely compromise and deft manoeuvring the landmark Oxford Improvement Bill to the delight of the town and his University constituents. As Joanna Innes and Louise Ryland-Epton have shown, Thomas Gilbert adopted a new mode of legislating. The result was that his poor law legislation reflected the results not only of his fellow MPs' deliberations but tapped the expertise of county magistrates and informed philanthropists. It was a uniquely collaborative approach that drew upon the wisdom of men who would ultimately have responsibility for implementing the legislation he hoped to secure. The method did not guarantee the passage of his measures, but it endowed them with greater legitimacy.[1]

Gilbert stands out also because he was perhaps the most versatile and active of the MPs who went beyond enclosure, turnpike, navigation and improvement bills and instead carried an array of general measures. These bills supplemented the finance bills, legislation to maintain the army and navy and the ever larger volume of bills relating to the empire that formed the core of a late eighteenth-century government's annual legislative output. Notably absent from that agenda were measures relating to the social

---

[1] See below pp. 106, 109–110, 113.

life of the nation. Generally, these bills were left to the initiative of backbench MPs, though if their bills affected the nation's revenue or commerce, the Treasury or Board of Trade were likely to become involved.[2] As noted in Chapters 2-5 this sort of legislation included measures initiated by Sir Charles Bunbury and Sir William Meredith to reform the penal code, by reducing the number of capital offences. Bunbury along with William Eden and Sir William Blackstone also introduced reforms of the penitentiary system in the 1770s and 1780s. Gilbert was the most notable poor law reformer, but he was one of many. Peniston Portlock Powney was one of several MPs to present legislation to prevent the vexatious removal of the poor. John Rolle introduced a series of bills for the relief of the Exeter poor and in 1788 proposed a fairly radical measure for 'a more comfortable subsistence for the poor', and a reduction of 'the very heavy and increasing poor rates', to be achieved by publicly funded annuities. His fellow knight of the shire, John Pollexfen Bastard, was an energetic legislator who introduced and secured the passage of a bill to curtail the powers of the ecclesiastical courts. Several members introduced legislation to relieve imprisoned debtors, and Burke attributed his support for Lord Beauchamp's Insolvent Debtors Bill in 1780[3] against the wishes of his constituents as a principal cause for his loss of support at Bristol. James Bland Burges' Debtors and Creditor Bill, apparently one of the eighteenth century's most effective attempts to deal with the problem of insolvency, was lost in the House of Lords. It is finally noteworthy that the creation of the militia and its establishment on a firm foundation was due the work of three knights of the shire: General George Townshend, Sir George Savile and Lord Strange.

Legislation was the essential business of MPs, and members lost their seats because they were insufficiently attentive to their constituencies or were otherwise delinquent. According to Linda Colley, Sir Richard Grosvenor's[4] opposition to a Whig proposal to restore Chester's diminishing trade by improving the River Dee so annoyed the town's 1500 voters that his seat became suddenly in jeopardy.[5] More severe problems faced John Albert Bentinck, member for Rye. The borough normally went to men who worked on behalf of their constituents. Bentinck, however, was on active service for several years and even with the restoration of peace, took little interest in the affairs of the constituency. Because he had not visited the borough since 1761, Rye's treasury manager informed Newcastle that 'the freemen are not a little angry'. Not surprisingly, the Duke dropped Bentinck before the 1768 election.[6]

---

[2] Peter Jupp estimates that between 1772 and 1838 private members contributed to a total of between 28 and 42 per cent of all general bills, including those which were unsuccessful, and to between 18 and 25 per cent of those which were successful. Jupp, *The Governing of Britain, 1688–1848*, p. 221.
[3] It did not pass. Hoppit, *Failed Legislation*, pp. 566–7.
[4] Linda Colley, *In Defiance of Oligarchy: The Tory Party, 1714–60* (Cambridge and New York, 1982), p. 163.
[5] Sir Richard Grosvenor, 4th Bt. (1689–1732), MP, Chester, 1715–32; Mayor, Chester, 1715–16.
[6] *HPC, 1754–1790*, ii, 83–4.

I: MPs and Representation

The histories of MPs cited in Chapter 9 demonstrate that while some may have acknowledged the legitimacy of Burke's vision of the position in which they stood in relation to their constituents, many of his colleagues were unwilling to translate that vision into invariable practice. This was not because they had succumbed to the views of radicals such as William Beckford or Henry Cruger, who in 1774 told his Bristol electors that they had 'a right to instruct their Members' who were obliged 'to be guided by [their] counsels and instructions'. Instead, like Sir John Hussey Delaval,[7] Thomas Prowse or Matthew Brickdale, these members, in the process of doing their constituents' legislative business, established ties with them that enabled them to survive differences on contentious local issues and sometimes on national ones as well.

Political relationships that lasted over extended periods and endured despite differences on issues did not arise so much out of a shared belief in reformist ideologies, except on a limited level in and around the metropolis. Instead, they grew out of the member attending in a timely and effective manner to the host of matters that neighbours and constituents brought to his attention session after session. It was this sort of business which, as Burke discovered during his time as Bristol's MP, commanded much of the member's attention and absorbed a good portion of his energies.[8] A fundamental conclusion of this study is that service of this sort gave rise in many instances to bonds of trust between the member and his constituents. Once the bond was formed, constituents were prepared to forgive the intermittent transgressions of a Delaval, a Brickdale or Isaac Gascoyne. Conversely a hide-bound MP such as General Sir George Howard was prepared to act upon that connection and vote against the government that had imposed the Receipts Tax as his constituents had instructed him to do.

In September 1774 Edmund Burke told his new Bristol constituents that:

> his unbiased opinion, his mature judgement, his enlightened conscience, he ought not to sacrifice to you; to any man, or to any set of men living. These he does not derive from your pleasure; no, nor from the Law and the Constitution. They are a trust from Providence, for the abuse of which he is deeply answerable. Your Representative owes you, not his industry only, but his judgement; and he betrays, instead of serving you, if he sacrifices it to your opinion.[9]

Most authorities regarded Burke's view as the norm adopted by eighteenth-century MPs. The late Paul Langford maintained that the vision of the relationship between member and constituents that Burke presented following his election at Bristol in 1774 'was eminently acceptable to MPs, and perhaps to electors who were wary of being

---

[7] Sir John Hussey Delaval, (1728–1808), MP, Berwick-upon-Tweed, 1754–61, 1765–74, 1780–6; cr. Bt. 1761; cr. Baron Delaval [I], 1783; cr. Baron Delaval [GB], 1786.
[8] See Chapter 3 for Burke's own reaction to his Bristol experience.
[9] *The Writings and Speeches of Edmund Burke: Party, Parliament and the American War, 1774–1780*, ed. W.M. Elofson and John A. Woods (Oxford, 1996), iii, pp. 68–9.

bound by instructions',[10] adding that 'it would have been impossible for Parliament to answer to the needs of a propertied society in its broadest and most flexible form if ordinary MPs had been controlled by their immediate constituents'.[11] Nevertheless, he acknowledged in his Ford lectures in 1990, that 'most legislators were likely to have considerations other than Burke's':

> For practical purposes they thought of those who elected, supported, and influenced them. Their constituency, their residence, their property, their neighbourhood, and their interests, as well as their relationship with political masters, were all in question.

And that 'for practical [purposes] most MPs were used to being instructed by their constituents. But the language in which these instructions were expressed was generally diplomatic'.[12]

In line with Langford's formulation, Matthew Brickdale, according to his biography in the *History of Parliament* volumes, not only paid attention 'to the requirements of the Bristol commercial interest but seems to have followed his own independent line, 'influenced only by the instructions and interest of his constituents'[13] He was never 'controlled' by constituents with whom he had a working partnership. His was the sort of relationship that John Hussey Delaval formed with Berwick-upon-Tweed constituents and John Rolle and Sir William Dolben had with theirs. All four were effective MPs who did justice to their constituents' opinions.

Manifestations of these ties emerge again and again in the speeches, correspondence and Parliamentary participation of MPs. During an early debate on Pitt's French commercial treaty, Isaac Hawkins Browne[14] remarked that in conversations with the manufacturers of Bridgnorth he learned that they 'were sincerely pleased with the Treaty and regarded it as a singular benefit to the trade and commerce of the kingdom', for which he eventually voted. Likewise, Captain Berkeley[15] reported that 'the woollen manufacturers of Gloucester had requested him to state their earnest wishes to have it [the Treaty] carried into execution'. Both MPs indicated that interactions with constituents were important in shaping their own views of the Treaty.[16] Their situations were quite in contrast to that of William Windham who alienated an influential group of his constituents when he misrepresented their positions on the treaty in a speech that he allegedly delivered in the House in 1787.

MPs remained in contact with their constituents in a variety of other ways. Some maintained an active correspondence with representatives of important groups and a

---

[10] Langford, *Private Life*, p. 189.
[11] *A Polite and Commercial People, England 1727–1783*, p. 713.
[12] Langford, *Private Life*, pp. 189, 191.
[13] *HPC, 1754–1790*, ii, 115–16.
[14] Isaac Hawkins Browne (1745–1818), MP, Bridgnorth, 1784–1812.
[15] Hon. George Cranfield Berkeley (1753–1818), MP, Gloucestershire, 1783–1818; R.N., 1766; Lt. 1774; Cdr., 1778; Capt. 1780; R.-Adm., 1799; V.-Adm. 1805; Adm. 1810; Surveyor Gen. of the Ordnance, 1789–95.
[16] *PH*, xxvi, 469, 480, 670.

range of individuals within their constituencies. The Warwickshire MPs who tended Birmingham's business in the House informed themselves on issues of importance to local manufacturers and merchants through the local press, correspondence with Boulton and Garbett and other businessmen and interactions with the recently established Commercial Committee.

The younger Bamber Gascoyne was accused by his Liverpool constituents of not answering letters he received and neglecting 'his public duties'. As a result, he gave up his seat in favour of his brother, Isaac[17] in 1796. Isaac dedicated most of the 1796 Parliament to tending the needs of his constituents; that sort of attention remained his distinctive attribute as an MP. According to Professor Samuel Beer, Isaac was said to have promoted at least 200 bills at the instigation of different Liverpool interests.[18] Though he differed with his constituents on points of public policy at various points, he retained his seat for 35 years because he was faithful and effective in dealing with issues of immediate concern to Liverpool, in the course of which he often placed constituency above party.[19]

The ability of Gascoyne and Sir George Savile to engage with their constituents on the business that came before the House shows that the local pervaded eighteenth-century political life. Frank O'Gorman argued in his book on the electoral system of the period that 'the source of electoral activity was overwhelmingly local, the election contest the expression of, not the solution to – local conflict. The study of electoral politics becomes the study of local communities'.[20] David Eastwood highlighted the popular role in the eighteenth-century electoral system along with O'Gorman, John Phillips and many others, but was cautious in evaluating the influence that constituents exercised over their MPs in the interim between elections. He acknowledged that in the last decades of the century the relationship could be sustained by formal mechanisms – petitions, instructions, county meetings, resolutions or, more vaguely, 'elements within constituencies'. He ignored, however, a variety of informal connections: correspondence between constituents and MPs; or conversations such as those I.H. Browne and Captain Berkeley had with their constituents on the French commercial treaty, or the informal 'focus groups' that Richard Tucker set between his brother John and his Weymouth friends, business associates and constituents. Mark Knights, in concluding his article on participation and representation stressed that the widespread participation in petitioning between 1780 and 1850 showed that:

> the 'triumph of elections' was never complete and often contested; that the electoral representation overlapped with a participatory structure of local authority; that

---

[17] Gen. Isaac Gascoyne (c.1763–1841), MP, Liverpool, 1796–1831; Ensign, 20 Ft., 1779; 2 Ft. Gds., 1780; Lt. and Capt. 1784; Capt. and Lt. Col. 1792; Brevet Col. 1796; Maj.-Gen. 1802; Col. W.I. Reg., 1805; Lt.-Gen. 1808; Col. 54 Ft. 1816–41; Gen. 1819.

[18] Samuel Beer, 'The representation of interests in British government: Historical background', *The American Political Science Review*, li (1957), 627.

[19] *History of Parliament 1790–1820*, www.historyofparliamentonline.org/volume/1790-1820/member/gascoyne-isaac-1763-1841; *The House of Commons, 1820–1832*, ed. David R. Fisher (7 vols, 2009), v, 261–6.

[20] Frank O'Gorman, *Voters, Patrons and Parties: The Unreformed Electoral System of Hanoverian England (1734–1832)* (Oxford, 1989), pp. 9–10.

participation and representation could thus (albeit sometimes uncomfortably) coexist; and that in Britain there were well established mechanisms for ensuring that it did.[21]

Knights focuses on petitions and addresses as the means by which electors and the disenfranchised could make their views known to Parliament and MPs between elections. My point is that there were other means, most of them informal and specific to the individual MP, which enabled him, his constituents and neighbours to maintain and solidify ties.

This book has not for the most part delved into the political connections of the MPs on whom it has focused. Instead it has concentrated on their careers as legislators, which were largely apolitical exercises because most legislation with which they were often involved was specific or local – turnpike, navigation, enclosure, estate bills or local improvement acts. Individual MPs, a Gilbert, a Bunbury or a Savile, presented general acts on their own initiative. For the most part these measures avoided becoming matters of political debate in the House of Commons. In doing so their authors drew upon the expertise of magistrates or militia officers, with whom many were in regular contact, or on their own experience as militia officers and working with militia colleagues. For these reasons their legislation provoked little controversy, except in the upper chamber.

The closer connections between MPs and their constituents were formed as they joined together to formulate and pass legislation that also contributed to the greater tension between Parliament's two chambers. By the 1780s it was evident that MPs were responding to constituents' instructions on pressing national questions as well as the specific issues that formed the core of their normal legislative agenda. As a result, they became less inclined to sit by passively as the Lords turned aside abolition bills supported by thousands of petitioners or to tolerate with indifference the Lords' rejection of legislation to eliminate the contested features of 'Old Corruption', which they had proposed with the general support of their constituents.

II: Smaller Constituencies and Representation

Intermittent electoral upsets were more likely to occur in boroughs with relatively large numbers of voters. At Maidstone, for example, where the Finch family had maintained one of the two predominant interests since 1715, theirs, according to John Phillips, ended with the defeat of the family candidate at the 1780 election.[22] Similar difficulties confronted the Onslow family at Guildford, a borough in which they had maintained the dominant interest since the Restoration. Nevertheless, they had to surrender one seat in 1766 to Sir Fletcher Norton. Thereafter the two interests returned their respective

---

[21] Knights, 'Participation and representation', 54.
[22] John A. Phillips, 'From municipal matters to Parliamentary principles: Eighteenth-century borough politics in Maidstone', *JBS*, xxvii (1988), 338.

candidates unopposed until 1790, but the subsequent five elections were all contested.[23] Even Malton, Burke's former safe constituency, experienced brief upheavals between 1804 and 1807 when several candidates challenged the Fitzwilliam nominees. Though the contests posed little threat to the Fitzwilliam interest, the invasive candidacies created a stir, as did the simultaneous challenges mounted by disgruntled voters against the Devonshire interest at Knaresborough between 1804 and 1806. Both challenges were beaten back but not forgotten.[24] Even the tiny Cornish borough of Liskeard was not untouched by discord. In 1802 the predominant Eliot interest was confronted with an unexpected challenge to the candidacy of the patron's two sons. Despite being turned back, Richard Sheridan continued to press the candidacy of his son with the support of the Prince of Wales. At the special election in 1804 there was a double return, which the House resolved in favour of the Eliot candidate, William Huskisson.[25] The Eliots then proceeded to re-establish their control of the borough. Though the contests were beaten back, they demonstrated to patrons that their hegemony was open to challenge, and to the members that the voters did, at the very least, have voices.

The contested races also raise the issue of small constituencies and their MPs to whom I have given little consideration – despite the fact most English members sat for constituencies with fewer than 500 electors. There are several reasons for my oversight. During my research in the archives I came across little material pertaining to 'rotten boroughs', their MPs and constituents. In addition, the data in Chapter 1 showed that members for constituencies with limited electorates predominated among legislators who promoted no more than one bill over the three sessions each decade during the 1760s, 1770s and 1780s, indicating that those constituencies generated little legislation. A substantial portion of that inactive group of legislators, however, also sat for constituencies with electorates of 1000 or more voters.

Thus, members for boroughs with limited electorates deserve consideration. It is notable that a number of small (with 200 or fewer voters) boroughs took strong stands on a range of public issues, either petitioning Parliament or dispatching instructions to their MPs. Sir Francis Dashwood's[26] unpopular Cider Excise Tax (3 Geo. III, c. 3) provoked an outcry throughout the west and southwest, initially causing farmers to destroy their orchards because they concluded they were no longer likely to be profitable. The tax also led to attacks in the press on despised excisemen.[27] As opposition to the tax became more

---

[23] *HPC, 1754-1790*, i 385–6; and http://historyofparliamentonline.org/volume/1790-1820/constituencies/guildford
[24] *HPC, 1790-1820*, i, 451–3.
[25] William Huskisson (1770–1830), MP, Morpeth, 1796–1802, Liskeard, 1804–7, Harwich, 1807–12, Chichester, 1812–23 and Liverpool, 1823–30; Under-Sec. of State for War, 1795–1801; Agent for Cape of Good Hope, 1795–1801 and for Ceylon, 1801–4 and 1807–23; Jt. Sec. to Treasury, 1804–6 and 1807–9; Commr. Woods, Forests and Land Revenue, 1814–23; Member, Board of Trade, 1814 and President, 1823–7; Treasurer of Navy, 1823–7; Sec. of State for Colonies, 1827–8.
[26] Sir Francis Dashwood, 2nd Bt. (1708–81), MP, New Romney, 1741–61 and Weymouth and Melcombe Regis, 1761–3; Treasurer of the Chamber, 1761–2; Chancellor of the Exchequer, 1762–3; Ld. Lt. Bucks, 1763–81; Keeper of the Great Wardrobe, 1763–5; Jt. Postmaster Gen. 1766–81; abeyance of the Barony of le Despencer terminated in his favour, Apr. 1763.
[27] Patrick Woodland, 'Extra-Parliamentary political organization in the making: Benjamin Heath and the opposition to the 1763 Cider Excise', *Parl. Hist.*, iv (1985), 116.

formalised in 1763-4, constituents in boroughs in the cider counties wrote to MPs thanking them for opposing the tax and instructing them to continue their resistance. Among these boroughs was Bodmin in Cornwall, one of whose members, Sir Christopher Treise, opposed the tax. Liskeard not only challenged its patrons' candidates in the early nineteenth century, but in 1763 petitioned against the tax, and Anthony Champion, a Liskeard MP, voted against it.[28] Both members for Callington and Fowey opposed the tax and received the thanks of their appreciative constituents.[29]

Similar processes occurred in three small Devon boroughs where the freemen of Plympton Erle thanked Sir William Baker for acting as teller for the opposition to the Cider Tax.[30] Bere Alston petitioned against the tax: both members, however, supported the Bute administration from time to time; because there are no division lists for the Cider Excise, it is unclear if they respected the instructions of the voters.[31] Both members for Plymouth, an Admiralty borough, opposed the Cider Excise and received the thanks of their constituents and instructions to continue to resist the imposition. Their opposition is notable, not only because they sat for an Admiralty borough, but because William Wildman Barrington held the post of Treasurer of the Navy under Bute and Grenville.[32]

Benjamin Heath,[33] the organiser of what became the broader anti-cider movement, disapproved of the informality of the initial letters and instructions. Instead, he promoted a 'constitutional union' to overturn the tax. The campaign was to be organised by county committees which would appoint paid agents to oversee their business and ensure that county committees acted in concert.

The plan was circulated in June 1763, publicised in the press and taken up at county meetings throughout the southwest and west. In all, seven counties, 19 boroughs and Bristol's Society of Merchant Venturers petitioned between 1763 and 1766 when the excise was finally repealed.[34] The five Cornish boroughs that petitioned – Bodmin and Callington, as well as East and West Looe and Lostwithiel,[35] had fewer than 200 voters.[36]

So strong was the reaction against the Cider Excise that when the administration recommended John Bindley, reputedly an author of the tax, to fill the vacant seat at West Looe in 1764, George Grenville agreed to withdraw his candidacy. As he told James Buller,[37] his candidacy 'would be attended with injury to your interest not only in that borough but in the county likewise'. Instead, Grenville nominated

---

[28] HPC, 1754-1790, i, 222, 225; Woodland, 'Extra-Parliamentary organization', p. 117. Anthony Champion (1725-1801), MP, St. Germans, 1754-61 and Liskeard, 1761-8. Sir Christopher Treise (1728-80), MP, Bodmin, 1762-8; sheriff, Cornwall, 1760-1.

[29] HPC, 1754-1790, i, 225-8; Woodland, 'Extra-Parliamentary organization', p. 117.

[30] HPC, 1754-1790, ii, 40; Woodland, 'Extra-Parliamentary organization', p. 117.

[31] HPC 1754-1790, i, 251; ii, 337-8, 627.

[32] Woodland, 'Extra-Parliamentary organization', 117.

[33] Benjamin Heath (1704-66), Devonshire merchant; author of *The Case of the County of Devon: With Respect to the Consequences of the New Excise Duty on Cyder and Perry* (1763).

[34] Woodland, 'Extra-Parliamentary organization', 126-7.

[35] HPC, 1754-1790, i. 252-3.

[36] Woodland, 'Extra-Parliamentary organization', 126.

[37] James Buller (1717-65), MP, East Looe, 1741-7 and Cornwall, 1748-65.

John Sargent,[38] a native of Devon and 'an eminent merchant of London'.[39] Altogether nine MPs who sat for West Country boroughs with 250 or fewer electors spoke and/or voted against the Cider Excise at one of the debates between March 1763 and 1766.[40]

Nor was it only cider that provoked small boroughs to instruct or petition their members. James Bradley showed that the patronage-dominated boroughs of the southwest reacted strongly to the addresses in support of coercion against the American colonies in 1775. The reaction manifested itself in petitions to Parliament and in support of conciliation. According to Bradley, the popular agitation resulted partially from the concentration of Parliamentary seats in the area which resulted in a higher number of elections in the southwest and a consequent elevation in political awareness. The right to vote had already become an issue because of the significant expansion of patronal influence throughout the area, so these grievances were gaining adherents as the American crisis came to the fore.[41]

Bradley demonstrates that seven boroughs (also with under 200 voters) responded to the developing American crisis by petitioning Parliament in favour of conciliation rather than coercion, and that in Hampshire the petitions supporting conciliation attracted more signatures than addresses to the Crown favouring coercion.[42] Moreover, in 1783 two additional small boroughs, Launceston in Cornwall and Lyme Regis in Dorset, petitioned in support of William Pitt's first reform bill. Launceston, with under 30 voters, was controlled by the Duke of Northumberland,[43] who returned both members in 1780 and 1784. Neither MP followed the lead of the voters and supported Pitt. The only novelty was provided by Charles George Perceval,[44] listed in Ginter's voting records as 'neuter', a unique classification for a division.[45] Another borough, Lyme Regis, with about 50 voters, was controlled by the Fane family, Earls of Westmorland. Though members of the constituency petitioned in favour of Pitt's bill, neither of the MPs, the Hon. Henry or Thomas Fane,[46] appear to have voted on the

---

[38] John Sargent (1715–91), MP, Midhurst, 1754–61 and West Looe, 1765–8.
[39] *Additional Grenville Papers*, p. 225.
[40] Woodland, 'Political atomization and regional interests in the 1761 Parliament: The impact of the Cider Debates 1763–1766', *Parl. Hist.*, viii (1989), 82–3.
[41] James Bradley, *Popular Politics, and the American Revolution*, pp. 128–9.
[42] Lymington (c. 50), Poole (c. 100), Portsmouth (c. 100), Wallingford (200), Westbury (69), Winchester (c. 70) and Yarmouth, I.o.W. (c. 50). James Bradley, *Popular Politics*, p. 67; and 'Parliament, print culture and petitioning in the late eighteenth century', in *The Print Culture of Parliament, 1600–1800*, ed. James Peacey (Edinburgh, 2007), pp. 110–12.
[43] Sir Hugh Smithson, 3rd Bt. (1715–86), MP, Middlesex, 1740–50; m. Elizabeth, da. and h. of the 7th Duke of Somerset; succ. father-in-law as Baron Wackworth and Earl of Northumberland, 1750; cr. Duke of Northumberland, 1766, and Lord Lovaine, Baron of Alnwick, 1784; Ld. of Bedchamber, 1753–63; Ld. Lt. Northumberland, 1753–86; Vice-Adm. Northumberland, 1753; Ld. chamberlain to the Queen, 1762–8; Ld. Lt. Middlesex, 1762–86; Ld. Lt. [I], 1763–5; Vice-Adm. N. America, 1764; Master of the Horse, 1778–80.
[44] Hon. Charles George Perceval (1756–1840), MP, Launceston, 1780–90, Warwick, 1790–6 and Totnes, 1796–1802; Ld. of Admiralty, 1783–1801; Registrar of Court of Admiralty, 1790–1840; Master of Mint, 1801–2; Commr., India Board, 1801–3; Ld. of Bedchamber, 1804–12; succ. as 2nd Baron Arden [UK], 1802.
[45] D.E. Ginter, ed., *Voting Records of the British House of Commons, 1761–1820* (6 vols, 1792), iv, p. 1150.
[46] Hon. Henry Fane (1739–1802), MP, Lyme Regis, 1772–1802; clerk in the Treasury, 1757–1762; Keeper of the King's Private Roads, 1772; Hon. Thomas Fane (1760–1807), MP, Lyme Regis, 1784–1806, army, Lt. 1 Ft. 1778; Capt. 2 Ft 1779 and Maj. 1783; Capt. 2 Ft. Gds. and Lt. Col.1783; ret. 1793; Groom of the Bedchamber, 1793–1807.

measure. Finally, George Page Turner, member for Thirsk, a Yorkshire borough controlled by the Frankland family, gave two reasons for supporting the motion for the repeal of William Pitt's Shop Tax in 1787 despite the fact he generally voted for the minister's proposals. First, he had been instructed by his constituents to do so, and secondly, he believed 'all persons ought to be taxed equally'.[47]

Thus, 20 small boroughs, more than three-quarters of which were dominated by patrons, either dispatched petitions to Parliament or instructions to their MPs against the Cider Excise, for conciliating American colonists, supporting William Pitt's reform proposals or instructing their members to vote against the Shop Tax. While not all of the members followed the instructions or acted according to the line recommended in the petitions, a majority of them voted according to the expressed wishes of their constituents or the signatories of petitions.

It is also notable that small boroughs produced their own legislative agenda. Lord Folkestone, discussed in Chapter 1, promoted road, enclosure and estate bills on behalf of his Salisbury constituents and went to considerable lengths to protect local weavers who petitioned against extending favours to the British linen industry in 1774. As noted in Chapter 3, Viscount Barrington faced considerable criticism from the town's officials and residents for helping to secure the passage of and then defending a series of controversial improvement bills.

The small borough of Tiverton[48] in Devon also generated but was not always able to implement a legislative agenda according to memoranda dispatched by Beavis Wood to Nathaniel Ryder.[49] In September 1768 Wood informed Ryder that the corporation would petition the House to press the administration to enlarge the nation's Asian commerce on behalf of local woollen manufacturers. The following January the Corporation sent a letter to the two MPs, Ryder and John Duntze,[50] instructing them to advocate for its views on the East India Company question. Ryder was attentive to the Corporation's instructions: on 21 November 1766 he reported the petition of the Mayor, burgesses, burgesses and trustees of an act of 21 Geo. II, to prepare and bring in a Bill[51] which he presented on the 22nd. He later reported the bill with amendments from its second reading committee on 9 December.[52] In 1777 and 1778 the corporation considered applying to Parliament for legislation to enable it to build a new town hall and was ready to send a proposal to Harrowby and Duntze until concerns about the costs and raising a mortgage resulted in a decision to drop the plan.[53] The same fate met Duntze's efforts in 1775 to get the borough to petition in support of shortening Parliaments. After some back and forth, the decision was 'to favour the continuance of

---

[47] *HPC, 1754–1790*, i, 441; ii, 244; *PH*, xxviii, 82.
[48] A corporation borough with about 25 voters. *HPC, 1754–1790*, i, 259–61.
[49] Nathaniel Ryder (1735–1803), MP, Tiverton, 1756–76; cr. Baron Harrowby, 1776.
[50] John Duntze (1735–95), MP, Tiverton, 1768–95; cr. Bt. 1774.
[51] 'To continue the term and render more effective, an Act of 31 Geo. II, for amending several roads leading from and widening the road from Bickley Bridge Cross to the sign of the Swan and from Bickley Wood Cross to Ford Village Water in Devon'.
[52] *CJ*, xxxi, pp. 19, 22, 40.
[53] *Georgian Tiverton: The Political Memoranda of Beavis Wood, 1768–98*, ed. John Bourne (Devon and Cornwall Record Society, n.s., xxix, 1986), pp. 44–6, 58.

Parliament as it stands'. In another example of a small borough promoting local legislation, Thomas Hunt,[54] in February and March 1786, carried the Bodmin Road Bill through all its stages in the House. The measure eventually reached the statute book as 26 Geo. III, c. 129.

Small boroughs produced their own legislation and had MPs who were effective in securing the passage of measures sought by the towns they represented. By no means all of the smaller Cornish or Devon boroughs, however, were fortunate enough to have members of the quality of a Ryder, Bastard or Folkestone. Many who sat for the small Cornish boroughs purchased their seats from a patron. Any obligation they had was often to the patron, not to the electors. Nor did most of them live in Cornwall or have an appreciation of Cornish issues.[55] These were not the circumstances likely to promote the sort of connection that gave rise to an implicit sense of representation. That sort of relationship could be nurtured, however, especially if the member came from one of the counties' families. Outsiders such as Lord Barrington or Nathaniel Ryder also proved themselves to be outstanding constituency MPs. As his brother, Samuel told Barrington, whose family seat was in Berkshire, 'I need not tell you what you already know, how much your constituents adore you'.[56] Barrington was a formidable constituency MP, who when pressed by his constituents on the Cider Excise, voted against an administration of which he was a member. Thomas Hunt, an outsider from Cheshire, resurrected a road bill that had languished for 17 years, so that by improving its roads, Bodmin could extend its links to the outside world.

In short, some smaller constituencies like their larger counterparts produced a legislative agenda and dispatched instructions to the MPs relating not only to turnpikes, navigations or local improvement acts, but to issues of broader importance. Most of the measures were of little importance, but in the process of dealing with improvement bills session after session, MPs and constituents, as Rosemary Sweet has noted, 'were locked into a much more complex set of relationships and reciprocal obligations'.[57] Sweet made this point specifically in reference to the relations that developed between residents of boroughs who promoted improvement commissions and the MPs who supported their projects and carried them through the House. I have argued earlier that the same complex ties developed in many of the constituencies that were fortunate enough to have MPs who were responsive to appeals for assistance in furthering a wider variety of projects whose implementation required the approval of Parliament. Between 1754 and 1790 there were a significant number of active and capable MPs willing to respond to the legislative needs of a range of England's Parliamentary constituencies who established Sweet's 'more complex set of relationships and reciprocal obligations', even in the tiny boroughs of the southwest.

For too long historians of Parliament focused their attention on political manoeuvrings at Westminster. Reading their biographies in the volumes of the *History*

---

[54] Thomas Hunt (c. 1723–89), MP, Bodmin, 1784–9.
[55] Josiah Tucker noted that most of the Cornish MPs 'have their chief Residence in the Metropolis, with Country-Seats perhaps in its Environs'. Quoted in Langford, *Public Life*, p. 193.
[56] *HPC, 1754–1790*, ii, 55.
[57] Rosemary Sweet, *The English Towns, 1680–1840*, p. 59.

of Parliament for the years from 1715 to 1790, it was difficult to remember the House of Commons was a legislative body that was in fact dealing with a surge in the volume of legislation. Somehow the two Houses dealt with that surge, though it would be impossible from those volumes to know how it was done. T.K. Moore and Henry Horwitz began to offer an answer in their 1971 article, by highlighting the work of one of their active groups of MPs, whose work chairing second reading committees resulted, they concluded, in legislation that made the Commons useful to the broader community. The same is true for the many legislators discussed in this book. Not only did they steer the proposals of constituents, neighbours, clients and interest groups through the House to passage, but they introduced their own measures, a number of them, national in their scope. In addition, they were active participants in the business of the nation, sometimes at the behest of their leaders, on other occasions at the behest of interest groups, increasingly in reaction to constituent pressure, sometimes on their own initiative. For any or all of these reasons, the great majority of MPs discussed in this book were formidable legislators. They ensured that the Commons was useful to broad swaths of the community. Few if any adorned the front benches; most, in fact, were quite obscure.

Bibliography

Manuscripts

Barnsley Archive: Walter Spencer Stanhope Papers, 60575
Birmingham Archive: Matthew Boulton General Correspondence 378212
Birmingham Central Library: Industrial Revolution; A Documentary History, Papers from the Boulton-Watt Archive and the Matthew Boulton Papers: Series One: Papers from the Birmingham Central Library, Box 30F, Samuel Garbett & Family, 1765–1785 (Box73), www.ampltd.co.uk
Boston College: John J. Burns Library, Boston College, Stephen Fuller Letter Books, Joseph J. Williams, SJ Ethnological Collection, MS.2009.030
Bristol Record Office: Jarrit Smith MSS, AC/JS/95; Society of Merchant Venturers MSS, SMV 2/4/2
British Archives Online: National Library of Wales: Slebech MSS
British Library:
    Althorp Papers, Add. MS 75580
    Auckland Papers, Add. MS 34419, 45728
    Barrington Papers, Add. MS 73673–73681
    Berkeley Papers, Add. MS 39312
    Bowood MS, 88906/01/011, 88906/01/012, 88906/01/013, 88906/01/014
    Bridport Papers, Add. MS 35202
    Camelford Papers, Add. MS 69293
    Chichester Papers, Add. MS 33090
    Dropmore Papers, Add. MS 58907, 58928, 69065
    Hardwicke Papers, Add. MS 35356–35360, 35609–35610
    Hertford Papers, Egerton MS 3262
    Holland House Papers, Add. MS 51710
    Leeds Papers, Add. MS 28064
    Liverpool Papers, Add. MS 38223, 38231, 38308, 38310, 38416
    Newcastle Papers, Add. MS 32936, 32966
    Sheffield Park Papers, Add. MS, 61867, 88906
    Windham Papers, Add. MS 37873
  Cambridge University Library: Vanneck-Arcedeckne Papers
  Devon R.O., Sidmouth Papers, 152n/c 1808/OZ
  Duke University: David M. Rubenstein Rare and Manuscripts Library: Fuller MSS 5462, 5463
  Essex Record Office: Strutt MSS, D/DRa o3, D/DRa o4, D/DRa 07, T/B 251/7, T/B 252/7
  Hampshire Archives and Local Studies:
    Hans Sloane Stanley MSS, 28 M57/54
    Malmesbury MSS, Parliamentary Diary of James Harris, 9M73
  Hertfordshire Archives and Local Studies: Verulam MSS, F27, F29
  Historical Manuscripts Commission:
    Ailesbury MSS

Carlisle MSS
Dartmouth MSS, ii, iii
Fortescue MSS, iii, vi
Lonsdale MSS
Kenyon MSS
Rutland MSS
Inspire Nottinghamshire Archives: Savile-Foljambe MS, DD/FG 11/1
Kent Archives and History Centre:
   Sackville Family Papers U169 C182
   Stanhope MSS, U1590/S5 C26
Lambeth Palace Library: Porteus Notebooks, MSS 2098, 2099
The National Archives:
   Colchester Papers, PRO 30/9/33
   Colonial Office Papers CO/137/87
   Pitt Papers, PRO 30/8
   Rail 806, Barnsley Canal Minutes Book
   Rail 810, Birmingham Canal Minute Book
National Library of Scotland:
   Delvine Papers, MS 1406
   Rose Papers, MS 3528
Northamptonshire Archives & Heritage Services: Fitzwilliam Papers, Box 38
Sheffield City Council, Libraries, Archives and Information: Sheffield City Archives: WWM/R1/1232
Somerset Archives and Local Studies: William Dickinson Papers, DD/DN/4/2/7
Staffordshire Record Office: Dartmouth Papers, D564/12
University of Bristol, Special Collections, Arts and Sciences Library: Matthew Brickdale Parliamentary Diary
University of Leeds Library, Brotherton Collection, MS Misc., Letters 1, Townshend
University of Nottingham, Manuscripts and Special Collections: Portland Papers: Pw F, 6884, 9003
Warwickshire Record Office:
   Denbigh Letterbooks: C2017/243
   Newdigate MSS, CR136/B2359–2340
Wiltshire and Swindon History Centre (Chippenham):
   Parliamentary Diary of Jacob Pleydell Bouverie, Viscount Folkestone, 1946/4/2F/1/3
   Prowse MSS

Newspapers and Periodicals

The Annual Register
Aris's Birmingham Gazette
Bath Chronicle and Weekly Gazette
Gentleman's Magazine
Jackson's Oxford Gazette
London Chronicle
Norfolk Chronicle
Staffordshire Advertiser
The Times

Parliamentary Sources and Reference Works

Almon, J. and Debrett, J., *The Parliamentary Register* (83 vols, 1775–1803).
Campbell, John, Lord, *Lives of the Lord Chancellors and Keepers of the Great Seal of England: From the Earliest Times till the Reign of Queen Victoria* (10 vols, 7th edn, New York, 1878).
Cobbett, W., *The Parliamentary History of England from the Norman Conquest... to the Year 1803* (36 vols, 1806–20).
Debrett, J., *History, Debates, Proceedings of Both Houses of Parliament, 1743–1774* (7 vols, 1792).
Journals of the Assembly of Jamaica.
Journals of the House of Commons, 1760–1811.
Journals of the House of Lords.
Judd, Gerritt P., *Members of Parliament, 1734–1832* (New Haven, CT, 1955).
Lambert, Sheila (ed.), *Commons' Sessional Papers of the Eighteenth Century* (London and Rio Grande, 1975).
Matthew, H.C.G. and Harrison, Brian (ed.), *The Oxford Dictionary of National Biography from the Earliest Times to the Year 2000* (60 vols, Oxford, 2004).
Namier, L.B. and Brooke, John (ed.), *The History of Parliament: The House of Commons, 1754–1790* (3 vols, 1964).
Sedgwick, Romney (ed.), *The History of Parliament: The House of Commons, 1715–1754* (2 vols, 1970).
Simmons, Richard G. and Thomas, Peter D.G., (ed.), *Proceedings and Debates of the British Parliament Respecting North America, Vol. II, 1765–1768* (Millwood, NY, 1983).
Thomas, Peter D.G. (ed.), *Parliamentary Diaries of Nathaniel Ryder, 1764–1767*, Camden Miscellany, vol. xxiii, Camden Society, 4th ser. Vol. 7 (Royal Historical Society, 1969).
—— and Simmons, Richard G. (ed.), *Proceedings and Debates of the British Parliament Respecting North America, Vol. II, 1765–1768* (Millwood, NY, 1983).
Thorne, R.G. (ed.), *The History of Parliament: The House of Commons, 1790–1820* (5 vols, 1986).
Torrington, F. William (ed.), *House of Lords Sessional Papers* (56 vols, Dobbs Ferry, NY, 1795).

Printed Primary Sources and Pamphlets

Albemarle, Earl of (ed.), *Memoirs of the Earl of Rockingham* (2 vols, 1852).
Aspinall, Arthur (ed.), *The Later Correspondence of George III* (5 vols., Cambridge, 1962-70)
Barnes, G.R. and Owen, J.H. (ed.), *The Private Papers of John, Earl of Sandwich* (3 vols, Naval Records Soc., 1932–8).
Baring, Mrs. Henry (ed.), *The Diary of the Right Hon. William Windham, 1784 to 1810*, (1866).
Bourn, John (ed.), *Georgian Tiverton: The Political Memoranda of Beavis Wood, 1768–98* (Devon and Cornwall Record Society, ns., xxix, 1986).
Bramwell, George, *The Manner of Proceeding on Bills in the House of Lords* (1831).
Carter, Harold C. (ed.), *The Sheep and Wool Correspondence of Sir Joseph Banks, 1781–1820* (London, 1979).
Christie, Ian R. et al. (ed.), *The Correspondence of Jeremy Bentham. Vol. III: January 1781 to October 1788* (10 vols, 1971).

Ditchfield, G.M. (ed.), *The Letters of Theophilus Lindsey (1723-1808). Vol. 1: 1747-1788* (3 vols, Church of England Record Society, Woodbridge, 2007).

Eden, William, *Principles of Penal Punishment* (1771).

Elofson, W.M. and Woods, John A. (ed.), *The Writings and Speeches of Edmund Burke: Party, Parliament and the American War, 1774-1780* (Oxford, 1996), ii.

Farrer, Lady, Katherine Eufemia (ed.), *Letters of Josiah Wedgwood* (3 vols, Manchester, 1903-6).

Finer, Ann and Savage, George (ed.), *The Selected Letters of Josiah Wedgwood* (New York, 1965).

Fox, Richard, 3rd Lord Holland, *Memoirs of the Whig Party during My Own Time* (2 vols, 1844-5).

Gilbert, Thomas, *A Scheme for the Better Relief and Employment of the Poor, Humbly Submitted to the Consideration of His Majesty and the Two Houses of Parliament* (1764).

——, *Observations upon the Orders and Resolutions of the House of Commons with Respect to the Poor, Vagrants and Houses of Correction* (1775).

——, *A Plan for the Better Relief and Employment of the Poor, for Enforcing and Amending the Laws Respecting Houses of Correction, and Vagrants; and for Improving the Police of this Country. Together with Bills Intended to Be Offered to Parliament for these Purposes* (1781).

——, *A Plan of Police: Exhibiting the Causes of the Present Increase of the Poor, and Proposing a Mode for their Future More Effectual Relief and Support* (1781).

——, *Observations on the Bills for Amending and Rendering More Effectual the Laws Relative to Houses of Correction; for the Better Relief of the Poor; and for Amending and Rendering More Effectual the Laws Relative to Rogues, Vagabonds and other Idle and Disorderly Persons* (1787).

Gilson, J.B. (ed.), *Correspondence of Edmund Burke and William Windham with Illustrative Letters in the Windham Papers in the British Museum* (Roxburghe Club, Cambridge, 1910).

Gray, Duncan and Walker, V.W. (ed.), *Records of the Borough of Nottingham, Being a Series of Extracts from the Archives of the Corporation of Nottingham. Vol. VII: 1760-1800* (Nottingham, 1947).

Gutteridge, George H. (ed.), *The Correspondence of Edmund Burke. Vol. III: July 1774-June 1778* (Cambridge, 1961).

Herbert, Lord (ed.), *Pembroke Papers (1780-1794): Letters and Diaries of Henry, Tenth Earl of Pembroke and his Circle* (1950).

Hogge, G. (ed.), *The Journal and Correspondence of William Lord Auckland* (4 vols, 1861-2).

Jarrett, Derek (ed.) *Memoirs of the Reign of George III* (4 vols, New Haven, CT, 2000).

Jucker, Ninette S. (ed.) *Jenkinson Papers* (1949).

Lewis, W.S., et al., *The Yale Edition of Horace Walpole's Correspondence* (48 vols, New Haven, CT, 1937-83).

Long, Edward, *The History of Jamaica, of General Survey of the Antient and Modern State of that Island: With Reflections on its Situation, Settlements, Inhabitants, Climate, Products, Commerce, Laws and Government* (3 vols, 1970).

Malmesbury, Earl of (ed.) *Diaries and Correspondence of James Harris, 1st Earl of Malmesbury* (4 vols, 1844)

——, *A Series of Letters of the First Earl of Malmesbury, his Family and Friends from 1745 to 1820* (2 vols, 1870).

McCahill, M.W. (ed.), *The Correspondence of Stephen Fuller, 1788-1795: Jamaica, the West India Interest at Westminster and the Campaign to Preserve the Slave Trade* (Chichester, 2014).
Meteyard, Eliza (ed.), *The Life of Josiah Wedgwood, from his Private Correspondence and Private Papers* (2 vols, 1865).
Minchinton, W.E. (ed.), *Politics of the Port of Bristol in the Eighteenth Century: The Petitions of the Society of Merchant Venturers, 1698-1805* (Bristol Record Society, xxiii, 1963).
Prest, Wilfred R. (ed.), *The Letters of Sir William Blackstone, 1774-1780* (Selden Society, 2006).
Rathbone, Hannah Mary (ed.), *Letters of Richard Reynolds and a Memoir of his Life* (Philadelphia, PA, 1855).
Redington, Joseph and Roberts, R.A. (ed.), *Calendar of Home Office Papers. Vol. I: 1760-1765* (London, 1878).
Savile, Sir George, *An Argument Concerning the Militia* (1762).
Steuart, A.F. (ed.), *Last Journals of Horace Walpole during the Reign of George III from 1771 to 1783* (2 vols., 1910).
Tomlinson, John R.G., *Additional Grenville Papers, 1763-65* (Manchester, 1962).
Tucker, Josiah, *A Review of Lord Vis. Clare's Conduct as Representative of Bristol* (Gloucester and Bristol, 1775).
White, A.W.A. (ed.), *The Correspondence of Sir Roger Newdigate of Arbury, Warwickshire* (Vol. XXXVII, Stratford-upon-Avon, 1995).
Wilberforce, R.I. and S., *The Life of William Wilberforce* (5 vols, 1338).
Woods, John A., *The Correspondence of Edmund Burke, 1778-1782*, IV (Cambridge, 1974).

Secondary Sources

Books

Albert, William, *The Turnpike Road System in England, 1763-1840* (Cambridge, 1974).
Anstey, Roger, *The Atlantic Slave Trade and British Abolition, 1760-1810* (Atlantic Highlands, NJ, 1975).
Armytage, Francis, *The Free Port System in the British West Indies: A Study in Commercial Policy, 1766-1822* (London, 1953).
Axon, W.E., *The Annals of Manchester: A Chronological Record from the Earliest Times to the End of 1885* (Manchester, 1886).
Barnes, Donald Grove, *A History of the English Corn Laws from 1660-1846* (1930).
Beastall, T.W., *History of Lincolnshire. Vol. VIII: The Agricultural Revolution in Lincolnshire* (Lincoln, 1978).
Beattie, J.M., *Crime and the Courts in England, 1660-1800* (Princeton, 1986).
Beckett, John V., *Coal and Tobacco: The Lowthers and the Economic Development of West Cumberland, 1660-1760* (Cambridge, 1981).
——, *The Aristocracy in England 1660-1914* (Oxford and New York, 1986).
Best, Geoffrey F.A., *Temporal Pillars: Queen Anne's Bounty, The Ecclesiastical Commissioners, and the Church of England* (Cambridge, 1964).
Bischoff, James, *A Comprehensive History of the Woollen and Worsted Manufactures* (2 vols, 1842).

Black, E.C., *The Association: British Extra-Parliamentary Organization, 1769–1793* (Cambridge, MA, 1963).
Bradley, James E., *Popular Politics and the American Revolution in England: Petitions, the Crown and Public Opinion* (Macon, GA, 1986).
Brewer, John, *Party Ideology and Popular Ideology at the Accession of George III* (Cambridge, 1976).
——, *Sinews of Power: War, Money and the English State* (Cambridge, MA, 1988).
Broadbridge, S.R., *The Birmingham Canal Navigations. Vol. 1: 1768–1846* (Newton Abbot, 1974).
Burnard, Trevor and Garrigus, John, *The Plantation Machine: Atlantic Capitalism in French Sainte-Domingue and British Jamaica* (Philadelphia, PA, 2016).
Cannadine, David, *Lords and Landlords: The Aristocracy and the Towns, 1774–1976* (Atlantic Highlands, NJ, 1980).
Cannon, John, *The Fox-North Coalition: The Crisis of the Constitution, 1782–1784* (Cambridge, 1969).
——, *Parliamentary Reform, 1640–1832* (Cambridge, 1973).
——, *Aristocratic Century: The Peerage of Eighteenth-Century England* (Cambridge, 1984).
Chalklin, Christopher, *The Provincial Towns of Georgian England: A Study of the Building Process, 1740–1820* (Montreal, 1974).
——, *English Counties and Public Building, 1650–1830* (London and Rio Grande, OH, 1998).
Cherry, Gordon E., *Birmingham: A Study in Geography, History, and Planning* (Chichester, 1994).
Christie, Ian R., *The End of Lord North's Ministry, 1780–1782* (1958).
——, *Wilkes, Wyvill and Reform* (1962).
——, *Myth and Reality in Eighteenth-Century British Politics and Other Papers* (1970).
Clark, J.C.D., *English Society 1688–1832: Ideology, Social Structure and Political Practice during the Ancient Regime* (Cambridge and New York, 1985).
Clark, Peter (ed.), *The Cambridge Urban History of Britain. Vol. II: 1540–1840*, (3 vols, Cambridge, 2000).
—— and Murfin, Lyn, *The History of Maidstone: The Making of a Modern County Town* (Stroud, 1996).
Coleridge, E.H., *The Life of Thomas Coutts, Banker* (New York, 1920).
Colley, Linda, *In Defiance of Oligarchy: The Tory Party, 1714–60* (Cambridge, 1982).
Compton, Hugh J., *The Oxford Canal* (Newton Abbot and North Pomfret, VT, 1976).
Copeland, Reginald, *The British Anti-Slavery Movement* (New York, 1964).
Corfield, Penelope, *The Impact of English Towns, 1700–1800* (New York, 1982).
Craton, Michael and Walvin, James, *A Jamaican Plantation: The History of Worthy Park, 1670–1970* (1970).
——, *Testing the Chains: Resistance to Slavery in the British West Indies* (1982).
Dickinson, H.T., *Radical Politics in the North-East of England in the Later Eighteenth Century* (Durham County Local History Society, 1979).
——, *The Politics of the People in the Eighteenth Century* (Basingstoke, 1995).
Dickinson, H.W., *Matthew Boulton* (Cambridge, 1937).
Doolittle, I.G., *William Blackstone: A Biography* (Haslemere, 2001).
Draper, Nicholas, *The Price of Emancipation: Slave Ownership, Compensation and British Society at the End of Slavery* (Cambridge, 2010).
Drescher, Seymour, *Capitalism and Antislavery: Mobilization in Comparative Perspective* (New York, 1987).

———, *Abolition: A History of Slavery and Antislavery* (Cambridge, 2009).
Dresser, Madge, *Slavery Obscured: The Social History of the Slave Trade in an English Provincial Port* (London and New York, 2001).
Duffy, Ian P.H., *Bankruptcy and Insolvency in London during the Industrial Revolution* (New York, 1985).
Eastwood, David, *Governing Rural England, Tradition and Transformation in Local Government 1780-1840* (Oxford, 1994).
Ehrman, John, *The Younger Pitt: The Years of Acclaim* (New York, 1969).
Emden, Cecil S., *The People and the Constitution, Being the History of the Development of the People's Influence in British Government* (Oxford, 1956).
Fitton, R.S. and Wadsworth, A.P., *The Strutts and the Arkwrights 1758-1830: A Study of the Early Factory System* (Manchester, 1958).
Flinn, Michael W., *The History of the British Coal Industry* (2 vols, Oxford, 1984).
Gauci, Perry, *William Beckford: First Prime Minister of the London Empire* (New Haven, CT, and London, 2013).
Gray, Arthur, *The Town of Cambridge* (Cambridge, 1925).
Grieve, Hilda, *The Sleepers and the Shadows: Chelmsford a Town, its People and its Past. Vol. 2: From Market Town to Chartered Borough (1608-1888)* (Essex Record Office, no. 128, Chelmsford, 1994).
Grigg, David, *The Agricultural Revolution in South Lincolnshire* (Cambridge, 1966).
Habakkuk, John, *Marriage, Debt and the Estates, English Landownership, 1650-1950* (Oxford, 1994).
Hadfield, Charles, *The Canals of the West Midlands* (Newton Abbot, 1966).
Hall, Douglas, *A Brief History of the West India Committee* (St. Lawrence, Barbados, 1971).
Hancock, David, *Citizens of the World: London Merchants and the Integration of the British Atlantic Community, 1735-1785* (Cambridge, 1994).
Harling, Philip, *The Waning of 'Old Corruption': The Politics of Economical Reform in Britain, 1779-1846* (Oxford, 1996).
Hayton, David, *Constituencies and Elections: 1690-1715* (2002). www.historyofparliamentonline.org/volume/1690-1715/survey/constituencies-and-elections
Hembry, Phyllis, *The English Spa, 1560-1815: A Social History* (London and Cranbury, NJ, 1990).
Herward, Edmund, *Lord Mansfield* (Chichester and London, 1979).
Hill, Sir Francis, *Georgian Lincoln* (Cambridge, 1966).
Hopkins, Eric, *Birmingham: The First Manufacturing Town in the World, 1760-1840* (1989).
Hoppit, Julian (ed.), *Failed Legislation, 1660-1800* (London and Rio Grande, 1997).
———, *Britain's Political Economies: Parliament and Economic Life 1660-1800* (Cambridge and New York, 2017).
Hyde, F.E., *Liverpool and the Mersey: An Economic History of a Port* (Newton Abbot, 1971).
Ignatieff, Michael, *A Just Measure of Pain: The Penitentiary in the Industrial Revolution* (New York, 1978).
Jackman, William T., *The Development of Transportation in Modern England* (1962).
Jackson, Gordon, *Hull in the Eighteenth Century: A Study in Economic and Social History* (London and New York, 1972).
Judd, Gerritt P., *Members of Parliament, 1734-1832* (New Haven, CT, 1955).
Jupp, Peter, *The Governing of Britain, 1688-1848: The Executive Parliament and the People* (Abingdon, 2006).

Kenyon, Hon, George T., *The Life of Lloyd, First Lord Kenyon, Lord Chief Justice of England* (1873).
King, Peter, *Punishing the Criminal Corpse, 1700–1840: Aggravated Forms of Death Penalty in England* (London, 1988).
King, Steven, *Poverty and Welfare in England, 1700–1850* (Manchester, 2000).
Lambert, Sheila, *Bills and Acts: Legislative Procedure in Eighteenth-Century England* (Cambridge, 1971).
Langford, John Alfred, *A Century of Birmingham Life; or A Chronicle of Local Events from 1741 to 1781* (2 vols, Birmingham, 1868).
Langford, Paul, *A Polite and Commercial People* (Oxford and New York, 1989).
——, *Public Life and Propertied Englishmen, 1689–1798* (Oxford and New York, 1991).
Lead, Peter, *Agents of Revolution: John and Thomas Gilbert – Entrepreneurs* (Stoke-on-Trent, 1989).
Lloyd, Sarah, *Charity and Poverty in England, c. 1680–1820: Wild and Visionary Schemes* (Manchester and New York, 2009).
Malet, Hugh, *Bridgewater, the Canal Duke, 1736–1803* (Manchester, 1977).
Mathias, Peter, *The Brewing Industry in England, 1700–1830* (Cambridge, 1959).
McCahill, Michael, *Order and Equipoise: The Peerage and the House of Lords, 1783–1806* (1978).
——, *The House of Lords in the Age of George III* (Chichester and Malden, MA, 2009).
McDowell, R.B., *Ireland in the Age of Imperialism and Revolution 1760–1801* (Oxford, 1979).
McGrath, Patrick, *The Merchant Venturers of Bristol* (Bristol, 1975).
Mingay, G.E., *Parliamentary Enclosure in England: An Introduction to its Causes, Incidence and Impact, 1750–1850* (Harrow, 1997).
Mitchell, B.R., *British Historical Statistics* (Cambridge, 1788).
Mitchell, Leslie, G., *Charles James Fox and the Disintegration of the Whig Party, 1782–1794* (1971).
Money, John, *Experience and Identity: Birmingham and the West Midlands, 1760–1800* (Montreal, 1977).
Morgan, Kenneth, *Bristol and the Atlantic Trade in the Eighteenth Century* (Cambridge and New York, 1993).
Namier, L.B., *England in the Age of the American Revolution* (1961).
——, *The Structure of Politics at the Accession of George III* (2 vols, 1963).
Neale, R.S., *Bath, 1680–1850: A Social History* (London and Boston, MA, 1981).
Newton, Robert, *Eighteenth-Century Exeter* (Exeter, 1984).
Norris, John, *Shelburne and Reform* (London and New York, 1963).
O'Gorman, Frank, *Voters, Patrons and Parties: The Unreformed Electorates of Hanoverian England, 1734–1832* (Oxford, 1989).
O'Shaughnessy, Andrew Jackson, *An Empire Divided: The American Revolution and the British Caribbean* (Philadelphia, PA, 2000).
Pares, Richard, *A West India Fortune* (London and New York, 1953).
Pawson, Eric, *Transport and Economy: The Turnpike Roads of Eighteenth-Century Britain* (London, New York and San Francisco, 1977).
Penson, Lillian M., *The Colonial Agents of the British West Indies: A Study in Colonial Administration, Mainly in the Eighteenth Century* (1971).
Pitkin, Hanna Fenichel, *The Concept of Representation* (Berkeley, CA, and Los Angeles, CA, 1967).
Pressnell, L.S., *Country Banking in the Industrial Revolution* (Oxford, 1956).

Prest, Wilfred, *William Blackstone: Law and Letters in the Eighteenth Century* (Oxford, 2008).
Radzinowicz, Sir Leon, *A History of English Criminal Law and its Administration from 1750. Vol 1: The Movement for Reform* (5 vols, 1948).
Raybould, T.J., *The Economic Emergence of the Black Country: A Study of the Dudley Estate* (Newton Abbot, 1973).
Reitan, Eric A., *Politics, Finance and the People: Economical Reform in the Age of the American Revolution, 1770-1792* (Basingstoke and New York, 2007).
Rogers, Nicholas, *Whigs and Cities: Popular Politics in the Age of Walpole and Pitt* (Oxford, 1989).
Ryden, David Beck, *West Indian Slavery and British Abolition, 1783-1807* (Cambridge and New York, 2009).
Rydz, D.R., *The Parliamentary Agents: A History* (1979).
Shave, Samantha, *Pauper Policies: Poor Law Practice in England 1780-1850* (Manchester, 2017).
Sheridan, Richard B., *Sugar and Slavery: An Economic History of the British West Indies, 1623-1775* (Kingston, Jamaica, 1974).
Slack, Paul, *The English Poor Law, 1531-1782* (Cambridge, 1990).
Smith, S.D., *Slavery, Family, and Gentry Capitalism in the British Atlantic: The World of the Lascelles, 1648-1834* (Cambridge, 2000).
Stephens, W.B. (ed.), *Victoria County History: The History of the County of Warwick, Vol. VII: The City of Birmingham* (1963).
——, *Victoria History of the Counties of England: A History of Essex, Vol. II* (1907).
Sweet, Rosemary, *The English Towns, 1680-1840: Government, Society and Culture* (Harlow and New York, 1998).
Taussig, Anthony, *Blackstone and his Contemporaries* (Austin, TX, 2009).
Thomas, Peter D.G., *The House of Commons in the Eighteenth Century* (1971).
——, *British Politics and the Stamp Act Crisis: The First Act of the American Revolution, 1763-1767* (Oxford, 1975).
Turner, Michael, *English Parliamentary Enclosure: Its Historical Geography and Economic History* (Folkestone, Kent and Hamden, CT, 1980).
Uglow, Jenny, *The Lunar Men: The Friends Who Made the Future* (New York, 2002).
Wadsworth, A.P. and Mann, Julia DeLacy, *The Cotton Trade and the Industrial Revolution 1600-1780* (Manchester, 1931).
Ward, J.R., *The Finance of Canal Building in Eighteenth-Century England* (1974).
Ward, W.R., *Georgian Oxford: University Politics in the Eighteenth Century* (Oxford, 1958).
Warden, Lewis, C., *The Life of Blackstone* (Charlottesville, VA, 1938).
Webb, Sidney and Beatrice, *English Prisons under Local Government* (New York, 1922).
——, *English Local Government. Vol. 5: The Story of The King's Highway* (Hamden, CT, 1963).
Western, J.R., *The English Militia in the Eighteenth Century: The Story of a Political Issue, 1660-1800* (Oxford, 1958).
Wilkinson, David, *The Duke of Portland: Politics and Party in the Age of George III* (Basingstoke, 2003).
Willan, Thomas S., *The Navigation of the River Weaver in the Eighteenth Century* (Manchester, 1951).
Williams, Eric, *Capitalism and Slavery* (Chapel Hill, NC, 1944).
Williams, Orlo Cyprian, *The Clerical Organization of the House of Commons, 1661-1850* (Oxford, 1954).

Wilson, Kathleen, *The Sense of the People: Politics, Culture and Imperialism in England, 1715–1785* (Cambridge and New York, 1995).
Wilson, Richard G., *Gentlemen Merchants: The Merchant Community in Leeds, 1700–1830* (Manchester, 1971).
Wordie, J.R., *Estate Management in Eighteenth-Century England* (1982).

Articles and Chapters

Anderson, B.L. 'The attorney and the early capital market in Lancashire', in *Capital Formation in the Industrial Revolution*, ed. Francois Crouzet (1972).
Beckett, John V., 'A back-bench MP in the eighteenth century: Sir James Lowther of Whitehaven', *Parlimentary History* (1982).
——, 'An industrial town in the making, 1750–1830', in *A Centenary History of Nottingham*, ed. Beckett (Manchester and New York, 1997).
——, 'Parliament and the localities: The borough of Nottingham', in *Parliament and Locality, 1660–1939*, ed. David Dean and Clyve Jones (Parliamentary Yearbook Trust, Edinburgh, 1998).
Beer, Samuel, 'The representation of interests in British government: Historical background', *The American Political Science Review*, li (1957).
Bowden, Witt, 'English manufacturers and the commercial treaty of 1786 with France', *American Historical Review*, xxv (1919).
——, 'The influence of the manufacturers on some of the early policies of William Pitt', *American Historical Review*, xxix (1924).
Brewer, John, 'The Wilkites and the law, 1763–74: A study of radical notions of governance', in *An Ungovernable People: The England and their Law in the Seventeenth and Eighteenth Centuries*, ed. John Brewer and John Styles (New Brunswick, NJ, 1780).
Brill, Herbert C., 'British colonial policy in the West Indies, 1783–1793', *English Historical Review*, xxxi (1916).
Christie, I.R., 'The Wilkites and the general election of 1774', in *Myth and Reality in Eighteenth-Century British Politics and Other Papers* (1970).
——, 'The Yorkshire Association, 1780–4: A study in political organization', in *Myth and Reality in Eighteenth-Century British Politics and Other Papers* (1970).
Coats, A.W., 'Economic thought and poor law policy in the eighteenth century', *Economic History Review*, xiii (1960).
Connors, Richard, 'Parliament and poverty in mid-eighteenth-century England', *Parliamentary History*, xxi (2002).
Craton, Michael, 'Hobbesian or Panglossian? Two extremes of slave conditions in the British West Indies', *William and Mary Quarterly*, 3rd Ser. xxxv (1978).
Devereux, Simon, 'The making of the Penitentiary Act, 1775–1779', *Historical Journal*, xl (1999).
——, 'Inexperienced humanitarians: William Wilberforce, William Pitt and the execution crisis of the 1780s', *Law and History Review*, xxxviii (2015).
——, 'Radicals and reformers in the age of Wilkes and Wyvill' in *British Politics and Society from Walpole to Pitt, 1742–1789*, ed. Jeremy Back (Basingstoke and London, 1990).
Ditchfield, G.M., 'Parliament, the Quakers and the tithe question, 1750–1835', *Parliamentary History*, iv (1985).
——, 'The subscription issue in British Parliamentary politics, 1772–79', *Parliamentary History*, vii (1988).
——, 'Lord Thurlow', in *Lords of Parliament. Studies: 1714–1914* (Stanford, CA, 1995).

——, '"How narrow will the limits of this toleration appear?" Dissenting petitions to Parliament, 1772–1773', in *Parliament and Dissent*, ed. Stephen Taylor and David Wykes (Edinburgh, 2005).

Duckham, Barron F., 'Canals and river navigation', in *Transportation in the Industrial Revolution*, ed. Derek H. Aldcroft and Michael J. Freeman (Manchester and Dover, NH, 1983).

Eastwood, David, 'Men, morals and the machinery of social legislation, 1790–1840', *Parliamentary History*, xiii (1994).

Fraser, Peter, 'Public petitioning and Parliament before 1832', *History*, xlvi (1961).

Gauci, Perry, 'Learning the ropes of sand: The West Indian interest, 1714–1760', in *Regulating the British Economy, 1660–1850*, ed. Gauci, (Farnham and Burlington, VT, 2011).

——, 'The attack of the Creolian powers: West Indians at the Parliamentary elections of mid-Georgian Britain', 1754–1774, *Parliament, Politics and Policy in Britain and Ireland, c. 1680–1832: Essays in Honour of D. W. Hayton*, ed. Clyve Jones and James Kelly (Chichester, 2014).

Gray, I.E., 'Ferdinando Stratford of Gloucestershire', *Transactions of the Bristol and Gloucestershire Archaeological Society* (1946, 7, 8).

Harling, Philip, 'Parliament, the state and "Old Corruption": Conceptualizing reform: c. 1790–1832', in *Rethinking the Age of Reform: Britain, 1780–1850*, ed. Arthur Burns and Joanna Innes (Cambridge, 2003).

Hay, Douglas, 'The state and the market in 1800: Lord Kenyon and Mr Waddington', *Past & Present*, clxii (1999).

Haydon, Colin, 'Parliament and popery in England, 1700–1780', in *Parliament and the Church, 1529–1960*, ed. J.P. Parry and Stephen Taylor (Edinburgh, 2000).

Hopkinson, G.H., 'Road development in South Yorkshire and North Derbyshire, 1700–1850', *Transactions of the Hunter Archaeological Society*, x (1971).

Hoppit, Julian, 'Patterns of Parliamentary legislation, 1660–1801', *Historical Journal*, xxxix (1996).

Hoppit, Julian, Innes, Joanna and Styles, John, 'Towards a history of Parliamentary legislation, 1660–1800', *Parliamentary History*, xiii (1994).

——, 'Petitions, economic legislation and interest groups in Britain, 1660–1800', in *Pressure and Parliament from Civil War to Civil Society*, ed. Richard Huzzey (Parliamentary History Yearbook Trust, Chichester and Medford, MA, 2018).

Innes, Joanna, 'Parliament and the shaping of eighteenth-century English social policy', *Transactions of the Royal Historical Society*, 5th ser., xl (1990).

Innes, Joanna, 'Parliament and the shaping of English social policy', in *Inferior Politics: Social Problems and Social Policies in Eighteenth-Century Britain* (Oxford and New York, 2009).

——, 'Local acts of a national Parliament: Parliament's role in sanctioning local acts in eighteenth-century Britain', in *Parliament and Locality: 1660–1939*, ed. David Dean and Clyve Jones (Edinburgh, 1998).

——, 'Politics and morals: The Reformation of manners movement in later eighteenth-century England' in *The Transformation of Political Culture: England and Germany in the Late Eighteenth Century*, ed. Hellmuth Eckhart (Oxford, 1990).

——, 'The State of the Poor: Eighteenth-Century England in European Perspective', in *Rethinking the Leviathan: The Eighteenth-Century State in Britain and Germany*, ed. John Brewer and Eckhart Hellmuth (1999).

——, 'Thomas Gilbert (c. 1720–98)', in *The Biographical Dictionary of British Economists*, ed. Donald Rutherford and Warren Samuels (2 vols, London, 2004).

——, 'The "mixed economy of welfare" in early modern England: Assessments of options from Hale to Malthus (c. 1683–1803)', in *Charity, Self-Interest and Welfare in the English Past*, ed. Martin Daunton (Abingdon and New York, 2016).

Kelly, Paul, 'Radicalism and public opinion in the general election of 1784', *Bulletin of the Institute of Historical Research*, xlv (1972).

——, 'Constituents' instructions to members of Parliament in the eighteenth century', in *Party and Management in Parliament, 1660–1784*, ed. Clyve Jones (New York, 1984).

Knights, Mark, 'Participation and representation before democracy: Petitions and addresses in premodern Britain', in *Political Representation*, ed. Ian Shapiro, Susan S. Stokes, Elizabeth Jean Wood and Alexander S. Kirshner (Cambridge and New York, 2009).

Langford, Paul, 'William Pitt and public opinion in 1757', *English Historical Review*, lxxxviii (1973).

——, 'The first Rockingham Administration and the repeal of the Stamp Act: The role of the commercial lobby and economic pressures' in *Resistance, Politics, and the American Struggle for Independence, 1765–1775*, ed. Walter H. Conser, Jr, Ronald McCarthy, David J. Toscano and Gene Sharpe (Boulder, CO, 1986).

——, 'Property and "virtual representation"', *Historical Journal*, xxxi (1988).

Lawson, Philip and Phillips, Jim, '"Our execrable banditti": Perceptions of nabobs in mid-eighteenth-century Britain', *Albion*, xvi (1984).

Little, Bryan, 'Gloucestershire spas: An eighteenth-century parallel', in *Essays in Bristol and Gloucestershire History*, ed. Patrick McGrath and John Cannon (Bristol, 1976).

Loft, Philip, 'Petitions and petitioners to the Westminster Parliament, 1660–1788', *Parliamentary History*, xxxviii (2019).

Lowe, W.C., 'Peers and printers: The beginnings of sustained press coverage of the House of Lords in the 1770s', *Parliamentary History*, vii (1988).

Marshall, P.J., 'The anti-slave trade movement in Bristol', in *Bristol in the Eighteenth Century*, ed. Patrick McGrath (Newton Abbot, 1972).

Martin, J.M., 'Members of Parliament and enclosure: A reconsideration', *Agricultural History Review*, xxvii (1974).

McCahill, Michael, 'Peers, patronage and the Industrial Revolution', *Journal of British Studies*, xvi (1976).

——, 'The House of Lords in the 1760s', in *A Pillar of the Constitution: The House of Lords in British Politics, 1640–1784*, ed. Clyve Jones (London and Ronceverte, WV, 1989).

——, 'Estate acts of Parliament, 1740–1800', in *Institutional Practice and Memory: Parliamentary People, Records and Histories. Essays in Honour of Sir John Sainty*, ed. Clyve Jones (Chichester, 2013).

McGrath, Patrick, 'Edmund Burke: The commissary of his Bristol constituents, 1774–1780', *English Historical Review*, lxxiii (1958).

Minchinton, Walter, 'The port of Bristol in the eighteenth century', in *Bristol in the Eighteenth Century*, ed. Patrick McGrath (Newton Abbot, 1972).

Mitchell, L.G., 'Politics and revolution, 1772–1800', in *The History of the University of Oxford. Vol. V: The Eighteenth Century*, ed. Lucy Sutherland and L.G. Mitchell (Oxford, 1986).

Moore, T.K. and Horwitz, Henry, 'Who runs the House? Aspects of Parliamentary organization in the later seventeenth century', *Journal of Modern History*, xliii (1971).

Morgan, Kenneth, 'Bristol West Indian merchants in the eighteenth century', *Transactions of the Royal Historical Society*, 6th ser., iii (1993).

Munby, Julian and Walton, Hugh, 'The building of New Road', *Oxoniensia*, lv (1990).

Namier, L.B. 'Country gentlemen in Parliament, 1750–1787', in *Crossroads in Power: Essays on Eighteenth-Century England* (1962).
Norris, John, 'Samuel Garbett and the early development of industrial lobbying', *Economic History Review*, x, 2nd ser. (1958).
O'Brien, Patrick, Griffith, Trevor and Hunt, Philip, 'Political components of the Industrial Revolution: Parliament and the English cotton textile industry, 1660–1774', *EcHR*, n.s., xliv (1972).
O'Shaughnessy, Andrew Jackson, 'The formation of a colonial lobby: The West India interest, British colonial policy and the American Revolution', *Historical Journal*, xl (1997).
Penson, Lillian, 'The London West India interest', *English Historical Review*, xxxvi (1921).
Phillips, John A., 'Popular politics in unreformed England', *Journal of Modern History*, lii (1980).
Richards, Eric, 'The industrial face of a great estate: Trentham and Lilleshall, 1780–1840', *EcHR*, xxvii (1974).
Richardson, David, 'The ending of the British slave trade in 1807 The economic context', *The British Slave Trade: Abolition, Parliament and People*, ed. Stephen Farrell, Melanie Unwin and James Walvin (Edinburgh, 2007).
Robinson, Eric, 'Matthew Boulton and the art of Parliamentary lobbying', *Historical Journal*, vii (1964).
——, 'James Watt and the law of patent', *Technology and Culture*, xiii (1972).
Ryden, David Beck, 'Spokesman for opposition: Stephen Fuller, the Jamaica Assembly, and the London West India interest during popular abolitionism, 1788–1795', *The Jamaican Historical Review*, xxvi (2013)
Seymour, S. Daniels and Watkins, C., 'Estate and empire: Sir George Cornewall's management of Moccas, Herefordshire and La Taste, Grenada, 1771–1819', *Journal of Historical Geography*, xxiv (1998).
Sheridan, Richard B., 'Simon Taylor, sugar tycoon of Jamaica, 1740–1813', *Agricultural History*, xlv (1971).
Sutherland, Lucy, 'Edmund Burke and relations between members of Parliament and their constituents', in *Politics and Finance in the Eighteenth Century*, ed. Aubrey Newman (1984).
——, 'The administration of the university', in *History of the University of Oxford. Vol. V: The Eighteenth Century*, ed. Lucy Sutherland and L.G. Mitchell (Oxford, 1986).
Sweet, Rosemary, 'Local identities and a national parliament, c. 1688–1835', in *Parliaments, Nations and Identities in Britain and Ireland, 1660–1850*, ed. Julian Hoppit (Manchester and New York, 2003).
Tate, William Edward, 'Parliamentary enclosure in the county of Nottingham during the eighteenth and nineteenth centuries (1743–1868)', *Thoroton Society Record Series*, v (1935).
——, 'Members of Parliament and their personal relations to enclosures: A study with special reference to Oxfordshire enclosures', *Agricultural History*, xxiii (1949).
Thompson, Andrew C., 'Toleration, dissent and the state in Britain', in *The Oxford History of Protestant Dissenting Traditions. Vol. II: The Long Eighteenth Century c. 1689–c.1828*, ed. Andrew C. Thompson (Oxford, 2018).
Tranter, Neil, 'The agricultural sector in the age of industrialization', *Historical Journal*, xxxiii (1990).
Tucker, Bob and Black, Jeremy, 'John Tucker, MP, and mid-eighteenth-century British politics', *Albion*, xxix (1997).

Underdown, Patrick T., 'Religious opposition to the licensing of the Bristol and Birmingham theatres in the eighteenth century', *University of Birmingham Historical Journal*, vi (1957–8).
——, 'Bristol and Burke', in *Bristol in the Eighteenth Century*, ed. Patrick McGrath (Newton Abbot, 1972).
Walvin, James, 'The public campaign in England against slavery, 1787–1835', in *The Abolition of the Atlantic Slave Trade*, ed. David Eltis and James Walvin (Edinburgh, 2007).
Ward, J.R., 'The profitability of sugar planting in the British West Indies, 1650–1734', *EcHR*, 2nd ser., 31 (1978).
——, 'The British West Indies, 1748–1815', in *The Oxford History of the British Empire. Vol. II: The Eighteenth Century*, ed. P.J. Marshall (Oxford, 1998).
Ward, Roger, 'Birmingham: A political profile, 1700–1840', in *Birmingham: The Workshop of the World*, ed. Carl Chinn and Malcolm Dick (Liverpool, 2016).
Westwood, Arthur, *The Assay Office at Birmingham. Part I: The Foundation* (Birmingham, 1936).
Wilson, Richard G., 'The Aire and Calder Navigation. Part III: The Navigation in the second half of the eighteenth century', *The Bradford Antiquary*, xliv (1969).
——, 'Newspapers and industry: The export of wool controversies of the 1780s', in *The Press in English Society from the Seventeenth to the Nineteenth Centuries*, ed. Michael Harris and Alan Lee (Cranbury, NJ and London, 1986).
Woodland, Patrick, 'Extra-Parliamentary political organization in the making: Benjamin Heath and the opposition to the 1763 Cider Excise', *Parliamentary History*, iv (1985).

Unpublished PhD Dissertation

Ramage, Jean H., 'The English woollen industry and Parliament, 1750–1830: A study in economic attitudes and political pressure' (PhD thesis, Yale University, 1970).

Index

Note: Page numbers followed by an italic *f* indicate a figure and *t* indicates a table.

Abbot, Charles 223
Abdy, Sir Anthony 119, 120, 121, 122, 124
Abingdon, Earls of 80, 95
active county legislators 32–6
active county MPs, in the 1780s 42–5
Adams, John 139
Addenbrooke Hospital 34
Affleck, Sir Edmund 134*t*
Aire and Calder Navigation 20, 39
alehouses 112
Allen, Benjamin 134*t*
Allen, James 132
Allen, Joseph 151
Almon, John 20
Alston, Bere 240
Amcotts, Charles 33
Amcotts, Wharton 202
Amyand, John 134*t*
Amyand, Sir George 134*t*
Anderson, B.L. 99
Anderson, James 178
Anne, Queen 103, 184, 220
Annual Register 230
Anson, Thomas 162
Apsley, Henry Bathurst, Lord Chancellor 219
Arcedeckne, Chaloner 134*t*, 156
Arden, Richard Pepper 50, 223
Argument Concerning the Militia, An, (Savile) 38
Aris's Birmingham Gazette 147, 164
Arkwright, Richard 17, 23
Armytage, Francis 144
Ashby, Shukburgh 206
Assay Office Bill 167
Atkinson, Richard 134*t*

backbench MPs, and general measures 7–8
Bacon, Anthony 134*t*

Bagot, Sir William 70, 162
Baillie, James 134*t*
Baker, Sir William 134*t*, 142, 240
Baker, William 9, 17, 134*t*, 228
Bampfylde, Sir Charles Warwick 135*t*
Bankes, Henry 231
banking crisis of 1772 63
Banks, Sir Joseph 44
Barnard, Sir John 135*t*
Barrington, Shute 225
Barrington, William Wildman, Lord 13, 55, 77, 119, 121, 122, 123, 204, 240, 242, 243
Barrow, Sir Charles 135*t*
Barwell, Edward 119, 120, 122
Bastard, Edmund 180
Bastard, John Pollexfen 46–7, 231, 234
Bath Improvement Act/Bill 21, 38
Bayly, Nathaniel 135*t*, 146–7, 148
Beauchamp, William, Lord 73, 163, 234
Beaufoy, Henry 36, 94, 178–9
Beckett, John 22, 204
Beckett, J.V. 29
Beckford, Julines 133, 135*t*
Beckford, Peter 133, 135*t*
Beckford, Richard 133, 135*t*
Beckford, William 61, 132, 133, 135*t*, 144, 193, 195, 196*f*, 235
  and free port proposal 143
  and reform movements 185, 186
  and the Stamp Act 140, 141, 142
Beckford II, William 135*t*
Bedford, Duke of 22
Bedworth, enclosure of 87
Beer, Professor Samuel 237
Bentham, Jeremy 82, 110
Bentinck, John Albert 234
Bentley, James 100
Berkeley, Captain George Cranfield 236

Bertie, Brownlow, Lord 9, 11, 12, 33–4, 43, 52, 204
Bertie family, Earls of Abingdon 79, 95
Bertie, Peregrine 124
Bethell, Slingsby 135*t*
Bindley, John 240
Birmingham 159–60
   Chamber of Manufacturers 177
   Commercial Chamber 174
   Commercial Committee 171, 172–3, 176
   'Priestley Riots' 1791 175
   Society of Constitution Information 175
Birmingham & Birmingham & Fazeley Canal Company 165
Birmingham and Fazeley Canal Navigation 164–5
Birmingham Assay Office 165–7
Birmingham Bill 70, 167
Birmingham Canal 101, 162–5, 220
Birmingham Canal Company 163, 164, 176
Birmingham Gazette 169
Birmingham Theatre Bill 197
Blackburne, John 135*t*
Blackett, Sir Walter 203
Black, Eugene 191
Black, Jeremy 205
Blackstone, Sir William 13, 15, 79–82, 95, 107, 142, 227, 234
Blake, Patrick 135*t*
Blakey, William 168
Bland Burges, James 234
Bodmin Road Bill 243
Bond, John 135*t*
Boston Tea Party 144
Botley Act 81
Botley Causeway 81, 82
Botley Turnpike Bill 87–8
Boulton, Matthew 97, 101, 105, 160, 168, 169, 173, 175–6, 177
   and Birmingham Assay Office 165, 166
   and Birmingham Canal 162
bounties 178
Bouverie, Hon. William 135*t*
Boyd, John 135*t*
Bradley, James 194, 241
Bramston, Thomas 124

Bramwell, George 216
Brand Hollis, Thomas 186, 190
Brewer, John 186, 188
brewers 18–19
Brickdale, Matthew 74, 135*t*, 204, 235, 236
   and Bristol's legislation 62–3, 64, 65, 68, 75, 76, 77
   political conduct of 206
Bridgewater, Francis Egerton, 3rd Duke of 90, 97, 98, 101
Bridlington Harbour Bill 47
Brindley, James 100
Bristol 13, 55, 59–60, 76, 77
   1780–90 75–6
   Edmund Burke and 65–74
   and its MPs 60–5
   soap duties 68, 70
   Society of Merchant Venturers (SMV) 60–1, 63, 68, 72, 76, 240
Bristol Bridge Act 75
Bristol Playhouse Bill 64
Bristol Port Bill 69
Bristol Quakers 70
Bristol Streets Bill 62
Bristol Turnpike Bill 51
British Caribbean islands 132
British Fisheries Act 1786 178
British Society for Extending British Fisheries, & Improving the Sea Coast of the Kingdom 179–80
British West Indies 62
   free port system in 65
Broadbridge, S.R. 164
Bromley, Hon. Thomas 135*t*
Bromley, William Throckmorton 160
Brougham, Henry 79
Browne, Isaac Hawkins 236
Brudenell, George Bridges 11, 12
Buckingham, George Nugent Temple Grenville, 1st Marquess of 212, 213
Buller, James 240
Bull, Frederick 135*t*, 188
Bunbury, Sir Charles 226, 234
Bunbury, Sir Thomas Charles 14, 15, 135*t*
Burdett, Sir Francis 50
Burges, James Bland 226, 234
Burgoyne, Montague 126
Burke, Edmund 2, 13, 46, 55, 135*t*, 170, 193, 194, 214, 226

and abolition bills 139
and Bristol 65–74, 77–8, 204, 235
and conflict between the House of Commons and the House of Lords 218
and constituents' instructions 195–6, 197
economical reform measures 138–9
and the India Bill 227
proposal to abolish the Board of Trade 111
on Sir George Savile 30
William Windham and 91
Burke, William 160, 217
Burney, Fanny 91
Burn, Richard 106, 112
Burrell, Peter 11, 12
Burt, William Matthew 135t
Bute, Lord 79

Calder-Kingsmill Navigation Bill 38
Cambridge Improvement Bill 36
canals 100, 162–5
Cannon, John 184, 189, 191–2, 206, 211
Capitalism and Slavery (Williams) 150
capital punishment
  for arson in dockyards 15
  hanging as punishment for capital crimes 49
Caribbean islands 75
Cartwright, John 186–7
Catholic Relief Act 53
Cavendish, George Augustus, Lord 42–3, 52
Cavendish, John, Lord 67
Chalklin, Christopher 20, 126
Chamber of Manufacturers, Birmingham 159, 170, 172–3, 177
Champion, Anthony 240
Champion, Richard 65, 70, 170, 197
Charles I, King 83
Charles II, King 193
Chelmer Navigation Bill 117, 118, 120, 121, 126, 127
Cheshire 190
Chilvers Coton parish 90
Cholmley, Nathaniel 11
Christie, Ian 187, 189, 212

Church of England 83
  Nullum Tempus privileges of the 83
Cider Excise Tax 195, 206, 239–41
civil list revenue, regulation of 202
Clare, Robert Nugent, Lord 60–5, 67, 68, 71, 72, 77, 137t, 142, 204
Clavering, Sir Thomas 9–10, 193
Clerkenwell, house of correction 50
Clerke, Sir Philip Jennings 135t
coal 89
Coal Tax 170
Cocoa Nut Duty Bill 216
Codrington, Sir William 135t
Coke, Daniel Parker 204, 207
Coldbath Prison 50
Colebrooke, Sir George 135t
Colleton, J.E. 135t
Colley, Linda 234
Colmore, William 163
Combe, Richard 15, 69, 74, 77
Commentaries on the Laws of England (Blackstone) 79, 80, 82, 95
Commission of Public Accounts 189
communications, improvements in 20–1
Connors, Richard 45, 230
constituencies, representation and smaller 238–44
constituent instructions 2, 184, 195–9
Con-Test (newspaper) 206
Cooper, Sir Grey 69, 215
Copyright Bill 223
Corn Bill 218
corn bill 76
Cornewall, Sir George 135t
Cornwallis, Archbishop 46
cotton cloth, duties on 17–18
Cotton, Sir John Hynde 12, 24–5
Counties and Public Building (Chalklin) 126
county elections, reform of 221, 225
county gaols 52–3
county MPs 233
  in the 1780s 42–5
  active legislators 32–6
  and general legislation 45–50
  number of bills promoted by, 1765–7, 1772–4, 1786–8 32t
Coventry Canal Bill 204
Craftsman 195

Craven, William, Lord 161
creditors' relief bill 82, 227
Crewe, John 42, 135*t*, 188
Crewkerne Turnpike Bill 51
Cricklade Election Bill 225
Criminal Laws Bill 1772 226
Crosby, Brass, Lord Mayor 201, 219
Cruger, Henry 64, 69, 73, 74, 76, 77, 135*t*, 197, 199, 235
    and abolition of the slave trade 156
    and Bristol's legislation 75
Cumbrian turnpike acts 29
Cunliffe, Ellis 135*t*
Cust, John 43
Cust, Sir Brownlow 33

Dance, George 123, 127
Dartmouth, William Legge, 2nd Earl of 161, 166, 168, 177
Dashwood, Sir Francis 239
Daubeney, George 135*t*, 206
Davers, Sir Charles 136*t*
Dawes, John 136*t*
Dawkins, Henry 136*t*
Dawkins, James 136*t*
Dawkins II, James 136*t*
death penalty 14
Debrett, John 20
Debtors and Creditors Bill 226, 234
Dee Navigation Bill 14
DeGrey, Thomas 12
Dehany, Philip 136*t*
Delaval, John Hussey, Lord 207
Delaval, Sir John Hussey 235, 236
democracy 199–204, 208
Dempster, George 179
Denbigh, Basil Feilding, 6th Earl of 34
Derbyshire 33
Devaynes, William 136*t*
Devereux, Simon 49
Devon 46
Devonshire, William Cavendish, 4th Duke of 99
Dicker, Samuel 136*t*
Dickinson, H.T. 129, 185
Dickinson, William 51, 136*t*
Dickinson II, William 136*t*
Ditchfield, Professor G.M. 103
Dixon, Gilbert 165, 166

dogs, licensing of 112
Dolben, Sir William 84, 202, 227, 230, 236
    bill for observance of the Sabbath 50
    Slave Trade Regulation Bills 48, 75, 76, 130, 155
Dominica 143, 144, 148
Dominica free port act 75
Dominica Society 62
Donnington Wood Canal 99
Dowdeswell, William 143, 226
Drax, Thomas Erle 136*t*
Dugdale, Dugdale Strafford 176
Duncombe, Henry 12, 47, 171
Dundas, Henry 152, 179
Dundas, Sir Thomas 58
Duntze, John 242
Durant, George 136*t*
Durbin, Sir John 73
Dyson, Jeremiah 217–18

East, Edward Hyde 136*t*
East India Company 144, 151, 227, 242
Eastwood, David 45, 192, 230, 237
ecclesiastical courts 46
Eden, William 14, 15, 82, 151, 154, 173, 203, 229, 234
Effingham, Thomas Howard, Lord 171, 225
Egerton, Francis *see* Bridgewater, Francis Egerton, 3rd Duke of
Egmont, John Perceval, Earl of 107
Ehrman, John 189
electors, rights of 41
Eliot, Edward 30
Emancipation Act 1833 150
Emden, Clive 195
enclosure acts/bills 18, 22, 32, 33, 42, 87
Essex Gaol 117
Essex Gaol Bill 123–7
estate acts 22
Estwick, Samuel 136*t*, 149
Ewer, William 155
excise crisis 195
Exeter 44
Eyre, Francis 136*t*

Failed Legislation (Hoppit) 226
Fane, Henry 106, 241

Fane, Thomas 241
Farr, Paul 69, 197
Feather's Tavern group of Church of England clergy and laity 39, 83, 85
Felix Farley's Bristol Journal 70
Felon's Anatomy Bill 26
Fergusson, Adam 215
Finch family 238
    Maidstone 238
fisheries 177–81
    bounties 178
Fisheries Acts 178, 179
Fitzherbert, William 136*t*
Fitzwalter, Lord 117
Fitzwilliam family 239
Fitzwilliam, William Wentworth, Earl 58, 77
Flood, Henry 94
flour, importation of 61
Folkestone, Jacob Pleydell-Bouverie, Viscount 15–17, 242
Fortescue, Matthew, Lord 225
Foster, Thomas 136*t*
Fothergill, John 166
Fothergill, Thomas 85
Fox, Charles 25, 94, 214, 227
Fox, Charles James 216, 225, 226, 228
Fox, Henry 118
Fraser, Peter 193
Freeman, Sambrooke 136*t*
Free Ports Act 143–4
French, Jeffrey 136*t*
Fry, Fripp & Co. 70
Fuller, John 136*t*
Fuller II, John 136*t*
Fuller, Rose 8, 136*t*, 140, 141, 142, 143, 144, 145, 209
Fuller, Stephen 45, 48, 131, 134, 140–1, 143, 148–9, 152, 158
Fuller, Thomas 152
fustian tax 45, 170

Gainsborough, establishment of a port at 57
Galway, Robert Monckton Arundell, Lord 199, 200
Gambles, Anna 178
Gamon, Richard Grace 136*t*
gaols, county 52–3

Garbett, Samuel 160, 161, 170, 171, 172, 173, 174, 175, 176, 207
Gardner, Alan 136*t*
Garrick, David 71
Gascoyne, Bamber 29, 117–18, 120–1, 122–3, 136*t*, 204, 237
    and the Essex Gaol Bill 123–5, 126, 127
Gascoyne, Isaac 237
Gem, Thomas 161
general measures 7–8, 233–5
    backbench MPs and 7–8
General Turnpike Act 102
George III, King 35, 77, 104–5, 144, 157, 158, 206, 213, 227, 228
Germain, George, Lord 147, 148, 188
Gibbons, Sir John 136*t*, 142
Gibbons, William 174
Gilbert, John 97, 98, 99, 167
Gilbert's Act 108–9, 110, 113
Gilbert, Thomas 1, 8, 12, 97–115, 162, 166, 188, 220, 234
    1765 poor law 80
    bills introduced by 114–15
    early general reforms 101–3
    obituary 101–2
    political and court reforms 103–6
    poor law legislation 106–15, 209, 233
    Rogues and Vagabonds Bill 226
Glover, Richard 17, 146
Glynn, Sir John 199
Glyn, Sir Richard 136*t*
Goddard, Ambrose 184
Gooch, Sir Thomas 22
Gordon, George, Lord 206
Gordon, James 136*t*
Gordon, Sir William 136*t*
Gower, Granville Leveson-Gower, Earl 90, 97, 98–9, 100, 107, 162, 228
Gray, Charles 112, 123, 124
Greatheed, Samuel 136*t*
Grenada 75, 148
Grenville, George 8, 67, 140, 141, 160, 213, 240
Grenville, George Nugent Temple *see* Buckingham, George Nugent Temple Grenville, 1st Marquess of
Grenville, James 51
Grenville, Lord 158, 231
Grenville, William 48

Grey, Charles 94
Grey, Charles Harry, Lord 162
Grieve, Hilda 117, 122, 127
Grigby, Joshua 199
Grosvenor, Richard Erle Drax 136*t*
Grosvenor, Sir Richard 234
Grosvenor, Thomas 136*t*
Growth of Silk Act 63
Guernsey, Heneage Finch, Lord 161, 167, 168
Gulston, Joseph 134, 136*t*
Gurney, John 94

Hanway, Jonas 109
Harbord, Sir Harbord 44, 96
Hard Labour Bill 82
Hardman, John 136*t*
Hardwicke, Philip Yorke, Chancellor 222
Hardy, Sir Charles 77
Harley, Hon. Thomas 136*t*
Harley, Thomas 167
Harris, Bob 178
Harris, Ian 20
Harris, James 20, 39, 198
Hastings, Warren 93, 96
Hawkers and Pedlars Bill 91
Hawkesbury, Robert Banks Jenkinson, Lord 152, 154, 180
Hawkins-Browne, Isaac 173
Haydon, Colin 40
Hayley, George 136*t*
Hayton, David 183, 208
Heath, Benjamin 240
Hewett, John 11
Heywood, James Modyford 136*t*
Highways Act 102
Highways Turnpike Roads Act 1766 102
Hill, Sir Richard 134, 136*t*
Hillyer, William 127
History of Birmingham (Hutton) 164
History of Parliament 3, 5, 47, 180, 183, 206, 236, 243–4
Hobart, Henry 92
Hoghton, Sir Henry 86, 198, 199, 226
Holbourne, Francis 77
Holdsworth, Arthur 180
Holdsworth, Sir William 82, 227
Holte, Sir Charles 161
Hood, Admiral Sir Alexander 212

Hoppit, Julian 3, 22, 130, 178, 181, 183, 226
Horne, Rev. George 86
Horwitz, Henry 4, 26, 210, 244
Hotham, Beaumont 11
House of Commons
  co-ordination between the House of Lords and 219–21
  institutional conflict between the House of Lords and 216–19
  legislative friction between the House of Lords and 221–5
  legislative partnership with the House of Lords 211–32
  privileges constraints 214–16
House of Lords
  constraints on peers' electoral interests 211–14
  co-ordination between the House of Commons and 219–21
  institutional conflict between the House of Commons and 216–19
  legislative friction between the House of Commons and 221–5
  legislative partnership with the House of Commons 211–32
  limits on the privileges of the House of Commons 229
  loss of House of Commons' bills in 226–9
  privileges constraints 214–16
Howard, General Sir George 200, 201, 202, 235
Howard, John 16, 126
Howard, Thomas *see* Effingham, Thomas Howard, Lord
Howe, Richard, Admiral Lord 17
Hulks Act 15
Hull 55, 57–9
Hull Dock Company 57
Hunt, Thomas 243
Huskisson, William 239

Ignatieff, Michael 50
Ihalainen, Pasi 183, 199, 208
improvement bills/acts 21, 36, 56
India Bill 35, 214, 227, 229
Innes, Joanna 3, 45, 108, 109, 111, 112, 230, 233
Innes, William 136*t*

Insolvent Debtors Bill 234
interest groups 129–58, 209
'Interludes Bill' 49
Ireland, relaxation of the restrictions on trade with 71
Irish salted provisions bill 68

Jackson, Richard 80
Jackson's Oxford Journal 81, 89
Jamaica 75, 131, 132, 140, 141
    Assembly of 157, 158
    Council of 157
    free ports 62, 144
Jebb, John 186
Jenkinson, Charles 137t, 153, 178, 230
Jennings-Clerke, Sir Philip 188
Jewish Naturalization Bill 1753 206
Johnstone, Sir James 137t
Joseph II of Austria, Emperor 170
Journals of the House of Commons 5

Kelly, Paul 206
Kent, electorate in 29
Kenyon, Lloyd 46, 224–5
Keyberry Road Bill 46
King, Steven 109
Kingston-upon-Hull 13, 76, 77
King Street Theatre, Birmingham 169, 170
Kirkman, John 137t
Knights, Mark 237–8
knights of the shire 23, 29–53, 191, 233
    active county legislators 32–6
    legislative activity among 31–2
Kynaston, Edward 7, 8

Labrador trade 73
Ladbroke, Robert 137t
Ladbroke, Sir Robert 137t
Lambert, John 71
Lancashire 13, 29, 44
landlord representation 181, 183
Lane, John 162
Langford, Paul 3, 24, 26, 67, 204, 205, 209, 235
    on burden of legislation on knights of the shire 30
    and 'landlord representation' 131, 183
    and role of Barlow Trecothick in the Stamp Act 140

Lansdowne, Lord 174
Laroche, Sir James 63, 69, 77, 137t
Lascelles, Daniel 137t
Lascelles, Edward 137t
Lascelles, Edwin 137t, 166
Launceston, Cornwall 241
Lawley, Francis 176
Lawley, Sir Robert 53, 161, 162, 173, 174, 176
Leeds, Francis Godolphin-Osborne, Duke of 216, 224
Leeds-Selby Canal Bill 30, 39
Leeward Islands 132, 140
Legge, William *see* Dartmouth, William Legge, 2nd Earl of
legislation 234, 244
    complexity of 50–2
    impact of specific and local 19–23
    number of bills promoted by county members, 1765–7, 1772–4, 1786–8 32t
    process of legislating 6–7
legislative activity
    among knights of the shire 31–2
    case studies 13–19
    of English county MPs 31t
Lethieullier, Benjamin 137t
Lewes, Sir Watkin 137t
Lincolnshire 13, 32, 33
Lindsey, Theophilus 40
linen trade, in Great Britain and Ireland 10
Lippincott, Sir Henry 137t
Liskeard, Cornwall 239, 240
Liverpool 13
Liverpool, Robert Banks Jenkinson, 2nd Earl of 232
lobbies 159–81
    background 130
    Birmingham Assay Office 165–8
    canals 162–5
    Chamber of Manufacturers, Birmingham 172–3
    fisheries 177–81
    indirect representation 161–2
    issues in Birmingham 168–70
local acts, by-products of 2
London, City of, Remonstrance of 193
London Goldsmiths 166

London's Company of the Mystery of
   Goldsmiths 176
Long, Beeston 141, 144, 145
Long, Charles 137*t*
Long, Dudley 137*t*
Long, Edward 131, 152
Loughborough, Lord 222–3, 230
Lowther, Robert 212
Lowther, Sir James 29, 30, 39, 137*t*, 184,
   212, 214
Lowther, William 212
Lucas, Thomas 137*t*
Luther, John 121, 123, 124, 125, 126
Luttrell, Henry Lawes 41, 186
Lyme Regis, Dorset 241
Lyttleton, Hon. George Fulke 137*t*
Lyttleton, Thomas, Lord 219

Macaulay, Catherine 197
Macdonald, Archibald 223
Mackreth, Robert 137*t*
Mackworth, Sir Herbert 11
Macleane, Lauchlin 137*t*
Mahon, Lord 190, 191, 226, 230
Maidstone 192, 238
Mainwaring, Richard 199
Mainwaring, William 12, 46, 49–50
Maitland, Lord 226
Malet, Hugh 112
Manchester 24
Manchester, George Montague, Duke of
   105, 217, 225
Mandamus 125
Manner of Proceeding (Bramwell) 216
Mansfield, Lord 216, 224, 229
Marchmont, Hugh Hume-Campbell, 3rd
   Earl of 217
Marine Society 202
Marlborough, Duke of 90
Marsham, Charles 19, 42, 137*t*, 156
Martin, Charles 137*t*
Martin, Henry 137*t*
Martin, James 199
Martin, J.M. 34, 87
Martin, Samuel 137*t*
Mathias, Peter 18, 188
Mawbey, Sir Joseph 12, 199
Maynard, Sir William 123–4, 125, 126
Memoirs of Wool (Smith) 43

Meredith, Sir William 14, 61, 63, 83, 85,
   137*t*, 141, 142, 226, 234
metropolitan policing reform 49
Michel, David Robert 137*t*
Middlesex 49
Mildmay, Sir William 117, 120, 121, 122,
   123, 124, 126, 127
militia 53, 234
Militia Act/Bill 38, 222
Miller, Sir Thomas 213
Mingay, Gordon 32
Mitchell, L.G. 95
Molineux, Crisp 137*t*, 156
Monckton, Robert 137*t*
money bills 216, 218
Money, John 159, 174, 175, 177
Monserrat 140
Montagu, Frederick 9, 17, 18, 41, 52,
   53, 84, 233
Moore, Daniel 137*t*
Moore, T.K. 4, 26, 210, 244
Morant, Edward 137*t*
Mordaunt, Sir Charles 34, 160, 162
Morgan, Kenneth 59
Morris, Robert 218–19
MPs
   holding on to their seats 24
   and legislation in late 18th-century
      parliaments 1–27
   level of legislative activity 8–13
   motivations for MPs to get involved in
      legislation 23–4
   numbers and percentage of MPs
      overseeing the passage of legislation
      in 1765–7, 1772–4, 1786–8 10*t*
   numbers of bills carried by active MPs
      in 1765–7, 1772–4, 1786–8 10*t*
   and representation 235–8
Muilman, Richard 137*t*
Mulgrave, Lord 48
Mutiny Act/Bill 228, 229

Namier, L.B. 8, 29, 34, 80, 82, 126, 211
Navigation Act 1660 150
navigation bills 32, 42
Neave, Sir Richard 149
Needham, Trench-Chiswell William 137*t*
Neild, James 126
Nesbitt, Arnold 137*t*

Nesbitt, John 137t
Nevis 140
Newdigate, Sir Roger 79, 83–90, 94–5, 233
Newfoundland fisheries 180–1
Newnham, Nathaniel 137t, 213
New Street Company, petition to licence 170
New Street Theatre, Birmingham 169
Noble, John 72–3
Norfolk 32
Norfolk Chronicle 92
Norfolk, Edward Howard, Duke of 166
Northampton 192
North, Lord 18, 57, 67, 83, 85, 89, 147, 188, 213, 218
   and Bristol brass makers 171
   and Commission of Public Accounts 189
   concessions to the Irish 72
   and definition of the Commons' privileges 215
   efforts to form an economic bond between England and Ireland 26
   fall in 1782 177
   legislation activity of 25
   legislation prohibiting trade with colonies in revolt 69
   support for 200–1
   and West India Interest Group 158
Norton, Sir Fletcher 215, 238
Norwich 192
Nottingham, Corporation of 204
Nowell, Thomas 84
Nugent, Robert *see* Clare, Robert Nugent, Lord
Nullum Tempus Bill 39
Nullum Tempus privileges of the Church of England 83

O'Brien, Patrick 22, 188
O'Gorman, Frank 24, 192, 237
'Old Corruption' 24, 230, 238
Oliver, Richard 137t, 145–6, 198, 219
Onslow, Colonel George 137t, 201
Onslow family 238
   Guildford 238
Onslow, George 137t, 142, 217
Onslow, Thomas 137t
Orwell, Francis Vernon, Lord 107, 112

O'Shaughnessy, Andrew 130, 202
outdoor relief 108
Oxford Canal 89
Oxford Canal Bill 25
Oxford Improvement Act 81, 82
Oxford Improvement Bill (Mileways Act) 81, 88, 95, 233

Page, Francis 84, 85
Page Turner, George 242
Page Turner, Sir Gregory 112
Parker, Joseph 89
Parker, Sir Peter 137t
Parliamentary History 42
parliamentary reform 183–210
   and democracy 199–204
   instructions from constituents 195–9
   modes of communication 204–10
   petitions 192–4
parliamentary representation 184
Parsons, Reverend John 169
Partridge, Robert 91, 92
patents 169
Payne, Ralph 137t
Pelham, Thomas, Lord 213
Pembroke, Henry Herbert, Earl of 224
Penal Laws Bill 14
Pengree, William 168
Penhryn, Lord 152, 154, 155
Penitentiary Act 1779 53, 82
Penitentiary Bill 15
Pennant, Richard 138t, 149
Penson, Lillian 139
Perceval, Charles George 241
Perceval, Spencer 232
petitions 6, 192–4
Phillips, John 94, 238
Phipps, James Farrell 138t
Pinney, John Frederick 138t
Pitt, Thomas 30
Pitt, William 13, 25, 35, 48, 58, 77, 91, 93, 154, 155
   and 1784 election 214
   and British fisheries 179
   efforts to form an economic bond between England and Ireland 26
   fustian tax 45
   and Henry Beaufoy 178
   and the India Bill 228

and the Mutiny Act 229
negotiations between Garbett, iron masters and 173
and observance of the Sabbath 50
plan for a new commercial relationship between Ireland and Britain in 1785 172
reform bills 241
and regulation of the disposal of the bodies of executed criminals 223
rise to power 205
Shop Tax 242
and the West Indies 152–3
Pitt, William, the younger 183, 191, 209
Plan for the Better Relief and Employment of the Poor (Gilbert) 109
Plumptre, John 17
Plymouth 13, 55–7, 76, 77
Plympton Erle, Devon 240
Pole, Charles 138*t*
poor law 80, 97
poor law reforms 103, 106–15
Popham, Alexander 16
Porchester, Henry George Herbert, Lord 231
ports 21
Powell, John 73
Pownall, Thomas 111, 167, 218
Powney, Peniston Portlock 234
Poyntz, Newdigate 81, 120, 122, 126
Prescott, George 81
Prest, Wilfred 80
Proclamation Society 48, 49, 50
Prohibitory Bill 146–7, 197
property rights 18
Protestant Dissenting Deputies 130
Protestantism 39
Prowse, Thomas 51–2, 235
public bills 7
Public Offices Bill 222
Pulteney, Sir William 21–2, 25, 138*t*
Pye, Henry James 42

Quaker Meeting of Sufferings 103
Quaker Tithes Bill 103
Queen Anne's Bounty 103, 220

Rawdon, Francis, Lord 171, 176
Rawlinson, Henry 138*t*, 150

Raybould, T.J. 22
Receipts Tax 170, 200, 204, 235
referees 122
reform movements 185–92
Relief of the Poor Act of 1782 97
religious liberty 40
Rennie, John 59
Residence House Acts 103
Reversion Bills 208, 232
Reynolds, Richard 99, 174
Richards, Eric 98
Richmond, Charles Lennox, 3rd Duke of 58, 225, 228
Ridley, Sir Matthew White 48
Rigby, Richard 120
Robinson, John 166, 212, 213, 228
Rochford, William Henry Nassau de Zuylestein, Lord 124
Rockingham, Charles Watson-Wentworth, Lord 18, 41, 166, 190, 213
Rodney, George 138*t*
Rodney, Lord 201
Rogues and Vagabonds Bill 226
Rolle, Denys 46, 138*t*
Rolle, John 42, 44, 46, 47, 138*t*, 200, 201, 226, 234, 236
Rolliad 47
Roman Catholic Relief Act 206
Roman Catholics, freedom from penal code 40, 86
Rose, George 138*t*
Royal Navy 151
Rutland, Charles Manners, 4th Duke of 214
Ryder, Nathaniel 242
Ryland-Epton, Louise 106, 109, 233

Sabbath, observance of the 50
St. Aubyn, Sir John 57
St. Kitts 132, 140
St. Leger Douglas, John 136*t*
St. Vincent 148
Salt Tax 179
Salusbury, Thomas 138*t*
Sandwich, Lord 55, 188
Sargent, John 241
Savile, Sir George 8, 12, 29–30, 36–42, 53, 79, 84, 166, 234, 237

Sawbridge, John 138*t*, 156, 183, 187, 196*f*, 198, 199, 226, 230
Scott, John 46, 213
Secker, Thomas, Archbishop 80
second reading committees 27, 52
Sedgemoor enclosure bill 19
select committees 6
Selwyn, George 19
Septennial Act 184
Seven Years War 131
Severn salmon fishery 73
Seymour, Henry 83
Sharpe, Fane William 138*t*
Sharpe, John 138*t*
Shave, Samantha 110
Sheffield, Lord 173–4, 203, 229
Sheffield Plate Bill 171
Shelburne, William Petty-Fitzmaurice, Lord 104, 105, 165, 216
Sheridan, Richard 143, 239
Shiffner, Henry 11
Shop Tax 91, 200, 203, 242
Shuckburgh, Sir George Augustus 53, 161, 170, 174, 176
Sibthorp, Coningsby 33
Sidmouth, Lord 232
Silks Act, 1769 63
Skipwith, Thomas 166, 167
Slack, Paul 110
slave trade 45
  abolition of 46, 48, 53, 75, 150, 154, 155–6, 230–1
Slave Trade Regulation Bill 230
Slave Trade Regulation Bills 48, 75, 130, 155
Smeaton, John 119
Smith, Adam 151
Smith, Jarrit 62, 68, 77, 138*t*
Smith, John 43
Smith, Robert 203, 204, 207
Smuggling Bill 73
Smyth, John 200, 201
Society for Constitutional Information 186
Society for the Support of the Bill of Rights (SSBR) 185, 186, 187, 206, 219
Society of West India Merchants 132, 148
Society of West India Planters and Merchants 145, 151
Somerset 29
Somerset, Henry, Marquess of Worcester 138*t*
Somerton Act 51
Sommerset Case 224
Span, Samuel 71, 72
Spencer-Stanhope, Walter 77
Spottiswood, John 150
Stafford, Lord 176
Staffordshire 33
Staffordshire Advertiser 1, 98, 101
Staffordshire Gaol Bill 111
Stamp Act 8, 140–3, 160, 161
standing orders 52
Stanhope, Charles, 3rd Earl of 221, 225
Stanhope, Lovell 138*t*
Stanhope, Walter Spencer 233
Stanley, Hans 138*t*, 142
Stanley, Hans Sloane 138*t*, 199–200
Stanley, Thomas 13, 44–5, 53, 138*t*, 233
Stapleton, Sir Thomas 138*t*
State of the Prisons (Howard) 126
statute book 4
Stephens, Philip 72, 73
Stockdale's Debates 181
Storer, Anthony 138*t*
Stormont, David Murray, Lord 222
Strange, James Smith Stanley, Lord 38, 53, 234
Stratford, Ferdinand 119
Streets Act 56
Strutt, John 118, 119, 120, 121, 123, 124
Suffolk 192
sugar 60, 131, 144
Sugar Act 139
Surrey 33
Sutherland, Lucy 185
Sweet, Rosemary 2, 243
Swymmer, Anthony Lagley 138*t*
Sydney, Thomas Townshend, Lord 152, 221, 226

Tarleton, Col. Banastre 138*t*
Tarleton, John 138*t*
Tate, W.E. 32
taxation, opposition to 200
Taylor, Michael Angelo 180

Taylor, Simon 156
Temple, George Nugent, Lord 227, 228
Test and Corporation Acts 35, 36, 94, 178
Test (newspaper) 206
Thomas, Peter 215
Thomas, Sir George 138*t*
Thornton, Henry 203, 231
Thornton, Samuel 58, 59, 77, 233
Thorold, Sir John 42, 43, 44
Thurlow, Lord 213, 224, 227, 228
Tierney, George 213, 231
Times, The 230
Tindal, Rev. John 123
Tiverton, Devon 242
Tobacco Bill 224
Toleration Act 86
toll bridge, at Swimford 81
Tomlinson, John 138*t*
Touchet, Samuel 138*t*
Town Moor enclosure bill 9
Townshend, George 38, 222, 234
Townshend, Jason 196*f*
Townshend, Thomas 80, 84
Townson, John 138*t*
Trade and Navigation Acts 131
Trade with America Act 1785 178
Trecothick, Barlow 138*t*, 140
Treise, Sir Christopher 240
Trent and Mersey Canal Bill 100, 101
Trevanion, John 138*t*
Tucker, Bob 205
Tucker, Dean 63, 84
Tucker, John 205, 237
Tucker, Rev. Josiah 64
Tucker, Richard 237
Tudway, Charles 138*t*
Tudway, Clement 138*t*
Turner, Michael 32
Turner, Sir John 121, 122
Turnpike Act/Bill 50, 102
turnpikes 1, 101
Tweed Fisheries Bill of 1771 207

Underwood, P.T. 67

Vaughan, Benjamin 139*t*
Vaughan, General John 201
Verney, Ralph, Lord 65

Walpole, Horace 104, 105, 141, 149, 195, 197–8
Walpole, Sir Robert 198
Walsingham, Thomas De Grey, 2nd Baron 221
Ward, John 139*t*
Ward, J.W. 231
Ward, William 139*t*
Warren, John, Bishop 46, 224
wars, economic burden of 188
Warwickshire 159
    enclosure bills 34
Watson, Brooke 139*t*
Watson, Richard 85
Watt, James 168, 169
Webb, Nathaniel 139*t*
Webster, Sir Godfrey Vassall 139*t*
Weddell, William 57, 77
Wedgwood, Josiah 32, 100, 160
Wenman, Philip, Lord 87
Wentworth, Paul 139*t*
Western, J.R. 38
West India interest group 129–58
    and the American War of Independence 144–9
    decline of 150–8
    early development of 130–1
    extent of 139–44
    structure of 131–3
    West Indian contingent in the House of Commons 133–9
West Indies, dependence upon Great Britain 157
Westmorland, John Fane, 10th Earl of 51
West Riding 20, 43
Wetherell, Nathan 84, 88, 89
Weymouth, Viscount 219
wheat, importation of 61
Whichcot, Thomas 12
Whitbread, Samuel 18, 19, 231
White, George 162
White, Sir Thomas 204
White Thomas, George 139*t*
Whittam, William 219
Whitworth, Charles 12
Whitworth, Richard 215
Wilberforce, William 1, 47, 48, 77, 129, 134, 209

and abolition of the slave trade 46, 53,
    154, 155
bill to regulate the disposal of the
    bodies of executed criminals 222,
    230
Wildman, William, 2nd Viscount
    Barrington *see* Barrington, William
    Wildman, Lord
Wilkes, John 183, 185, 186, 199, 212, 213,
    217, 218, 219
    parliamentary reform proposals 187
    proceedings against 40–1
Wilkinson, Jacob 139*t*
Williams, Eric 150
Williams, John 139*t*
Willoughby, Thomas 41
Wilson, Richard 25, 44
Windham, William 13, 79, 90–4, 95–6, 236
Windward Islands 132
Wood, Beavis 242
Woodley, William 139*t*
woollen fleeces, export of 26
woollen industry 43–4
workhouses 108, 109
Wray, Sir Cecil 11, 12, 199
Wrottesley, Sir John 167
Wyvill, Reverend Christopher 189,
    190, 192

Yates, Richard 70, 169
Yates, Robert 130
Yeomans, Thomas 120
Yonge, Sir George 200
Yorke, Charles 82
Yorke, Philip 35–6, 53, 204
Yorkshire
    economical reform movement 189–90
    electorate in 29
    enclosure bills 32
Young, Sir William 139*t*

www.ingramcontent.com/pod-product-compliance
Lightning Source LLC
Chambersburg PA
CBHW052218300426
44115CB00011B/1739